THE COMPLETE
GARDENER

HAMLYN

THE COMPLETE
GARDENER

INTRODUCTION BY
ALAN TITCHMARSH

HAZEL EVANS   RON MENAGE
JOHN NEGUS   DAVID SQUIRE
ALAN TOOGOOD   MICHAEL UPWARD

This edition published in 1988 by
The Hamlyn Publishing Group Limited
Bridge House, 69 London Road, Twickenham, Middlesex, England

© 1987 Hennerwood Publications Limited

ISBN 0 600 55770 7

Printed in Czechoslovakia
50669

CONTENTS

INTRODUCTION

Here, in one volume, is a guide to practically every kind of gardening job you can think of. Michael Upward sets out the basic guidelines within which you can work out original ideas for the kind of garden *you* want.

John Negus and Hazel Evans then get down to the business of stocking the ornamental garden with annuals, perennials, shrubs and trees in an amazing variety of sizes, shapes, colours and textures. Ron Menage shows how to choose a greenhouse for your particular needs and how to grow a comprehensive range of flowers, fruit and vegetables in it.

Alan Toogood nudges you into all-year-round gardening action – not just to keep the garden tidy but to turn your plot into a cheerfully interesting place in every season.

With a weekly mailbag that can run well into three figures, I know how confusing this gardening lark can be, and David Squire provides answers to hundreds of the sort of questions that crop up most often in gardening magazines and programmes.

All in all, a book to dip into or immerse yourself – and one to inspire you to enjoyable action in the open air!

Alan Titchmarsh

PART 1

CREATING A GARDEN

This section shows you how to design and build a garden, whether you are working with a small basement area in town or a rolling country acre. Starting from scratch, it takes you through each step, from levelling the plot to creating and stocking ornamental borders, vegetable plots and fruit-growing areas, and it includes detailed advice on how to build hard-surfaced structural features such as boundary walls, paths, patios and steps.

ASSESSMENT AND INSPIRATION

When people move, they expect to impart their personalities to the new home, perhaps by redecorating but certainly with their own possessions. Yet all too often the garden stays just as it was. However, if you assess your site thoughtfully, considering all the factors which come with it such as climate and soil, you can make a garden as individually suited to you as any other part of your home.

The essence of good garden design lies in creating an area that is visually pleasing, functional, within the bounds of maintenance by the owner and not outrageously expensive to instal.

Maintenance is controlled by the amount of work that any owner is prepared to put into the upkeep of the garden – and the key rule here is to be realistic. Expense is a comparative matter – it simply depends on how much you are prepared to spend, have to spend or want to spend. If finance

An attractive garden which includes all the necessary adjuncts to gardening. The greenhouses and shed have been well 'planted out' so that they do not intrude into the overall garden design. The planting has been thoughtfully planned to screen off the railway.

is not available immediately, you can work in stages of development, even in a small area, with temporary cheap answers for the time being, such as sowing the whole site with grass seed, parts of which are then later removed to create beds and borders. At the other end of the scale, you may consider employing a landscape architect. If you are a novice gardener, then this may be a wise move, but a rapport has to be established, so that whoever is submitting the proposals can be confident of understanding your wishes.

WHAT DO YOU WANT FROM YOUR GARDEN?

Other factors enter into the consideration of a design, such as the age of a family – whether playing areas are needed in the initial years, which can later become different features in the overall design. Is entertainment a high priority for you so that an outside living area is needed, complete with barbecue facilities? Are you keen gardeners, with a knowledge of plants or are you complete beginners? Some husbands and wives garden harmoniously and enjoy working together; others have separate areas where neither dares trespass. However limited the duration a child's enthusiasm for gardening may be, he or she must never be given a plot in the furthest corner of the garden where nothing else will grow, for how can that encourage the young gardener?

Fresh vegetables may be the heart's desire of the cook of the household; soft fruit may also be a preference; it may even be economics that dictate that you grow your own.

The site and situation of a garden are relevant to any design – north-facing aspects will not accommodate sun-loving plants; shade-loving plants will not be happy if the garden faces south. The ground may be permanently damp or excessively drained; the soil may be alkaline or acidic – this factor often being overlooked by new gardeners with disastrous and expensive results. It is no use, for example, trying to grow rhododendrons on chalk downs or in limestone areas. Neither is there any point in trying to create beds of imported soil to overcome the problem, for lime will always seep in somehow and the water supply is bound to be tainted. Accept your lot, garden accordingly, working with, rather than fighting against, nature.

You may want a greenhouse, cold frame or shed in your garden. The former will want good sunlight. Such structures should be serviced by hard dry paths and should not be placed anywhere near overhanging trees if you live in an area of high snowfall.

Below left Clever use of brickwork has created a pattern which complements the colourful planting and seems to broaden the site. The shy nymph draws the viewer's eye and gives the impression of enlarging the garden by adding focal interest in the distance.

Below An example of a terraced border, which could be adapted for smaller gardens. Trailing plants both provide colour, and help disguise the straight lines of the wall.

FIRST CONSIDERATIONS

Planning may seem unnecessary or daunting to the new gardener. Not everyone is able to commit to paper their ideas or evaluate the different possibilities systematically. But it does pay to be sensible and, particularly with the smaller site, to have some sort of plan in mind so that you do not make time-consuming and expensive mistakes in laying out your garden.

The first priority to consider must be the site itself: its existing good points, amenities or problems. Decisions will have to be made to remove or retain whatever is already on site.

The current design vogue is to disguise the existing shape of your site but it is also fashionable to accentuate the squareness or elongate the length of the site you possess. I personally feel that lines in landscape need to be softened and long narrow gardens need to be broadened visually to give a more substantial look to them. So your main style decision is whether you want a 'formal' garden based on regular shapes such as straight lines and circles or whether your garden should rely on more apparently random shapes to look 'informal' or natural.

The next priority is to think about the climate, aspect and the condition of the soil in your garden.

PREPLANNING

As you assess the basic considerations of your site, you will want to review the kind of plants you will grow in your garden, but be patient. Any existing features will usually influence how the garden shall proceed. You work from a recipe in which the ingredients are your own taste, your soil, the climate, aspect and the features of your site.

What a sad sight is presented by this derelict garden. But an attractive plot could result from careful planning as the illustration on the right demonstrates.

It may be that you have a superb specimen tree; or in fact, this tree may well overshadow the entire garden. Other features should be considered; for instance, you may be overlooked by an unpleasant building. Conversely, you may have a view which needs to be accentuated and so all your planning needs to lead the eye to the view in question.

If your new garden has a summerhouse, shed or greenhouse, you will need to consider whether the structure is pleasing or useful to you, whether it wants to be masked or moved. Similarly, you will need to question the permanence of other large features. Paved areas may be enlarged upon, planted up with alpines or tubs, or removed.

ASSESSING YOUR DESIGN
There is one point which I would like to stress at the beginning. This is that one of the mistakes that we all make when planning a garden is to imagine that it is ever finished. I estimate that a garden can take five years to mature, after which a good hard look is necessary because some things will have got too large or mistakes will have been made. To quote a personal example, we thought we had bought a small Pampas Grass which would not misbehave. It grew and grew, together with *Thuja occidentalis* 'Rheingold', until one day I looked behind them and found that there was a huge gap that could be planted up so they were both thrown out. About 100 interesting plants such as hellebores, snowdrops and euphorbias were planted in their place to give an attractive late winter garden, followed by hostas in the summer. So always review how your garden is growing, your own changing needs and ideas and don't be afraid to rework the design.

The derelict garden transformed to give an illusion of space and width. The yellow conifer and small pond make focal points.

1. *Magnolia soulangeana*
2. *Berberis thunbergii* 'Atropurpurea'
3. *Caltha palustris*
4. Primulas
5. *Houttuynia cordata*
6. Astilbes
7. Hostas
8. Irises
9. *Juniperus tamariscifolia*
10. *Chamaecyparis ellwoodii*
11. *Hydrangea hortensis*
12. *Alchemilla mollis*
13. *Fuchsia magellanica*
14. *Hypericum patulum* 'Hidcote'
15. Upright conifer – *Juniperus chinensis* 'Aurea'
16. *Forsythia × intermedia*
17. *Kerria japonica* 'Flore Pleno'
18. *Hebe pageana*
19. *Viburnum bodnantense*

ASPECT

Before considering your design likes and dislikes and your favourite plants, take a good hard look at the site and adapt your thinking accordingly. A garden facing south will give you full sun for most of the day, most of the year. If your site faces slightly to the east, it will give you sun early in the morning, and conversely, to the west, late in the evening. The disadvantage of an eastern aspect is that the sun will damage the frosted flowers of winter-flowering plants. It is not actually frost which kills flowers but the rapid melting of the ice that does the most damage. A north-facing garden is not the end of the world as there are some lovely woodland plants that can be accommodated in what will probably be a chilly aspect.

SOIL TYPES

The type of soil in your garden will determine what sort of preparation is necessary before planting. Clay soils will grow good plants but will be brutish to dig and may hold the moisture too readily. Depending on the degree of stickiness of the clay, a good deal of well-rotted garden compost should be incorporated.

SOIL CONDITION

Plants that thrive on acid soils include rhododendrons, camellias, certain primulas, meconopsis and as a wide generalization, members of the heath and heather botanical grouping known as Ericaceae. Usually, a quick look at neighbouring gardens will indicate the type of chemical structure you have – if rhododendrons and ericaceous plants are growing locally, the answer is obvious. If you are in a known limestone area, or on the chalk downs, then it will be obvious that the soil is alkaline and you must choose plants accordingly. There are many plants that will tolerate both conditions. Soil acidity is measured on the pH factor, neutral being 7.0, below being acid, above alkaline.

Sometimes the natural drainage of a soil has become impeded by building works and improvement is required. A permanently damp soil quickly becomes stagnant and offensive to plant life, so it is essential to make sure that surplus moisture is able to be removed or will remove itself naturally from the site. It may be necessary to construct a sump – this would be a large hole filled with rubble, towards which land drains can be led. Land drains are short 30cm (12in) clay pipes that should be kept cleared to maintain an efficient system. Conversely, a soil might be too quick-draining, in which case more moisture may have to be channelled its way, or the physical properties of the soil improved by the addition of peat, leafmould, compost or manure, to give it more moisture retentive properties.

COMPOST AND HUMUS

Clay soil is easily waterlogged after rain and a handful will roll into a solid ball. Sandy soil drains very quickly and tends to be lacking in goodness. A handful will run through your fingers. Loamy soils are a good blend of sand, clay and humus. I am a great believer in garden composting. At home we have a fairly scientific, but simple system of throwing all vegetable rubbish (household and garden) into a brick bay with corrugated iron above so that the compost rots in a dry condition – this allows the correct bacteria to work on the decomposition of the waste products of the garden. All vegetable matter is thrown on, with an occasional sprinkling of sulphate of ammonia, which helps activate the compost. The heap is turned once and then bagged up into small polythene bags, easy to handle and stored ready for use. In our establishment we use it as a top dressing but in a new garden it will be useful to dig it in. Obviously when you begin on a site you do not have your own ready-made compost and so will have to rely on something like leafmould, cow manure or peat, but the latter is expensive so it is best to look for natural materials that cost you less. The same principle of digging in rotted vegetable matter applies to a well-drained sandy soil too in that this needs humus material in it to bind it and so the same materials are used for the opposite

A garden in an area of beautiful mature trees has been planted in a natural way that complements the fine backdrop. Herbaceous plants, with foliage interest, are growing under shrubs and trees.

reasons. In clay soil the compost makes the whole more friable, in sandy soil it adds 'body'. In really heavy clay conditions, more drastic forms of drainage may need to be considered, but usually the incorporation of good compost lightens the soil. Fortunate is the person who picks a site that has been cultivated for some while, for the action of plants growing will improve the soil's fertility from its original condition.

CLIMATE

Few countries have a uniform climate. In Britain it is accepted that it is generally colder in the north and warmer in the south but there is also an east/west difference in that the west has more rainfall and the east is drier. Exposure to strong winds is a factor which influences what will grow quite as much as temperature. Many plants will not thrive without some shelter from wind, particularly near the sea because the wind will carry salt. The proximity of other houses also affects your garden. City gardens often receive some warmth and protection from surrounding buildings but may also be shaded by them, especially in winter.

The fault committed by most of us is to plant plants that are on the tender side because they are attractive or a challenge to grow. Come a hard winter and these less hardy specimens are damaged or lost to us which is very sad. For those who are determined to grow tender plants in cold areas then the most sensible solution is to have a greenhouse in which rooted cuttings are placed each year.

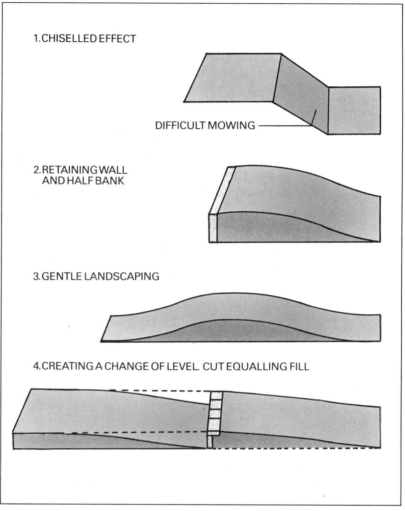

1. CHISELLED EFFECT

DIFFICULT MOWING —

2. RETAINING WALL AND HALF BANK

3. GENTLE LANDSCAPING

4. CREATING A CHANGE OF LEVEL. CUT EQUALLING FILL

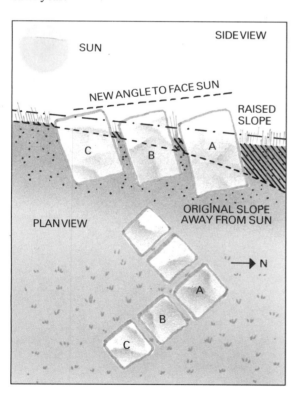

SIDE VIEW

SUN

NEW ANGLE TO FACE SUN

RAISED SLOPE

C   B   A

PLAN VIEW

ORIGINAL SLOPE AWAY FROM SUN

→ N

A

B

C

LEVELS

Not all gardens come flat, and not all slope in the right direction. However, a change of level can greatly add to the interest of your site. Gentle slopes can be used for rock garden features; turned into shady woodland areas; stepped and terraced to provide formal levels and, in fact, offer perhaps more than does a flat site. An area that has gently undulating levels or a ghastly mess left by the builders can be landscaped to give you sunken features below the average level of the surrounding ground and, again, provide some interesting aspects and cool corners for plants that are happy in such situations.

Level changes may complicate your planting because of course a south facing garden may have a slope towards the house, which means that the slope itself faces north. This can be corrected by terracing and turning the levels so that they tip into the slope and therefore get some of the warmth from the sun. Any major amount of heavy earth moving may well prove to be too gargantuan a task, so you will need to adapt your thinking to accommodate the slope as it stands (see also pages 17 and 30–1).

Above The diagrams illustrate some of the solutions for dealing with a garden on more than one level. An angular level change is harder to mow. A retaining wall and bank look good, as does the rolling landscaping which demands space. The cut and fill treatment is demanding to achieve.

Left Rocks A, B and C have been tilted to convert a north-facing slope into a south-facing aspect. The rocks in this illustration have been 'stepped' but their tops could be level to create a larger planting area.

AREA AND SHAPE

Before thinking about the shape of your garden you will have to consider your boundary. Generally, when you move to your property, the boundary fence has been put in place for you, or there is a hedge or brick wall. Alternatively, there may be an open plan for the estate or locality, in which case you must discover whether you are allowed to create screens, if you wish to divide yourself from your neighbour. Remember that any form of division is expensive, be it wooden fencing, chain link fencing or most of all, brick or stone walling. On a tight budget, building a boundary may take up a great deal of the available finance, but it does ensure the balance you want between privacy and public display. Boundaries are discussed in more detail on page 26–9.

PLANNING SCALE AND SHAPE

If your design is going to be relatively simple, you may prefer to dispense with paper plans. In this case, use trails of sand or rope to mark on the cleared site or grass the intended outline of beds, borders, paving or other features.

For any larger or more sophisticated garden you would be wise to attempt a paper plan, perhaps with several alternatives, until you are happy with the balance of hard and soft surfaces, the shape of planting areas etc. Make your plans on graph paper on a scale of 1/50 or 1/100. Translate the garden measurements on to it so that you can calculate the ultimate size of trees and shrubs and overcome future problems. Ideas can be put down on paper and translated roughly on to the ground to give you an idea of how the whole will look.

A lecturer in landscape design in my student days stressed that you needed to go into the bedroom in order to see how your garden will look. Whilst this sounds slightly jokey, it is nevertheless a good idea to view the garden from above and from every aspect before you take the final plunge. Check that the features you want are incorporated in your garden – flowerbeds, borders, vegetables, soft fruit, fruit trees and so on – remembering that some cause more work than others. Do not, however, try to create a 'labourless garden' because there is no such object. All gardens need some regular maintenance.

BUDGETING

If the landscaping of the site is costly in terms of putting the soil to rights and making a decent feature of what was a total wilderness, then there may be little left over to spend on trees and shrubs. It cannot be emphasized enough that the preparation of the garden is far more important than the actual planting. Skimped preparation will lead to years of heartache and disappointment.

Remember that features such as rock gardens and pools and waterfalls are expensive to construct and maintain. Water adds movement to the garden and is exceedingly attractive, but if the budget is limited, then its use as a feature should not be considered.

Budget priorities are thus easily summarized: the first expense is to make the site clean, the second is to consider the boundaries and the third is to consider the planting costs, both in terms of the plants themselves and in terms of any extra labour involved. Having said all this, you need to go back to the planning stage to consider the amount of maintenance that you have created, whether you can cope with this physically and, if not, whether you can cope with it financially by employing someone as necessary.

This typical suburban garden has a rather fussy layout which is demanding to keep up, does not effectively mask the houses at the end and fails to make the most of the space.

Above *A flat site that has been planted to give shape, form and colour in addition to height. The different foliage textures and colours alone make the garden interesting.*

it creates informality. There is no crime in having a flat, square or rectangular lawn if you so desire. There is a formal school of gardening, which, with the addition of garden features such as urns and statues, can produce very imposing results and can be much simpler to maintain than the informal garden. Likewise, it is not necessary to create your ups and downs artificially. Clever planting can do this, leading the eye along a gradient by the use of well planted upright growing conifers and small trees. Use heathers or ground cover plants to create a wider space. Remember that many different colours will make a flat space look smaller than if you use a more limited range.

COMBINING EXCAVATION

If you choose to construct a pond, the soil excavated therefrom can, of course, be employed in making a rock garden nearby. Rock gardens and pools seem to be a natural, attractive and practical combination. Sound planning is the key to a successful rock garden.

A simplified version of the garden opposite – the basic planting has been thinned out and a pergola with roses planted to screen the greenhouse. The uncluttered expanse of grass gives a spacious feeling.

1. Cedar
2. *Chamaecyparis lawsoniana*
3. Pergola
4. Weeping tree
5. Golden conifer
6. *Genista*
7. *Dianthus*
8. Yucca
9. Dwarf pine

SLOPES

I wish I had a slope in my garden. With a slope you can create many aspects and you can, in effect, turn round the slope position to face a different point of the compass. South facing slopes on sandy soils will, of course, be very well drained and the moisture will evaporate considerably.

Terracing a slope can be an expensive undertaking, but there are various ways of doing it: by building a series of retaining brick walls and having each level absolutely flat; by creating a dry stone wall effect or, in a larger garden, you can instal a series of steps going up the slope with wider beds incorporating shrubs and herbaceous plants.

If you want to create slopes in a flat area, this is easily done by digging out soil and replacing it in banks, but in a small area this would look bitty; it needs bold thinking and should only be attempted in the larger garden. Remember to put the topsoil aside before making your mound, then replace the topsoil. Raised beds are a good way of adding interest to flat gardens.

FLAT AREAS

It is relevant to say here that if you are seeking a formal style of gardening, and have a flat area, then it is best left flat. When slopes are introduced

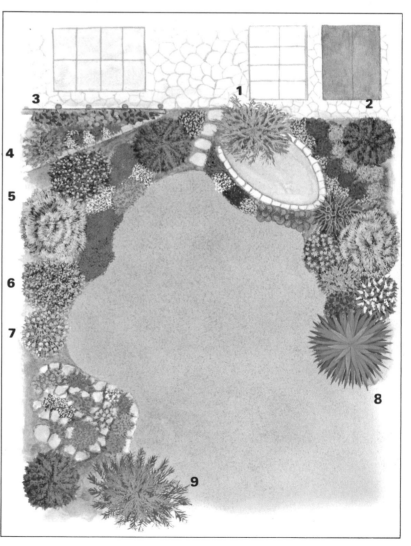

FOCAL INTEREST

What immediately springs to mind under this heading is the garden on the grand scale with magnificent statuary placed at the end of a long vista, or a temple erected on a knoll, Capability Brown-style. But you do not need to work on country house scale! For the smaller garden there are some very reasonably priced statues in re-constituted stone, glassfibre or even concrete. There is also a profusion of urns and vases in different sizes to choose from. Attractive garden seating is a feature in its own right; a pergola, entrance arch or a piece of trellis work could be a feature, especially if you wished to screen a compost heap, shed or greenhouse. But focal points do not need to be artificial as there is such a wealth of rich colourful plant material that sparkles even in the far distance. An upright growing golden conifer placed on the corner of a border is always a pleasant point of interest. The variegated

shrub *Elaeagnus pungens* 'Maculata' makes a brilliant colourful display at the end of a path, and as it is evergreen it could easily hide a compost heap or similar feature. Evergreens are the best choice for year-round focal points. Deciduous trees and shrubs can look slightly sparse in winter but a possible exception to this is the twisted hazel, *Corylus avellana* 'Tortuosa'. This has curiously twisted stems and large, slightly gross leaves during the summer but come February time, its branches are clothed in delicate, pale fawny, yellowish catkins which are a most attractive feature at a thin time of the year for interest. Underplanted with dwarf *Iris reticulata*, this tree provides a very interesting sight. A bed of heathers, which grow best in acid or peaty soil, can, by careful choice, give an eye-catching display throughout most of the months of the year. If you want to have an arresting feature in the summer, and the garden is large enough, then a

This is a very clever blending of colours, with a deeper background in the same tones. Both border and backdrop are focal points of interest.

Containers can in themselves be focal points and may provide seasonal displays. Here full dramatic use has been made of summer-flowering plants, but in the spring they might be planted with daffodils to give bold splashes of colour.

bed cut out of the lawn filled with self-supporting herbaceous plants (i.e. that do not need supporting stakes) can be most attractive. In principle I prefer to leave the lawn as a vast expanse rather than have it broken up by beds.

If the garden faces south and a summerhouse can be incorporated, there are some very attractive standard designs that can be found. If placed in an arbour of surrounding trees and shrubs, these can be made to look very cool and restful in the summer. If you have a pergola, train clematis and roses or wisteria to clamber through it and your garden will have a beautiful centre of interest. Do not neglect seasonal interest when choosing focal plants.

INTERESTING CAMOUFLAGE
A focal point can also be made to take the eye away from a less pleasant feature and so consideration might be given to the placing of, say, a vegetable garden conveniently nearer the house which can be screened easily by fruit trees or roses and the real centres of interest placed at the further end of the garden. Likewise, a shed at the end of the garden is inconvenient on a time and motion basis. The best place for the tool shed is in the centre of your plot, so that wherever you walk from the shed is equidistant. Your shed may be hidden for most of the summer behind a magnificent screen of sweet peas or honeysuckle, with a forsythia shrub to do the job in spring.

SMALL TOWN GARDENS

The vast majority of us live in towns and cities, where space is at a premium, and consequently we have small gardens. These present a number of particular problems which are considered here, together with some imaginative solutions. They show how successful and creative you can be with even a tiny awkward-shaped yard.

Bringing the garden indoors! The extremely imaginative planting of this patio area is rather overcrowded, but succeeds in the use of different foliage forms. The placing of the statue to draw attention past the clutter is very clever. Plants indoors 'marry up' with those outside.

At this stage we should perhaps look at small town gardens because they frequently pose special problems to the designer. There are numerous external factors that will influence any design and these must be looked at first.

One of the most familiar kinds of town garden lies at the back of old terraced property, probably with a party wall going down either side and finishing up with a dividing wall between your own plot and the garden of the property backing on to you. This may mean that the buildings overshadow each other's gardens and suitable plants must be considered for shady areas. You

may also have a wish to mask any unpleasant property that is nearby if you have the misfortune to be overlooked by commercial premises.

The other main style of urban garden is one on an open estate where there may well be a covenant restricting fences being erected in the front of a property and so the front garden has to be open plan. If the estate is on entirely open virgin land you do, of course, have a complete opportunity to start from scratch. You can make a virtue of this and plant appropriate trees and shrubs.

There are practical problems that can be encountered. There may be old foundations in the

garden which have to be removed, or more cleverly, incorporated in your garden design. Similarly manhole covers, access to dustbins and garden storage may need different treatment in small town gardens because light and space are at a premium.

Service areas for a garden, such as side entrances, are often unsightly and so these should be screened as best as possible with either natural hedging material or trellis work or railings which can form supports for attractive climbing plants.

SEASIDE PLANTS

This is just a small selection to encourage the gardener who has been put off by wind and salt-shrivelled species. Your local nursery will suggest others. These are particularly good for small gardens.

	Height
Armeria maritima Sea thrift. There are several named cultivars of this evergreen perennial that forms tufts of leaves in sandy soils and which produces a round pink flowerhead on a short stem.	15–30cm (6–12in)
Elaeagnus × ebbingei An evergreen shrub with grey-tinted foliage, silvery flowers and red or orange fruits.	3–4.5m (10–15ft)
Eryngium spp. A large genus of herbaceous perennials. *E. maritimum* is the sea holly. Silvery green leaves and bright blue flowers.	30–45cm (12–18in)
Hebe These are the shrubby veronicas and most species do well by the sea. Wide range of flower and leaf colour. Not all are hardy.	Most 60–90cm (2–3ft)
Hippophae rhamnoides Sea buckthorn. A most attractive grey shrub that grows well on the edges of salt marshes. Orange berries are produced if planted in mixed groups with male and female plants.	2.5–3m (8–10ft)
Lavatera maritima Mallow. This is not as robust as some so requires a warm sheltered position. The pale lilac flowers are produced from mid-summer to late autumn.	1.2m (4ft)
Limonium latifolium Sea lavender. Has evergreen foliage and produces long sprays of light violet blue flowers in summer.	60cm (2ft)
Nepeta × mussinii Catmint, so-called because cats are reputed to love it. It forms a loose grey-foliaged herbaceous plant with blue spikes in summer.	30cm (12in)
Spartium junceum An informal broom that produces long sprays of fragrant yellow pea flowers.	2.5–3m (8–10ft)
Tamarix spp. Several tamarisks have naturalized along southern coasts of Britain. They form loose shrubs of fine foliage which carry sprays of light or deep pink flowers, in early summer.	3–4.5m

If your garden is going to be used a lot and is really too small to use a mower, then crazy or formal paving, brick or gravel can form a good hard surface. This can be broken up with small shrubs and ground cover plants to relieve the flatness of this type of surface. If, on the other hand, there is going to be very little wear and tear on the ground, then a camomile lawn might be considered. When walked on gently, it exudes a fragrance that is pleasant and requires relatively little maintenance.

You will also want to consider whether the house and garden are well placed to spend some time eating out in the summer months. Have you allowed yourselves sufficient shelter, sun and a pleasant outlook so that you can relax on your patio or terrace?

Seaside town gardens suffer particularly from salt spray damage and wind, but there are quite a number of plants that will tolerate such conditions. Some suggestions are given in the chart.

A seaside garden looking colourful in late summer with hydrangeas, the African lily or Agapanthus *and* Montbretia.

BASEMENT GARDENS

Basement gardens can provide much charm and pleasure. Your main problem is likely to be too much or too little sun, for most basements are either sun traps or are shaded by buildings. If you have a bright basement, you might consider building a pergola to provide a sun filter, and choose plants which are reasonably drought resistant. If, as is more frequently the case, you lack sun, then if possible, paint walls white to reflect the light. Remember not to block access to drainage by your planting and don't construct raised beds against a house wall or you may cause damage.

Basement gardening is necessarily restricted by space and rather artificial, but these restrictions do not have to stifle your creativity. Ideally you want to have somewhere, perhaps inside, where you can propagate plants to provide seasonal colour. Otherwise you will need to replace flowering displays from time to time. Contrasting foliage and interesting climbing plants will offer you more lasting interest than if you aim only for colour. Train your climbers with care and feed

and water them regularly or you will find that the lower stems tend to become bare as the upper ones search for light.

In the autumn you can plant tubs with wallflowers and bulbs but do not have entirely bulbs and wallflowers. Choose short varieties of bulbs or they will become long and leggy. Tubs planted up with snowdrops and crocuses to precede dwarf daffodils and narcissi are a wonderful harbinger of spring. Camellias and azaleas are good subjects for tubs too with hostas and begonias planted round the edge. Continuity of flower is obviously desirable and following on from the bulbs and wallflowers in the spring you can have bedding plants for the summer. Busy Lizzies, pansies and fuchsias do well in tubs and can provide several months of colourful bloom. If you live in the centre of a town, the protected environment might enable you to get away with some house plants on your patio, such as the heather *Erica canaliculatus* which is found in florists around Christmas time. Likewise, some of the chrysanthemums may provide a splash of colour throughout the winter.

LONG NARROW GARDENS

A long, narrow site does not have to look long and narrow unless you want it to, but a thin garden will inevitably look thin if you design along the boundaries.

You might devise borders that intrude across the centre of the garden to stop your eye part of the way down, together with a feature such as an upright shrub, conifer, statue or arbour suitably clothed with climbers. Even an urn with flowers tumbling down out of it may form an arresting sight which gives an illusion of width. Rather than plant trees along the boundaries, bring them into the garden to give a bit of height in the centre. Tuck taller plants into the backs of the borders and do not leave them bare. There is nothing worse than looking into a border and finding hollows. In a long, narrow strip you might like to dispense with grass altogether; or you can plan for a small circular or irregularly shaped piece of lawn.

Left A long lawn with mowing lines that accentuate the narrow shape. *Below* The borders should be brought forward and planted to blend in with the woodland.

1. *Parrotia persica*
2. *Syringa vulgaris* 'Congo'
3. *Philadelphus* 'Virginal'
4. *Ericas*
5. *Chamaecyparis* 'Columnaris'
6. *Forsythia × intermedia*
7. *Daphne mezereum*
8. *Viburnum tomentosum mariesii*
9. *Rhododendron* 'Hinomayo'
10. *Ceratostigma willmottianum*
11. *Viburnum carlesii*
12. *Hydrangea paniculata*
13. *Eucryphia glutinosa*
14. *Robinia pseudoacacia* 'Frisia'
15. *Euphorbia polychroma*
16. *Rhododendron* 'Praecox'
17. *Hydrangea hortensis*
18. *Hamamelis mollis*
19. *Geranium psilostemon*
20. *Lysimachia punctata*
21. *Monarda* 'Cambridge Scarlet'
22. *Solidago* 'Golden Mosa'
23. *Stachys lanata*
24. *Brunnera macrophylla*
25. *Senecio greyii*
26. *Ceanothus thyrsiflorus*
27. *Buddleia alternifolia*

SMALL SHRUBS

Abelia schumanii Lilac-pink flowers are produced in late summer. — 60–90cm (2–3ft)

Andromeda polifolia Clusters of pink flowers in May/June. Acid soil. Loose habit. 'Compacta' is neater. — 30cm (12in)

Azara microphylla Dainty foliage with clusters of fragrant yellow flowers in spring. — 1.5m (5ft)

Berberis thunbergii 'Atropurpurea' Tall, but elegant arching sprays of reddish-purple foliage. Flowers pale and insignificant followed by red autumn berries. The cultivars 'Atropurpurea Nana' and 'Aurea' are much smaller. — 45–120cm (1.5–4ft)

Calluna vulgaris Ling There are too many cultivars to detail any here; all make excellent ground cover in association with Erica q.v. — 30cm (12in)

Camellia A genus with many species and named varieties which are best chosen when in flower. All are evergreen and should be protected from winter sunshine. — 2–4m (6–12ft)

Ceratostigma willmottianum Blue flowers from summer through to autumn, when the foliage has red tints. — 90cm (3ft)

Chaenomeles Japonica Another genus with many named varieties. Does well against a wall and produces flowers early in the year. — 90–183cm (3–6ft)

Cornus alba Dogwood Does well in wet or dry situations, grown for its red bark in winter with additional bonus of autumn colour. Prune in early spring to encourage young growth and keep bush at 90–122cm (3–4ft). — 2–3m (8–10ft)

Cotoneaster horizontalis A ground-covering species with red berries in autumn. — 60cm (2ft)

Cytisus Broom A large family with a preference for light soils and full sun. Larger species need pruning to prevent legginess. — 0.3–1.8m (1–6ft)

Daphne A large genus with many species suitable for the smaller garden. — 0.3–1.8m (1–6ft)
  D. odora 'Aureomarginata' Has heavily scented pinkish-white flowers in spring and yellow-edged leaves. — 1.5–2m (5–6ft)
  D. 'Somerset' Forms a neat shrub with deliciously scented pink flowers in summer. — 1.2m (4ft)
  D. tangutica Rose-pink to purple scented flowers appear in spring. Evergreen. — 0.6m (2ft)

Deutzia A large genus with many named cultivars. Prune after flowering for best results. — 1–2m (4–6ft)

Erica Heather A genus with a wide range of coloured foliage, flowers and form. Some are ideal for ground cover. Specialist catalogues should be consulted. — 0.6–6m (2–20ft)

SMALL SHRUBS

Forsythia A valuable plant for its early yellow flowers. Rather large and vigorous, but try the delicate F. suspensa against a wall. — 2–3m (8–10ft)

Fuchsia An invaluable summer-flowering shrub with many cultivars – not all of which are completely hardy. Try F. riccartonii. — 0.6–1.5m (2–5ft)

Genista Broom A genus with a wide variety of low-growing and prostrate shrubs. All require acid soils and all have yellow flowers. — 0.9–2.4m (3–8ft)

Hebe This now covers all the shrubby veronicas. There is such a variety of leaf form and habit that it is an essential genus to consider for the smaller garden. Most are evergreen, some with grey, variegated or yellow foliage. Some tend towards legginess, but this can be controlled by pruning. — 0.6–1.5m (2–5ft)

Hibiscus Some cultivars are too big, but the genus is worth considering, as plants flower in late summer. They are slow-growing enough to be considered for the smaller garden. — up to 3m (10ft)

Hydrangea hortensia This has so many named varieties that it is difficult to choose any. They are excellent subjects for containers and are valuable for their flowers in late summer/early autumn. — average 1.5–3m (5–10ft)

Hypericum St John's wort There are many small shrubs that should be seen in growth before planting. H. calycinum is a weedy groundcover plant that should be avoided at all costs. All have yellow flowers in summer. — 30–90cm (1–3ft)

Kerria japonica Usually seen in its double form 'Pleniflora', which has orange balls throughout summer. However, the single flowered species is attractive and more so in the form 'Variegata' with variegated foliage. — 1–2m (4–6ft)

Lavandula Common lavender may be a choice for the small garden, but it needs good drainage and full sun to succeed. — 30–90cm (1–3ft)

Magnolia Another large genus both in size and choice of species. The best for small gardens is M. stellata, with white many-petalled flowers in March and April. — up to 3m (9ft)

Mahonia aquifolium An invaluable evergreen shrub that produces clusters of yellow flowers early in the year. — 90–150cm (3–5ft)

Olearia Daisy bush A useful genus of which some species are tolerant of atmospheric pollution. Evergreen, they are wind-resistant in maritime conditions. Some are tall, but generally could be accommodated in the smaller garden. The species need to be seen before purchase. — up to 1.8m (6ft)

Berberis thunbergii
'Atropupurea'

Hebe gauntletti

SMALL SHRUBS

Osmanthus delavayii An evergreen, slow-growing shrub bearing fragrant white flowers in April. — up to 1.8m (6ft)

Pernettya mucronata A dwarf evergreen with attractive autumn berries varying from white to purple. — 60cm (2ft)

Philadelphus Mock Orange Most are larger but one or two smaller selections: 'Beauclerk' is medium-sized; 'Manteau d'Hermine' has creamy-white double flowers. — 90cm (3ft)

Pieris An evergreen genus that requires similar treatment to rhododendrons. The flowers are borne in white panicles, but the main attraction is the spectacular young red foliage which appears in spring. Susceptible to frosts. — 1.8m (6ft)+

Pittosporum Grown for its foliage, more a small tree than a shrub, but the cultivars of *P. tenuifolium* such as 'Purpureum' or 'Silver Queen' have neat habits in tune with a small area. — up to 4.5m (15ft)

Potentilla fruticosa A valuable shrub with yellow flowers in summer. — 90cm (3ft)

Rhododendron This is too large a genus to be dealt with here, but there are a number of smaller species that do well on acid soils; the Kurume hybrid azaleas are evergreen; the Ghent hybrids are deciduous – a specialist nursery or garden centre should be visited before purchase. — 1–2m (3–6ft)

Santolina chamaecyparissus Cotton lavender A grey-leaved shrub with not particularly attractive yellow flower heads that is useful for foliage contrast. Thrives on a poor soil. — 45–60cm (18–24in)

Senecio greyi Another grey-leaved low-growing shrub, with daisy-like clusters of flowers. Spreads to 90cm (3ft). — 60cm (2ft)

Skimmia japonica A dome-shaped evergreen with fragrant flowers in April or May. If the right sexes are planted, berries follow. — 1–1.5m (3–5ft)

Spiraea japonica A variable plant, with flat heads of pink flowers. It has several smaller cultivars. — up to 90cm (3ft)

Syringa velutina (syn. *S. palibiniana*) This, the smallest of the lilacs, has undergone some name changes but despite that, its size warrants including in a list of small shrubs. It has pink flowers, not particularly scented. — 1–1.5m (3–5ft)

Viburnum farreri A shrub of slender behaviour, which begins flowering in the late autumn. Its fragrant pale pink flowers are produced in small clusters. — 2m (6ft)

Weigela florida 'Variegata' This form has a more compact habit than the species, making a small neat shrub. The flowers are pink and the leaves edged creamy-white. — 90–120cm (3–4ft)

TREES AND SHRUBS OF SPECIAL MERIT FOR TOWN GARDENS

The plants you choose should be interesting as well as appropriate in size. Ascertain the final spread and growth of the mature plants of particular species or cultivars.

Acer palmatum Japanese maple Selections have both leaf and colour variations and are sufficiently slow-growing.

Buddleia These shrubs require some attention because not all are hardy. Average height 2.75m (9ft). Prune well in April.

Caryopteris × clandonensis A very attractive grey-leaved, blue-flowering 90cm (3ft) shrub that again needs to be pruned hard in April to give flowers late in the summer. It needs a sunny spot.

Ceanothus This family produces blue-flowered shrubs from early summer to autumn. They can be either deciduous or evergreen but some are tender and may be hit very badly by hard winters.

Choisya ternata Mock orange Can reach 1.8m (6ft), has strongly fragrant white flowers in summer, is evergreen and fairly hardy.

Garrya G. *elliptica* grows to 3m (10ft) but does very well against a wall and the male plants produce some quite spectacular grey tassels in winter.

Prunus There are some very attractive prunus, apart from the showy, double-flowered pink 'Kanzan' Japanese cherry. Consider another ornamental cherry *P. sargentii* which does rise to 7.6m (25ft) but has pink flowers in March and April and good autumn colouring. *P. subhirtella* 'Autumnalis' autumn cherry grows to 6m (20ft) and has semi-double white or (in the rosea form) pink flowers from November to February.

Pyracantha Firethorn A shrubby genus that is evergreen and prickly, hardy and grown for its autumn berries. *P. coccinea* 'Lalandei' has marvellous orange berries and is particularly good against a wall.

Pyrus Pear trees are easy to manage if well trained when young. *P. salicifolia* 'Pendula', although it reaches 7.6m (25ft) has most attractive slow-growing weeping branches of silver leaves.

Ribes The flowering currant is a deciduous shrub flowering very early in the spring. *R. sanguineum* reaches 2.4m (8ft) and has one or two named cultivars. They grow anywhere and are very accommodating but, once they have flowered, have not much to offer.

Rosmarinus A well-known culinary herb with aromatic leaves. It has an upright form entitled 'Miss Jessops' which makes it slightly more tidy for the small garden.

Santolina Cotton lavender Another aromatic shrub with grey foliage that tends to become leggy if not cut back. It is best in full sun and poor dry soil.

Tamarix Seaside gardeners find Tamarisk useful. The branches bear soft foliage and rose-pink flowers from July onwards and should be pruned back after flowering.

Forsythia × intermedia 'Spectabilis'

Choisya ternata (Mexican Orange Blossom)

FULFILLING THE PLAN

Once you know what shapes and forms you want in your garden, you are ready to start creating it. You need to decide what materials to use and to construct your boundaries, to level and lay hard surfaces and so on. Before doing any major construction work, remember to check that you are not breaking local bye-laws or uprooting a tree with a preservation order on it.

BOUNDARIES

Your boundary construction serves a number of purposes as well as delineating the limits of your property. It may keep your children or pets safe and provide privacy but it can also be an attractive feature in its own right, in the way it complements and extends the character of your home.

There are, of course, many different materials. Choose from brick, stone, concrete or block unit walls; fencing; hedges or frame and planting barriers. On modern housing estates, there may be a covenant restricting the erection of boundaries. Otherwise the nature of your boundary is a matter of taste and weather conditions. Strange as

it may sound, in really windy areas a solid wall often causes wind to whip down over, resulting in great damage to plants underneath it. A hedge or pierced screen wall may offer your plants more effective protection than any solid wall as the wind is broken up rather than concentrated.

WALLS

The type of material used, if you are contemplating a brick or stone wall, should, if possible, match with any surrounding buildings. If you have access to old bricks, they are perfectly serviceable for walls and may look better than new brick by a period house.

This page A dry stone boundary wall made interesting by the planting of alpines in pockets left for the purpose during construction. Lewisia cotyledon hybrids are looking most effective here.

Opposite page, top right An example of a formal boundary hedge (yew) that has been used here to give framework for a sitting-out area and topiary work.

Opposite page, left This brick wall shows what you can do with a combination of different kinds of brick. Prefabricated screen blocks can be bought in a variety of patterns.

Opposite page, bottom right A selection of the different types of brick available for garden walls.

FOUNDATIONS AND SUPPORTS

All walls, apart from stone walls, need a foundation, usually of concrete, to avoid the risk of subsidence. The depth of the foundation required depends on the nature of the ground and the height of the wall but it rarely needs to be deeper than 500mm (20in). The width of the foundation should be at least double the width of the wall. 100mm (4in) thick brick or block walls can be built without further support up to a height of 600mm (24in). Above that height, the wall will need strengthening by piers (regularly spaced thickened sections) or must be built 200mm (8in) thick throughout. Zig-zag or crinkle-crankle walls take their strength from their horizontal deviations. If you want a low brick wall which is strong, you could leave a hollow trench in the top of a three-brick thick wall to be planted up.

STONE WALLS

These take slightly more skill and patience to build than a brick wall but can be very attractive. Reconstituted stone, split blocks, concrete and local stone are all effective walling materials.

One of the most attractive types of walling is dry stone with recesses for plants (see left). All stone walls should be built to a batter, that is wider at the bottom than the top. A raised bed should have sloping sides lest the soil push out the top layers of stone. Raised beds or raised walls with planting areas in them are ideal for disabled gardeners. When building a wall against a slope remember that it is vital to have some drainage space – there should be at least a 75mm (3in) gap from time to time along the bottom layer of any retaining walls. Likewise, take note of any trees nearby in case roots are damaged in the construction of your wall, or conversely, whether the roots will in future cause your wall to crack.

FENCES AND GATES

FENCES

Fencing serves the same functions as walls do but is obviously less massive, less durable and much cheaper. Be careful to place your fence exactly on your boundary in the interest of good neighbourly relations. Wood, metal and concrete are the usual materials. Plastic fencing is also available. It looks neat and urban; hurdles, the other extreme, look very rural. The environment and purpose of the fence should guide your choice of material. You could use trellis or netting as a temporary stop gap or plant support.

Fence and gate posts must be firmly mounted or they will quickly rot in damp earth. If you inherit a fence you like but which is not structurally sound, sink metal or concrete spur posts into concrete to splint the main posts.

When erecting a new fence, use wood posts if possible; concrete looks artificial and is heavy to handle. Oak posts are very durable but expensive. Treated larch is a good alternative. You need a line, spirit level, hammer, nails and a spade or post-hole borer. Position the posts carefully and, if possible, let them stand until concrete sets around the base before attaching the panels. If you do not want to use concrete, steel spike post holders are available.

If you use wooden fencing, choose the best

Right An attractive gate that gives the hint of further delights. Wrought-iron is long-lasting, but expensive to buy.

Opposite Panelled fencing supported at intervals by stout posts that could be wood or concrete. The plants growing in front are too small – taller subjects would make the fence less dominant.

quality you can afford and it must be well treated with preservative (ask for a non-creosote preservative if you want to plant close up to the fence). Well maintained by annual preservative treatments, your fence should last well.

GATES

The gate to your property is often the first thing a visitor will see, so make it attractive, durable and easy to open and close. Ask yourself whether the gates function to keep children or pets in, to provide privacy, whether it is for pedestrians or cars, do you prefer wood or metal? The style should complement the style of your house and the boundary – if you have a wood fence, it is sensible to have a wooden gate. Town gates tend to be more formal and of tighter construction than country ones but this is a matter of taste.

Gates and posts, if of wood, must be of well-treated timber. Gate posts, as fence posts, must be firmly set and made rigid by good ramming down of the infill material. Wooden gates should, as far as possible, be constructed with mortise-and-tenon joints fixed by wooden dowels. Ensure that hinges and latches are really strong and serviceable.

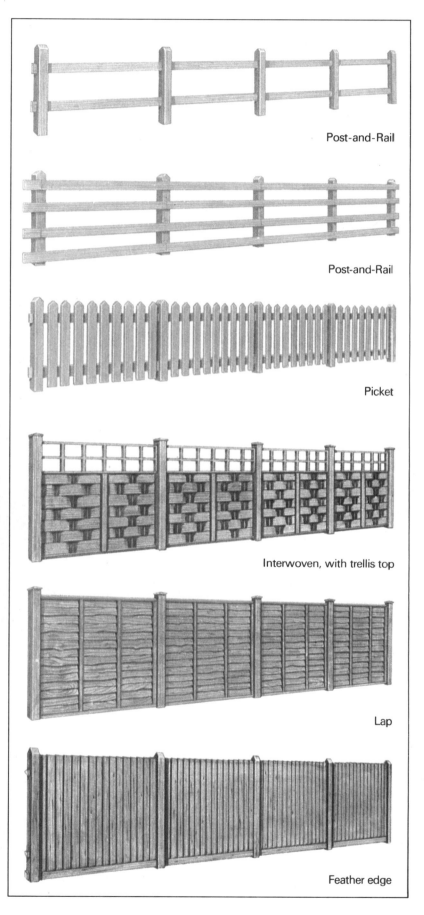

Post-and-Rail

Post-and-Rail

Picket

Interwoven, with trellis top

Lap

Feather edge

TERRACING

On a really steep site it may be advisable to terrace the land. Although this is a costly and laborious way of dealing with the landscape, it can be extremely effective and, on an awkward site, a good way of allowing light to reach lower windows. The depth of each 'step' in the terrace depends on the steepness of the slope – the steeper the deeper. It is best not to have too many little steps but fewer, wider steps in the terracing, linked, if necessary by stone steps to each level. One of the best terraced gardens in Britain is at Powis Castle in Wales where the terraces are wide enough to have paths and grass borders edged by balustrades, making the whole landscape look most spectacular. The average garden does not

Right *An example of a steep slope that has been terraced and in effect placed the house on a 'platform'. Once again trailing plants soften the hard outlines.*

Below *Different ways of tidying up slopes and level changes.*

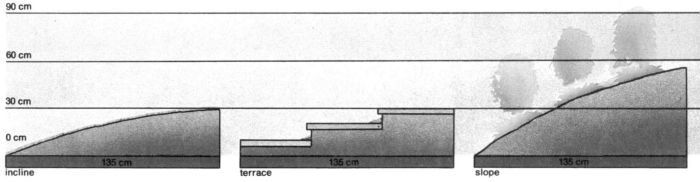

90 cm

60 cm

30 cm

0 cm

incline   135 cm   terrace   135 cm   slope   135 cm

have enough room to construct such terracing, so we have to keep the levels in proportion, remembering the wider the level, the more spacious the appearance of the garden.

The materials used in terracing should match any other feature in the garden or incorporate the same materials that have been used elsewhere to give a unity to the whole design. A brick wall interspersed with the same stone used on an exterior boundary wall would look attractive and in keeping. The lines of a terrace can especially complement the angularity of modern architecture. Planting can soften up some of the harshness if you prefer. If you want the planting to be permanent rather than seasonal, then small shrubs and low-growing herbaceous plants are the order of the day, rather than bedding plants. A good way to lead the eye from level to level is to have plants hanging down over the edges of steps. Lawn and terracing look good together and grass carried right up to the foot of a terrace wall is a good contrast if the upper terraces are planted.

RETAINING WALLS

Dry-stone walling is an attractive natural way to retain a bank but it does have to be very carefully constructed and lean in sufficiently so that the pressures from further up the hill do not push it out. The plants that can clothe a retaining wall are much more varied than you might think. In the spring you have *Alyssum*, *Arabis* and *Aubrieta* but colourful displays can be continued into the summer with *Saponaria*, *Dianthus* (pinks), *Campanula* and into the autumn with *Polygonum affine* and *Polygonum vacciniifolium*. The latter can even be in flower on Christmas Day. Peat blocks can be used for retaining banks but should not be used if more than 2 or 3 layers of blocks are being contemplated as they would not hold a bank for many years. Peat banks are constructed on much gentler slopes and are mentioned here as they provide a very attractive feature and medium for growing peat and acid-loving plants, such as dwarf rhododendrons, primulas and heathers.

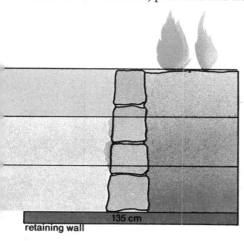

135 cm
retaining wall

Ramonda myconi: *enjoying the sunshine in a raised bed in a trough here, but it would do equally well placed in a wall in semi-shade.*

RAISED BEDS

These can be used in conjunction with terracing. Raised beds work much better than rockeries in most city gardens. Alpine and rockery plants look good in them and it is pleasant to be able to appreciate the delicate shape of such small flowers nearer to eye level.

BEDS AND BORDERS

Any bed or border must have been well dug or well prepared and be totally free of any perennial weeds before a single plant can be planted.

There are three main types of general garden beds: a shrub border, a herbaceous perennial border or a mixture of the two. The last is perhaps the happiest compromise. Annuals which are hardy or half-hardy, provide glorious splashes of colour but are time-consuming and can be expensive. Use them with discretion.

A herbaceous perennial is a plant which lives for an indefinite period, producing woody stems during the spring and summer, dying down in the autumn, then reviving in the spring. They provide a spectacular display throughout the summer, especially if the planting is devised to be successive, but during the rest of the year look somewhat flat and lacking architectural interest.

Above Bold-leaved hostas and green-flowered spurge contrast well with the soft pinks of common valerian. A good illustration of plant association.

Below A neat vegetable plot, with soft fruit and cordon fruit trees, and herbs in the foreground. An example of intensive cultivation.

round interest for a mixed border. The maintenance of mixed borders consists mainly of forking over in late winter or spring and top dressing with manure or compost if possible. If this can be done earlier in the year, a further top dressing of bark chippings can be applied in order to suppress weeds.

If perennial weeds persist, then apply selective weedkiller to the growing tips of the weeds, but extreme care should be taken not to get any on nearby plants. It should be remembered that herbaceous borders need to be lifted and divided every three to five years. This is a chore but a necessary one because perennials grow quickly. A shrub border, once planted, requires no replacement for several years.

VEGETABLE PLOTS

There are many good reasons for growing vegetables. It is usually cheaper than buying them, they can be organically grown if you prefer, and the fruits of your labours can be eaten when they are fresh enough to be at their most delicious.

A well-planned vegetable garden will yield crops throughout the year, especially if there is some form of glass protection. In very small gardens, plants have to be grown in odd spaces, tubs or growing bags. Many herbs, strawberries, tomatoes, peppers, lettuces etc. thrive in containers, which easily enable you to control soil pests and diseases. Runner beans form an attractive screen or climber even in a tiny garden. But if you have the space to grow more than summer salad plants and herbs, then you need to think out your plot before you plant. Where it is sited depends on whether you find a display of vegetables attractive, in which case site it within convenient reach of the kitchen, or whether you prefer it discreetly hidden away from the house. Try, however, to select open, sunny land.

The quantity and quality of your crops will reflect the thoroughness of your soil preparation. Dig the soil over very methodically, really clear it of weeds and if possible, plant a cleaning crop of potatoes. Rotational cropping is the system whereby closely related vegetables with similar soil and nutritional needs are grown on different plots each year. If they were grown on the same site continuously, then essential minerals might become exhausted and pests and diseases increase. The illustration opposite shows how this rotation works in practice.

By making small-scale repeated sowings throughout the season of crops such as carrots, beetroot and cabbages, you achieve a longer cropping period of ripe vegetables than by one annual sowing. To make the best use of your plot you should inter-crop, that is, plant a quick crop like lettuce between rows of slower growers like beans or peas. Seed packets give sound instructions for sowing, planting, thinning and distances and it is important to follow these for successful cropping.

HERBS

Herbs can be considered an adjunct to the vegetable garden and you could make an attractive edging to beds with chives, parsley or thyme. However, it is advisable to plant your herbs in the vegetable patch only if it is sited near the kitchen. If possible, select a part of the garden which faces west for greatest sunshine, and treat the ground with compost or manure before planting. Most herb plants are easy to cultivate and you may need to cut back rampant growers. Many herbs produce attractive foliage, colourful flowers or a strong perfume.

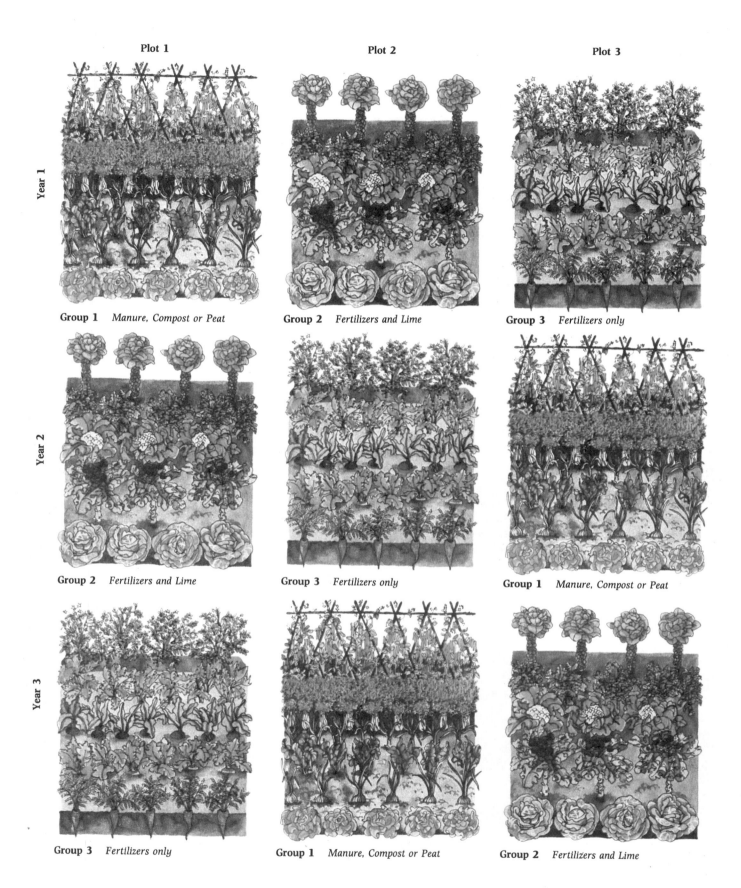

Plot 1   Plot 2   Plot 3

Year 1

Group 1   *Manure, Compost or Peat*   **Group 2**   *Fertilizers and Lime*   **Group 3**   *Fertilizers only*

Year 2

Group 2   *Fertilizers and Lime*   **Group 3**   *Fertilizers only*   **Group 1**   *Manure, Compost or Peat*

Year 3

Group 3   *Fertilizers only*   **Group 1**   *Manure, Compost or Peat*   **Group 2**   *Fertilizers and Lime*

A simple crop rotation lasts three years and involves dividing the vegetable garden into three plots. This ensures that crops are moved round methodically so that no group of soil nutrients is exhausted in any area. The groups are: 1) peas, beans, salad crops and onions; 2) the cabbage family; and 3) potatoes and root vegetables.

FRUIT PRODUCING AREAS

Most gardens are not big enough to devote much of an area to fruit-growing, so space should be used economically. If you move into a garden which already has some mature fruit trees, you will want to design the garden around them, but if you are able to plan from the beginning then, by careful choice, a succession of fruits can be enjoyed. When planting new trees or soft fruit, buy only quality stock or stock which is certified virus free. All fruits prefer a sheltered sunny situation.

FRUIT TREES

The development of dwarfing rootstocks has enabled gardeners to place top fruits such as apples and pears, cherries and plums in very small spaces. These varieties can be trained against walls or fences or act as divisions in the garden, making attractive features. For instance, cordon apple trees, that is, apples trained onto a single stem and planted at an angle of 45°, can be used this way. Espalier-trained trees can serve the same decorative and space-saving functions. You can also train plums and cherries as fans (see illustration). The advantage with cordons is that

they can be planted as little as 0.75 metres (2.5ft) apart, making them ideal for gardens where space is limited.

Pruning of trained trees is important as they will only flourish in their intended shape if they are properly trimmed and supported. Cordons need cutting back several times a year for the whole crop to remain within reach. An espalier is trained as one vertical stem with the side branches tied on to wires in a horizontal position; the pruning of the horizontal branches is conducted in the same way as a cordon. Fan training is a variation of espalier and is particularly popular for cherries. Fan-trained trees have a basic point from which the stems are trained outwards. This arrangement is most useful for limited space and against a wall.

SOFT FRUIT

Raspberries, blackcurrants, blackberries and gooseberries will usually crop in most situations. Other soft fruit favours sunny protected planting, and most fruit prefers a slightly acid soil. Plant where you can take some action against birds, if possible by netting, if necessary with a fruit cage. Soil should be well drained and properly dug over before planting. Some feeding with compounds

A mixed garden where precedence has been given to the soft fruit and vegetable areas. Strawberries in the foreground have been strawed to keep the fruits clean and the successive crops continue down the path.

Left A fan-trained apple tree against a wall is an attractive way of growing fruit in a confined space. Care should be taken not to put plants in front of the tree.

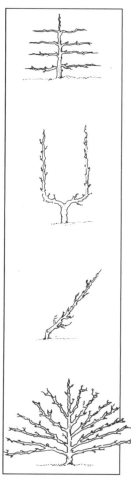

Below Ways of training fruit trees. Top to bottom: espalier, double cordon, single cordon and fan. Take expert advice about correct pruning.

of nitrogen, phosphates and potash will improve growth, hardiness and resistance to disease.

What you grow will, of course, depend on your own preferences but these may be influenced by space and maintenance. Strawberries can be planted in rows 60cm (2ft) apart with 45cm (1.5ft) between plants. They need mulching with plastic or clean straw in spring. Strawberries are very suitable for growing under cloches, in polythene tunnels, or in tubs.

For those protected in this way, late-July is the time for planting. They need humus-rich soil, so add well-rotted compost if necessary. Varieties that bear a single crop are harvested in mid-summer; but the so-called perpetual types, now widely available, crop from June to mid-autumn. Detach the fruits by cutting the stalks; the flesh bruises easily.

Currants are very easy to look after. Place them at least 1.2 metres (4ft) apart and when planting make sure that the crown of the plant is just below the soil level. After blackberries crop, cut out all the wood on which fruit has been borne and leave the new growth for next year. This should be carried out annually. Redcurrants are grown on a short stem and the fruit appears on the old wood so the branches should be trained to form a permanent frame, cutting back the laterals to form fruiting spurs. In later years, thinning can be undertaken. Gooseberries are grown in the same manner as red and white currants.

Raspberry canes are planted 45cm (1.5ft) apart in rows 1.8 metres (6ft) apart or along a boundary or fence but they should have plenty of wire support. After planting, cut canes to 23cm (9in) and thereafter remove the fruiting stems to ground level immediately after fruiting and train in the new shoots for the following year.

The young raspberry canes are planted in November in well-drained but moisture-retentive soil. Mulch the plants in April and keep them well watered in dry summer weather. The summer-fruiting varieties flower in May and June and the fruit are ready for harvesting in July and August; the autumn-fruiting types bear fruit from mid-September onwards. Harvest the fruit regularly during the fruiting season; the ripe fruit soon deteriorates on the canes.

Blackberries, loganberries and hybrid berries can be trained along fences but in the small garden care should be taken as they are somewhat vigorous and should be pruned after fruiting.

Unfortunately, there are many pests and diseases of fruit that cause top fruit in particular to become unsightly. Pests can be eliminated by spraying, but do not spray crops that are about to be picked. Aphids are a particular nuisance on a number of fruits and these should be sprayed whenever they are seen, as they are carriers of viruses which infect and reduce crop yield. Any fruit that is found to be infected with virus should be burnt immediately and a fresh virus-free stock planted. Strawberries and raspberries are particularly susceptible.

ROCK GARDENS

Rockeries can form the most delightful features of any garden and, contrary to general belief, can give colour throughout the year. They begin flowering with dwarf bulbs in January and finish in December with more dwarf bulbs and late autumn-flowering carpeting plants. Naturally, there are highlight periods of bloom, but a rockery's overall contribution to the colour and variety of a garden cannot be over-emphasized, especially when used in combination with water. But it must also be stressed that to keep them looking attractive, the amount of maintenance required by rock gardens is high compared to other forms of gardening.

PREPARATION

As with a vegetable garden, preparation of the site is of paramount importance. The entire area should be dug and any perennial weeds dealt with. Remove persistent offenders by chemical means if necessary, for once the rocks are in place it is extremely difficult to eradicate weeds. If you are keen to make a rock garden but have no natural slope on which you can begin, then you will have to set to and dig, throwing up the soil to make mounds and hollows of suitable size and shapes.

Rock is expensive and so must be used sparingly and sensibly. The great illusion is to make it look as if there is more rock than in fact exists. However, rocks should be set into the earth solidly to ensure stability, often to at least half their depth.

CONSTRUCTION

In my experience the most economical form of rock construction is the outcrop method, where the stone looks like little outcrops emerging from a gentle slope. This occurs in nature, as in the limestone hills of northern England for example. It helps to remember that all rock starts off as a solid lump, which is then split horizontally and vertically by natural weathering. So when you construct a rock garden avoid placing the rocks as if they are bonded, like a brick wall. Continue any strata lines right down through the design in one direction, either horizontally or vertically, to make the whole look more natural.

Building a rock garden can be strenuous work and to prevent injuring yourself, various items of equipment are quite useful: a sack truck for transporting rock; wooden planks to prevent

An extremely colourful spring rock garden with aubrieta, alyssum, iberis and saxifrages that will be over in a flash and leaving no room for colour later in the year. Much more varied planting is essential to give continuity of colour.

wheels sticking into soft soil; and a crowbar to manoeuvre the rock into position at the last point of resting. Do remember that once in place a rock garden is a permanent feature. Get the setting of the stones correct the first time. They should be tilted backwards slightly to allow rainwater to trickle down to the roots of plants. Rocks should be rammed into place and firmed with a wooden rammer or the reverse end of a cold hammer or trowel. Check carefully that they are stable and properly balanced before stepping on them.

CHOOSING THE STONE

Choice of stone is very important; I share the dislike of many in seeing the wrong stone in the wrong area. For instance, in a limestone area I consider that limestone is the best material to use. But if your local natural stone is sandstone, then limestone can look out of place. Local stone will be cheaper to use as transport distance will be less. It is transport that increases the cost of rock. There is one local stone that is welcome in almost any rock garden. This is the soft porous rock

called tufa. It has no strata lines and so is easy to use. There are also man-made 'rock' materials.

SOIL

If you wish you can construct little beds of rocks into which can be placed different soil mixtures. Then, for example, you can grow peat-loving plants in a slightly alkaline soil area by adjusting the soil accordingly.

If your soil is heavy, then a tremendous amount of drainage material in the form of chippings should be incorporated with the soil. The essential thing about the alpine plants mainly grown in rock gardens is that they all require good drainage.

When the rock garden is complete and planting undertaken, the whole area can be top dressed with chippings. These have a three-fold effect: they conserve moisture; look neat, tidy and natural; and they protect the collars of the plants from rot at soil level. Ideally, the chippings should be of the same material as the stone, but this again is an expensive undertaking. In most instances

A colourful example of how a rock garden can look – the drawing illustrates plants that flower over a long period – a point often overlooked, as alpines are considered to be spring plants only.

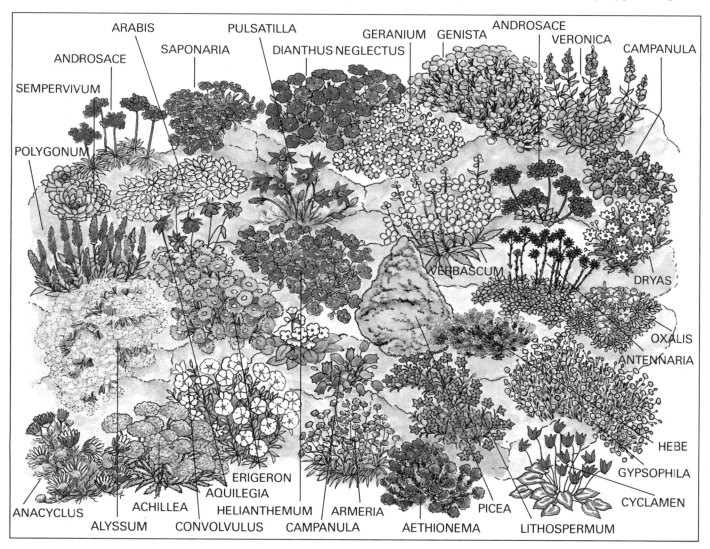

washed river gravel is just as acceptable.

When planting, remember one golden rule: in nature you never see an upright tree at the top of a mountain, so always place upright-growing plants at the base of a rockery. Conversely, plant only low-growing conifers or alpine species on the top of the rocks.

If it is not possible to create a rockery in your garden, you can still grow alpines very effectively in troughs and raised beds.

WATER GARDENS

Water makes an attractive feature in the garden because it is always moving. Even a slight breeze will ripple the surface of a still pool, while a waterfall creates a visual delight.

Water can be used in contrasting ways, either formally or informally. In a small town garden a formal rectangular pond looks most effective edged with square paving. Suitable planting can add height to avoid too 'flat' a look. Should you be fortunate enough to have a natural source of water in your garden, note the way in which it behaves before deciding to incorporate it in your overall garden design. For instance, in mid-winter a natural pool may be full of water, but in summer it may be just a dry hollow. The cause may be excessive drainage, and you will need to decide whether or not to impede this drainage to retain the water. Likewise, if a stream flows through your property, good use can be made of it. But first check the source of the water supply; if it flows through an area that is polluted, it will not support much plant and fish life. Before deciding to include a water feature, you should consider whether it will be safe if children are to be regular users of the garden.

POOLS

The level of any natural water will, of course, determine the style of garden design; and with natural water too, the shape of a pool will often be determined for you. Shape is also decided in advance if you use the prefabricated glassfibre pools which are readily available. These have many advantages for the small garden, tending to be on the small side themselves, and have an estimated life of about ten years. But they also tend to constrict your design as available shapes are not very varied.

Informal pools or ponds are usually edged with broken natural stone to hide the pool liner or cement, while plants grown at the side of the pool are designed to flop over the stone and disguise any severe lines. Remember that geometric

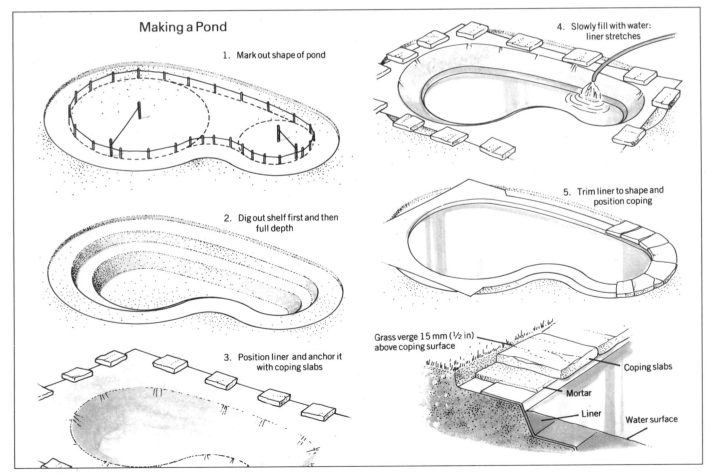

Making a Pond

1. Mark out shape of pond

2. Dig out shelf first and then full depth

3. Position liner and anchor it with coping slabs

4. Slowly fill with water: liner stretches

5. Trim liner to shape and position coping

Grass verge 15 mm (½ in) above coping surface

Coping slabs

Mortar

Liner

Water surface

A suggestion for a small garden on a gentle slope – two levels have been created and linked by steps. The pool has been raised from ground level to reduce the effect of a sloping site. Raised pools are safer than low pools if the garden will be used by children or old people.

shapes tend to produce formality; irregular-shaped ponds are more informal.

A more formal style of pool requires more detailed construction and there are certain steps to be followed. The diagram opposite gives you the basic ones. A great advantage today is the use of butyl, rubber or plastic liners, which save the chore of creating a concrete pool. Concrete may be more prone to leakage unless really well constructed but offers you the advantage of overflow and outlet pipes. Think through the mechanics of managing control of water before construction begins. If you want to have a waterfall, for example, particular thought must be given to use of a circulatory pump for the return of the water. You would be well advised to seek professional advice before starting work.

It must be remembered that water freezes in winter, so any equipment likely to be damaged by severe weather should be buried at least 40cm (16in) beneath the surface of the ground or be in a position to be removed for winter storage.

A water course of descending pools is a lovely sight but tricky to construct and maintain. Only consider installing one if you are yourself a very skilled handyman or are employing a professional landscape architect.

PLANTING

Consider carefully the planting of a pool. If, for instance, a rectangular pool is to be viewed from one of the narrow ends, do not plant it so as to obscure the far end: put the taller subjects at the back rather than in the foreground, much as you would when planting a border.

The edges of a more informal pool or pond can include a bog garden, where plants such as hostas, astilbes, iris and the like enjoy having their roots in water. If you have a simple pool, without running water, make sure the level is kept topped up during hot spells in summer. Dead leaves must be removed in autumn and when the pond needs a thorough cleaning-out, all the plants should be removed and temporarily placed in a bucket of water in order to remove all the accumulated rubbish.

Keeping fish is an attractive idea to many water-gardeners, but fish must be given plenty of space and oxygen to keep healthy. Oxygen is supplied by oxygenating plants and by movement of the water. In winter, oxygen will be denied to the fish when the water is frozen. A simple remedy is to keep something floating on top of the water to hinder ice from forming. If ice does form, never break it sharply, as the shock can kill the fish; it is better to melt a hole gently with boiling water from a kettle.

Herons are very fond of pond fish and may well visit your garden. It may be necessary to stretch a net across the water to prevent the birds from taking your fish; the same net will deter cats which also like to lift tasty fish dinners out of pools.

LAWNS

A new lawn can be made either by sowing seed or laying turf. The latter is more expensive but provides a usable lawn more quickly; the former enables you to choose your seed, depending on what use the lawn will be put to. If the lawn will be used primarily by children for playing, a strong mixture such as a rye grass selection should be used. For the average lawn you can buy an inexpensive mixture of several species without such broad blades of grass. Or you can purchase a flower seed/grass mix if you plan a garden meadow area. You can also purchase mixtures suitable for different types of soil and for shady conditions.

PREPARATION

Seed is best sown in September as this gives the lawn a chance to establish itself during the winter, when there is less likelihood of 'traffic' walking across it. Turf can be laid at any time of the year but is best done in the autumn or mid-spring. The preparation for lawns is the same for both seed and turf. As much care should be taken in preparing the soil as for any other part of the garden. It should be dug, raked, rolled, raked again, and the soil made fine, if necessary treating it with chemicals to reduce the perennial weeds (but see also below). Raking and rolling should be undertaken when the ground is dry—never when it is wet.

SOWING SEED

Preparation should take place during the summer, so that continual cultivation of the site can eliminate weed seedlings. Do not use a hormone weedkiller at this stage as it will affect germination of the grass seed. Apply general fertilizer at the rate of 55g per square metre (2oz per sq yd) about ten days before sowing or turfing. Scatter the seed uniformly over the surface of the ground, if possible using a distributor; rake it in and if

The informal treatment of a grassed area, where one waits for the bulb foliage to die down before mowing, which may well be done only twice a year.

The formal lawn, showing how the mower has been used in different directions. This gives a neater appearance to the lawn than if it was mown in the same direction each time.

birds are likely to be a problem, net the area or use bird scarers. Always sow at the rate recommended by the supplier – fine seed will need many more seeds to the square metre than a coarser variety. Some seed is specially treated to be distasteful to birds. Water well if no rain falls. When the grass is about 4cm (1.5in) high, roll it lightly to consolidate the soil and then, in a dry spell, mow with the blade set high.

LAYING TURF

Laying turf is simple. First lay the turf around the edge of the site, so that you have the outline of the lawn. Then fill in the centre with turves, laying them as you would a brick wall—that is, interlocking so that lines do not run straight across. This can be done quite simply. Lift a turf on a fork and unfold each end, then press it into place firmly with the fork, tapping it down lightly afterwards. When you come to the end of a row, cut any surplus that lies over the edging turf with

a sharp garden knife. Use pieces for filling in.

Always work facing the bare soil, so that your weight is on the grass you are laying. For this you need two planks; one to stand on and another to move forward. Using these prevents constant raking of the soil which you would otherwise tread on. A light rolling when the turf is laid helps to consolidate it, with a top dressing of soil or peat to fill in the joints. Before mowing, roll again and fill in any gaps. Then mow in the same way as for a grass-seeded lawn, with the blades set high.

Subsequent maintenance involves an annual top dressing of fertilizer, which can usually be applied at the same time as a selective weed-killer.

A well maintained lawn is well worth the time and money spent on it, as an attractive feature of any garden and a background to set off plants. Remember that flower beds created in a lawn will break up an open space and in the small garden will produce a fussy look rather than the open appearance you need to give a feeling of space.

PATIOS AND PAVING

Patios have never been more popular than they are today, as we become more and more aware of the value of precious living space out of doors. Somewhere to sit, to play, to entertain out in the open extends the living area of your house and adds another dimension to leisure life, especially if you are able to cook outside, too, on occasions.

Opposite page *Basic patio layout at the rear of the house, with mixed paving and including a mini-pool. At left the pergola and overhead beams, offering support for climbing plants, provide partial shade for the table and bench seating, built-in barbecue and storage units.*

A patio is an expensive item to construct, so it's important to get the design and the planning right. But before you get to the actual planning stage, there are a few questions to ask yourself about the site. Traditionally we think of the patio as an area alongside the house, but this need not necessarily be so: it all depends on how you are going to use it. Is it to be an outdoor room? It could be that you are overlooked, or that the garden is in shade all the time, or that the street is so noisy that you are not likely to want to stay outdoors for long. In this case, you may decide to use your patio mainly as an area filled with attractive plants that can be viewed from the window. A paved area is a very good way of showing off a series of tubs, boxes and baskets of flowers that can be switched around with the seasons and replenished with bedding plants.

Many people have to use their patio primarily as a service area. For instance, you may have to store dustbins in it, or hang out the washing across it, or use at least part of the total space to keep a bicycle, scooter, or push-chair under cover. In such cases you may want to arrange for trellises or other types of screens to hide all the impedimenta and still leave you room for a deckchair or for sunbathing. So the patio may need to be larger than you might otherwise have envisaged. A patio that is to be a young children's playground, on the other hand, does not necessarily need the sun; but it should have a non-slip surface and be near enough to the kitchen door for you to be able to keep an eye on things.

Work out which way your plot faces in relation to the sun's position at various times of the day and how it might affect your use of a patio. You may find, for instance, when you come to chart the sunshine, that the spot where you are planning to sunbathe in the afternoon, in a small backyard or garden, will be in the shade at that time of day; in which case you will have to think again. Remember that in summer the sun climbs higher in the sky and you get longer hours of heat and light. The ideal patio faces south or west for the maximum warmth and sunshine. If it is sunbathing at all costs that you want from your patio you may find you need to

Right *An archway, well clothed with climbers, creates a sense of anticipation by concealing what lies beyond in this Leeds council-house garden.*

site it away from the house, perhaps even at the far end of your garden. This might have the bonus of giving you more peace and quiet, distanced from the hurly-burly of the house.

Screening off the area from the eyes of the neighbours and ensuring privacy plays its part in the planning of most patios; but it should be done in such a way that it does not put the garden or the patio itself into shade or make it feel cramped. This can often be done by using a see-through structure such as trellis or pierced-screen concrete blocks, rather than a solid wall. But remember that the higher the fence, the less sunshine it will let in. In cramped city conditions a 'ceiling' of laths or planks suspended on their edges, with creepers growing over and between them, can block out the upstairs neighbours' view of you and give you the feeling that you are in your own outdoor dining room. If you want to, you can add clear, corrugated PVC sheeting on top, which will shut out the worst of the weather and act as a greenhouse over the climbers beneath; but it will be very noisy when it rains hard. Any such roofing, incidentally, should have a slight slope so that the rain runs off it. You can also use the space under the planks to suspend plant pots and hanging baskets.

42

PLANNING THE PATIO

No matter how small your patio is going to be, it pays to make a plan. But first of all, if you are doing anything drastic, you need to check that you are not contravening local bye-laws or a landlord's agreement. It is far better to find out beforehand than to have to put things right afterwards – expensively. Remember that many trees now have preservation orders on them, especially in towns; this is a point that needs checking too. It is useful at this stage to find out what type of soil you have – acid, alkaline (limy), or neutral. And find out whether it is sticky clay or a lightweight sand that will let the moisture drain through. If you are gardening solely in containers then you can choose your own compost to suit yourself and the plants you wish to select. Otherwise, a chat with the neighbours or the use of a soil-testing kit will give you a guide-line when it comes to choosing plants. If you have no-one else to turn to, your local town parks department may be of help.

DESIGN

Note any existing features that are there and plan to make the most of them. Even a dead woody shrub or tree may be useful as a host to climbing plants or to suspend hanging baskets from. Other factors must also be taken into consideration. Are you overlooked by a high-rise building, for instance, which shuts out a lot of light? Is yours a site that gets more than its fair share of wind? Decide, too, whether you want to block out your surroundings or make a feature of them. Often an item like a church spire or a magnificent tree across the road can make a punctuation point outside your garden that you want to keep in view, while an ugly factory or lines of neighbours' washing will need screening from sight.

Fences and walls are a precious bonus to the confined gardener: they are the features where you can get some of your most spectacular effects with climbers planted in half baskets; you can even exploit them to deceive the eye by painting murals on them or by using mirrors. Think carefully about the patio 'floor'. What is it going to be used for? Heavy-duty traffic may dictate the use of concrete or natural stone paving; but they can be jazzed up by growing little crevice plants between them – a point to bear in mind when laying the slabs. Remember, though, that the use of paving under a deciduous tree or a bush that bears lots of berries may mean that you will have a great deal of sweeping up to do when autumn comes if it is not to look unsightly, and it may pay you to have grass or a grass substitute instead.

If a patch of lawn is out of the question, but you yearn for one, then you can have a miniature patch of green chamomile or some other creeping plant that makes a good grass substitute simply by leaving out one or two of the paving stones at random and planting up the spaces.

Even the smallest patio needs a focal point of

some sort – something that focuses your attention when you view it. A small statue, if it is carefully chosen, can lead the eye to the end of a small courtyard. A sundial makes a good centre point to a paved garden. A small pool looks good, especially if it is raised above ground level for dramatic effect. Water makes an ever changing centre of interest, especially in confined surroundings.

Patio lighting is another item to be taken into consideration at this stage, since it is much easier to instal right at the beginning, when wiring can be hidden, than having to disguise trailing flexes later on. If you are planning a barbecue, remember that you will need to provide suitable lighting around it for evening cook-outs. A permanent fixture above head height is best.

While you are still at the planning stage it is a good idea to develop an overall theme for your patio. It could be a particular colour scheme: small patio areas look best with one, rather than a liquorice-allsorts mix of every conceivable colour. Or it could be a particular 'look'. If you wanted to make your plot look like a Mediterranean-style patio, for instance, you could plan for some large terracotta pots, and make up a shopping list of plants like the yucca, and the Chusan palm (*Trachycarpus fortunei*) or New Zealand flax (*Phormium tenax*) to give a spicy, sub-tropical look. A country-garden patio can easily be achieved by heavy interplanting among the paving slabs and with old-fashioned flowers like foxgloves (*Digitalis*) and hollyhocks (*Althaea*) against the wall.

Left *A series of terraces answers the problem of paving this large, sloping site.*

Below *Large sliding garden doors allow this living room and patio to become fully integrated on warm summer days.*

45

MAKING YOUR PLAN

Drawing up a plan of your patio gives you a chance to make your mistakes on paper rather than more expensively on the site. The easiest way to do this is to make a large-scale plan of your plot on graph paper. Using the squares to count, rather than measuring each time, saves a great deal of effort. And you can sketch in the approximate size of fully grown specimen plants to see how they will look. Better still, cut them out of pieces of paper and move them around on your plan to find the best position for them. If you are proposing to include deckchairs, cushions, or a table and chairs, cut out scale outlines of the furniture separately and move them around on your plan to see if they will fit. You will need to attend to such details as making sure that it is actually possible to push a chair back from the table when you want to stand up, especially if you are building a terrace in a confined space or planning to cram a number of containers onto it. For a really comfortable sitting-out area that will take a table seating four people, you need a width of at least 2.5m (8¼ft) and as much length as is available.

As a general rule, keep the centre of the patio open, otherwise the immediate outlook from the house will seem cluttered. Bear in mind, too, if you are planning raised flowerbeds or putting plants against a house wall where there has never been a bed before, that you must not go above the damp-course line or you may be plagued with moisture problems on the inside of the house. You will find the damp-course if you look for a layer of tarred felt or other material inserted between courses of bricks near the ground on newer houses or, on older properties, such features as a series of holes bored in the wall. Where no damp course is evident, follow the general guide that the soil level should be a good 150mm (6in) below the floor level inside the house. If you do come up against the problem of damp, you must move the flower-bed away from the wall, put your plants in free-standing containers, or instal some sort of permanent waterproof sheeting between the soil and the brickwork. Another simple idea is to use growing bags. You can disguise these useful but unattractive plastic containers in various ways – for instance, with a row of pot-grown herbs.

If, when you have drawn up your plan and put it on paper, you are still a little doubtful how the

The patio can be a place of restful relaxation. Here, for instance, a small paved area is separated from the noise and bustle of the house by a pierced-screen-block wall and the lawn beyond.

Tiny town gardens can provide a colourful display with space-saving 'vertical' plantings, narrow borders and small container plants.

overall plan or some of its main features will look in reality, it's a good idea to take photographs of the site from several angles. You can then sketch the major features you are proposing, like specimen trees, raised beds, a barbecue, or walls and screens, on to the photos. This will help you to see what your plan will look like in a third dimension. Now try your plan out on the actual site, using buckets as containers and pieces of wood and any other props you please. You may find that what seemed to work on paper does not quite work out in practice. Perhaps the door or window will not open fully, for instance, because something is in the way. Mark out paved areas, flower beds, and so on with a string and wooden pegs. Keep the string above ground level to give a more realistic feel of that third dimension, height: a planned area picked out in chalk on the ground may seem to work out nicely – but may become obtrusive when you see it in terms of growing plants. If your plot slopes, do not be in too much of a hurry to level it up. Think carefully first: it might be better to turn it into a series of terraces. Or the slope could be exploited by installing a feature with an attractive trickle of water down to a pool.

A small, steep-sloping site has been cleverly converted here into intimate upper and lower terraces, whose circular form is echoed in the shape of the pool and flights of steps.

MATERIALS

The materials for your patio are likely to be the largest single expenditure you will make on your garden, so it is as well to make the right choice. There is a wide range of surfaces available now, each with its own advantages and disadvantages. You need to list your own particular requirements in order of importance, then choose the material that suits you best.

Used creatively, a hard surface outside can enhance the look of your house. But you must at all costs avoid producing a desolate, hard-ground cover reminiscent of a shopping precinct. So think, in general, about breaking up the hard-surface layout into fairly small areas, varying the surfacing materials, and incorporating plants.

The nature and design of hard surfacing should be assessed carefully for its functional and aesthetic qualities. In functional terms the surface may be used for access (for people, bikes), for children's play, for entertaining, and for sitting and sunbathing. The materials can vary widely according to function; but whatever it is used for, the best patio surface should be hard, clean, smooth, quick-drying, and weed-

free. And, of course, whatever the material and the use to which it is put, it must be durable and not unreasonably expensive.

From the point of view of appearance, a potentially dull-looking hard-surfaced area can be made interesting and attractive by careful choice of colours, by breaking up the floorscape (for instance, with tubs or small beds of flowers), by changing levels, and by attention to the detailed finishing both within the surfaced area and particularly around the margins. Paving made up of small units, such as brick pavers, can both add character and create an illusion of space within a small garden. If the same type of brick is associated with materials also used in the house or its boundaries, a pleasingly co-ordinated effect may be achieved. Colours and textures are very important: bright colours that look attractive in the catalogue sometimes look garish on site, especially if they are mixed, and they tend to attract the eye away from the subtle, natural colours of your plants. Large expanses of light grey concrete are not only boring to look at but can cause glare in bright sunlight. On the other hand, lighter colours can help to reflect light into shaded areas.

The rather severe appearance of square paving can be alleviated if plantings are encouraged to overgrow the line of the edging slabs.

NATURAL STONE

York stone, limestone, granite and other kinds of natural stone have one big advantage: once laid they look instantly mellow, as if they have been in place for a long time – a good selling point if your house is an old one. But they are extremely costly, even when bought second-hand, and are not always readily available. If you are buying second-hand from a demolition yard – the cheapest source – you may find that the slabs vary greatly not only in size but in thickness too. So if you are paying a great deal for your materials it is worth shelling out still more to get a professional to lay them, rather than trying to tackle this job yourself.

PREFABRICATED SLABS

These are now the most commonly used materials for hard surfacing in the garden. Prefabricated concrete slabs are available in a vast range of colours and textures, and vary in shape from the 600 × 600mm (2 × 2ft) common grey slab to polygonal and circular forms; most of them are 50mm (2in) thick or less. More expensive types are made of reconstituted stone, and you can even find them in a texture reminiscent of

Above *Natural stone slabs, though beautifully weathered in appearance, are expensive and sometimes difficult to obtain.*

Left *Prefabricated concrete slabs are available in a variety of sizes, shapes, colours and surface textures.*

water-worn stone. It is important, however, to make sure that the surface finish is non-slip: a smooth finish encrusted with algal growth can be treacherous in wet weather. Incidentally, it is quite easy to make your own concrete paving slabs. If you construct a wooden framework from 50 × 50mm (2 × 2in) section timber with multiple 'cells' you can form several slabs at once. Prefabricated slabs come in a wide range of colours and, if you are making your own, you can colour the concrete easily with the mix-in

powder. But remember not to be too heavy handed: coloured slabs when laid, and particularly when wet, tend to look brighter than they did in the builder's yard or garden centre. If you are laying a large area, it pays to use two colours, chequerboard fashion, to avoid monotony. But again, be careful in your use of combined colours. For instance, although grey and honey-beige slabs are uninteresting if used by themselves over a large area, when combined they can look very attractive.

CRAZY PAVING

Although crazy paving has often been sneered at, there is a great deal to be said for it, provided that the broken stone of which it is constructed is natural and also that it is properly laid. It is those bits of broken concrete or synthetic paving, or stretches of concrete marked out in a random pattern, or poorly fitted paving with ugly, thick mortar joints that have given crazy paving a bad name. Properly laid random paving can look perfect in a country setting, although it is inclined to seem out of place in towns or with avant-garde architecture.

Bear in mind, if you intend to use natural stone for your crazy paving, that the pieces are likely to vary considerably in thickness. This means that you must prepare the ground carefully if the paving is to present a flat, even surface.

Below *The mellow colours of old brick paving look especially good in the gardens of older properties.*

Above *Crazy paving is best made from natural stone. Although rock of a single type is safest, different colours and textures can be attractive if carefully selected.*

BRICKS

Bricks are among the most versatile of paving materials. There is an enormous range of colours and the small unit size is particularly well suited to the smaller garden. They can match the bricks used for the house and serve visually to link the house and garden and give a very pleasant appearance.

Two sorts of brick are available for garden paving. You can use standardized bricks which are frost resistant and generally, therefore, will need to be of 'special' quality. Alternatively, you can buy specially made paving bricks, which are usually thinner in section but are very hard and dense. Engineering bricks are suitable, too, but choose muted colours.

Standard bricks can be laid flat on their bedding faces or, more traditionally, you can lay them on edge (but this requires more bricks). Perforated bricks must, of course, be laid on edge. There are many bonding patterns to choose, from the simple stretcher bond to the more decorative basket weave and diagonal herringbone, but the latter pattern will entail cutting the bricks diagonally at the edges.

BLOCKS

A paving material recently introduced to this country, although it has been used for many years in continental Europe, is the concrete block, which is now available in Britain in many colours and a variety of shapes. The rectangular blocks are 200 × 100 × 65mm (8 × 4 × 2½in) in size – that is, similar in shape to, but slightly smaller than, a brick.

In the last few years too, special concrete paver blocks, in various shapes and colours, have come on the market. One of the attractions of using these is that they can be laid in a wide variety of patterns to create visual interest and sometimes also an illusion of extra space, width, or depth. They are extremely hardwearing and are usually easier for the amateur to lay than conventional bricks.

CONCRETE

Used in mass form as a garden surfacing material, concrete is hard, durable, and fairly easy to lay, and once laid it is more or less permanent. To many people, the colour of concrete is harsh, to others merely boring; certainly large, bare areas of concrete are pretty unexciting. Colouring agents can help to relieve the monotony if the concreted area is fairly small and the colours chosen with care; but a more interesting effect can be achieved by modifying the surface texture – for example, by exposing the coarse stone aggregate. Alternatively you can mark it out into mock paving squares, although, unless this is done neatly, it is likely to look worse than a plain surface. You may find that the best solution is to concentrate on stocking the surroundings with colourful plants.

A potentially gloomy conservatory can be brightened greatly by vividly coloured container-grown plants.

COBBLES

These smooth rounded stones look very attractive if you use them on a small scale, setting them around a tree for instance, or infilling an odd corner, where it might be difficult to cut larger paving materials. But they are not suitable for a large area, since they become dangerously slippery when wet, and they are totally unstable to stand garden furniture on. However, they can look very attractive when used to break up a large expanse of concrete – set in a circular swirl for instance, or ranged into a square. Granite setts, too, can be used in the same way, to provide patterns on what might otherwise be a dull expanse of paving or concrete. Bed them in carefully to achieve a flat surface.

Cube-shaped granite setts, though expensive, make a hard-wearing paved surface of distinctive colour and texture.

GRAVEL

Although it is used a great deal on the Continent, particularly in France, gravel is seldom used over here for patios, though it has many advantages. It makes a relatively inexpensive and quickly laid surfacing material. Curves are much easier to form with gravel than with paving slabs, and slight changes in level are readily accommodated. Gravel offers the advantage, too, that it can easily be taken up and later re-laid if underground piping and other services need to be installed at any time. Finally, if you become bored with it, the gravel is likely to form a good base for an alternative surface. The main disadvantage is that, unless it is carefully graded, the surface will be loose: pieces of gravel spilling on to an adjacent lawn could cause serious damage to a mower, while they are easy to bring into the house on the soles of shoes.

Gravel is available in two main forms: crushed stone from quarries, and pea gravel from gravel pits. The former is of better quality, but will be very expensive unless the stone is quarried locally. Gravel occurs in a variety of attractive natural colours, and your choice should if possible complement any stone employed in the garden for walling or rock gardens. The alternative, washed pea gravel, comes in shades from near white to almost black. Whichever type is used, ensure that the stones are neither too large (which makes walking uncomfortable), nor too small (they will stick to your shoes). For most purposes the best size is in the range 10 to 20mm (⅜ to ¾in) in diameter. Be sure that it is all of one grade; a mixture tends to settle out into layers and looks less effective.

Gravel is good at suppressing weeds. The only maintenance it should need is an occasional raking over to keep it looking trim and to remove any bumps or indentations.

DECKING

Little used in this country, but popular in the United States, decking can solve problems as an alternative to paving if you are laying a patio over several different levels or a very uneven surface. It looks particularly good in country surroundings or with modern houses and it feels pleasantly warm to walk on. But it is very expensive, and its life-span is not as great as that of concrete. You need to use hardwoods (or softwoods that have been really thoroughly treated with preservative) and the fastenings are expensive, as they must be of the very best quality. But decking is quite easy to construct yourself, unless it has to be built high off the ground, and you can get some pleasing patterns by arranging the planks in different designs. If you cannot afford to deck the entire area, see if a corner of the patio could be decked.

Timber decking makes a warm, handsome surface, especially suitable for use with modern buildings.

A FINAL THOUGHT ON PLANNING

You need to choose your patio surface as you would a good carpet: you are looking for something that is going to wear well, of course, but it must also be attractive to the eye and blend in with the surroundings. In other words a solid, unimaginative, grey concrete slab would detract from rather than add to the charms of a period house, whereas herringbone brick paving, or large slabs of (albeit imitation) York stone could look very attractive indeed.

If your patio is any size at all, vary the paving materials you use – don't stick to just one type. Give your patio 'professional' touches by breaking up the line of the paving, here and there, with something else – cobbles set around a newly planted tree on the patio, for instance, or small, narrow pavers outlining a large square of paving stones, or even a selection of decorative ceramic tiles (make sure they are suitable for outdoor use) forming a stone 'rug' in front of the back door. One of the easiest ways to add variety to the smaller patio is to mix small and large size slabs of the same material; most of them are made in modules that can mix so it is quite easy to do this.

If you are using slabs the easiest way to finalise your design is to buy graph paper and work it out on that. Don't feel that you have to pave the entire area; if there is space for it, why not plant a decorative tree or, at the least, a flowering bush? (But ensure that it is located where it is not going to be in the way of the main traffic runs, and where it can be seen and appreciated.) Think carefully, too, about what you are going to do with the edge of the patio, where it meets the lawn, if there is one. Avoid that 'station-platform' look at all costs by legislating for a low wall, at the very least, to finish it off.

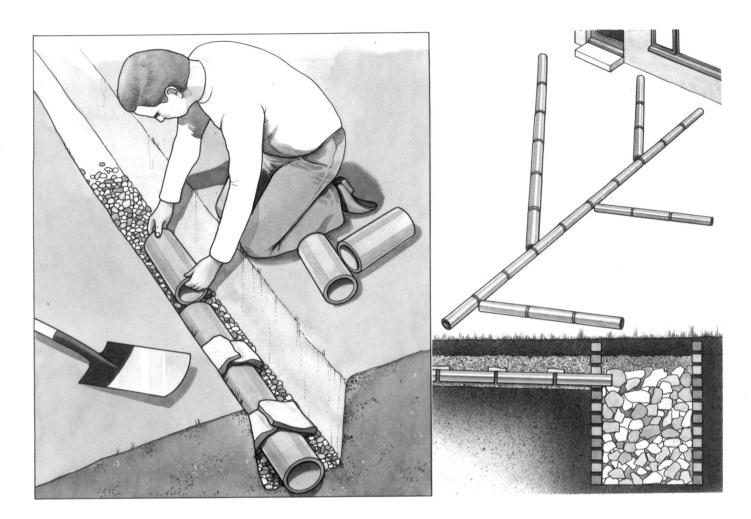

Above *Before laying paving material, make sure that the underlying surface is properly drained. The drawing at left shows installation of drainage pipes, with joints between pipe-lengths covered with slates.*

Right, above and below *A herring-bone pattern of main and tributary drainage pipes with coarse aggregate topped with finer material.*

CONSTRUCTION HINTS

Laying your own patio can be hard work. By doing so, you save a good deal of money, if not time; and for many people there is great satisfaction in doing it yourself.

Whatever form of surface you decide on, make sure that it is laid on a well-drained stable base; this will avoid problems of sinkage and water-logging. All topsoil must be removed because it contains organic matter, which will decompose and may settle. The surfacing material can sometimes be laid directly onto well-compacted subsoil, but usually a well-consolidated layer of hardcore (such as fragments of brick) is needed, covered with sand, ash, or hoggin (screened gravel).

Begin by drawing a scale plan on which are marked the lines of all the drains and the positions of manholes and water pipes. Now using manufacturer's plans and leaflets work out an appropriate layout using standard paving sizes; try to avoid having to cut slabs.

LAYING PAVING SLABS

The easiest way of laying paving slabs is to put them directly on to the soil; but this requires a light sandy soil and a comparatively level site. It is not easy to get a good level on heavy clay soils, and uneven levels can cause shifting or even cracking of the slabs. On these soils, it is best to lay the slabs on a bed of sand; this saves the effort and expense of using a mortar base.

You need a firm and level base on which to work, so first prepare the ground. Dig down deep enough to bring the finished patio to the level you want. Allow for a slight slope across the paved area to drain rainwater away from the house. If the ground is firm, you need dig out only the softer areas and replace the soil there with well-compacted hardcore. On soft clay soils, however, it's best to roll or firmly compact a 100mm (4in) thick layer of hardcore over the whole area, finishing it with a 50mm (2in) layer of sharp sand to fill in larger gaps. Mark out the edges of the patio with pegs and string to ensure that the edges of the slabs make straight lines (individual slabs vary slightly in size) and use a builder's square to make sure that your corners form right angles. Try to plan the paving in such a way that you will not have to cut any of the slabs; cutting is tricky work. Begin bedding slabs at one corner. You can lay a mortar bed under the whole of the slab; or you can lay five pads of mortar about 50mm (2in) high, one under each corner and one in the middle of the slab. Mortar used should be a 1:4 mix of cement and sand. Tap down each slab with a wooden mallet or with a hammer on a piece of softwood: treat the slabs gently to avoid breaking them. Level each slab against its neighbour and against your wooden peg reference points (which you take out progressively as work proceeds). Leave 12mm (½in) wide joints between slabs and insert wooden spacers of that width to stop the slabs closing up. Joints can be filled in various ways. You can, for instance, mix a cement/sand solution and pour it into the joints. Or you can mix the cement and sand dry (the sand needs to be very dry) and brush the dry mix into the gaps; then you sprinkle the joints with a watering can fitted with a fine rose. Generally, the easiest way is to mix up a very stiff mortar and press it firmly into the joints with the edge of a pointing trowel. Don't walk on the slabs for at least three days. If the patio is bounded by a wall at the bottom of the slope, leave a small gap between the slabs and the wall, filling the gap with pebbles to help drainage.

If your patio is going to have really heavy use, it's best to lay the slabs in a wet concrete mixture (1 part of cement to 6 of sand) at least 100mm (4in) deep. Use ready-mixed concrete to avoid hard work but make sure the site is ready when it is delivered. Guard against concrete burns by protecting your hands with gloves. The paving slabs are laid on the wet surface of the concrete after it has been tamped down and levelled.

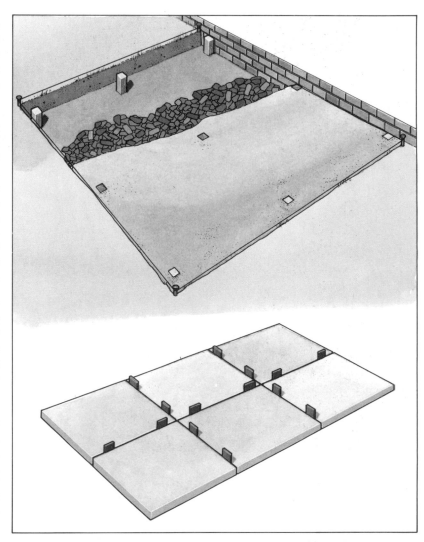

Above *Laying patio paving. In the upper picture, the site has been prepared with a sand layer over compacted hardcore; the sand surface is level with the tops of the wooden pegs, which determine the height and slope of the paving. The slabs (lower picture) are separated by spacers; the gaps are then filled with mortar.*

Left *Add interest to your hard surfacing by using more than one material.*

Solid concrete makes efficient paving – but it's a good idea to relieve its monotonous appearance with more colourful materials – and, as here, with a rich array of flowering plants.

LAYING CONCRETE

Contrary to popular belief, concrete can be laid directly on to subsoil, so long as it is firm and stable. The only preparation you need to do is to make sure the ground has the necessary slope for drainage, and then to roll it thoroughly. Any soft spots should be dug out and replaced with rammed hardcore. If the subsoil is not so suitable, prepare the ground as if you were laying paving stones, with hardcore and sand.

You will now need to set shuttering, or formwork, at the sides to keep the concrete in place when it is poured and keep it straight at the edges. Special steel shuttering and holding pins can be hired, but a cheaper alternative is to use old planks of timber, at least 25mm (1in) thick, set on their edges and held in place with pegs. Set a straight edge and spirit-level between the formwork on either side and hammer the shuttering down with a mallet until you get a level reading on the spirit level; then make fine adjustments in order to achieve a drainage slope.

Concrete is basically a mixture of cement (usually ordinary Portland cement), sharp (concreting) sand, coarse aggregate (stones), and water. For good quality concrete the proportions of these materials should be carefully measured and mixed. Always store the materials separately, and use heavy-duty plastic buckets to mea-

sure the ingredients (measuring by shovelfuls is not accurate enough). Avoid laying concrete in frosty weather. The standard mixture for this type of application is 1 part of cement, 2½ parts of sharp sand, and 4 parts of 20mm (¾in) coarse aggregate.

CRAZY PAVING

Again, you need a firm base for laying, and it is generally best to lay the broken pieces of slab on to a continuous mortar bed rather than on to mortar pads; the pieces are often triangular in shape and the mortar pad method would not give enough stability for these.

The first thing to do is to sort out the larger pieces with straight edges and to lay a number of these to give you a straight line along the edges of the path or patio. Then you can infill with the smaller, irregular pieces in the middle. However, a more informal approach can also be attractive. This can be achieved by laying the paving with a deliberately ragged edge, over which trailing plants can grow. Whichever method you adopt, first lay the broken pieces loose, fitting them together in attractive combinations of shape and colour, before you begin to fix them in their mortar bed. Try to make your paving 'jig-saw' fit as neatly as possible, so that the joints are not unattractively wide.

BRICKS

Set some sort of edging around the area – timber for instance – then lay your bricks into a 37-50mm (1½-2in) layer of mortar, leaving a 10mm (⅜in) gap between them, then grout them carefully with a dryish mix. Blocks and pavers should be set in the same way; though if arranged in interlocking patterns, they can be laid on a carefully levelled bed of sand, then bedded down with a plate vibrator.

COBBLES

These should be packed as close together as possible on a bed of mortar or concrete. Another method is to set them in a dry bed of mortar or concrete mix, then water them thoroughly with a sprinkler to set them. You can lay the cobbles at random or you can create patterns, by exploiting colour differences or by laying them in concentric circles or squares.

Far left *Brick lends itself to a huge variety of paving patterns.*

Near left *Cobbles, too, can be used to create pleasing patterns, though preferably over small areas.*

Below *Crazy paving looks best in informal settings. The site needs to be carefully prepared to ensure a level paving surface.*

Above *Formal brick
and concrete steps.*

STEPS

Well-chosen, well-suited steps are more than just a necessary adjunct to a patio – they can actually enhance it if you give a little time and thought to their design. They don't have to be totally utilitarian: you could, for instance, build them with 'pockets' at either side of the treads to accommodate trailing and bedding plants, or make crevices in the risers in which you could grow alpine plants to give a waterfall of colour when viewed from below. Built-in lighting is not only a decorative trick but a safety measure, too, if you use your patio and garden at night.

The way you design your steps will depend very much on the slope that they are bridging, but there are so many attractive materials available that there is no need to make them dull. Ideally, the steps should echo or complement the material used on the patio. If the latter is paved, reserve enough additional slabs to use as the treads; the risers can be made of bricks, reproduction dry-stone walling, or any other suitable material that will blend in with a building material used elsewhere in the garden.

Discarded railway sleepers (if you can get hold of them) make interesting and unusual steps, as do rustic half-logs and old bricks; but they should not be used for a steep flight since they are all likely to become covered with algae and moss and can be slippery. If you are using paving slabs or other similar material, the flight of steps will look much more handsome if you make the treads overhang the risers by about 35mm (1½in).

Remember to keep your steps in scale with their surroundings – a grandiose sweep, complete with balustrades, would look out of place in the typical suburban garden, but there's no reason why you shouldn't have twin plinths at the top and/or bottom on which to place bowls of bedding plants.

Your first job is to work out the design of the steps on paper. Draw up cross sections from the front and from the sides to work out the number of steps that you need, for a given height of riser and a depth of tread, to fill the overall space. The area the steps cover should be twice as long as it is high. Garden steps need to be broad and shallow for safety's sake. The treads should ideally be about 375mm (15in) from front to back, and the risers 100-150mm (4-6in) high. In other words the depth of tread should be at least twice the height of the riser, and the treads should all be of equal depth, otherwise they make walking up the steps an uncomfortable business and might cause children to stumble and fall.

Left *Informal steps
made of railway
sleepers.*

CONSTRUCTING YOUR STEPS

First shape and firm the bank up which the steps are to go, cutting out the steps in the compacted soil. Then set in the first set of risers on the base. Now sit the first tread on a bed of concrete laid over a layer of hardcore. From now on each riser is set in mortar at the back of a tread, overlapping it by about 25-50mm (1-2in) to prevent the tread from tipping. Set each tread at a very slight angle, falling about 6mm (¼in) in every foot to the front or one side to allow rainwater to drain off.

Below *Garden steps, however formal, need not lack decorative qualities. These old steps down to a gloomy basement 'area' have been given colour and character merely by hanging a basket of flowers from the hand-rail.*

PLANTING YOUR STEPS

In order to make the steps look established as soon as possible, the bank that surrounds them should be planted up quickly with basic ground cover that will give it a mature appearance. The periwinkle (*Vinca major*) grows quickly and produces pretty blue flowers in summer; or, if the area is large the bushier Rose of Sharon (*Hypericum calycinum*) gives close cover. Alternatively, ivy (*Hedera*) gives a mature look in double-quick time; and, if the steps are built alongside a retaining wall rather than a bank, ivy tumbling over the top, enlivened by ivy-leaved geraniums (*Pelargonium*) in summer, will give a very attractive display. If you do not mark your steps by pillars or some other sort of 'furniture', consider placing twin standard bay trees in tubs at the top for a formal look, or small pieces of topiary that have been grown in pots. The steps might also make a good excuse for a rose-covered arch at top or bottom; suitable arch frames which are easily assembled can be found in most garden centres.

Another idea is to make a mini-waterfall by installing parallel but narrower steps down which a greatly moving sheet of water cascades; the steps will need to be lipped at each side to avoid spillage onto either the bank or the footsteps. The water can be circulated by a pump.

Above *The cut-away drawing shows a typical structure for garden steps, with brick risers and concrete-slab treads. The bottom-step risers are laid on a concrete foundation.*

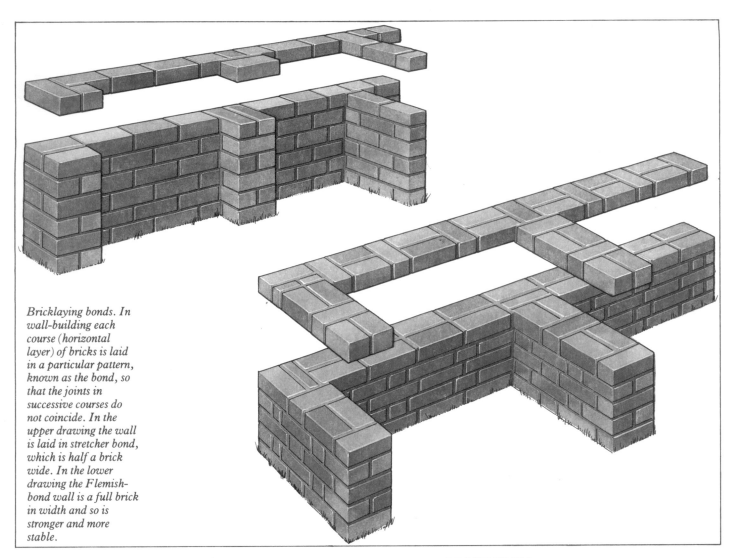

Bricklaying bonds. In wall-building each course (horizontal layer) of bricks is laid in a particular pattern, known as the bond, so that the joints in successive courses do not coincide. In the upper drawing the wall is laid in stretcher bond, which is half a brick wide. In the lower drawing the Flemish-bond wall is a full brick in width and so is stronger and more stable.

BOUNDARIES

Walls and fences do more than just act as boundaries around a patio: they give shelter against prevailing winds for both people and plants, and confer a feeling of privacy; they are also useful for screening things like dustbins and sheds. Something is often needed, too, to make a natural break between paving and grass. Although hedges can look very attractive, they take up a great deal of room, and rob the soil of nutrients for a foot or more on either side. They also need constant maintenance if they are to look trim. All things considered, a man-made barrier is usually the best solution. Solid screens made from brick or close-boarded wood are expensive but will last a long time. If you are planning a brick wall you need to dig a trench for the foundation; in the case of a fence, the posts need to be set in a concrete base.

Although a solid fence gives maximum privacy it can create considerable air turbulence on either side of it on a windy day. A more 'porous' structure may be kinder to your plants and make the patio more comfortable to sit in.

BRICK WALL

This is expensive but, once in place, will last a life-time. If you want to build your own, a low wall is certainly within the scope of the beginner. For best appearance use facing bricks, not 'commons'. Even a low wall needs a concrete foundation. As a general guide a 375mm (15in) wide strip should be excavated for a wall up to 600mm (2ft) high. Dig until firm ground is found: if stability is in doubt, lay a bed of well-compacted hardcore. Allow for a 35mm (3in) layer of concrete (1 part cement to 2½ parts sharp sand, 4 parts aggregate) with the first course of bricks to be below ground level. If the wall is to be more than 1.2m (4ft) high, lay a 100mm (4in) layer of concrete, with the first two courses of bricks below ground level. Mark out the line of the wall with two string lines pulled taut and tied to stakes. Use a mortar mix of 1 part of cement to 5 parts of builders sand. The mortar should be buttery (not too dry, nor too wet). A few drops of washing-up liquid will improve its workability, but do not mix up more mortar than you can use in an hour.

SCREEN-BLOCK WALL

This can look very attractive around a patio. It is made of precast concrete blocks, usually 300mm (1ft) square and 100mm (4in) thick. You need to provide a firm concrete foundation, using a mixture of 1 part cement to 5 parts 20mm (¾in) ballast. For the mortar use 1 part cement to 6 parts sand plus plasticizer. The foundation should be a minimum of 200mm (8in) deep, including bricks or rubble where needed. At each end of the wall, pilaster blocks are used. Loose-lay the screen blocks between the pilasters to ensure they fit, then lay the blocks as for brickwork except that you should work from both ends to the middle. Check each block for level, and again build up the corners before completing successive courses.

Drawings *Building a screen-block wall. Special pilasters (top) are built up from individual blocks. The screen blocks are laid (centre) between the pilasters, the mortar joints being strengthened by incorporating strips of expanded metal. The wall is finished (bottom) by topping off the blocks with special coping slabs and pilaster caps.*

Photographs, far left *The pierced-screen-block wall (above), though perhaps over-used in recent years, makes an efficient screen while admitting light and air. The brick wall (below) achieves a similar effect by leaving gaps between each brick in the central courses.*

PATIO FEATURES

Much of the individuality of your patio will be found not so much in its basic structure as in the way you equip and furnish it for the particular uses to which it will be put. In this chapter we have a look at some of the ways to get maximum usefulness and enjoyment from your paved area.

PERGOLAS

This modern structure, combining pergola with overhead beams, represents a large open-air extension to the living room.

Add a pergola to your patio and you make it look much more like an outdoor room, for it gives an instant illusion of walls and, sometimes, a ceiling too if you include some cross-pieces overhead. It is also a useful way of showing off climbers that would otherwise be relegated to side walls.

Pergolas look impressive if built with pillars of stone or brick, but they are more usually made from timber. In that case oak or cedar are the ideal choice for uprights; but both these woods are extremely expensive, so most people use cheaper larch or pine instead. Pergolas are often available from garden centres in kit form.

MAKING YOUR OWN PERGOLA

The timber for a home-made pergola can be squared or 'rustic'. In the latter case larch poles are the best choice. Leave the bark on only if the larch has been felled during the winter; otherwise the bark will eventually fall off. It is probably better to remove it with a knife or spoke shave, and to apply varnish or a wood preservative to the underlying surface. Only butt joints are possible with rustic poles, and both joint faces must be squared before they are nailed together.

Although slim poles may look better when the pergola or arch is bare, be fairly generous with the thickness as the structure may eventually have to bear a considerable weight of foliage. Moreover, high winds, or high-spirited people swinging on the poles, can put a severe strain on the structure so err on the side of safety. Uprights should be treated like fence posts: they must be well preserved and set firmly at least 450mm (18in) in the ground. Uprights should be spaced no more than 2.4m (8ft) apart, and should not be less than 100mm (4in) in diameter or square. A variety of possibilities exists for the cross rails, but they should be a minimum of 75mm (3in) in diameter or square; a pleasing effect is produced if they extend each side of the uprights, with shaped ends. Some people who prefer a more sturdy appearance use wider but thinner cross rails, such as planking 150 × 25mm (6 × 1in). Side members should be about the same size as the cross rails, or perhaps a little smaller.

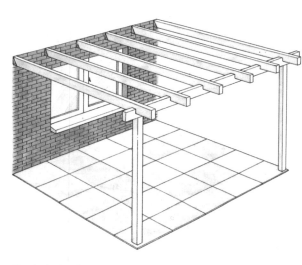

Basic design for a pergola and overhead beams. The vertical posts must be sunk at least 900mm (3ft) into concrete foundations beneath the paving. The overhead beams shown here are made from 150×50mm (6×2in) floor joists; at the house end they slot into joist hangers set into the wall.

PLANTING A PERGOLA

Vines of all kinds look good when trained up a pergola; so do climbing roses, especially if they are twinned with clematis. And, if you have the space to include them, scented plants like honeysuckle (*Lonicera*) add an extra dimension of fragrance in the air when you sit out on the patio in the evening.

If the pergola forms part of an overhead structure attached to the house, it is best to train deciduous rather than evergreen climbers up it, otherwise in the winter months it may shut too much light out of the rooms nearby. Be sure to build in adequate support vine-eyes and wires before you plant your climbers: it is much easier to do it at that stage than when you have to struggle with fully grown plants. If, for some reason, you cannot have ordinary beds around the base of the pergola – for instance, the support poles may be built into the patio itself – then a series of rectangular troughs could be fitted around the base of the supports instead and planted with shallow-rooting climbers. For a permanent planting, wisteria looks very attractive, while if you need quick cover you can't beat the Russian vine or mile-a-minute (*Polygonum baldschuanicum*), though it will need frequent and fairly ruthless cutting back once established if it is not to take over.

This simple lean-to pergola offers ample support even for a large, mature climber.

BARBECUE DESIGNS & SITES

If you are constructing a patio, why not build in a barbecue at the same time? It will cost very little – you probably have the materials to hand – and, apart from being something of a status symbol, it's great fun to use when the weather is kind.

Choose a sheltered spot on which to site it – you don't want a howling wind fanning the flames, and make sure that it is away from precious shrubs or climbers; evergreens, on the whole, stand up better than deciduous shrubs to being scorched occasionally. The ideal site is against a brick or concrete wall, where it can do little or no harm. If this is not possible (the walls of the house are not suitable because of smoke drifting indoors), then consider making an island site for it on the patio, if there is space; then everyone can gather round and help (or hinder) the cook. Keep it reasonably near the kitchen so that dishes and foodstuffs can be shuttled back and forth without too long a walk.

You can now buy barbecue kits which can be built in as a permanent fixture. They consist of a grid and tray to take the charcoal and a grill on which to put the food. An attractive extra is a battery-operated rotisserie which fits over the top. This equipment is incorporated into a simple three-sided brick wall which anyone can make and which requires only a little over 100 bricks. Alternatively, you can buy an attractive small triangular barbecue kit that will go into an odd corner and occupy little usable space.

If you have the space, it pays to build two more brick piers at either side of your barbecue and continue the bricks at the back, then to fix ceramic tiles on a wooden base on top. You then have an area on either side on which to prepare and serve food. Cupboards can be built underneath, not only to house charcoal and other cooking items, but the odd flower pot or two as well.

Make the most of your barbecue. Plant essential herbs around it so that guests can help themselves to flavourings – mint, tarragon, and especially chives can then be snipped over salads, while fennel goes well with fish, and lamb is particularly good when cooked over rosemary. The herbs can be grown in tubs as part of the decoration of the patio, or in a specially raised bed nearby.

Remember that you will need some good lighting so that the cook can see what he or she is doing. A discreet spotlight set high will do the trick or you could floodlight the whole area.

CONSTRUCTING A BASIC BARBECUE

Set the bricks out, dry, on the patio where the barbecue is to be, making two courses. Then, using the barbecue grill as a guide, check that the dimensions are correct and square, and draw a line around the inside of them as your guide.

Then mix up your mortar so that it is workable and not runny, adding a spot of

A built-in barbecue with storage cupboard. The barbecue grill can be adjusted for height. The cupboard has quarry tiles on top to provide a durable working surface.

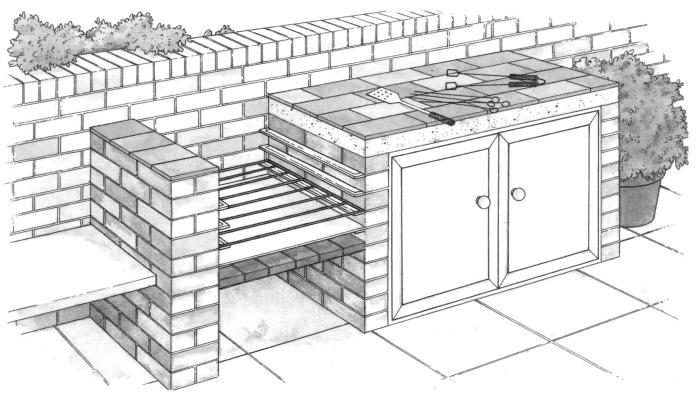

A barbecue/storage cupboard design basically similar to that on the opposite page. For alfresco meals a table can be used with the L-shaped seating built into the brick structure.

washing-up liquid to it, to make it easier to work. Lay the bricks along the back wall first, then add the side wall bricks, checking all the time against your pencil guide, making sure they are square and level. Then start the second course – the corner bricks will have to be placed to make a half bond – and continue round, ending with two half bricks to finish off the front at either side. When you get to the height where the charcoal tray is to go, put three bricks sideways on so that they project as half-bricks from the centre of each side wall, to form a ledge on which the tray can sit. An average barbecue is 11 courses high, but you can vary it to suit yourself.

A more elaborate barbecue could be constructed, Spanish style, with a brick arch overhead, culminating in a chimney. This sort of thing would become a focal point of the patio and should be treated accordingly; the wall at the back could be covered in decorative tiles, and lighting could play its part in adding drama to the setting (wrought-iron outdoor lamps can be found that would go very well in this scheme).

To extend the usefulness of a barbecue beyond the summer season, consider the possibility of building some sort of overhead protection against the weather. A pergola could be extended and roofed in, for instance; and provided the barbecue itself had an arch and chimney over it, or some other method of avoiding a fire hazard, you could eat alfresco for many more evenings of the year.

Right *On a small patio, built-in benching is a space-saving alternative to chairs and loungers.*

Opposite page *These simple slatted chairs can be folded for compact storage.*

Below *There is now a huge range of patio furniture available in a variety of prices.*

PATIO FURNITURE

The first thing you have to decide, when choosing furniture for your patio, is whether it is to stay out all year round or be stored away in winter. Furniture that can be left out of doors is made from wood – usually hardwood – plastic or metal. Furniture that must be taken indoors is made from cane or bamboo, unpainted and untreated softwood and, of course, anything that is upholstered. Storing garden furniture indoors or in a garage can sometimes present problems, unless you buy something that can actually be used as indoor furniture too. But there is a third category – items like loungers, chairs and tables that are collapsible or can be easily dismantled, and take up very little space when stored.

Choose your furniture to go with the style of your house and patio. Rustic, rough-hewn benches and tables usually look out of place in a town setting, unless you have deliberately created a country garden look to go with them. Bamboo and cane look good with 'tropical' plants like the yucca, but they are less happy in stark modern surroundings. Wooden furniture should be strongly made, especially if it is to stay outside all year round. Check that any metal screws, hinges or fittings on them are made from stainless steel or brass rather than steel, which will rust. Plastic furniture, including that made

from glass-fibre, is usually trouble free, but it should be heavy enough to be stable so that it will not topple over easily.

Metal furniture ranges from antique reproductions in cast aluminium to stackable folding chairs in bright colours and modern designs. Cast aluminium chairs and tables are expensive to buy but last indefinitely and will not rust. Most other metals need to be painted regularly unless they have been enamelled or coated with plastic. Most of the better-quality metal furniture has the disadvantage of being heavy to move around, so it is better chosen for a large patio, where it can stay permanently in place.

Upholstered chairs and loungers – and there are some very sumptuous ones around – and swing seats should all have detachable cushions. Even so, it's a good idea to have a rainproof cover of some sort for the larger items so that, should there be a sudden shower, you can quickly shield them from it, rather than have to pull off canopies and cushions and bring them inside.

If you have the space for it, it's a good idea to build in some of your patio furniture. A very attractive bench-seat can be constructed, for instance, around a large tree, or an arbour with a seat built into it can be established in a corner of the patio. But it is for dining that built-in furniture really comes into its own. A brick-built bench seat along one wall, and possibly going round a corner too, takes up far less space than a set of chairs. It can be made in several different ways: it could have a hinged wooden seat, for instance, which lifts up to reveal storage space for garden tools; or it could have a tiled top with cupboards underneath. A brick-built bench of this kind could have two deep troughs built into it at each end in which you could plant flowers.

A built-in table can be made quite simply if you can get hold of a very large piece of slate or marble that would make a top; these can sometimes be picked up in junk shops. Two simple brick piers usually suffice to take the place of legs, or, if the table top is very small, you might be able to get away with just one acting as a central plinth.

Junk shops are also a source of temporary patio furniture – things like old kitchen chairs and tables – which you can get for a very low price. Unified by a coat of bright paint – bright blue, green, or scarlet, for instance – several odd chairs will go together perfectly happily, an old table, perhaps with a laminated plastic top, can be painted to match; then cover the painted top with a heavy sheet of glass to keep it good-looking. Indoor furniture that has been thoroughly painted should last outdoors for a year or so; though if the joints are glued they may need re-doing after a time.

DESIGNING FOR CHILDREN

A patio that is going to be used by children needs careful thought, at the planning stage, so that it can lead a useful life throughout the day and, eventually, revert to being purely ornamental as the family grows up. With play in mind, the basic structure of the patio should offer as few hazards as possible. It might be better, for instance, to provide access by a ramp instead of shallow steps to the garden to facilitate use of tricycles and other wheeled toys.

If the patio is large enough to take it, it would be a good idea to provide one corner especially for the children. If enough play space and attractions are concentrated in this area, it may reduce the temptation to run wild in the more precious ornamental areas. Storage could also be built along one wall to park toys that could be kept permanently out of doors, to avoid having to trundle them into the house.

When you are providing facilities for the children, use a little cunning and site them so that they can be adapted, later on, for other uses. A sand-pit could be built into the patio itself by leaving out some of the paving in a square, rectangular, or even free-form shape. (If you do this, line the bottom of the pit with un-mortared bricks to allow drainage.) Then, when the family have grown up it can be turned into an attractive ornamental pond, or a bed for flowers or herbs. If the sand-pit is of a regular shape and not too large, you could build a simple box-like structure to go on top of it when not in use. This would not only keep the rain and family pets out, but would act as a simple seat, made more attractive by addition of brightly coloured cushions. A sand-pit can also make a convenient spot to site the holder for a whirlygig washing line, so that its pole can be slotted in and out when needed.

If the children have their own corner, it's a good idea to encourage their interest in plants at an early stage by giving them some growing space of their own. Packets of annual flowers, generously sprinkled on the soil, covered and watered, usually oblige, but children also enjoy growing novelty things. The sensitive plant (*Mimosa pudica*) can be grown as an annual (it won't survive a winter out of doors) and its leaves fold up, instantly, if you touch them. The squirting cucumber (*Ecballium elaterium*) literally fires its seeds at you as if from a gun. And gourds, decorative squashes and the loofah plant are all interesting curiosities for children to grow. On the edible front, radishes grow with amazing speed, provided they are well watered, and vegetable spaghetti (a marrow with flesh that looks just like spaghetti when you cook it) is well worth trying. Tiny tomatoes like 'Gardener's Delight' are also fun for children, as are alpine strawberries, used for ground cover.

For the rest of the patio, it's best to plant a framework of trees and shrubs on and around it that are relatively child-proof. But this doesn't mean that you have to give up flowers: viburnums, olearias, philadephus, and shrub roses will give you an attractive range of flowers and foliage, while shrubs with coloured foliage such as the purple-leaved hazel (*Corylus maxima* 'Purpurea'), the golden elder (*Sambucus nigra* 'Aurea'), or the smoke tree (*Cotinus coggygria*) will provide colourful focal points all through the summer. With a boisterous family it is better to legislate for some degree of accidental damage and plant multi-stemmed trees such as birch (*Betulus*), alder (*Alnus*), or hornbeam (*Carpinus betulus*) so that even if part of the tree is injured, the rest will survive to form an attractive clump.

A children's sand-pit made from railway sleepers. Secured by a vertical bolt at each corner, the timber walls are less painful to young shins and knees than brick or concrete.

PLANTS POISONOUS TO CHILDREN
Aconite, aquilegia, box (*Buxus*), cotoneaster, daphne, beech (*Fagus sylvatica*), hellebore, iris, ivy (*Hedera*), juniper (*Juniperus*), laburnum, oleander, and pulsatilla are a few among many.

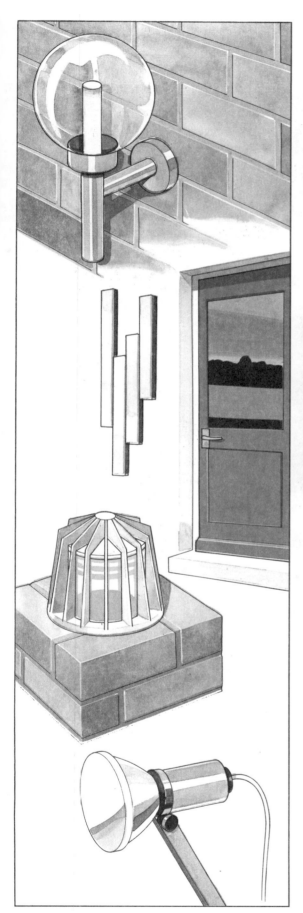

PATIO LIGHTING

Lighting, if it is properly used, can completely change the look and atmosphere of your patio at night. At the touch of a switch the whole scene is illuminated, and you are in control. You can draw attention to the things that you want people to see, such as flowering plants, an attractively shaped specimen tree, a climber in bloom, and leave items such as dustbins or an untidy bed in darkness.

There are several different types of lights to choose from, depending on the effect that you want to make. Floodlights can be fixed to light up the entire patio area or to illuminate one end wall. They are usually fixed high up on the house itself and angled. Spotlights give a far more intimate effect and are usually fixed on brackets on a wall or on spikes that you can

insert into a flower bed. They are very effective for drawing attention to one particular item – a statue, for instance, or a tree or plant with striking foliage. They can also be used as down-lighting over a barbecue so that the cook can work more easily.

LIGHTING PONDS
Moving water is the most spectacularly rewarding of all patio features when lit up after dark. By far the best effects come from submerged lamps – which must, of course, be a type made specifically for that purpose. Water looks at its best lit from below and behind. A lamp shining up behind a fountain, for instance, turns it into a rippling sheet of molten coloured glass.

TEMPORARY LIGHTS
Candles in barbecue lanterns or jamjars can make attractive occasional or temporary lighting if you are eating outdoors. Giant church candles are also excellent and they are stable enough to be stood on their own on the patio floor. Coloured flares and nightlights, which are now obtainable almost everywhere, give the patio a gala look and are particularly good for parties. They are generally available on thin canes.

Far left *Examples of exterior lighting. Halogen bulbs have allowed the introduction of more powerful lamps for garden use.*

Near left *Imaginatively sited, patio lights can achieve delightful effects.*

PART 2

STOCKING THE GARDEN

Selecting plants for the ornamental garden involves much more than rummaging through the nurserymen's catalogues. This section shows how to choose plants for beds, borders and containers of every kind. The criteria include plant shape, size, colour and growing habit; sunny, shady, exposed and sheltered sites; different types of soil; and the selection of varieties that will create interest and beauty in every season of the year.

FLOWERS IN THEIR SETTING

An imaginative blend of well-chosen plants is the key to a successful and beautiful flower
garden. The candidates are annuals and biennials, and perennials,
which include herbaceous plants, bulbs and shrubs.

The garden in bloom. The picture represents a period from spring to summer, with a fine array of colour contributed by bulbs, bedding plants, perennials, shrubs and trees. Key to numbers on plan: 1 Pansy, 2 Crocus, 3 Tulip, 4 Daffodil, 5 Polyanthus, 6 Helenium, 7 Rose-of-Sharon (Hypericum), 8 Pink (Dianthus), 9 Clematis, 10 Canadian spruce (Picea), 11 Lavender, 12 Rose 'Pink Perpetue', 13 Rose 'Paul's Scarlet Climber', 14 Laburnum, 15 Hyacinth, 16 Alyssum, 17 Petunia, 18 Variegated plantain lily (Hosta), 19 Hollyhock, 20 Lobelia, 21 Antirrhinum, 22 St John's wort (Hypericum), 23 Periwinkle (Vinca), 24 Paper-bark maple (Acer), 25 Grape hyacinth (Muscari), 26 Foxglove (Digitalis), 27 Japanese azalea, 28 Variegated ivy (Hedera), 29 Deutzia, 30 Corylopsis, 31 Plantain lily (Hosta), 32 Forget-me-not (Myosotis), 33 Bergenia, 34 Japanese spurge (Pachysandra).

LOCATION

Assessing the site is one of the first things to do when planning a garden. All plots are different; even if they are the same size and in the same road, the conditions found in each will demand differing approaches. One plot may be bathed in sun while, next door, a tall tree may plunge part of that garden into deep shadow. Winds may make it necessary to install a windbreak in one garden, while in another breezes may he hardly noticeable. Each plot must be judged on its own characteristics.

SITE & SOIL

The type of vegetation already growing in a plot is often a good indicator of the nature of the soil. If gardens are lush with rhododendrons and azaleas in the spring and there is an abundance of heathers throughout the year, it is certain that the soil is acid. On the other hand, if the surrounding countryside is supporting luxurious growths of traveller's joy (old man's beard), whose botanical name is *Clematis vitalba*, the soil is definitely chalky. The point to bear in mind is that some plants are lime-haters while others cannot thrive in acid soils. If you are starting a garden from scratch it's a good idea to buy an inexpensive soil-testing kit. Test the soil in several places all over the garden: it is possible that it will prove to be acid in one spot and alkaline at a point only a few yards away. Mark your results on your site plan.

Right *Clematis grow naturally on chalky (limy) soil. But lime is not essential for success with garden hybrids, such as this* Clematis *'Ville de Lyon', which flowers from July to October.*

Above *Heather or ling* (Calluna vulgaris) *enriches many of our upland moors with a cloak of purple in early autumn, thriving on acid soil. Garden forms have buttercup-yellow and coppery red leaves that colour borders in winter.*

Sometimes a barren site will have a small area where water collects, so that the soil remains permanently wet or water-logged. If this spot is covered in vegetation it may not be easy to detect; but a preponderance of marsh plants – rushes, reeds and sedges – among the wild flora will give a good indication of such a problem. If the whole plot shows signs of being wet, the ground will need to be drained. Such a spot in only one part of the site, however, provides the opportunity to have a marsh garden or natural pool as a special feature. Indicate any such wet areas on the site plan.

It is also important to mark the position of any places where the soil appears to be exceptionally dry, so that planting can be carried out accordingly.

ASPECT

How the site is positioned in relation to the points of compass is the next consideration. The aspect bears on the 'well-being' of a garden in two main ways. First, it determines how much sun the garden enjoys and at what time of the day certain parts of the area are in sun or shade. Second, the aspect of a plot will in some cases – coastal districts and very exposed inland areas in particular – determine what spots in the garden are exposed to strong winds and so need to be screened.

The best aspect for a rear garden in the northern hemisphere is south or, better still, south-west. It will get the maximum amount of sun during the day: if the garden is not over-shadowed, the sun will shine on it from early or mid-morning until evening. The principal draw-back to such an aspect is that in some districts it may be exposed to strong south-westerly winds, although these are usually relatively warm.

The worst aspects for a garden are east and north. In the case of the latter, the amount of sun that shines directly on the garden may be restricted, while a garden that faces east is likely to be in shade during the afternoon. In addition, the winds that blow from north and east are often strong and biting, and if the site is in a very open position, such as on the outskirts of a town, this could have a damaging effect on plants. West and north-west are much more favourable aspects as they provide a certain amount of warmth, shade and moisture.

Above *Perfect for planting in gaps in crazy paving or on rock garden screes in full sun, stonecrop* (Sedum) *quickly forms a weed-proof carpet and flowers profusely in summer. This version is* S. lydium.

Left Skimmia japonica *is a handsome evergreen shrub that thrives in partial shade. Its glossy leaves and brilliant berries bring autumn and winter colour to the garden.*

KNOW YOUR SOIL

Soil has to be improved, modified or manipulated so that the best conditions for plant life can be created. Good soils offer anchorage and support, sufficient food, warmth, moisture and oxygen, and room for plants to develop.

The critical soil factors for effective gardening are: land drainage, moisture retention, food content, acidity or chalkiness, and temperature. Fertile soil is easily worked and crumbly. It is dark in colour, well-drained and yet retains moisture for growth. It contains reserves of plant food to support sturdy, balanced plant growth. Examination of good soil will show moist crumbs of solid matter, pieces of old root-fibre, small pebbles, a worm or two – and innumerable tiny life-forms.

SOIL TESTING

A trial dig to a spade's depth or more will reveal much about a piece of ground. Under wet conditions, clay soils will have puddles on the surface, and be greasy to the touch, and will stick tenaciously to your spade. A sandy soil will be well drained and gritty; feet and spade are easily cleaned, and the hole dug with comparative ease. Loams lie between the two extremes.

Under dry summer conditions clay soils become cracked, hard to cultivate, and lumpy. Conversely, sandy soil is easy to dig and is dry and dusty.

Digging chalk soils will reveal the tell-tale whitish subsoil of chalk or limestone, and whitish coloured lumps in the soil. Peat soils are usually dark, spongy and fibrous.

WHAT'S YOUR GARDEN MADE OF?

SOIL	APPEARANCE	PHYSICAL QUALITIES	CHEMICAL STATUS
CLAY	Soil lies under water in wet weather. Sedges, rushes, buttercup, alder, willow in evidence.	Very slow to drain. Adhesive, greasy if wet or hard and lumpy when dry.	Naturally rich in plant food.
HEAVY LOAM	Intermediate between clay and medium loam		
MEDIUM LOAM	Strong-growing roses, shrubs and grasses.	Drains moderately quickly. Worked fairly readily.	Usually well supplied with plant food.
LIGHT LOAM	Intermediate between medium and sandy soil.		
SANDY	Light coloured soil. Gorse, broom and Scots pine, heather and rhododendrons.	Quick draining. Easily worked in most conditions. Gritty to the touch.	Low in nutrients. Often very acid. Needs regular feeding.
CHALK OR LIMESTONE	White or whitish subsoil. Dogwood, viburnum and clematis flourish.	Chalk is pasty when moist. Limestone is gritty to the touch.	Low in organic matter. Alkaline.
PEATY	Dark fibrous soil. Alder and willow trees often present.	Spongy and fibrous.	Low in phosphates. Usually acid.
STONY	Often light-coloured. Many stones on surface. Sparse vegetation. Mountain ash present.	Shallow soils with large proportion of rock and stone.	Low nutrient content. Needs regular and heavy feeding.

It's important to know whether your soil is acid, alkaline or neutral. You can easily find out by using a soil-testing kit (left), which depends on the colour a chemical solution turns when mixed with a soil sample. The electronic meter (right) indicates the soil's pH (relative acidity or alkalinity) on a dial.

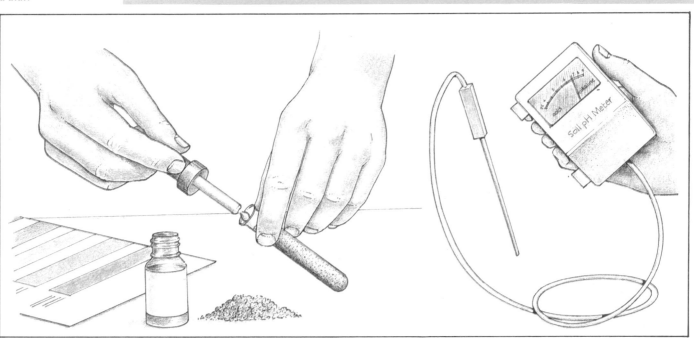

DRAINAGE

When making a new garden or improving an established site, check the drainage by making a test dig. During the winter, dig out a hole 600 mm (2 ft) deep and cover it to prevent rain falling in. Inspect the hole daily, replacing the cover each time. If after 48 hours following heavy rain, less than 450 mm (18 in) of soil shows above the water table or water level, then attention to drainage is needed, especially if trees are to be planted. Surplus moisture in gardens is best drained by means of a soakaway or underground pipes or channels.

ENRICHING THE SOIL

There are two groups of manure: those which breakdown readily to release plant food; and those, such as peat, which are much slower to decompose, providing little by way of plant nutrients, but, like the former, improve the soil's humus content. The first group includes farmyard manure, composted straw or garden waste material, spent mushroom compost, and seaweed. Peat, pulverized tree bark, leaf mould, and spent hops belong in the second group.

FERTILIZERS

Some fertilizers are used as a base dressing *before* planting; others are applied as a top dressing while plants are growing. Base and top dressings usually provide the main needs of nitrogen, phosphate and potash.

Base fertilizers are mostly available as ordinary or high-potash types. The ordinary grades contain equal proportions of nitrogen, phosphate and potash, and are used for general feeding. The high-potash types are designed for fruit and flower crops and contain twice the amount of potash.

Top dressings are applied dry or as a liquid feed. Proprietary brands are sold as three grades: *high nitrogen*, used for celery and cucumbers; *ordinary grade*, for bringing on young plants; and *high potash*, for fruit and flowers.

PROPRIETARY FERTILISERS

MATERIAL	INGREDIENTS (%)			TYPE
	N	P	K	
Bonemeal	4	21	—	Base
Hoof-and-horn	13–14	—	—	Base
Potassium nitrate	15	—	45	Top
Nitro-chalk	15.5	—	—	Top
Sulphate of ammonia	21	—	—	Base and top
Sulphate of potash	—	—	48–50	Base and top
Super-phosphate	—	16–18	—	Base and top

N = nitrogen, P = phosphorus, K = potassium

WHAT GROWS WHERE

Situation and aspect govern plant selection; so to a lesser extent does soil type. Fortunately, most plants are very adaptable: although they may prefer a particular kind of soil, they will usually tolerate most reasonably fertile ones that are neither too wet nor too dry for long periods. Most fussy are the lime haters, such as enkianthus, gentians, lithospermum, rhododendrons and azaleas, and most heathers (with the exception of some ericas).

Your garden's situation affects its exposure to wind and temperature, factors which influence growth. There are hillside and seaside gardens in which it is almost impossible to develop a planting scheme until winds have been softened by shelter belts of evergreen trees and shrubs and carefully sited filter-fences.

Before you buy any plants, look in neighbours' gardens and note what grows well. Talk to local experts and attend gardening-club meetings to glean all you can about the kind of plants that thrive in your district.

PLANTS FOR ACID SOIL

Lime-hating plants thrive on acid, peaty loam soils. Some, such as camellias, rhododendrons and azaleas, also enjoy dappled shade and need shelter from spring frosts which can blacken their blooms. If you are trying to grow acid-soil lovers on ground which contains a trace of lime, water the foliage with sequestered-iron solution.

Many garden plants are lime-haters and do best in acid soils. Typical of these are the rhododendrons and azaleas, of which this example is R. 'King George'. Such plants can sometimes be persuaded to grow in marginally chalky soil if it is given an annual dose of sequestered iron, a spring feed of seaweed fertilizer, and a generous mulch of peat or forest bark.

Clove-scented pinks (Dianthus) love a sunny bank to sprawl upon. Easily propagated by pegging down shoots, which root where they press against the soil, pinks flower for most of the summer. This one is the modern garden variety 'Show Celebrity'.

PLANT	IN FLOWER	COLOURS
Calluna (S)	Summer, autumn	Pink, purple, red, white
Camellia (S)	Spring	Pink, purple, red, white
Clethra (S)	Summer	White
Daboecia (S)	Autumn	Pink, red, white
Enkianthus (S)	Spring	Bronze
Erica (most) (S)	Winter, spring, summer	Mauve, pink, red, white
Eucryphia (S)	Summer	White
Fothergilla (S)	—	Autumn foliage colours
Gaultheria (S)	—	Purple or red autumn fruits
Gentiana sino-ornata (R)	Autumn	Blue
Hamamelis (S)	Winter	Orange, red, yellow
Kalmia (S)	Spring, summer	Pink
Lithospermum diffusum (R)	Summer	Blue
Magnolia (S)	Spring	White
Rhododendron (S)	Spring, summer	Various

(H) = Herbaceous, (R) = Rock plant, (S) = Shrub

PLANTS FOR CHALKY SOIL

Many plants that are reputedly lime-haters will grow in alkaline (chalky) soil if the fertile topsoil is reasonably deep. The following will do well if the soil has been well dug and enriched.

PLANT	IN FLOWER	COLOURS
Agapanthus (H)	Summer	Blue, violet, white
Aster (A), (H)	Summer, autumn	Many
Aubrieta (R)	Spring	Blue, pink, purple
Campanula (H)	Summer	Blue, pink, purple, white
Cheiranthus (Bi)	Spring, summer	Orange, pink, red, yellow
Clematis (C)	Spring, summer, autumn	Many
Daphne (S)	Winter, spring	Pink, red, purple
Deutzia (S)	Summer	Pink, white
Dianthus (H)	Summer	Many
Eranthis (B)	Winter, spring	Yellow
Erica (some) (S)	Autumn, winter	Various
Hebe (S)	Summer, autumn	Pink, purple, white
Hypericum (S)	Summer	Yellow
Papaver (A), (H)	Summer	Various
Saxifraga (R)	Spring, summer, autumn	Various
Syringa (H)	Spring, summer	Pink, purple, white

(A) = Annual   (C) = Climber   (S) = Shrub
(B) = Bulb   (H) = Herbaceous
(Bi) = Biennial   (R) = Rock plant

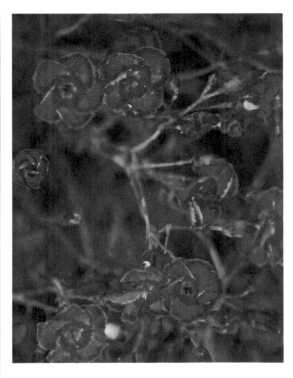

PLANTS FOR SUNNY PLACES

Most plants enjoy an open, sunny position and the majority that compose the framework of the flower garden will benefit from maximum light at all times. The following are very colourful kinds that cheer us through spring and summer. They are also tolerant of partial shade: they will thrive if they receive direct sunlight for only half the day, provided there is strong indirect light for the other half.

PLANT	IN FLOWER	COLOURS
Achillea (H)	Summer	Yellow
Agapanthus (H)	Summer	Blue, white
Alstroemeria ligtu (H)	Summer	Orange, pink, white
Centaurea (H)	Summer	Blue, pink, purple, red, white
Cistus (S)	Summer	Pink, red, white
Choisya (S)	Spring, autumn	White
Cytisus (S)	Spring	Pink, purple, white, yellow
Dianthus (H)	Summer	Pink, red, white
Eryngium (H)	Summer	Blue, white
Escallonia (S)	Summer	Pink, red, white
Genista (S)	Spring, summer	Yellow
Geranium (H)	Summer	Blue, pink, red
Helianthemum (S)	Summer	Pink, red, white, yellow
Hemerocallis (H)	Summer	Bronze, yellow
Iris germanica (H)	Spring	Various
Kniphofia (H)	Summer	Orange, red, yellow
Lavandula (S)	Summer	Blue, purple

PLANT	IN FLOWER	COLOURS
Linum perenne (H)	Summer	Blue
Oenothera (H)	Summer	Yellow
Rosmarinus (S)	Spring	Blue
Spartium (S)	Summer	Yellow
Santolina (S)	Summer	Yellow
Verbascum (H)	Summer	Biscuit, pink, yellow

(H) = Herbaceous; (S) = Shrub

PLANTS FOR SHADE

All plants need light to survive, but not all of them need brilliant sunshine. Natives of woodland, in particular, are happiest when given some protection from the sun's rays. All the plants listed below will tolerate shade to a greater or lesser degree. If the soil is too dry – that, for instance, under a large tree usually is – improve its moisture-retaining properties by digging in plenty of organic manure. Rhododendrons, azaleas, camellias and hydrangeas are a few of many superb plants that thrive in little sunshine. If the right plants are chosen, there is no reason why shady spots should be dull places. Many foliage plants grow well in shade, including ferns, of which there are many fully hardy and highly ornamental kinds.

PLANT	IN FLOWER	COLOURS
Acanthus (H)	Summer	Purple, white
Aconitum (H)	Summer	Blue
Ajuga (H)	Spring, summer	Blue
Alchemilla (H)	Summer	Yellow
Allium moly (B)	Summer	Yellow
Anemone blanda (B)	Spring	Blue
Aruncus (H)	Summer	White
Asperula odorata (H)	Spring	White
Astilbe (H)	Summer	Pink, red white
Astrantia (H)	Summer	Pink, white
Bergenia (H)	Spring	Pink, red
Brunnera (H)	Spring	Blue
Camassia (B)	Summer	Blue
Camellia (S)	Spring	Various
Convallaria (H)	Spring	White
Corydalis (H)	Spring, summer	Yellow
Cyclamen (B)	Spring, summer	Pink
Daphne mezereum (S)	Winter, spring	Red, violet, white
Dicentra (H)	Spring	Pink
Digitalis (Bi)	Summer	Rose-pink
Endymion (B)	Spring	Blue
Epimedium (H)	Spring	Pink, yellow
Erythronium (B)	Spring	Mauve
Euonymus (S)	—	Foliage only
Euphorbia robbiae (H)	Spring	Green
Gaultheria (S)	—	Foliage, berries

PLANT	IN FLOWER	COLOURS
Geranium endressii (H)	Summer	Pink
Helleborus (H)	Spring	Green, plum
Hosta (H)	Summer	Mauve, white
Hypericum calycinum	Summer	Yellow
Liriope (H)	Autumn	Purple
Lysimachia clethroides (H)	Summer	White
Mahonia (S)	Winter, spring	Yellow
Meconopsis (H)	Summer	Blue
Ornithogalum nutans (B)	Spring	White
Pernettya (S)	—	Red berries
Polygonatum (H)	Spring	White
Polygonum (some) (H)	Summer	Cream, pink, red
Primula (some) (H)	Spring	Pink, yellow
Prunella (H)	Spring, summer	Blue, pink
Pulmonaria (H)	Spring	Blue, pink, red
Sanguinaria (H)	Spring	White
Sarcococca (S)	Winter	White
Skimmia (S)	Summer	White; red berries
Symphoricarpos (S)	—	White or pink fruits
Symphytum (H)	Spring	Blue, yellow
Thalictrum dipterocarpum (H)	Summer	Lilac, yellow
Tiarella (H)	Spring, summer	White
Trillium (H)	Spring	White

Flowering from February to April, when it brightens a shady corner under trees or in the lea of a building, the windflower (Anemone blanda 'Atrocaerulea') grows happily in deep, leafy soil.

PLANT	IN FLOWER	COLOURS
Trollius (H)	Spring	Orange, yellow
Viburnum (S)	Spring	White; blue or red berries
Vinca (H)	Spring	Blue, purple, white
Viola (H), (A)	Spring, summer	Various

(A) = Annual	(H) = Herbaceous
(B) = Bulb	(S) = Shrub (Bi) = Biennial

PLANTS FOR DRY SOIL

Light and sandy soils have many advantages: they are easy to cultivate, they warm up quickly in spring, and they drain well after wet weather.

If sandy soil is all you have, and you want to grow plants that enjoy a modicum of moisture at the roots, there is only one thing for it: you must enrich your earth with plenty of organic matter – peat, compost, manure, leaf-mould and the like.

The plants in this list can usually tolerate dry conditions, but they will all need a helping hand in their youth. It is no good pushing their roots into dust and expecting them to survive. During the first year of establishment they will need to be soaked in dry spells so that the root system they develop is far-reaching and capable of searching for moisture. Organic matter is useful for these plants, too. And remember that when water is able to pass quickly through a soil, it often takes nutrients with it. Sandy soils are hungry soils: feed them regularly.

Revelling in poor, well-drained, even dry soil in full sun, broom (this one is Genista lydia) *unfolds its wealth of blossom in May and June. It looks particularly lovely when cascading over a low wall or rock-garden outcrop.*

PLANT	IN FLOWER	COLOURS
Acanthus (H)	Summer	Purple, white
Achillea (H)	Summer	Pink, yellow
Ageratum (A)	Summer	Blue, mauve, white

PLANT	IN FLOWER	COLOURS
Agrostemma (A)	Summer	Pink
Alchemilla (H)	Summer	Yellow
Anthemis (H)	Summer, autumn	White, yellow
Artemisia (H)	—	Silver leaves
Astrantia (H)	Summer	Pink, white
Aubrieta (R)	Spring	Mauve, pink, purple, red
Berberis (S)	Spring	Orange, yellow; red berries
Bergenia (some) (H)	Spring	Pink, red, white
Borago (A)	Summer	Blue
Buddleia (S)	Summer	Blue, mauve, red, white
Calluna (S)	Summer	Pink, purple, red, white
Campanula (Bi), (H)	Summer	Blue, violet, white
Cistus (S)	Summer	Pink, red, white, yellow
Clarkia (A)	Summer	Pink
Corydalis (R)	Spring, summer	Blue, yellow
Cosmea (A)	Summer	Orange, scarlet, yellow
Cotoneaster (S)	Summer	White; red berries
Crocosmia (H)	Summer	Orange, scarlet, yellow
Cytisus (S)	Spring	Cream, pink, red, yellow
Dierama (H)	Summer	Pink, purple, white
Digitalis (Bi)	Summer	Various
Echinops (H)	Summer	Blue
Echium (A)	Summer	Blue
Erigeron (H)	Summer	Blue, orange, pink
Eryngium (H)	Summer	Blue
Eschscholzia (A)	Summer	Orange, red, yellow
Gazania (A)	Summer	Yellow
Genista (S)	Summer	Yellow
Geranium (H)	Summer	Blue, pink, purple, white
Godetia (A)	Summer	Orange, salmon
Gypsophila (A), (H)	Summer	White
Hebe (S)	Summer	Blue, purple, red, white
Helianthemum (S)	Spring, summer	Pink, red, white, yellow
Helichrysum (A)	Summer	Orange, pink, red
Hibiscus (S)	Summer, autumn	Blue, mauve, red, white
Hypericum (S)	Summer	Yellow
Kniphofia (H)	Summer	Orange, red, yellow
Lathyrus (C)	Summer	Pink, red, white
Lavandula (S)	Summer	Blue, purple
Lavatera (S)	Summer, autumn	Pink, purple, white

PLANT	IN FLOWER	COLOURS
Liatris (H)	Summer	Purple
Limnanthes (A)	Summer	White, yellow
Linaria (A), (H)	Summer	Pink, violet
Linum (A), (H)	Summer	Blue
Lychnis (H)	Summer	Pink, red
Macleaya (H)	Summer	Cream, white
Myrtus (S)	Summer	White
Nepeta (H)	Summer	Blue
Nigella (A)	Summer	Blue, pink, red, white
Oenothera (H)	Summer	Yellow
Olearia (S)	Summer	White
Osmanthus (S)	Spring, summer	White
Physalis (H)	Summer	White; red seed pods
Santolina (S)	Summer	Yellow; silvery leaves
Sarcococca (S)	Winter	White
Sedum (H)	Summer	Pink, red
Sempervivum (R)	Summer	Pink, red, yellow
Solidago (H)	Summer, autumn	Yellow
Stachys (H)	Summer	Pink, purple; silvery leaves
Tagetes (A)	Summer, autumn	Bronze, orange, yellow
Tamarix (S)	Summer	Pink
Vinca (H)	Spring	Blue, red, violet, white
Yucca (S)	Summer	White

(A) = Annual　　*(H) = Herbaceous*
(Bi) = Biennial　*(R) = Rock plant*
(C) = Climber　　*(S) = Shrub*

PLANTS FOR MOISTURE-RETENTIVE OR CLAY SOIL

There's no denying that clay soil is the most unpleasant kind to work, and the most back-breaking, too. But once plants are established within it they often do well, sinking their roots into a medium which seldom dries out at depth and so offers sustenance in dry summers, when plants on lighter soils are suffering.

Dig heavy soils in autumn so that the winter frosts can help shatter the clods and break them into more workable crumbs, and add as much organic matter and sharp grit as you can. Planting on soils like these is nearly always best carried out in spring.

PLANT	IN FLOWER	COLOURS
Ajuga (H)	Spring, summer	Blue
Alchemilla (H)	Summer	Yellow
Astilbe (H)	Summer	Pink, red, white
Astrantia (H)	Summer	Pink, white
Brunnera (H)	Spring	Blue
Cimicifuga (H)	Summer	White
Dicentra (H)	Spring	Pink, white

PLANT	IN FLOWER	COLOURS
Dodecatheon (H)	Spring	Lilac, yellow
Fritillaria meleagris (B)	Spring	Purplish-green
Hemerocallis (H)	Summer	Bronze, yellow
Heuchera (H)	Summer	Pink, red
Hosta (H)	Summer	Blue, mauve, white
Iris (many) (H), (B)	Spring	Various
Lamium (H)	—	Foliage: silver, gold variegation
Leucojum aestivum (B)	Summer	White
Leucojum vernum (B)	Spring	White
Liriope (H)	Autumn	Purple, violet
Ligularia (H)	Summer	Yellow
Lysimachia (H)	Summer	White, yellow
Lythrum (H)	Summer	Pink
Mimulus (H)	Summer	Yellow
Monarda (H)	Summer	Lavender, pink, red
Myosotis (Bi)	Spring	Blue, pink, white
Narcissus cyclamineus (B)	Spring	Yellow
Ornithogalum nutans (B)	Spring	White
Polygonatum (H)	Spring	White
Polygonum (H)	Summer	Cream, pink, red
Primula (many) (H)	Spring	Various
Pulmonaria (H)	Spring	Blue, red; variegated foliage
Ruscus (S)	—	Red berries
Sidalcea (H)	Summer	Pink
Symphytum (H)	Spring	Blue, yellow
Thalictrum (H)	Summer	Lavender, purple, white, yellow
Trollius (H)	Spring	Orange, yellow

(B) = Bulb　　　*(R) = Rock plant*
(Bi) = Biennial　*(S) = Shrub*
(H) = Herbaceous

Prized by flower arrangers for its sprays of sulphur-yellow summer flowers, and by gardeners for the way its leaf hairs cause droplets of dew to gather like balls of quicksilver, lady's mantle (Alchemilla mollis) is a firm favourite on clay soils.

There are few more heartening sights on a chilly late-October day than the icing-sugar-pink flowers of the Guernsey lily (Nerine bowdenii). Colonising happily in a south- or south-west-facing border where summer sun has warmed the bulbs, it comes into flower in autumn.

TENDER PLANTS FOR WARM, SHELTERED POSITIONS

A good selection of frost-tender plants from warm countries will thrive in sheltered southern and western regions of the British Isles if we site them carefully. Their big enemy is wind frost, the killer that shrivels leaves and bites deep into the soil. The answer is to shield such exotics as bottle-brush (*Callistemon*) and lobster's claw (*Clianthus*) by setting them at the foot of a south or west facing wall, or in some sun-drenched corner.

PLANT	IN FLOWER	COLOURS
Agapanthus (H)	Summer	Blue, violet-purple, white
Amaryllis belladonna (B)	Summer, autumn	Pink
Ballota pseudodictamnus (H)	Summer, autumn	Foliage: woolly white leaves
Berberidopsis (C)	Late summer	Crimson, yellow
Buddleia fallowiana (S)	Summer	Lavender
Callistemon (S)	Summer	Red
Camellia sasanqua (S)	Spring	Pink, red, white
Campsis (C)	Summer, autumn	Orange
Centaurea gymnocarpa (H)	—	Foliage: silvery leaves
Chrysanthemum ptarmacaefolium (H)	—	Foliage: lacy white leaves
Clerodendron (S)	Summer, autumn	Red
Clianthus (C)	Spring, summer	Red
Crinum (B)	Summer, autumn	Pink
Convolvulus cneorum (S)	Summer	White
Dimorphotheca ecklanis (H)	Summer	Purple, white
Eccremocarpus (C)	Summer	Orange, red
Gazania (H)	Summer	Brown, orange, red, pink, yellow
Hebe hybrids (S)	Summer	Pink, purple, red, white
Helichrysum petiolatum (H)	—	Foliage: grey-green leaves
Indigofera potaninii (S)	Summer, autumn	Pink
Jasminum officinalis (S)	Summer	White
Lampranthus (Mesembryanthemum) (S)	Summer	Red
Mutisia clematis (S)	Summer	Orange-pink
Nerine (B)	Autumn	Pink, red, white
Olearia semidentata (S)	Summer	Purple
Passiflora caerulea (C)	Summer	Blue/white
Piptanthus (S)	Spring	Yellow
Teucrium fruticans (S)	Summer	Blue
Tigridia (B)	Summer	Red, white, yellow
Trachelospermum (C)	Summer	White
Tropaeolum tuberosum (C)	Summer, autumn	Red, yellow

(B) = Bulb　　**(H) = Herbaceous**
(C) = Climber　　**(S) = Shrub**

PLANTS FOR GROUND COVER

Gardeners have been planting things closely together for hundreds of years, both for the mat-like effect of growth as well as to keep down weeds. Today the idea has caught on as a labour-saving device.

The earth must be well cultivated, weeded and fertilised and the plants given every encouragement to grow well from the outset. This means that they will have to be thoroughly watered in dry spells, and that they will have to be weeded among until their leaves meet to form an impenetrable rug of growth.

When it comes to calculating how many plants you will need, bear in mind the ultimate spread of the species chosen. Plant so that the individuals will overlap slightly when they have been growing for a season or two.

PLANT	IN FLOWER	COLOURS
Acaena (R)	—	Metallic blue leaves
Ajuga (H)	Spring, summer	Purple
Alchemilla (H)	Summer	Yellow-green
Arundinaria (dwarf species) (S)	—	Feathery bamboo
Bergenia (H)	Spring	Pink, red, white
Brunnera (H)	Spring	Blue
Calamintha (H)	Summer	Lavender
Calluna (S)	Summer, autumn	Mauve, pink, purple, white
Cistus (S)	Summer	Pink, red, white, yellow
Convallaria (H)	Spring	White
Cornus canadensis (H)	Summer	White
Cotoneaster 'Skogsholm'	—	Red berries
Epimedium (H)	Spring	Pink, red, yellow
Erica (S)	Winter, spring, summer	Mauve, pink, red, white
Euonymus fortunei (S)	—	Variegated foliage
Euphorbia (some) (H)	Spring, summer	Yellow
Gaultheria (S)	—	Purple or red autumn fruits
Hebe (S)	Summer	Blue, purple, red, white
Hedera (S)	—	Varied foliage
Helianthemum (S)	Spring, summer	Pink, red, white, yellow
Hosta (H)	Summer	Blue, mauve, white; decorative leaves
Hypericum (S)	Summer	Yellow
Iberis (A)	Spring	White
Juniperus (some) (S)	—	Foliage: blue, green, grey or yellow
Lamium (H)	—	Foliage: varieties in gold, silver

PLANT	IN FLOWER	COLOURS
Lavandula (S)	Summer	Blue, purple
Liriope (H)	Autumn	Purple, violet
Lysimachia nummularia (H)	Summer	Yellow
Mahonia aquifolium	—	Black berries
Nepeta (H)	Summer	Blue
Pachysandra terminalis (S)	—	Foliage: pale green or variegated
Pernettya (S)	—	Pink, red or white berries
Potentilla (H), (S)	Summer	White, yellow
Pulmonaria (H)	Spring	Blue, red; variegated foliage
Ruscus (S)	—	Red berries
Santolina (S)	Summer	Yellow; silvery foliage
Sarcococca (S)	Winter	White
Skimmia (S)	Summer	White; red berries
Stachys (H)	Summer	Pink, purple; silvery leaves
Symphytum (H)	Spring, summer	Red, yellow
Thymus (R)	Summer	Lilac
Tiarella (H)	Spring	White
Vaccineum (S)	Spring	Pink
Vinca (H)	Spring	Blue, red, violet, white
Viola (A), (H)	Spring, summer	Various

(A) = Annual   **(R) = Rock plant**
(H) = Herbaceous   **(S) = Shrub**

Valued for its exquisitely marbled leaves, which even in winter remain dry and leathery, barrenwort (Epimedium) forms a carpet of foliage no weed can penetrate. There are species with white, yellow, red and orange columbine-like flowers in late spring. This one is E. perralderianum.

PLANTS FOR SEASIDE GARDENS

Coastal gardens have the great advantage of a fairly stable climate, thanks to the presence of the sea, whose temperature fluctuates very slowly. Such gardens, however, are apt to suffer at the hands of the wind, which lashes them with salt spray in autumn and winter.

Some plants can cope with this kind of treatment, and even though many of them look badly burned after a severe gale, they will soon produce new leaves when favourable weather returns.

Gardens right on the sea front are the most difficult to plant, and it is essential that some form of windbreak is provided before planting gets underway. Wattle hurdles and other semi-permeable barriers should be erected before salt-tolerant hedges, such as tamarisk and juniper, are established to make a more durable shield.

That done, the gardener can experiment with a varied group of plants, even though his season may be shorter than that of gardens inland. The first gales of autumn are always awaited with dread!

Provided you shield it from the direct onslaught of a salty wind, the Peruvian lily (Alstroemeria aurantiaca) will colour a border in summer with a multiplicity of fiery orange blooms. It spreads by underground stems, and within a few years a single plant becomes a thriving colony if its soil is enriched with bone-meal and peat.

PLANT	IN FLOWER	COLOURS
Achillea (H)	Summer	Pink, yellow
Agapanthus (H)	Summer	Blue, white
Alstroemeria (H)	Summer	Orange, pink, red
Anemone (H)	Summer, autumn	Pink, red, white
Artemisia (H)	Summer	Foliage: silvery white
Berberis (S)	Spring	Orange, yellow
Bergenia (H)	Spring	Pink, red, white
Buddleia (S)	Summer	Blue, mauve, red, white
Carpenteria (S)	Summer	White
Caryopteris (S)	Summer, autumn	Blue
Catananche (H)	Summer	Blue
Ceanothus (S)	Spring, summer	Blue, pink
Centaurea (H)	Summer	Blue, pink
Choisya (S)	Spring, autumn	White
Chrysanthemum (H)	Autumn	Various
Cistus (S)	Summer	Pink, red, white, yellow
Clematis (C)	Spring, summer, winter	Various
Cotoneaster (S)	Summer	White; red berries
Crocosmia (H)	Summer	Orange, red, yellow
Cytisus (S)	Spring	Purple, red, white, yellow
Dianthus (H)	Summer	Pink, red, white
Dierama (H)	Summer	Pink, purple, white
Eccremocarpus (C)	Summer	Orange, red
Echinops (H)	Summer	Blue
Elaeagnus (S)	—	Foliage: variegated
Endymion (B)	Spring	Blue, pink, white
Erigeron (H)	Summer	Blue, orange, pink
Eryngium (H)	Summer	Blue
Escallonia (S)	Summer	Pink, red, white
Euonymus japonicus	—	Foliage: green or variegated
Euphorbia (H)	Spring, summer	Lime, orange, yellow
Festuca (H)	—	Foliage: blue-grey
Fremontia (S)	Summer	Yellow
Fuchsia (S)	Summer, autumn	Pink, red, white
Garrya (S)	Winter	Silver catkins
Gazania (H)	Summer	Orange, yellow
Genista (S)	Spring, summer	Yellow
Geranium (H)	Summer	Blue, pink, red, white
Gypsophila (H)	Summer	White
Hebe (S)	Summer	Blue, pink, purple, red
Hedera (S)	—	Foliage: variegated
Heuchera (H)	Spring, summer	Pink, red

PLANT	IN FLOWER	COLOURS
Hibiscus (S)	Summer, autumn	Blue, mauve, red, white
Hydrangea (S)	Summer, autumn	Blue, pink, red, white
Hypericum (S)	Summer	Yellow
Iris (H)	Spring	Various
Juniperus (S)	—	Foliage: blue, green, grey, yellow
Kniphofia (H)	Summer	Orange, red, yellow
Lathyrus (C)	Summer	Pink, red, white
Lavandula (S)	Summer	Blue, purple
Lavatera (S)	Summer	Pink, red
Leycesteria (S)	Summer, autumn	Red/white; purple berries
Linaria (A), (H)	Summer	Pink, violet
Lychnis (H)	Summer	Pink, red
Myrtus (S)	Summer	White
Oenothera (H)	Summer	Yellow
Olearia (S)	Summer	White
Osmanthus (S)	Spring	White
Passiflora (C)	Summer	Blue/white
Penstemon (H), (S)	Summer	Blue, pink, red
Phormium (S)	—	Foliage: sword-like leaves
Polygonum (H)	Summer	Cream, pink, red
Potentilla (S)	Summer	Cream, yellow
Primula vulgaris and hybrids (H)	Spring	Various

PLANT	IN FLOWER	COLOURS
Pyracantha (S)	Summer	White; red or yellow berries
Ribes (S)	Spring	Pink, red
Romneya (S)	Summer	White, yellow
Rosmarinus (S)	Spring	Blue
Sambucus (S)	Spring, summer	Cream; cut foliage; black or red fruits
Santolina (S)	Summer	Yellow; silvery leaves
Scabiosa (H)	Summer	Mauve, pink, white, yellow
Scilla (B)	Spring, autumn	Blue, white
Sedum (H)	Summer	Pink, red
Skimmia (S)	Spring	White; red berries
Solanum (C)	Summer	Blue, purple
Spartium (S)	Summer	Yellow
Symphoricarpos (S)	—	White or pink fruits
Tamarix (S)	Summer	Pink
Tradescantia (H)	Summer	Blue, red, violet
Tropaeolum (C)	Summer	Orange, red, yellow
Veronica (H)	Summer	Blue
Viburnum tinus (S)	Winter, spring	Pinkish white
Weigela (S)	Spring	Pink
Yucca (S)	Summer	White

(B) = Bulb **(H) = Herbaceous**
(C) = Climber **(S) = Shrub**

Known as elephant's ears on account of its large leathery leaves, Bergenia 'Ballawley' is a robust member of the clan and its spring-flowering stems grow 600–750 mm (2–2½ ft) high in heavy, moist soil.

HEIGHT, SPREAD AND SHAPE

When you plan your flower garden, think carefully about the various elements in the total scheme and how they will relate to each other. There is, for instance, a great and obvious contrast between the hard, angular lines and solid mass of the house and the slender, flowing shapes of flowering plants. The visual transition from one to the other can be made less abrupt in many ways – by training climbers on the house walls, for instance, or by extending paving outward from the house and stocking it with container plants. In the same way, different parts of the garden can be made to merge into one another, the eye being led from one to the next by carefully sited visual 'signals' – a decorative urn, perhaps, or stepping stones curving across the margins of a lawn.

The view from the house windows is important, especially in winter. Here flowers come into their own, whether they are herbaceous plants, bulbs, flowering shrubs or roses. When you are choosing them, their season of flowering, as well as their colours, are important.

VARYING THE LEVELS

A variation in levels and a variation of plant heights all help to add interest; for instance, a herbaceous border can all too easily have a single horizontal level. Break it up with the smaller, vertically growing conifers, juniper 'Skyrocket', the fastigiate Irish yew or evening primroses (Oenothera). Use shrubs as a change from herbaceous plants; go in for bulbs – these can vary from the tiny front-of-border snowdrops and crocuses to the 900 mm (3 ft) crown imperials and summer hyacinths (Galtonia).

The herbaceous border, when first conceived, contained plants graded in height so that the lowest were in front and the tallest at the back; it was meant to be looked at from only one side. When successful it was superb, but it was difficult to achieve and often difficult to cultivate. The modern idea has commuted this a little to the 'island border'. This is a bed of irregular curving shape, cut in turf or surrounded by paving, containing perennials arranged so that the tallest are more or less in the middle, and the carpeters at the edges. The shapes of these beds can be very pleasing and, being islands, they are more easily cared for, particularly if no-staking perennials are grown.

This last point is not to be overlooked in planting. The more time you have to spare, the more you can improve the garden, and enjoy it, too; a garden which is always needing attention becomes a tiresome job which has to be done, instead of being a place for pleasure and interest, as it should be. Shrubs are plants which do not need a lot of care, on the whole, but which can provide much in the way of flowers, fruits and foliage. Ground-cover plants will fill in spaces between perennials and shrubs so that the weeds cannot spread; ivy, periwinkle, heathers, London pride, St John's wort (*Hypericum*), creeping thyme and saxifrages, once established, need virtually no attention.

LAYING OUT A MIXED BORDER

The size, shape and levels of a mixed flower border will be largely influenced by the existing site. Depth and breadth of the bed should be taken into account as much as the proposed colour schemes and season of interest, and the height and character of the plants should relate to each other and their surroundings.

A simple plan for a border in front of a hedge could have tall plants placed at the back and shorter subjects to the fore. With large borders it is better to set plants in groups rather than individually, or a spotty effect may be created. Tall spiky plants like delphiniums and verbascum contrast well with round-headed flowers like achillea and phlox, or with plants such as helenium that form a mounded clump.

The duration and times of the flowering season are important: borders close to the house need subjects that provide year-round colour, although a traditional herbaceous border usually has a short but splendid season in summer. Small evergreen shrubs introduced in a mixed border provide a useful framework and give year-round interest.

Strong hues of red or yellow contrast well against shades of green and blue. White and cream blend harmoniously with most flower colours. Bronze, orange and pinks create a warm effect, compared with the coolness of blues and lavenders. Grey foliage blends or contrasts with red, cerise, pink and white shades.

Above *A handsome raised trough such as this creates interest for much of the year, especially in spring and early summer. It can feature permanent plant residents or be used to display a changing parade of colourful bedding plants.*

Left *The stately evening primrose (Oenothera) makes a handsome sentinel to punctuate a border and elevate an otherwise flattish planting scheme. This one is O. tetragona 'Fireworks'.*

Berberis darwinii
Evergreen. April flowers
followed by berries. Any
soil; open site. Height
1.8–2.4 m (6–8 ft).

Euonymus japonicus
'Aureus' Evergreen.
Well-drained soil;
sunny site. Height
3–4.5 m (10–15 ft).

Daisy bush
(Olearia × haastii)
Evergreen shrub.
Scented flowers in July.
Prune in spring. Well-
drained, fertile soil; full
sun. Height 1.2 m (4 ft).

THE BACKCLOTH

SHRUBS

An herbaceous or mixed border of shrubs and hardy perennials needs a contrasting backcloth – a wall, fence, hedge or informal arrangement of evergreen trees or shrubs.

A yew (*Taxus*) or arbor-vitae (*Thuja*) hedge is ideal. Clipped once a year, in August, it doesn't grow out of hand and the deep-green foliage contrasts superbly with the orange-red tones of crocosmia and kniphofia, the sun-yellow blooms of achillea and helianthus, and the snow-white of the bellflower (*Campanula lactiflora* 'Alba').

Other evergreen shrubs include berberis, attractive and easy-to-grow. One of the best is the charming *B. darwinii*. Californian lilacs (*Ceanothus*) are blue-flowered shrubs which bloom in spring, summer or autumn.

Another very attractive flowering shrub is Mexican orange blossom (*Choisya ternata*). Grown mostly for the beauty of their foliage, *Elaeagnus* are hardy, with tiny, scented flowers in spring or autumn. The oleaster (*E. commutata*) has deciduous silver leaves and bears small, silvery fruits.

Escallonia grow particularly well in seaside gardens. *E.* × *edinensis* has pink flowers in arching sprays; *E.* × 'Apple Blossom' pink and white, 'Donard Brilliance', crimson. All flower in June–July. Another good shrub for seaside gardens is *Euonymus japonicus* 'Aureus', with glossy, gold-centred leaves.

Yet another good hedging and backcloth plant for seaside gardens (and towns) is the daisy bush (*Olearia*). Probably the best is the hybrid *O.* × *haastii*, whose flattish clusters of daisy-like flowers bloom in July.

Osmanthus delavayi, a rounded evergreen shrub, has strongly scented small white flowers in April, and small glossy, dark green leaves.

The firethorns (*Pyracantha*) are evergreen in reasonable winters, and very spiny. They are quite hardy and grown mostly for their fruits.

Most garden senecios have grey or silvery foliage and yellow flowers in summer and early autumn. The best garden species is *Senecio* 'Sunshine', whose leaves are white-felted.

HERBACEOUS PLANTS

Point up your medium-size and low-growing border plants with a backcloth of tall, elegant herbaceous types, preferably self-supporting up to a height of 1.5 m (5 ft) to 2 m (6½ ft), depending on the size of the border.

Delphiniums, reliable and popular herbaceous border plants in English gardens, are also among the most handsome; they contribute some of the most vivid blues to the garden scene. The blues of the large-flowered hybrids show infinite variation, from the palest powder blue to deepest navy, with violet, lilac, mauve and pink tingeing the petals; white, cream and yellow are also represented. Outstanding amongst the magnificent Pacific Hybrids, which reach at least 1.8 m (6 ft) high, are the blue 'Ann Page', pink 'Astolat', and white 'Pacific Galahad'. The Belladonna cultivars are smaller.

The plume poppy (*Macleaya microcarpa*) is quite unlike a poppy in its flowers. It is a tall plant whose habit of growth provides a welcome airiness amongst the denser foliage and flowers of most perennials. The large rounded, scalloped-edged leaves have silvery undersides; the small, yellowish buff-coloured flowers grow in large feathery clusters at the top of each stem.

Herbaceous Plants

NAME	DESCRIPTION	HEIGHT/SPREAD	IN FLOWER	SOIL AND SITE	REMARKS	PROPAGATION
Acanthus spinosus bear's breeches	Distinctive, deeply cut foliage and spectacular spikes of mauve-purple flowers	H: 1.2 m (4 ft) S: 600 mm (2 ft)	July–Sept	Deep, well-drained loam, sunny or slightly shaded	Dislikes disturbance	Root cuttings in Jan. or Feb. Large clumps can be divided between Oct. and April
Achillea	Attractive divided foliage, and flat yellow flower-heads. 'Coronation Gold' (deep yellow; H: 0.9–1.2 m/ 3–4 ft, S: 750–900 mm/ 2½–3 ft); 'Moonshine' (silvery foliage, pale yellow flowers; H: 600 mm/2 ft, S: 45 cm/1½ ft)	See description	June–Aug	Stony, gravelly or chalky soils, full sun	Trouble-free plants in right conditions. Flower-heads retain colour for many months when cut and dried	Divide established clumps in Sept. or spring. Keep young plants moist until established
Alstroemeria ligtu Hybrids Peruvian lily	Small lily-like flowers. Pink, scarlet, orange and yellow	H: 60–90 cm (2–3 ft) S: 300 mm (1 ft)	June–Aug.	Fertile, well-drained soil, sheltered from cold winds	Always plant pot-grown specimens: root disturbance resented	Divide established clumps in spring. Raised from seed

NAME	DESCRIPTION	HEIGHT/ SPREAD	IN FLOWER	SOIL AND SITE	REMARKS	PROPAGATION
Artemisia lactiflora white mugwort	Plumes of fragrant creamy-white flowers, deeply divided leaves	H: 1.2 cm (4 ft) S: 600 mm (2 ft)	Aug.–Oct.	Well-drained soil, sun or part shade	In autumn, cut plants down to soil level	Divide clump from Oct. to March
Campanula lactiflora bellflower	Light blue bells 25 mm (1 in) across on tall, leafy stems. Cultivars include 'Loddon Anna' (lilac-pink)	H: 1.2 m (4 ft) S: 900 mm (3 ft)	June–Aug.	Fertile, well-drained soil, sun or partial shade	Support may be necessary in windy areas	Divide in March or April
Delphinium (garden hybrids)	Many good cultivars: 'Ann Page' (semi-double, cornflower blue), 'Black Knight' (dark blue), 'King Arthur' (purple, with white eye) and 'Startling' (deep violet, white eye)	H: 1.8 m (6 ft) S: 750–900 mm (2½–3 ft)	June–Aug.	Deep fertile soil, sunny position, sheltered from strong winds	Staking essential. After flowering, cut stems back to soil level.	Take cuttings in April. Root in equal parts peat and sand in a cold-frame. Divide established plants in spring. Raised from seed.
Eupatorium purpureum joe-pye weed	Clustered heads of purple-crimson flowers	H: 1.5 m (5 ft) S: 900 m (3 ft)	Aug.–Sept.	Ordinary soil, sun or partial shade	Ensure soil is kept moist. Cut foliage down to ground in autumn	Divide in Oct. or March
Helianthus 'Loddon Gold' perennial sunflower	Double, golden-yellow flowers	H: 1.5 m (5 ft) S: 1 m (3¼ ft)	Aug.–Sept.	Well-drained soil, full sun	May need support in exposed places	Divide in Oct. or April
Inula magnifica	Very large, with hoary leaves, bright yellow daisy-like blooms	H: 1.8 m (6 ft) S: 900 mm (3 ft)	July–Aug.	Moisture-retentive soil, full sun	Ensure plants do not become dry	Divide in March or April
Kniphofia (garden hybrids) red-hot poker	Stiff spikes in shades of glowing orange, red or yellow	H: 1–1.2 m (3½–4 ft) S: 450 mm (1½ ft)	June–July	Good soil, full sun	Plant in Sept or Oct, mulch in spring	Divide established plants in April
Ligularia dentata (syn. *L. clivorum*, *Senecio clivorum*)	'Desdemona' has large, vivid orange daisy-like heads and large flushed purple leaves	H: 1.2 m (4 ft) S: 900 mm (3 ft)	July–Sept.	Moist, deeply cultivated soil, full sun	May require support and protection from winds	Divide established plants in April
Macleaya cordata (syn. *Bocconia cordata*) plume poppy	Creamy-white, 12 mm (½ in) long flowers carried in sprays above lobed, glaucous leaves	H: 1.2 m (4 ft) S: 900 mm (3 ft)	Aug.–Sept.	Deep soil, sunny but sheltered position	Support young growth with twiggy sticks	Divide established plants from Oct. to April
Sidalcea	Spires of attractive mallow-like pink flowers. Cultivars include 'Pink Pinnacle' (clear pink), 'Rose Queen' (clear rose), and 'William Smith' (salmon)	H: 1.2 m (4 ft) S: 600 mm (2 ft)	June–Aug.	Ordinary garden soil, full sun	Cut flowering stems down to 300 mm (1 ft) immediately after blooming	Divide in spring. Can also be grown from seed

Far left Osmanthus delavayi's *arching shoots are clad with scented tubular white flowers in April and May. It reaches a height and spread of up to 6 m (20 ft).*

Near left *Possessing great charm, 'Pink Sensation' – one of the Belladonna group of delphiniums – looks superb in front of cream-coloured climbers. It grows up to 1.3 m (4½ ft) high.*

CLIMBERS & TRAILERS

You can almost double the potential growing space of your patio or garden if you use the boundary walls or fences in an imaginative way. Climbers on the walls of a house, for instance, can turn them into part of the garden scheme and bring flowers close to the windows. Climbers can also be used to hide unsightly items.

A climber can be used to frame a window. Morning glory (*Ipomoea*), grown in pots, for instance, can be trained up lines of twine around the window. Or you can build a narrow trellis and grow climbers up that. Even a humble chain-link fence can have a climber, such as common ivy (*Hedera helix*), trained and tied to it so that it is completely covered and becomes a lush green 'wall'.

A warm and sheltered wall, which usually retains heat either from the house or from the sun can be used to give protection to the more tender plants which might perish if grown in the open. Climbers trained to scale a post, archway or pergola can provide an accent or a focal point. Similarly, an ugly dead tree can be turned into an object of beauty if it has an attractive plant growing over it.

Climbing shrubs do not always have to be grown upwards: training them in the reverse direction can be decorative as well as useful. A somewhat plain bank can be covered effectively by planting several climbers at the top and allowing them to trail downwards.

Some evergreens should be included in a planting scheme of this type to ensure that walls and fences do not become bare in winter. During the summer, when flower-beds are blooming, it is not so important to plant climbers on the boundaries to give bright colours. In winter, however, when most plants are bare, some winter- or autumn-flowering climbers and wall plants give great pleasure. Examples are flowering quince (*Chaenomeles speciosa*), which has rosy red flowers in January, at least in mild winters; its cultivar 'Aurora', which has salmon-pink blooms in October; the winter sweet (*Chimonanthus praecox*), which has sweetly scented, pale yellow flowers from December to February; and *Clematis cirrhosa balearica*, which produces pale yellow blossoms, spotted reddish purple, throughout the winter.

Climbing roses should be sited with care if space is restricted, as their prickles may become a nuisance. They grow best of all on open trellis or laths set slightly away from a brick wall,

Typical planting scheme for the backcloth, with the tallest plants trained against a wall. Key to numbers: 1 Delphinium, 2 Passion-flower (Passiflora), 3 Yarrow (Achillea), 4 Red-hot poker (Kniphofia), 5 Trumpet vine (Campsis), 6 Garrya elliptica, 7 Shrubby euphorbia, 8 Clematis, 9 Day lily (Hemerocallis), 10 Bellflower (Campanula).

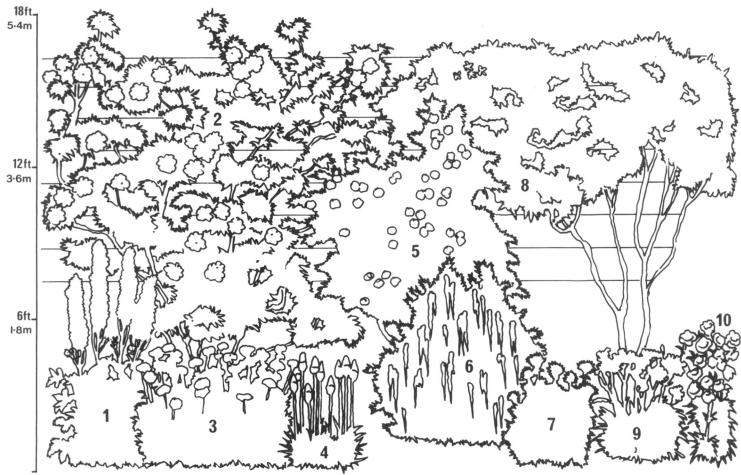

because they need plenty of air around them to discourage the scourge of mildew. For a small wall the 'Lemon Pillar' rose (which is in fact white) or 'Crimson Coral Satin' is a good choice. If you prefer pink, 'Conrad F. Meyer', a rugosa rose, is a pretty one to choose. Ramblers, on the other hand, behave exactly as their name suggests – ramble all over the place and are not so suitable for a small area.

Clematis and other 'softer' climbers, such as winter jasmine (*Jasminum nudiflorum*) and honeysuckle (*Lonicera*) will need plenty of wire-netting or trellis to cling to and climb over and to protect them from strong winds. But they do tend to make fast growth and flower quickly and they do not need tying in. They can also be grown easily in pots, as can the passion flower (*Passiflora caerulea*), which actually flowers better if it has some root restriction.

If you are planning on climbers for pergolas and posts around a terrace, a vine, traditionally, makes an attractive network of leaves under which to dine out or sit. The most vigorous variety to choose is *Vitis vinifera* 'Brandt', which has foliage that colours in the autumn and tempting dark red grapes that can be used for desserts or for making wine.

If you have a wall, or an unsightly building that you want to cover rapidly, then the fastest, most vigorous climber you are likely to come across is Russian vine (*Polygonum baldschuanicum*), which can cover 6 m (20 ft) of wall in one season. However, the trouble is that once having started it, it is difficult to get it to stop. It is deciduous, too, so you are left with bare branches in winter. But if judiciously clipped and pruned back, it quite quickly forms a thick network of trunks which makes it an attractive proposition for, say, a pergola where you want leaves overhead; and its long delicate racemes of white flowers hang down in an attractive way. It is a good choice to compensate for a slower-growing, more attractive climber like a vine or wisteria, provided you keep it under control. Two other rapid climbers to look for are *Clematis montana* varieties and *Rosa filipes* 'Kiftsgate', a very vigorous rambler with white flowers that will eventually need checking. Clematis can also be used to scramble over an existing bush or tree. More instant cover is provided by the perennial climbing nasturtium, Scottish Flame (*Tropaeolum speciosum*), which grows fast while permanent climbers are becoming established.

Tall plants to consider putting against a wall to brighten it up on a temporary basis include sunflowers (*Helianthus annuus*), tall delphiniums, foxgloves (*Digitalis purpurea*), hollyhocks (*Althaea rosea*), and black-eyed susan (*Rudbeckia hirta*).

North walls can be a problem, but fortunately there are a number of attractive climbers that will cope with them, notably *Hydrangea petiolaris*. This bears little or no resemblance to the ordinary hydrangea, having delicate lace-like white flowers and dark, glossy green leaves; it reaches a height of 14 m (46 ft).

Do not be tempted to choose the tallest plant in the garden centre: take a good hard look at it first for it may be drawn out and straggly. A climber that is shorter but has several stems may be a better bet and will soon catch up in height when it is in the ground. If it is container-grown, make sure that it is not pot-bound (that is, with overcrowded roots).

Captivating daisy-like blooms of the coneflower or black-eyed-susan (Rudbeckia hirta) are borne freely on sturdy stems in early autumn when the main summer display of border plants has dwindled. Contrasting effectively with a red brick wall, it is perfect for planting close to the house.

CLIMBERS FOR A SUNNY WALL

Wisterias are among the most showy and colourful climbing shrubs. They support themselves by twining stems, and their long tassels of pea flowers, lilac purple in most forms, are a magnificent sight in May and June. *Wisteria sinensis* is the most popular species, with flower clusters 200–300 mm (8–12 in) long. These appear before the leaves. The white form, 'Alba', is also well worth growing. *W. floribunda*, the Japanese wisteria, has the most striking cultivar of all, 'Macrobotrys', with pendant lilac flower trusses up to 1 m (3¼ ft) long. Wisteria flowers have a spicy scent, reminiscent of lupins.

Summer jasmine (*J. officinale*) is a vigorous twiner which produces masses of small white, intensely fragrant flowers from June to September. Its rather untidy and straggling habit of growth makes it most suitable for growing through trees or over sheds or other outbuildings.

Honeysuckles (*Lonicera*) are grown as much for their perfume as for their decorative display. Cultivars of our native woodbine (*L. periclymenum*) are among the most fragrant, although some other species and hybrids are showier and more colourful.

SELF-SUPPORTING CLIMBERS

Most garden climbers attach themselves to supports by means of twining stems or leaf tendrils. A few, however, require no support, gripping walls or other vertical surfaces with aerial roots or self-clinging pads. The following are typical self-supporters.

North American trumpet vine (*Campsis radicans*), a deciduous shrub, has light green leaves, and in August and September produces brilliant orange and scarlet, trumpet-shaped flowers. It

*Right Scented early or late Dutch honeysuckle (*Lonicera periclymenum*) is perfect for draping a pergola or cascading from a patio's overhead beams. Happy in sun or light shade, it flowers in July–September.*

grows to a height of about 12 m (40 ft) and likes enriched, well-drained soil in shelter and full sun. The much less vigorous *C.* × *tagliabuana* 'Madame Galen' has large, pink-red trumpets.

Among the ivies the Canary Island form (*Hedera canariensis* 'Gloire de Marengo') is a rapid-growing evergreen with leathery leaves, dark green in the centre, becoming silvery grey

and then white at the margin. Older leaves are sometimes flecked crimson. Thrives in any soil in sun or shade but is not hardy in severe winters. It grows to about 6 m (20 ft) and needs pruning to keep it in bounds.

Persian ivy (*H. colchica*) is strong and quick-growing, with dark green leaves, glossy and leathery and grows in any soil. Needs pruning in

Passion flower (Passiflora caerulea) *Climbs by means of leaf tendrils; best for a south- or west-facing wall. Yellow, egg-shaped fruits follow flowers. Height 3–4 m (10–13 ft). Take stem cuttings in July–August.*

Trumpet vine (Campsis radicans) *Self-clinging by aerial roots; likes a sunny wall. 'Madame Galen' is an impressive salmon-red flowered cultivar. Height 6–7 m (20–23 ft). Take semi-hardwood cuttings in August.*

Virginia creeper (Parthenocissus quinquefolia) *Makes a vivid curtain of autumn tinted leaves. Climbs by limpet-like sucker discs. Height 7–8 m (23–26 ft). Take hardwood cuttings in November.*

late winter to control its size. Height 7.5 m (25 ft). Its variety 'Dentata Variegata' has large, shiny leaves soft green in colour with marked, deep yellow variegations; and grows to less than half the height.

Common ivy (*H. helix*) is a hardy evergreen with glossy dark green leaves. Happy in any soil, it needs pruning to control shape and size. Height 30 m (100 ft). Its varieties 'Buttercup', 'Golden Cloud' and 'Russell's Gold' have small, yellow, evergreen leaves, and are very slow-growing; 'Purpurea' has small evergreen leaves, green-coloured during the summer, turning deep purple in winter; 'Sagittaefolia Variegata' has small, evergreen leaves, shaped like an arrowhead with creamy white markings.

Climbing hydrangea (*Hydrangea petiolaris*) is deciduous and strong-growing, with rich, dark green, serrated leaves, pale green and downy underneath and turning lemon-coloured in autumn, and reddish-brown, peeling bark. Produces white flowers in June. Thrives on a north wall. Height 15 m (50 ft).

Chinese Virginia creeper (*Parthenocissus henryana*) is deciduous and not quite hardy. Its dark green leaves, with white and pink veinal variegations, turn red in autumn. Height 9 m (30 ft).

True Virginia creeper (*P. quinquefolia*) is hardy and deciduous, with green leaves that change to bright orange and red in autumn. Grows in moist, rich soil. Needs pruning in summer to control its denseness and spread. Height 21 m (70 ft).

ROSES

Apart from *Rosa filipes* 'Kiftsgate', already mentioned, there are many attractive roses suitable for growing against vertical supports. They can be divided into three main types. The first are the large-flowered climbers, of which the following are typical: 'Aloha' yields large, very full, fragrant flowers, deep rose-pink suffused with orange-salmon, from June onwards. Excellent for small gardens; moderately vigorous, it will grow on a north wall to a height of 1.8 m (6 ft). 'Casino' is repeat-flowering, has soft yellow, very fragrant flowers that open from deeper yellow buds, and dark green foliage. Vigorous and grows to a height of 2.7 m (9 ft). 'Compassion' has pale salmon-orange flowers with apricot shading that is lighter on the reverse. They are full and very fragrant and appear from June onwards. Very vigorous, grows to a height of 3 m (10 ft). 'Danse de Feu' produces full blooms of bright orange-red from June throughout the summer. Moderately vigorous, it will grow on a north wall and reaches a height of 2.4 m (8 ft). 'Parkdirektor Riggers' has dark green leaves and blood-red, semi-double, recurrent flowers borne in clusters from mid-June onwards. It will grow

on a north wall and is vigorous, reaching a height of 3.5 m (12 ft).

Rambler roses have vigorous but looser growth than the climbers but can readily be trained to take up the shape of their supports.

Four good ones are: 'Albéric Barbier', a veteran, having been introduced in 1900, with white, yellow-centred, fragrant flowers in June. The shiny foliage is semi-evergreen. Grows to a height of 7.5 m (25 ft). 'Crimson Shower' has clusters of small, rosette flowers in July and August. Vigorous; grows to a height of 2.4 m (8 ft). 'Emily Gray' has golden-buff, scented blooms in early summer, and semi-evergreen foliage. Very vigorous: grows to a height of 3.5 m (12 ft). 'New Dawn' is a repeat-flowering rambler with pale flesh-pink, full, perfumed flowers. Moderately vigorous: grows to 3 m (10 ft).

Sprawling roses are particularly good for covering tree stumps, training up steep banks, or using as ground cover. Two recommended varieties: 'Max Graf', a modern hybrid Rugosa shrub, has bright pink, single flowers with white centres and golden stamens in mid- to late-June. Vigorous and trailing, it reaches a height of 300 mm (1 ft). Good for quick ground-cover. 'Nozomi' has trusses of pearl-pink, single flowers. It has a spreading habit and will extend to a width of 600 mm (2 ft). Unsupported it grows to a height of 450 mm (1½ ft); supported it will grow up to 1.5 m (5 ft).

Above *Roses around a door (or a window) evoke cottage-garden tranquillity. There are dozens of repeat-flowering climbers and ramblers to choose from. Dead-head them regularly to encourage strong new shoots and a recurrent display of blooms.*

THE CENTRE

The middle of a border should dominate. Plants chosen for their shape and leaf texture, compatible colours and longevity of bloom should be the focus of an admiring and critical eye. The plants you choose should be about 450–750 mm (1½–2½ ft) high and carefully graded so that the smaller are not overshadowed by the larger.

HERBACEOUS PERENNIALS

The following are a few among many species of excellent permanent residents.

The deciduous African lilies (*Agapanthus*) have proved to be surprisingly hardy, considering their country of origin. Clusters of blue, bell-like flowers 50 mm (2 in) wide, appear at the top of stems 600–900 mm (2–3 ft) long from July to September. The strap-shaped leaves are profusely produced in a long arching rosette at the base of the plant from fleshy, rather brittle roots. The Headbourne Hybrids have a good range of blues, from sky-blue to deep blue and violet-blue. African lilies prefer a sunny site and rich but well-drained soil.

Among the astilbes the garden hybrids grouped under *A. × arendsii* are most commonly seen nowadays. They are erect, bushy plants with finely divided, fern-like leaves – some tinged bronze or purple – and sprays of tiny flowers in June–August. Good examples of medium-sized forms are 'Fire' (salmon-red), 'Irrlicht' (white), and 'Ostrich' (pink). All these grow to about 750 mm (2½ ft) in height.

The masterwort (*Astrantia carniolica*), 600 mm (2 ft), popular with flower-arrangers, has white pink-tinged flowers in July–August. *A. major* has similarly starlike flowers, but greenish pink in colour; while in *A. maxima* the flowers are rich pink. Sun and light shade are equally suitable sites; any reasonably fertile soil will do.

There are several good varieties of the Shasta daisy (*Chrysanthemum maximum*), with flowers comprising a yellow disc, and white rays. Typical are 'Everest', 'Mayfield Giant' and 'Wirral Supreme', all 600–900 mm (2–3 ft) tall.

Two good cultivars of baby's breath (*Gypsophila paniculata*) are 'Bristol Fairy' and 'Compacta Plena'. Both have large misty clusters of white flowers from June to August, and are particularly good for floral arrangements. They thrive in good soil in sun 90 cm (3 ft); 45 cm (1½ ft) respectively.

The sea hollies (*Eryngium*) are fascinating for their somewhat thistle-like prickly and spiny stiff leaves and stems, and their coned flowers with a prickly ruff of bracts round each. The overall colouring of the plants is silvery blue. *E. alpinum* grows to 600 mm (2 ft) tall and 300 mm (1 ft) wide; its variety 'Violetta' is blue to violet-blue, growing to about 750 mm (2½ ft) tall and 450 mm (1½ ft) wide. The original sea holly, *E. maritimum*, is native to Britain, so the plants are not difficult to grow, though they like a very well-drained, rather poor soil.

The cultivars of *Phlox paniculata* bloom between July and September and may reach a height of 1.2 m (4 ft). There are some marvellous colours amongst them and excellent examples are 'White Admiral', cherry-red 'Starfire', and lavender-blue 'Skylight'. Another excellent variety is pink *P. maculata* 'Alpha'. For late-summer flowering, border phlox are hard to beat, but they must be watered well to ensure plenty of blossom that will not fade quickly. Plants flourish in rich, fertile soil.

The 'Gainsborough' variety of mullein (*Verbascum × phoeniceum*) is a beauty. Its clear, light yellow spires of bloom rise to 900 mm (3 ft). Another, 'Pink Domino', has rose-coloured flowers that contrast well with the yellow forms.

Ox-eye daisies (Chrysanthemum maximum) flower for weeks in summer and create an imposing focus. Use them to separate 'hot' colours, such as reds and purples. Happy in any soil, though more vigorous on heavy clay, they come in single and double flowers; some have attractive 'anemone' centres.

ELBOW ROOM

One of the commonest mistakes with perennials is to underestimate the amount of room they need. Any plant which grows in the same place year after year must be expected to become bigger. If, in the early days, you are afraid the bed will look empty, fill in with annuals. Do not, however, overcrowd the perennials, which need room to expand by bushing out. Crowding will create tall and spindly growths and weak stems. In general, gardeners who find a great deal of staking is necessary have only themselves to blame.

Be sure that your borders are wide enough. It is a good basic rule to have a border twice as wide as the height of the tallest plants that it is to contain. This means that for plants 1.5 m (5 ft) high (delphiniums, for example, can easily exceed this height), a bed at least 3 m (10 ft) wide is necessary. If your borders are much narrower than this you should consider widening them by any means possible.

Herbaceous Perennials

NAME	DESCRIPTION	HEIGHT/SPREAD	IN FLOWER	SOIL AND SITE	REMARKS	PROPAGATION
Anchusa azurea Alkanet	Brilliant blue flowers. Outstanding cultivar is 'Loddon Royalist' (H: 900 m/3 ft, S: 600 mm/2 ft)	See description	May–July	Deep, fertile soil, sunny position	Support with twigs	Root cuttings in Jan. or Feb.
Aster novi-belgii Michaelmas daisy	Good types: 'Ada Ballard' (mauve-blue, H: 900 mm/3 ft), 'Carnival' (semi-double, red, H: 600 mm/2 ft)	See description	Sept–Oct	Fertile soil, sunny position. Soil must not dry out during the flowering season	Tall cultivars may need twiggy supports. Replace with fresh stock every three years.	Divide in April or March
Astrantia maxima Masterwort	Star-like white or rose-pink flowers with greenish-pink bracts	H: 750 mm (2½ ft) S: 600 mm (2 ft)	June–July	Moist soil, shady or sunny	Staking may be necessary in exposed places	Divide between Oct. and March
Anemone × hybrida Japanese anemone	Magnificent for late flowering colour in the garden. Cultivars include 'Bressingham Glow' (rosy-red), 'September Charm' (pink and gold flowers), and 'White Queen'	H: 450–900 mm (1½–3 ft) S: 300–600 mm (1–2 ft)	Aug–Oct	Fertile, moisture-retentive, well-drained soil, slight shade	May take a year or two to settle down.	Divide between Oct. and March
Campanula persicifolia Peach-leaved bellflower	Beautiful spires of blue or white flowers. 'Telham Beauty' is one of the best blues	H: 1 m (3¼ ft) S: 600 mm (2 ft)	June–Aug	Well drained, full or part sun	May need staking. Divide clumps in Oct.	
Chrysanthemum maximum Shasta daisy	Large white daisy flowers. 'Esther Read' (double, white) and 'Wirral Supreme' (large double white) are good	H: 900 mm (3 ft) S: 450 mm (1½ ft)	July–Sept	Best in well-drained soil in a sunny position	Divide clumps after three years	Divide established plants in spring
Dicentra spectabilis Bleeding heart	Drooping cascades of heart-shaped rosy-red flowers with white inner petals. Fern-like foliage	H: 600 mm (2 ft) S: 450 mm (1½ ft)	May–June	Rich, well drained soil, sheltered position	Trouble-free, self-supporting plants	Divide in spring
Erigeron (garden hybrids) Fleabane	Like a low-growing and summer-flowering Michaelmas daisy. Cultivars include 'Amity' (lilac-pink), 'Charity' (clear pink), and 'Darkest of All' (violet-blue)	H: 600 mm (2 ft) S: 450 mm (1½ ft)	June–Aug	Moist, well-drained soil, full sun	Trouble-free plants	Divide established plants in spring or autumn
Eryngium × oliverianum Sea holly	Attractive, jagged-edged leaves, bright blue teasel-like flower-heads	H: 900 mm (3 ft) S: 750 mm (2½ ft)	June–Aug	Well-drained soil, full sun	Twiggy sticks may be necessary for support. Cut down in autumn	Take root cuttings in Feb, inserting in boxes of peat-sand in a cold-frame

Size and shape arrangements of plants suitable for the centre of the border, with a height range of 450–900 mm (1½–3 ft). Key to numbers: 1 Poppy (Papaver), 2 Antirrhinum, 3 African lily (Agapanthus), 4 Phlox, 5 Anemone, 6 Peony (Paeonia), 7 Chrysanthemum, 8 Lupin (Lupinus), 9 Tobacco plant (Nicotiana).

NAME	DESCRIPTION	HEIGHT/ SPREAD	IN FLOWER	SOIL AND SITE	REMARKS	PROPAGATION
Helenium	Rayed flowers in shades of yellow, orange and red	H: 600– 900 mm (2–3 ft) S: 450–600 mm (1½–2 ft)	July–Aug	Ordinary garden soil, full sun	Support in exposed positions	Divide in Oct or March
Hemerocallis (garden hybrids) Day lily	A long succession of lily-like flowers in many colours. 'Black Magic' (ruby and purple), 'Buzz Bomb' (velvety-red), 'Fandango' (rich orange)	H: 600– 900 mm (2–3 ft) S: 450 mm (1½ ft)	June–Sept	Good garden soil in sun or part shade	Dislike disturbance	Divide in Oct or April
Iris (flag or German type)	Many superb cultivars, such as 'Berkeley Gold' (rich yellow), 'Braithwaite' (lavender standards, purple falls) and 'Jane Phillips' (flax blue)	H: 900 mm (3 ft) S: 450 mm (1½ ft)	May–June	Well-drained, sunny position. Lime is appreciated	Plant in late June or early July, with the rhizomes just below the surface	Divide old clumps immediately after flowering
Lupinus (garden hybrids) Lupin	Fine cultivars include 'My Castle' (brick-red), 'The Pages' (carmine), and 'The Governor' (blue and white)	H: 600– 900 mm (2–3 ft) S: 450–600 mm (1½–2 ft)	June–July	Light soil, full sun or part shade. Avoid rich soil	Remove dead spikes after flowering	Cuttings in March or April. Sow seed in spring or summer
Lychnis chalcedonica Maltese cross	Spectacular plant with heads of brilliant scarlet flowers, shaped like a Maltese Cross	H: 900 mm (3 ft) S: 450 mm (1½ ft)	June–Aug	Ordinary garden soil, full sun or part shade	Support young growth with twigs. Mulch with peat or compost in spring	Raised from seed or by division. Cuttings 2.5–5 cm (1–2 in) long can be taken in April and rooted in a cold-frame
Paeonia (garden hybrids) Peony	Spectacular, like large, full, roses. Many cultivars, in shades of pink, red and white	H: 750– 900 mm (2½–3 ft) S: 600 mm (2 ft)	June–Aug	Moist, rich, well-drained soil, sun or part shade	Mulch in spring. Support plants with stakes	Divide in Sept.
Phlox paniculata (garden hybrids)	Typical cultivars 'Dorothy Hanbury Forbes' (clear pink), 'Endurance' (salmon-orange), 'Prospero' (pale lilac), 'White Admiral' (white)	H: 900 mm (3 ft) S: 450 mm (1½ ft)	July–Sept.	Fertile, moisture-retentive soil, sun or part shade	Mulch annually in March or April. Water freely in dry weather	Divide in Oct. or April
Salvia × *superba*	Branching spires of violet-purple flowers	H: 900 mm (3 ft) S: 600 mm (2 ft)	July–Sept	Ordinary well-drained soil, full sun	Mulch with well-rotted compost in spring	Divide clumps in autumn or spring

African lily (Agapanthus) *Deciduous evergreen perennials; Headbourne Hybrids are the hardiest forms. Well-drained, chalky soil preferred; full sun and sheltered site. Flowers in July and August. Height 900 mm (3 ft). Sow hybrid seeds in March–April.*

Anemone × hybrida *Early-autumn-flowering herbaceous perennial. Colonises well. Likes free-draining moist soil; light shade preferred. Height 1.2 m (4 ft). Take root cuttings in November–January.*

Molly-the-witch peony (Paeonia mlokosewitschii) *Herbaceous perennial. Flowers in April–May. Needs rich, moisture-retentive soil; sunny or lightly shaded site. Height 750 mm (2½ ft). Sow in September.*

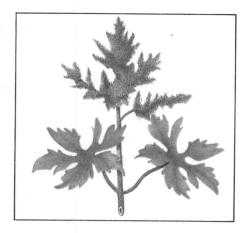

Astilbe × arendsii *Herbaceous perennial hybrid. Sprays of tiny flowers in various colours in June–August. Cool, moist (even boggy) soil preferred; cool site. Height 450 mm–1.2 m (1½–4 ft). Increase by division in April.*

Mullein (Verbascum × phoeniceum) *Hardy herbaceous perennial hybrid. Tall, slender flower stems in June–August. Rich, well-drained soil; sunny, sheltered site. Height 1–2 m (3¼–6½ ft). Increase by root cuttings in February.*

Cornflower (Centaurea cyanus) *Hardy annual. Erect plant; flowers in various colours in summer. Likes fertile, well-drained soil; sunny site. Height up to 900 mm (3 ft). Sow in April or September.*

BEDDING PLANTS

Although a mixed border consists principally of hardy perennials (herbaceous plants) and shrubs, there are usually gaps after the initial plantings and these may be filled with spring and summer bedding plants and bulbs.

There are many kinds of hardy annuals to choose from. Taller kinds from the focal, middle-of-the-border spot include the corn-cockle (*Agrostemma githago* 'Milas'), which sports soft lilac-pink or purple flowers on stems up to 1 m (3¼ ft) high; *Mentzelia lindleyi* (syn. *Bartonia aurea*), up to 600 mm (2 ft) high, with deep-lobed leaves and scented, saucer-shaped, golden flowers; tick weed (*Coreopsis drummondii* 'Golden Crown'), with golden yellow flowers with chestnut-brown centres. Others include *Chrysanthemum carinatum* 'Court Jesters', a vigorous grower to 600 mm (2 ft) with brightly zoned flowers in different colours; the graceful *Clarkia elegans* with its long spikes of salmon-pink, mauve, carmine or red flowers up to 600 mm (2 ft) high; and the Giant Imperial varieties of larkspur (*Delphinium consolida*), such as 'Blue Spire' (deep violet blue), 'White Spire', and 'Tall Hyacinth-Flowered'; the Spire forms grow to 1–1.2 m (3¼–4 ft) and the 'Hyacinth-Flowered' to 750–900 mm (2½–3 ft); the earlier, not quite so tall Stock-flowered group are also popular; 'Rosamund' is a bright pink variety.

The second group for summer bedding are the half-hardy annuals, of which the following are typical:

Love-lies-bleeding (*Amaranthus caudatus*) bears huge, showy, plum-red flower tassels in late summer; variety 'Viridis' has vivid green tassels. Cosmea (*Cosmos bipinnatus*), which grows up to 1.2 m (4 ft) high, has fern-like leaves and brightly coloured flowers up to 125 mm (5 in) in diameter in late summer or early autumn. The garden hybrid dahlias are among the most showy and popular hardies. Best-known of the bedding types are the 'Collerette Hybrids', which include single and double-flowered forms in single and mixed colours and grow to a height of 300–500 mm (12–20 in). The bells-of-Ireland or shell-flower (*Moluccella laevis*) is an intriguing-looking plant in which the tall spine carries tiny white flowers, each enclosed within light green bowl-shaped calyces. The spine is 750 mm (2½ ft) or more tall; it dries well and so is popular for winter-flower decorations. The velvet trumpet-flower (*Salpiglossis sinuata*), which reaches up to 600 mm (2 ft) in height, has pale green, narrow leaves and tall, graceful stems of trumpet-shaped red, pink, orange, gold, yellow or blue flowers from mid-summer to early autumn.

Love-lies-bleeding (Amaranthus caudatus) impresses with its extraordinary flowering tassels. A half-hardy annual, it must be raised in heat in early spring and planted out when frosts finish.

Bred to withstand poor weather, Zinnia elegans 'Early Wonder' makes a stunning show from early summer to first frosts if fed regularly and watered in dry spells.

Bedding Plants

NAME	DESCRIPTION	HEIGHT/SPREAD	IN FLOWER	SOIL AND SITE	REMARKS	PROPAGATION
Antirrhinum majus Snapdragon	Half-hardy. Yellow, red, pink, orange, white: 'Madame Butterfly', 'Wedding Bells', 'Bright Butterflies' Medium-sized: 'Cheerio' (mixed), 'Coronette' (mixed), 'Little Darling' (mixed), 'Black Prince' (crimson, bronze leaves), 'Monarch' (mixed), 'Rembrandt' (orange, with gold tips)	H: 600–900 mm (2–3 ft) S: 450 mm (1½ ft) H: 450 mm (1½ ft) S: 250 mm (10 in)	June–Oct	Rich, well-drained soil, sunny position	May require support	Sow under glass in Feb. or March. Plant out from late May onwards
Campanula medium Canterbury bell	Biennial. Large bell-shaped flowers. Double and single-flowered sorts available in blue, mauve, rose, and white, growing to 750 mm (2½ ft) high and 450 mm (1½ ft) wide. There is also a 'Dwarf Bedding' mixture at 450 mm (1½ ft) high and 300 mm (1 ft) wide	See description	May–July	Fertile, well-drained soil, sunny position	Keep ground free of weeds during early stages of growth	Sow outdoors from April to June, and set the plants 15 cm (6 in) apart in nursery beds before moving to the flowering positions in Sept or Oct
Centaurea cyanus Cornflower	Hardy annual. 'Polka Dot', 450 mm (1½ ft) high, 300 mm (1 ft) wide, in blue, red, purple, pink, white	See description	June–Sept	Fertile, well-drained soil, full sun	Support tall cultivars	Sow in April or Sept. where they are to flower

NAME	DESCRIPTION	HEIGHT/ SPREAD	IN FLOWER	SOIL AND SITE	REMARKS	PROPAGATION
Chrysanthemum carinatum (syn C. tricolor) Annual chrysanthemum	Hardy annual. Bright, daisy-like flowers, red, yellow or white banded with contrasting colours. Examples: 'Double Mixed', 'Merry Mixed', 'Monarch Court Jesters'	H: 450–600 mm (1½–2 ft) S: 250–375 mm (10–15 in)	June–Sept	Fertile, well-drained soil, sunny position	Nip out growing tips to encourage bushiness. Good for cutting	Sow outdoors from March to May, where plants will flower
Cosmos bipinnatus Cosmea	Half-hardy annual. Thread-like leaves, pink, rose, crimson or white flowers. Examples: 'Candy stripe' (white, crimson-splashed), 'Gloria' (large, rose-pink), 'Sensation Mixed'	H: 450–1200 mm (1½–4 ft) S: 600 mm (2 ft)	Aug–Sept	Poor, light dry soil, full sun or semi-shade	Support the plants with twiggy sticks. Remove dead flower heads	Sow in a greenhouse in March or April. Set out young plants from May onwards
Gypsophila elegans Baby's breath	Hardy annual. Dainty, graceful white flowers. 'Covent Garden' (white) is good cultivar; 'Rosea' is a pink form	H: 600 mm (2 ft) S: 450 mm (1½ ft)	May–Sept	Well-drained, alkaline soil, full sun	Support plants with twiggy sticks	Sow in March–May where the plants are to flower – for summer flowering; sow in Sept for spring flowers
Helianthus annuus Sunflower	Hardy annual. 'Tall Yellow' (H: 2.4 m/8 ft, S: 750–900 mm/2½–3 ft) produces enormous yellow flowers; 'Sunburst' (H: 1.2 m/4 ft, S: 450–600 mm/1½–2 ft) has medium-sized flowers, varying from primrose to bronze and maroon.	See description	Aug–Oct	Well-drained soil, sunny position	Stake tall cultivars	Sow in March–May where the plants are to flower
Lavatera trimestris Mallow	Hardy annual. Showy long-flowering plant. 'Silver Cup' (H: 600–900 mm/2–3 ft, S: 750 mm/2½ ft) has trumpet-shaped flowers of bright, deep pink	See description	July–Sept	Most garden soils, but avoid excessive richness; sunny, sheltered position	Seeds itself freely	Sow where the plants are to flower, from March to May
Zinnia elegans	Half-hardy annual. Zinnias resemble small dahlias in white, pink, orange, yellow, scarlet, crimson, purple. Typical is 'Giant Double Mixed'	H: 600–750 mm (2–2½ ft) S: 300–1450 mm (1–½ ft)	July–Sept	Fertile soil, warm, sunny position	Nip out growing tips to induce plants to branch	Sow March or april in heated greenhouse; plant out in late May.

Tulips, especially the flamboyant 'botanical varieties', are a highlight of spring, but it's important to plant bulbs no earlier than October or they will push through the soil prematurely and risk infection from tulip-fire disease.

BULBS

Although all but the smallest bulbs can be used in a bedding display, hyacinths and tulips are the most satisfactory and the latter can be used at the front of the centre of the border. Their flowers are symmetrical, show up boldly and look well from any angle.

Tulips, which are planted in October, can be had in a vast range of colours, many of them attractively marked or shaded with a second colour. The time of flowering will depend on the type chosen. Early Single and Early Double tulips bloom in April and are followed by the mid-season Mendel and Triumph divisions of cultivars in late April-May, to be succeeded in turn by the traditional Darwin and Cottage types in May. Unusual flower shapes are provided by the Fringed, Parrot, and Lily-flowered tulips, which also bloom in May.

FRONT OF BORDER

HERBACEOUS FAVOURITES

Lady's mantle (*Alchemilla mollis*) has very attractive pleated leaves, rounded in outline, and grey-green in colour. The star-shaped, lime-green flowers, appear in June-August. The plant looks especially effective if associated with grey or sand-coloured paving.

Michaelmas daisy (*Aster novi-belgii*) is a boon for the autumn, its blooms lighting up the border in September and October. Choose the dwarf forms that grow not more than about 300 mm (1 ft) high.

Bergenia cordifolia is a good evergreen perennial for the front of border, its rounded, glossy leaves contrasting well with other foliage. It produces lilac-rose heads mainly in March and April, but can start to flower in January.

Border pinks are hybrids of *Dianthus plumarius* (don't confuse them with the border carnations, which are mostly a little too tall for the front of the border). Good examples are 'Doris' (pale salmon pink), 'Excelsior' (pink), 'Mrs Sinkins' and 'Sam Barlow' (both white).

BEDDING PLANTS: HALF-HARDY

The following front-of-border bedders will make a colourful show, but must be planted out only when all risk of frost is past.

The ageratums have hairy, heart-shaped leaves and mounds of small, fluffy flowers in June–October. The best forms are F_1 hybrids of *A. houstonianum* and include 'Bengali' (rose-carmine), 'Blue Danube' (blue), 'Ocean' (light blue), 'Summer Snow' (white). None is more than 250 mm (10 in) high.

The antirrhinums include many attractive forms for both the centre and the front of the border. Those for the latter are forms of the variety *A. majus* 'Pumilum', which rarely exceed 150 mm (6 in) in height. They include 'Delice' (pale apricot), 'Floral Carpet' (mixed), 'Pixie' (mixed), 'Trumpet Serenade' (mixed).

Marigolds are available in two main forms – African (*Tagetes erecta*) and French (*T. patula*). Most of the African varieties are too tall for the front of the border except for the dwarf forms, such as the double-flowered 'Inca Orange' and 'Inca Yellow', which are less than 300 mm (1 ft) high. The French varieties include 'Honeycomb', 'Naughty Marietta', 'Spanish Brocade' and 'Tiger Eyes'.

BEDDING PLANTS: HARDY

The clarkias are graceful plants with sword-shaped leaves with flower-spikes bearing double or semi-double flowers in July–September. *C. pulchella* is best for the front of border.

California poppy (*Eschscholzia californica*) has fern-like grey-green foliage and delicate orange flowers; it is 300–600 mm (1–2 ft) high. Good cultivars include 'Ballerina' (pink, orange and yellow with white), 'Cherry Ripe' (cerise), and 'Monarch Mixed' (crimson, cream, orange, red and yellow). If these are too tall, try the cultivars of *E. caespitosa* – notably 'Sundew' (lemon yellow) and 'Miniature Primrose' – which are not more than 150 mm (6 in) high.

Godetias (close relatives of clarkias) are compact, with mid-green pointed leaves and trumpet shaped reddish purple flowers in June–August. Cultivars include 'Azalea-Flowered Mixed', 'Crimson Glow', 'Dwarf Bedding Mixed', 'Sybil Sherwood' (salmon pink edged with white); all are about 375 mm (15 in) tall.

Plants for the front of the border, ranging in height from 100 to 400 mm (4–16 in). Key to numbers: 1 Alyssum, 2 Pelargonium, 3 Petunia, 4 Cyclamen, 5 Geranium, 6 Lobelia, 7 Linum, 8 Pink (Dianthus), 9 Ageratum, 10 Godetia.

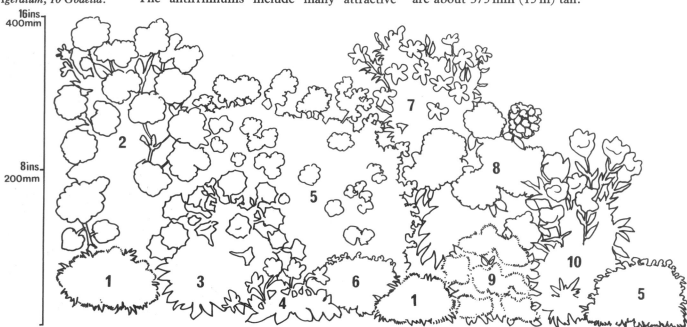

Bedding Plants

NAME	DESCRIPTION	HEIGHT/ SPREAD	IN FLOWER	SOIL AND SITE	REMARKS	PROPAGATION
Ageratum houstonianum	Half-hardy annual. Heads of tiny blue powderpuff flowers	H: 150– 450 mm (6–8 in) S: 250–450 mm (10–18 in)	July–Oct	Moist soil, sheltered site	Remove dead flower heads to prolong flowering	Sow in warmth from Feb to April, and plant out from May onwards
Anchusa capensis Alkanet	Hardy annual. Resembles giant forget-me-not; a good cultivar is 'Blue Angel' (brilliant ultramarine)	H and S: 230–300 mm (9–12 in)	June–Sept	Deep, fertile and moist soil, full sun	Do not allow soil to become dry	Sow outdoors in March or April
Begonia semperflorens Bedding begonia	Half-hardy annual. Bushy tender perennial grown as half-hardy annual for bedding out. Flowers in shades of pink, red, and white.	H: 150– 230 mm (6–9 in) S: 150–230 mm (6–9 in)	June–Oct	Light, well-cultivated soil in full sun or part shade	After flowering plants should be discarded	Sow in late winter in a temperatue of 20– 25°C (68–78°F), to produce plants large enough to bed out in late May
Bellis perennis Daisy	Biennial. Large, double, highly decorative forms of common daisy. Many cultivars	H: 100– 150 mm (4–6 in) S: 100–175 mm (4–7 in)	April–June	Fertile soil, sun or part shade	Dead-head plants to prevent them seeding	Sow 6 mm from April to June in cold-frame or outdoors; move to flowering positions in Sept or Oct
Calendula officinalis Pot marigold	Hardy annual. Bright, rayed pompon flowers in shades of orange or yellow.	H: 300– 600 mm (1–2 ft) S: 300–375 mm (1–1¼ ft)	May–Sept	Ordinary garden soil, good light.	Nip out terminal shoots to encourage branching; remove dead heads	Sow outdoors March– May for summer flowers, September for spring flowers
Cheiranthus cheiri Wallflower	Biennial. Fragrant spring bedding plants. Tall cultivars include 'Blood Red' (dark velvety crimson), 'Primrose Monarch' (primrose), and 'Ruby Gem' (violet-purple). Dwarf cultivars include 'Fair Lady' (charming mixture of pastel shades), and 'Tom Thumb'	H: 450 mm (1½ ft) S: 300 mm (1 ft) H: 230– 300 mm (9–12 in) S: 200–300 mm (8–12 in)	March–May	Alkaline soil, full sun	Protect young plants from cold winds	Sow in open ground during May–June; prick out seedlings in nursery rows. Plant in final positions as early as possible in autumn.
Clarkia elegans (syn. *C. unguiculata*)	Hardy annual. Graceful spikes of double flowers in shades of pink, red, mauve, purple, white	H: 375 mm (15 in) S: 300 mm (1 ft)	July–Sept	Light, acid soil, full sun	Do not feed the plants	Sow thinly from March to May where to flower
Convolvulus tricolor	Hardy annual. Open bell flowers in pinks and blues	H: 150– 375 mm (6–15 in) S: 230mm (9in)	July–Sept	Ordinary, well-drained soil, sunny position	Remove dead flower-heads	Sow where plants are to flower
Dianthus barbatus Sweet William	Biennial. Many good mixtures in shades of pink, salmon, crimson, and white	H: 450 mm (1½ ft) S: 230 mm (9 in)	June–July	Well-drained preferably alkaline soil, full sun	Good for cutting, colourful and fragrant	Sow outdoors from April to June. Prick off seedlings in nursery rows and set plants in position in Sept–Oct
D. chinensis 'Heddewigii' Indian or Chinese pink	Half-hardy annual. Brightly-coloured single or double 'pinks'. 'Baby Doll' is one of the best singles	H: 200– 300 mm (8–12 in) S: 150–250 mm (6–10 in)	June–Sept	As *D. barbatus*	Very bright and free-flowering	Sow under glass in Feb–April. Plant out from May onwards
Dimorphotheca African daisy	Hardy annual. Apricot, orange, primrose and salmon	H: 300 mm (1 ft) S: 230 mm (9 in)	June–Sept	Will grow in poor, dry soil, full sun, shelter	Remove all dead heads to encourage further flowering	Sow outdoors in April–June
Echium plantagineum Viper's bugloss	Hardy annual. Loose sprays of blue, mauve, pink or white flowers. Dwarf forms preferred	H: 300 mm (1 ft) S: 300 mm (1 ft)	June–Oct	Light soil, open, sunny site	Easy to grow and long-lasting	Sow outdoors in March–May
Eschscholzia californica Californian poppy	Hardy annual. Brilliant shades of orange, red, yellow, rose, white	H: 300 mm (1 ft) S: 300 mm (1 ft)	June–Oct	Poor soil, full sun	Self-seeds readily	Sow in March–May where it is to flower

Above *Half-hardy annual French marigolds* (Tagetes patula) *come in an array of warm colours, from palest yellow to deepest bronze-red. There are single- and double-flowered varieties and, latest offering from the breeders, Giant Crested forms.*

Above right *Rich blue ageratums (this one is* A. houstonianum) *are among the few annual summer-bedding plants that tolerate dry soil and light shade. Use them to make a carpet around the base of trees and large shrubs. Plants raised in early spring and planted out in May can be expected to flower for about five months.*

Bedding Plants (continued)

NAME	DESCRIPTION	HEIGHT/ SPREAD	IN FLOWER	SOIL AND SITE	REMARKS	PROPAGATION
Godetia grandiflora	Hardy annual. 'Dwarf Bedding Mixed' (H: 300 mm/1 ft, S: 200 mm/8 in)	See description	July–Oct	Light, moist soil, sunny position	Do not feed, as it may encourage lush growth at expense of flowers	Sow in March or April where plants are to flower
Helichrysum bracteatum Strawflower	Half-hardy annual. Papery 'everlasting' flowers. Good strain is 'Bright Bikini'. H: 300 m/1 ft, S: 230 mm/9 in).	See description	July–Sept	Light, well-drained soil, sunny site	Remove dead flower-heads	Sow under glass in March or April; plant out in May
Iberis umbellata Candytuft	Hardy annual: Flattish heads of small but bright pink, lavender, purple and white flowers	H: 300 mm (1 ft) S: 300 mm (1 ft)	June–Sept	Ordinary soil, sunny site	Remove dead flower-heads	Sow where plants are to flower from March to May
Impatiens wallerana Busy-lizzie	Half-hardy perennial grown as an annual. Scarlet, pink, orange and white flower colours. 'Imp' and 'Futura Mixed' are both dependable F1 hybrid mixtures (H: 230 mm/9 in; S: 230 mm)	See description	June–Oct	Good garden soil, shade or semi-shade	Useful for difficult shady spots	Sow from Feb to March in a temperature of 15–20°C (60–68°F). Germination is usually slow: Plant out from late May onwards
Linaria maroccana Toadflax	Hardy annual. Tiny snapdragon flowers in several colour combinations.	H: 230 mm (9 in) S: 150 mm (6 in)	June–July	Ordinary soil, sunny position	Cut plants back after first flush of flower – a second may follow	Sow thinly, where the plants are to flower, from March to May
Lobelia erinus	Half-hardy annual: Neat, free-flowering annual, frequently planted with alyssum. The compact cultivars (H: 100–150 mm/4–6 in, S: 150 mm/6 in) include 'Cambridge Blue' (pale blue) and 'Crystal Palace' (dark blue, bronze foliage)	See description	May–Oct	Rich, moist soil, sun or part shade	Ensure roots do not become dry	Sow in a heated greenhouse from Jan to March. Prick off seedlings as small clusters. Plant out from late May

NAME	DESCRIPTION	HEIGHT/ SPREAD	IN FLOWER	SOIL AND SITE	REMARKS	PROPAGATION
Lobularia maritima (syn. *Alyssum maritimum*)	Hardy annual. The most widely known cultivar is the white 'Little Dorrit', but there are carmine-red, violet-pink and deep violet-purple varieties	H: 100 mm (4 in) S: 200 mm (8 in)	June–Oct	Ordinary soil, full sun	Trouble-free plants, easy to grow	Sow where plants are to flower, from March to June,
Myosotis Forget-me-not	Biennial. Among best cultivars are 'Miniature Blue' (H: 15 cm/6 in, S: 15 cm/6 in),and 'Royal Blue' (H: 30 cm/ 300 mm/12 in, S: 200 mm/8 in)	See description	March–June	Moist soil, partial shade	Keep young plants moist at roots. Self-seeds easily	Sow outdoors from May to July; plant in flowering position in autumn
Nemesia strumosa	Half-hardy annual. 'Carnival Mixed' is bronze, cerise, crimson, pink, orange, scarlet and yellow	H: 200 mm (8 in) S: 150 mm (6 in)	June–Aug	Ordinary soil, full sun or part shade	Do not allow plants to become dry at roots	Sow from Feb. to May in heated greenhouse. Plant out from late May
Nigella damascena Love-in-a-mist	Hardy annual. Spidery flowers set amid feathery foliage. 'Miss Jekyll' (H: 450 mm/ 1½ ft, S: 300 mm/1 ft) has cornflower-blue flowers, 'Persian Jewels' (H: 375 mm/15 in, S: 300 mm/1 ft) is mixture of blue, mauve, pink, purple and rosy-red flowers	See description	June–Aug	Any well drained soil, full sun	Remove dead flower-heads to prolong flowering period	Sow where plants are to flower, from March to May for summer flowering, or in Sept for spring flowering
Petunia × *hybrida*	Half-hardy annual. Invaluable bedding plants, with masses of bright open trumpet flowers in many colours. Multiflora 'Resisto' types best; Grandiflora forms have larger flowers	H: 300– 375 mm (12–15 in) S: 300 mm (1 ft)	July–Sept	Light, well-drained soil, sheltered position, in full sun	Dead-head regularly	Sow from Feb to March under glass. Plant out in late May.
Tagetes erecta African marigold	Half-hardy annual. Fine bedding plant with large globular yellow or orange flowers.	H: 250– 300 mm (10–12 in) S: 230 mm (9 in)	June–Oct	Rich soil, sunny site	Remove dead-heads to prolong flowering period	Sow in slightly heated greenhouse in Feb– April; plant out in May–June
T. patula French marigold	Smaller than African forms. Dwarf single 'Naughty Marietta' (yellow boldly splashed with maroon) and 'Tiger Eyes' (ruffled orange crest within bronze-maroon petals)	H: 150– 250 mm (6–10 in) S: 150 mm (6 in)	June–Oct	Rich soil, sunny site	Very prolific; often flowers while still in seedbox. Hybrids between French and African forms are available	As *T. erecta*
Viola Pansy, violet, viola	Biennial. Both pansies (cultivars of *V.* × *wittrockiana*) and violas (cultivars of *V. cornuta*) are short-lived perennials best treated as biennials. Violas have smaller flowers and more upright habit than pansies. Good pansies include 'Majestic Giants' (H, S: 200 mm/ 8 in, mixed) and 'Roggli Swiss Giants' (H: 175 mm/7 in, S: 230 mm/9 in, mixed). Good violas: 'Alba' (H: 230 mm/9 in, S: 300 mm/12 in, white); 'Blue Heaven' (H: 150 mm/6 in, S: 200 mm/8 in, blue)	H: 150– 230 mm (6–9 in) S: 200–300 mm (8–12 in)	April–July	Moist, rich soil, semi-shade	Dead-head regularly	Sow in cold-frame or open ground in June-July; prick out into nursery beds. Move to flowering positions in Sept–Oct

Opposite page
Combined version of the border plants on pages 24, 29 and 34. Plants could, of course, be less densely packed than here, but the drawing indicates how different sizes and shapes can be exploited to lend structural character to a border.

Herbaceous Perennials

NAME	DESCRIPTION	HEIGHT/ SPREAD	IN FLOWER	SOIL AND SITE	REMARKS	PROPAGATION
Alchemilla mollis Lady's mantle	Sulphur-yellow flowers carried above rounded leaves	H: 450 mm (1½ ft) S: 300 mm (1 ft)	June–Aug.	Sunny or partly shaded, well-drained soil	Support plants in early stages of growth	Divide between Oct and March
Bergenia cordifolia Elephant's ears	Large leaves resembling elephants' ears, and sprays of pink flowers	H: 250 mm (10 in) S: 300 mm (1 ft)	April–May	Moist soil, full sun or partial shade	Leave undisturbed unless plants spread excessively	Divide overcrowded plants in March after flowering
Dianthus caryophyllus Carnation	Parent of many border carnations. Typical cultivars are 'Cherry Clove' (strongly scented, cherry-red); 'Robin Thain' (white flecked crimson)	H: 230 mm (9 in) S: 300 mm (1 ft)	July–Sept	Well-drained limy soil preferred, sunny site	Support with split bamboo canes	Layer stems in July or Aug
Heuchera sanguinea Alum root, coral bells	Slender stems of tiny bell-shaped, pink or red flowers, carried clear of basal leaves	H: 450 mm (1½ ft) S: 300 mm (1 ft)	June–Sept	Well-drained soil, sun or part shade	Mulch annually. Divide every four years	Lift and divide old plants in Oct or March
Linum narbonnense Flax	Brilliant blue flowers carried above narrow, grey-green leaves	H: 450 mm (1½ ft) S: 300 mm (1 ft)	June–Sept	Ordinary garden soil in full sun	Plant March–April or Oct. Cut off dead growth in Nov	Take cuttings of soft basal shoots in April
Mertensia virginica Virginian cowslip	Drooping clusters of purple-blue bells. Foliage dies down in July	H: 450 mm (1½ ft) S: 300 mm (1 ft)	April–June	Moist, rich soil, preferably in partial shade	Lift and replant every three or four years	Divide established plants in Oct or March
Nepeta × faassenii Catmint	Narrow, grey-green leaves and spikes of lavender flowers. Varieties include 'Blue Beauty' and 'Six Hills Giant'	H: 300–450 mm (1–1½ ft) S: 600 mm (2 ft)	May–Sept	Well-drained soil, sun or partial shade	Cut down plants in autumn	Divide in April. Can also be grown from seed
Physostegia virginiana 'Vivid' Obedient plant	Rose-lilac tubular flowers carried on stiff stems	H: 600 mm (2 ft) S: 300 mm (1 ft)	Aug–Nov	Ordinary soil, sun or part shade	Water and mulch in dry summer weather	Divide in Oct or April
Polygonum affine Knotweed	Forms mat of narrow leaves which become coppery in autumn. Pink flowers	H: 150–250 mm (6–10 in) S: 250mm (10in)	June–Sept	Moist fertile soil, sun or part shade	Young plants must not be allowed to become dry at roots	Divide in Oct or April
Sedum spectabile	Fleshy leaves and flat heads of long-lasting pink or red flowers	H: 300–600 mm (1–2 ft) S: 300–450 mm (1–1½ ft)	Aug–Oct	Ordinary, well-drained soil, full sun	Remove dead flower-heads in spring	Divide established plants in autumn or spring

Snapdragon (Antirrhinum majus) *Half-hardy annual. 'Pumilun' form here is smallest type, good for edging. Flowers June–September. Rich, well-drained soil needed; sunny site. Height 100–150 mm (4–6 in). Sow in January–March.*

Clarkia pulchella *Hardy annual. Flowers in mixed colours, double or semi-double, in July–September. Light, slightly acid soil preferred; sunny site. Height 300–450 mm (12–18 in). Sow in March–May.*

Love-in-a-mist (Nigella damascena) *Hardy annual. Blue, violet, pink, red or white flowers in June–August, followed by pretty seed pods. Well-drained soil; full sun. Height 150–450 mm (6–18 in). Sow in March.*

Bergenia cordifolia *Evergreen perennial. Large, wavy edged leaves. Flowers in March–April. Moist, fertile soil needed; sun or shade. Height 300–450 mm (12–18 in). Divide and replant single-root pieces in autumn.*

Pot marigold (Calendula officinalis) *Hardy annual. Large pompom flowers in May–September. Any well-drained soil; bright sun. Height 300–600 mm (1–2 ft). Sow in March–April.*

Wallflower (Cheiranthus cheiri) *Biennial. Erect, wiry-stemmed plant. Scented flowers in May–June. Well-drained chalky soil best; full sun. Height 300–600 mm (1–2 ft). Sow in May–June for flowers following year.*

COLOUR AND TEXTURE

Colour is the most obvious part of an ornamental plant's attraction. A dazzling, riotous display of colour from spring to autumn is generally the idea for beginner gardeners. But as time goes on and experience accumulates, this aim gradually changes as you realize that more subtle but more satisfying blendings can be obtained in which colour is mixed with white, or cool greys and silvers, or with plants whose leaves come in a variety of greens.

HARDY BORDER PLANTS

These are mainly herbaceous plants which 'perform' between April and October, die back in the winter and reappear the following spring. A few have evergreen leaves. Dead heading spent flowers will encourage new buds. Stake the taller varieties.

ANNUALS & BIENNIALS

Annuals and biennials fill the summer garden and patio with bold and brilliant blocks of colour. Following are easily grown from seed. Annuals flower the year they are planted, biennials the following year. Follow instructions on the seed packet for sowing depth.

BULBS

Bulbs take up little space and will give colour in the garden almost all year round. Most appreciate a well-cultivated soil and look better planted in clumps or drifts. Allow the leaves of narcissi to die back naturally to encourage healthy growth and flowering the following year.

QUICK COLOUR

When you are planning for quick colour remember that a small plot in a one-colour theme looks larger and better planned that a hotch-potch, so it is best to stick to pinks with blues or oranges with reds for a more co-ordinated look. On the other hand, if you are creating a 'cottage-garden look', you can use a wide variety of colours.

Many popular annuals come in several different forms. Half-hardy African marigolds (*Tagetes erecta*) make a patch of instant sunshine with their large, orange, pompon heads and range from dwarf to giant forms.

Cornflowers (*Centaurea*) are usually seen in bright blue but also come in pinks and whites; and love-in-a-mist (*Nigella*) can be found in pink and white as well as the usual dark mauve-blue. There are all sorts of new varieties of low-growing nasturtiums (*Tropaeolum majus*), some of them with double blooms. Look for the compact 'Jewel Mixed' if you do not want the plants to spread too far.

'Orange King' is the finest form of Berberis linearifolia, *a prickly shrub whose flowers unfold in April. It has a leggy, upright habit, so is best sited behind a round, spreading shrub.*

ORANGE

Hot and fiery orange is an exciting, vibrant colour, but use it sparingly or it will scream at you. It blends with yellow and should be interplanted with white-flowered plants to relieve the intensity. Orange, together with red, are assertive colours and a small space can be made to look larger by planting flowers of this hue in the foreground, with blues at the farther end of the garden.

Some of the most striking border plants with flowers in this colour are day lily (*Hemerocallis* 'Fandango'), lighting up summer from June to August; shrubby cinquefoil (*Potentilla fruticosa* 'Tangerine'), a shrub spreading to 600 mm (2 ft) that flowers from May to November; *Berberis linearifolia*. 'Orange King', a robust shrub that grows about 1.8 m (6 ft) high, but is a little on the upright, gaunt side, so is best positioned in a corner; and deciduous azaleas, specially 'Gibraltar', 'Gloria Mundi' 'Peter Koster', and 'Klondyke'. These look superb in front of a deep green hedge or clumps of evergreens such as *Cotoneaster lacteus* and Mexican orange blossom (*Choisya ternata*).

Other dashes of orange are contributed by *Crocosmia* × *crocosmiiflora* 'Emily MacKenzie', whose glowing heads of bloom are borne from July to September among sheaves of sword-shaped leaves. The euphorbias also have an orange-flowered member in the form of *E. griffithii* 'Fireglow', at its most colourful from May to June. Gaillardias with their bright, daisy blooms from June to September are vital to the summer beauty of an herbaceous border and orange-flame *G. grandiflora* 'Mandarin' associates well with the scarlet of red-hot pokers (*Kniphofia*).

Orange is also well represented among the

bedding plants, particularly by the marigolds. Specially fine are the African varieties (*Tagetes erecta*), such as 'Superjack Orange', large flowers on 600 mm (2 ft) stems, 'Inca Orange', and 'Gay Ladies'. The French dwarf doubles (*T. patula*) include 'Orange Boy', a beauty for edging, growing just 150 mm (6 in) high.

Lilies, enjoying light woodland shade and, ideally, the presence of small shrubs such as azaleas growing among them, are a delight. Or you can grow them in deep tubs. Orange-flowered varieties include 'Prince Constantine', with outward-facing petals, that blooms from June to July; and 'Mrs R. O. Backhouse', which also flowers then and is remarkable for producing up to 30 beautiful blooms on a strong pyramidal stem.

Subtle hints of green and orange in the 'Fireglow' variety of spurge (Euphorbia griffithii) make it a favourite for the flower arranger's border.

Shrubby cinquefoil (Potentilla fruticosa) *Orange variety 'Tangerine' flowers in May–August. Well-drained soil; sunny site. Height 450–600 mm (18–24 in). Take cuttings in autumn.*

Blanket-flower (Gaillardia grandiflora 'Mandarin') *Perennial. Flowers in June–October. Likes well-drained soil; sun or light shade. Height 600–900 mm (2–3 ft). Sow February–March.*

African marigold (Tagetes erecta 'Inca Orange'). *Dwarf form of half-hardy annual. Flowers in July–October. Well-worked soil; sunny open site. Height 200–250 in (8–10 in). Sow in March–April.*

YELLOW

We are lucky with yellows: Not only is there a vast choice of flowers in that colour, but there are many gold-leaved and gold or yellow variegated evergreens, too. A yellow border can be warmed by adding a touch of orange or cooled by introducing blue. White-flowered 'dot' plants relieve the intensity. An effective contrast is obtained by interplanting with purple flowers or shrubs, such as the purple-leaved smoke bush (*Cotinus coggygria* 'Royal Purple'). Some yellow-flowered shrubs are happy in shade, and the free-flowering *Forsythia* × *intermedia* 'Lynwood', a blaze of gold in early spring, will brighten a gloomy corner. So will a planting of winter aconites, specially the larger flowered *Eranthis* 'Guinea Gold', and all kinds of daffodils, including the diminutive *Narcissus cyclamineus*, a little charmer whose tiny trumpet blooms rise from a crown of swept-back petals.

The yarrow makes a stately subject for the middle or back of a border. Try *Achillea filipendulina* 'Gold Plate'; growing to 1.2–1.5 m (4–5 ft), its broad flower-heads not only colour the garden from July to August, but can then be cut and dried for winter decoration. It looks superb in association with the taller blue delphiniums.

Other border plants valued for their cheering yellow hues are the deep-yellow tickseed *Coreopsis grandiflora* 'Goldfink', in bloom from summer to autumn; *Kniphofia* 'Yellow Hammer'; leopard's bane (*Doronicum plantagineum* 'Spring Beauty'), prized for its neat, edging habit and double golden flowers; and *Oenothera missouriensis*, a flamboyant trailing form with massive cup-shaped flowers from June to August.

Among bedding plants, *Erysimum* 'Golden Gem', an alpine wallflower for rock gardens, makes a vivid splash in early spring. As for *Gazania* 'Mini-Star Yellow', its bright, starry, daisy flowers shine up at us all summer long. There are also the rich yellow French or African marigolds (*Tagetes*) and the carpeting poached-egg plant (*Limnanthes douglasii*), whose profusion of blooms are white with rich butter-yellow centres.

Cheering spring with its golden daisy flowers, leopard's-bane (Doronicum plantagineum) has a double-flowered form called 'Spring Beauty'. Both thrive in cold, draughty places so are excellent candidates for the more gloomy border.

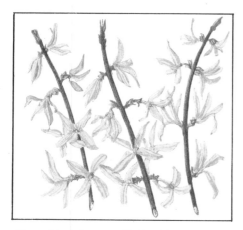

Forsythia × intermedia *Deciduous shrub hybrid. Flowers in March–April, before foliage. Free-draining fertile soil, sun or shade. Height 1.8–2.4 m (6–8 ft). Plant October–March.*

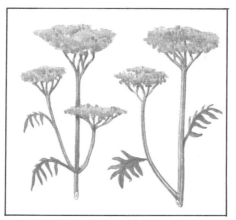

Yarrow (Achillea filipendulina *'Gold Plate') Hardy perennial. Flowers in June–September. Well-drained soil; sunny site. Height 900 mm–1.5 m (3–5 ft). Sow in March.*

Tickseed (Coreopsis grandiflora *'Goldfink') Perennial. Flowers in June–September. Fertile, well-drained, chalky soil preferred; full sun. Height 600–900 mm (2–3 ft). Take offsets in July–August.*

SHRUBS
YELLOW OR ORANGE FLOWERS

NAME AND HEIGHT	FLOWERS	SITE	NOTES
Kerria japonica (jew's mallow) 1.5 m (5 ft)	April–May	Shade	Any soil; easy to grow
Mahonia japonica to 1.5 m (5 ft)	Jan–March	Shade	Needs space; best at back of border
Potentilla fruticosa 'Tangerine' (cinquefoil) 600 mm (2 ft)	May–Nov	Sun or part shade	Many varieties; produces best colour in light shade
Ruta graveolens 'Jackman's Blue' (rue) 600 mm (2 ft)	July	Sun or part shade	Dense rounded shape; blue-grey leaf. Clip to keep shape
Senecio × 'Sunshine' 1 m (3¼ ft)	June	Sun	Silver-grey leaves. Spreading.

HARDY BORDER PLANTS
YELLOW FLOWERS

NAME AND HEIGHT	IN FLOWER	SITE	REMARKS
Achillea × 'Moonshine' (yarrow) 600 mm (2 ft)	June–Aug	Full sun	Silvery foliage
Alchemilla mollis (lady's mantle) 450 mm (1½ ft)	June–July	Sun or part shade	Pretty leaf; good for ground cover
Coreopsis verticillata (tickseed) 600 mm (2 ft)	June–Sept	Sun	Good for cutting
Epimedium perralderianum (barrenwort) 300 mm (1 ft)	April–May	Part or full shade	Ground cover; needs cool moist soil
Euphorbia polychroma (spurge) 450 mm (1½ ft)	April–May	Sun or part shade	Mound-forming
Hemerocallis (day lily) 450 mm (1½ ft)	June–Aug	Sun or shade	Needs moist soil. Plant in clumps

Solidago 'Caesia' (golden rod) 900 m (3 ft)	Sept–Oct	Sun or part shade	Good for back of border
Verbascum × 'Gainsborough' 1.2 m (4 ft)	July–Aug	Sun	Good on chalk. Felty leaves

ORANGE FLOWERS

Alstroemeria aurantiaca (Peruvian lily) 600 mm (2 ft)	June	Full sun	Rich soil
Crocosmia masonorum 'Firebird' 750 mm (2½ ft)	July–Aug	Full sun	Lovely by paths or front of border
Kniphofia 'Ada' (red-hot poker) 450 mm (1½ ft)	Sept–Oct	Sun	Moist, well-drained soil

ANNUALS & BIENNIALS
YELLOW/ORANGE FLOWERS

NAME	SOW	FLOWERS	HEIGHT	NOTES
Calendula (A) (pot marigold)	March–May	May–Aug	300 mm (1 ft)	Sun or part shade
Cheiranthus (B) (wallflower)	June	May–June	300 mm (1 ft)	Sun or part shade
Cosmos (A) (cosmea)	April–May	July–Sept	900 m (3 ft)	Sun or part shade
Tagetes patula (A) (French marigold)	April–May	July–Oct	150 mm (6 in)	Sun

BULBS
YELLOW/ORANGE FLOWERS

NAME AND HEIGHT	PLANT	FLOWERS	NOTES
Crocus ancyrensis 'Golden Bunch' 100 mm (4 in)	Sept–Oct	Dec–Jan	Well-drained soil, full sun
Eranthis hyemalis (winter aconite) 50 mm (2 in)	Aug–Sept	Jan–Feb	Moist soil
Narcissus (daffodil) to 450 mm (18 in)	Sept	March–April	Full sun. Many varieties

RED

When planning a red scheme, combine it with coppery-leaved plants, such as the purple-leaved cobnut (*Corylus maxima* 'Purpurea'), cutting the shrub back to a stump each winter to encourage a display of extra-large leaves. Or set red-flowered plants against a coppiced Pissard's purple plum (*Prunus pissardii*).

There are a few reds to choose from early in the year, and we rely on tulips, specially the *Tulipa greigii* hybrids, such as scarlet 'Red Riding Hood', and the *T. kaufmanniana* beauties renowned for their big blooms.

As spring advances the rock rose (*Helianthemum*) makes a carpet of bloom, and scarlet 'Red Dragon' and 'Mrs C. W. Earle' light up sunny patches. They have a sprawling, creeping habit, so arrange them on banks or use them to clothe rock-garden outcrops where their charm can be seen to advantage.

In summer, the field widens. Crocosmias, day lilies (*Hemerocallis*) and roses make their debut. Break up these zones of scarlet with arching, green-leaved grasses. Most striking of these are the feathery plumed *Pennisetum alopecuroides* and *Stipa pennata* (feather grass). Scarlet combines beautifully with white and a bed of floribunda roses: brilliant red 'Evelyn Fison', for instance, looks magnificent if interplanted with 'Iceberg', the purest white.

Another exciting contrast is achieved when scarlet-flowered *Crocosmia* 'Lucifer' or 'Vulcan' is planted close to the golden-leaved black-locust tree, *Robina pseudoacacia* 'Frisia'.

There are many contenders for this colour in bedding plants, too, and a tub or trough of *Pelargonium* 'Cherry Diamond' or 'Red Elite' positioned against a white wall hints of the Mediterranean.

Tulip (T. greigii *'Red Riding Hood') Bulb. Flowers in April. Leaves characteristically marbled. Fertile, well-drained soil; full sun. Height 300 mm (1 ft). Plant bulbs in mid-autumn.*

Rock rose (Helianthemum *'Red Dragon') Evergreen dwarf shrub. Flowers in May–July on trailing shoots. Likes chalky, well-drained soil; full sun. Height 250 mm (10 in) Take soft cuttings in June–July.*

Pelargonium 'Cherry Diamond' *Tender perennial. Flowers in summer, two to three weeks earlier than other seed-raised varieties. Well-drained soil; full sun. Height 300 mm (1 ft). Take soft cuttings in March–April.*

Hydrangea 'Europa' *Shrub. Mophead (Hortensia) variety; flowers in July–September. Flowers blue in acid soils. Fertile soil; sheltered site, part shaded. Height 1.2–1.8 m (4–6 ft). Take cuttings in summer.*

Rose 'Louise Odier' *Richly scented, blooms throughout summer. Well-drained, moisture-retentive soil; open, sunny site. Height 1.5 m (5 ft). Take ripe-wood cuttings in September–November.*

Mallow (Lavatera trimestris 'Silver Cup') *Hardy annual. Flowers continuously in July–October. Well-drained soil, chalk tolerated; bright sun. Height 1–1.2 m (3¼–4 ft). Sow in April or September.*

PINK

Tranquil and accommodating, pink is an 'easy' colour and there is a wide range of plants that provide it. Associating naturally with white, blending with red, and contrasing effectively with yellow, it reflects light well. Pink-flowered plants should be set against a dark, green background, such as a holly or yew hedge, or clumps of white-flowered hostas.

Pink looks well in tubs. Hydrangeas, such as 'Europa' and 'Holstein' (mophead kinds that bloom in late summer), stay compact and free-flowering when their roots are confined.

Among roses, coppery-pink 'Albertine', a robust rambler flowering in midsummer, makes a colourful backcloth and is ideal for clothing a chain-link fence or section of trellis. The floribunda 'Dearest', in salmon-pink, has a vigorous nature, grows about 750 mm (2½ ft) high, and looks well flanking a path or drive. The Bourbon roses are also well represented (with the bonus that most are sweetly scented). Finest are rich pink 'La Reine Victoria', whose exquisite cupped blooms are set against light green foliage; 'Kathleen Harrop', a beautiful shell-pink form of the bright carmine 'Zéphirine Drouhin'; and, most glorious of all, 'Louise Odier', deep rose-pink, and robust. All these flower in midsummer.

Border perennials with pink blooms include hybrids of the Peruvian lily (*Alstroemeria ligtu*), a sun-lover for a warm, wind-free border. In early summer, it becomes a mass of blooms.

Brightening spring and early summer are oriental poppies (*Papaver orientale*), especially 'Mrs Perry', which is pink with dark blotches, and the peonies, whose beautiful pink forms include 'Edulis Superba' and rose-scented 'Lady Alexandra Duff'.

Summer bedding annuals can be found in many pink shades: the corn-cockle (*Agrostemma githago* 'Milas') has large pink flowers and makes an impressive clump in the middle of a border; *Cosmea* 'Sensation Mixed' contains many powder-pink hues and it flowers for many weeks in summer; and lovely mallow *Lavatera trimestris* 'Silver Cup', with silver-pink blooms.

Opposite page, top
Day lily (Hemerocallis 'Burning Daylight'), *with its large, richly coloured flowers, blooms in mid-summer.*

SHRUBS

NAME AND HEIGHT	FLOWERS	SITE	NOTES
PINK OR RED FLOWERS			
Kolkwitzia amabilis 'Pink Cloud' (beauty bush) 1.5 m (5 ft)	May–June	Sun or part shade	Broad and twiggy; free-flowering
Ribes sanguineum 'Pulborough Scarlet' (flowering currant) 2 m (6½ ft)	April–May	Shade	Upright; fast grower; good for quick effect
Viburnum fragrans 2 m (6½ ft)	Nov–Feb	Sun or part shade	Slender, upright. Winter flowering

HARDY BORDER PLANTS
RED FLOWERS

Aquilegia 'Crimson Star' (columbine) 600 mm (2 ft)	May–June	Sun or part shade	Needs moisture
Aster novi-belgii 'Carnival' (Michaelmas daisy) 900 mm (3 ft)	Sept–Oct	Sun or part shade	Good for back of border
Lychnis chalcedonica (campion) 900 mm–1.2 m (3–4 ft)	June–July	Sun	Good for back of border
Stachys olympica (lamb's tongue) 300 mm (1 ft)	June–Aug	Sun or shade	Good for ground cover. Silver felty leaf

HARDY BORDER PLANTS

PINK FLOWERS

NAME AND HEIGHT	IN FLOWER	SITE	NOTES
Anemone × hybrida 600 mm (2 ft)	Aug–Oct	Sun or shade	Late-flowering
Lamium maculatum 'Chequers' (dead-nettle) 300 mm (1 ft)	May	Shade	Marbled leaf. Good ground cover under trees.
Paeonia 'Lady Alexander Duff' (peony) 750 mm (2½ ft)	June	Sun	Deep rich soil. Leave undisturbed
Phlox paniculata 'Balmoral' 600 mm (2 ft)	June	Part shade	Light, moist soil

ANNUALS & BIENNIALS
PINK/RED FLOWERS

NAME	SOW	FLOWERS	HEIGHT	SITE
Clarkia (A)	March–April	July–Aug	300 mm (1 ft)	Sun
Digitalis (B) (foxglove)	July	June–July	1.2–1.5 (4–5 ft)	Part shade
Godetia grandiflora 'Sybil Sherwood' (A)	March–April	July–Aug	300 mm (1 ft)	Sun or part shade
Linum (A) (flax)	March–April	July–Aug	450 mm (1½ ft)	Sun or part shade
Lavatera (A) (mallow)	April	July–Sept	900 mm (3 ft)	Sun or part shade
Tropaeolum majus (A) (nasturtium)	April–May	July–Sept	300 mm (1 ft)	Sun or part shade
Papaver (A) (poppy)	March–April	June–Sept	750 mm (2½ ft)	Sun or part shade
Phlox drummondii (A)	March–April	July–Oct	150 mm (6 in)	Sun or part shade

BULBS
PINK/RED FLOWERS

NAME	SOW	FLOWERS	NOTES
Amaryllis belladonna 450 mm (18 in)	Aug–Sept	Aug–Oct	Needs warm south-facing wall, moist, well-drained soil
Cyclamen neapolitanum 100 mm (4 in)	Sept–Oct	Aug–Nov	Partial or full shade. Good under trees
Tulipa 250–450 mm (10–18 in)	Nov	March–April	Well-drained soil in full sun.

Right *Brightening rock-garden pockets, window-boxes and tubs in February and March, crocuses repay generous planting. Here 'Warley Rose', a fine purple cultivar of C. chrysanthus, blends nicely with white and yellow varieties.*

Right *Dead-nettle (Lamium maculatum) adds a touch of floral pink to its ground-cover role, for which its attractive silver-splashed leaves are a boon. Rather aggressive, the plant may need to be curbed in smaller borders.*

BLUE

An open, sunny situation is best for blue flowers: in light shade they absorb light and are difficult to see. Delphiniums, meconopsis and gentians contribute the purest blues, and generous beds of them, if possible backed with green-leaved shrubs or the tall, arching leaves of grasses and day lilies, can make a wonderfully relaxing show.

Blue associates pleasingly with yellow or white, and also with its close relatives in the spectrum – mauve, lavender, purple and violet.

Blue-flowered bulbs aplenty brighten early spring. Two of the most reliable are lobelia-blue *Crocus chrysanthus* 'Blue Pearl' and flax-blue grape hyacinth, *Muscari armeniacum* 'Blue Spire'.

Among shrubs, *Hydrangea serrata* 'Bluebird', a lace-cap type, and its mophead cousin *H. macrophylla* 'Générale Vicomtesse de Vibraye', colour to a deep ultramarine-blue on acid soil. If your soil is neutral or limy, you can induce a colour change by treating the root area with a hydrangea colourant sold at garden centres, or by burying pieces of iron among the roots. Two late summer/early autumn flowering shrubs valued for their attractive blue flowers are the blue spiraea (*Caryopteris* 'Ferndown') and *Hibiscus* 'Blue Bird'.

Summer would not be the same without a clump or two of rich blue African lilies, notably *Agapanthus* 'Headbourne Hybrids', which are ideal for borders or for tubs to enhance the patio. Among annuals, the glorious *Salvia farinacea* 'Victoria' looks superb when interplanted with ferny-leaved sea ragwort (*Senecio cineraria*), of which 'Silver Dust' is a fine dwarf form.

Of blue-related colours, purple (like red and orange) is an extravagant colour and should be used in moderation – for instance, in small patches, or at the far end of the garden, or in combination with yellow, where its richness won't appear to foreshorten the view. Among the most striking purple-flowered border perennials are *Salvia nemorosa* 'Superba', a mass of fetching spikes up to 1 m (3 ft) tall; *Delphinium*

'King Arthur', to 1.8 m (6 ft); and the purple cone-flower, *Echinacea purpurea*, to 1.8 m (6 ft). These light up the border in summer.

Violet-purple can be found in the 'Hidcote' variety of lavender, which grows some 600 mm (2 ft) high, and that choice little edger, lily turf (*Liriope muscari*), especially the cultivar 'Majestic', whose dense racemes of rounded flowers bloom in autumn.

Below *'Hidcote' is one of the best of the compact forms of old English lavender (Lavandula angustifolia). Richly scented, its purple flowers attract butterflies.*

SHRUBS

NAME AND HEIGHT	PLANT	SITE	NOTES
BLUE FLOWERS			
Ceanothus × 'Cascade' (Californian lilac) 1.2 m (4 ft)	May–June	Sun	Best against sunny wall; spreading habit
Hibiscus syriacus 'Bluebird' 2.1 m (7 ft)	Aug–Sept	Sun	Sheltered position, well-drained soil
Lavandula spica 'Hidcote' (lavender) 300 mm (1 ft)	July–Sept	Sun	Well-drained light soil. Trim in April and August

HARDY BORDER PLANTS
BLUE FLOWERS

Ajuga reptans (bugle) 150 mm (6 in)	May–June	Sun or part shade	Good for ground cover. Bronze leaf
Brunnera macrophylla 450 mm (1½ ft)	May–June	Sun or shade	Ground cover
Campanula persicifolia (bellflower) 900 mm (3 ft)	June–Aug	Sun or part shade	Needs moisture
Geranium (*grandiflorum*) (crane's-bill) 300 mm (1 ft)	May–June	Sun or part shade	Ground cover

Willow gentian (Gentiana asclepiadea) *Perennial. Flowers in July–September. Likes damp soil; prefers a cool, shady, moist site. Height 400–600 mm (16–24 in). Sow in summer.*

Hibiscus syriacus 'Blue Bird' *Hardy deciduous shrub. Large-toothed leaves. Flowers in August–October. Well-drained, fertile soil; full sun, open site. Height and spread 1.8 m (6 ft). Take cuttings in July.*

Salvia farinacea 'Victoria' *Half-hardy annual. Intense blue flowers in June–July. Fairly rich, free-draining soil; open, sunny site. Height 450 mm (1½ ft). Sow in March–April.*

ANNUALS & BIENNIALS
BLUE FLOWERS

NAME	SOW	FLOWERS	HEIGHT	NOTES
Centaurea cyanus (A) (cornflower)	March–April	June–Sept	600 mm (2 ft)	Sun or part shade
Delphinium chinensis (A)	Sept	June–Sept	450 mm (1½ ft)	Sun or part shade
Echium plantagineum (A) (viper's bugloss)	March–April	July–Aug	300 mm (1 ft) 230 mm (9 in)	Sun or part shade
Lobelia erinus (A)	Feb–March	May–Oct		Sun or part shade
Myosotis sylvatica (B) (forget-me-not)	June–July	April-May	150 mm (6 in)	Sun or part shade
Nemesia (A)	May	July–Sept	300 mm (1 ft)	Sun or part shade
Nigella damascena (A) (love-in-a-mist)	March–April	June–Aug	230 mm (9 in)	Sun or part shade

BULBS
BLUE FLOWERS

NAME AND HEIGHT	PLANT	FLOWERS	NOTES
Chionodoxa (glory-of-the-snow) 150 mm (6 in)	Oct	Feb–March	Well-drained soil in full sun
Hyacinthus orientalis 300 mm (1 ft)	Oct	March–April	As above
Muscari armeniacum (grape hyacinth) 200 mm (8 in)	Sept–Oct	March–May	Full sun
Scilla sibirica (squill) 150 mm (6 in)	Oct	Feb–March	Moist, well-drained soil, part shade

PURPLE FLOWERS

NAME AND HEIGHT	PLANT	FLOWERS	NOTES
Erythronium denscanis (dog's-tooth violet) 150 mm (6 in)	Sept	March–April	Moist soil; part shade
Fritillaria meleagris	Sept–Nov	April–June	Moist soil. Looks best in rough grass.

Opposite page
King of the hellebores, Helleborus lividus corsicus greets late-spring days with massive heads of cup-shaped flowers.

Below *'Paper White' is one of many excellent daffodils with white petals and yellow cup. Member of the tazetta group, it can be forced for winter flowering in a bowl on a windowsill.*

WHITE & GREEN

White is indispensable: we use it to break up and tone down fierce orange, red and yellow flowers; to create a cool, single colour bed or border; to lighten a gloomy spot. The famous white border at Sissinghurst Castle (Kent) cleverly interposes silver- and grey-leaved plants between the flowers and the backing green-leaved hedge.

There is a tremendous choice of 'whites' and, by careful selection, it is often better to choose creamy rather than the starched 'white' forms as the former are more restful on the eye. There are white forms of most border plants – delphinium, campanula, dianthus, chrysanthemum, armeria, aster, kniphofia, iris and many others. Shrubs with white flowers are well represented, with magnolia, deutzia, philadelphus and viburnum.

Creamy white roses are a joy – but finding varieties resistant to black spot and other diseases can be difficult. Happily, the hybrid musks seldom let you down, and white-flushed lemon 'Moonlight' is sweetly scented.

There are plenty of white-flowered annuals. Pick from *Ageratum* 'Spindrift', *Alyssum* 'Snowdrift', *Arctotis grandis*, candytuft *Iberis* 'White Spiral', and *Dianthus heddewigii* 'Snow Fire'.

Among bulbs we are spoilt for choice, with white-flowered tulip, narcissus, crocus, grape hyacinth (*Muscari*), hyacinth, and anemone.

Green-flowered plants have special charm and are best used on their own. Favourites among them are winter-flowering hellebore (*Helleborus foetidus*) and its spring-flowering cousin (*H. corsicus*). The euphorbias are a delight, too, with *E. robbiae*'s pea-green blooms enriching light shade in early spring. A plant popular with flower arrangers is the 'Lime Green' variety of the sweet-scented tobacco plant, *Nicotiana alata*. A bedding plant with a difference is bells-of-Ireland (*Moluccella laevis*), which is prized by flower arrangers for winter displays.

SHRUBS

NAME AND HEIGHT	PLANT	SITE	NOTES
WHITE FLOWERS			
Magnolia stellata 900 mm (3 ft)	March–April	Sun	Needs sheltered site.
Philadelphus 'Sybille' (mock-orange) 1.2 m (4 ft)	June–July	Sun or part shade	Fragrant flowers marked with purple
Pieris 'Forest Flame' 1.5 m (5 ft)	May	Shade	Lime-hater; needs sheltered site
Pyracantha rogersiana (firethorn) 2.1 m (7 ft)	June	Sun or shade	Good for dark walls. Scarlet berries
Spiraea thunbergii 300 mm (1 ft)	March–April	Sun or part shade	Small and twiggy. Free-flowering

Giant bellflower (Campanula latifolia) *Perennial. Flowers 65 mm (2½ in) long in July. Likes well-drained, chalky soil; sun or light shade. Height 1.2 m (4 ft). Sow in March–April.*

***Iris germanica* 'Cliffs of Dover'.** *German or bearded type; perennial. Flowers in May–June. Free-draining soil, must be alkaline; open, sunny site. Height 1 m (3 ft). Plant after flowering.*

Spurge (Euphorbia robbiae) *Evergreen perennial. Flowers in March–June. Light, peaty soil; tolerates some shade. Height 450–600 mm (1½–2 ft). Root basal cuttings in spring and autumn.*

Tobacco plant (Nicotiana alata 'Lime Green') *Half-hardy annual. Scented flowers in June–October. Well-drained soil; sun or partial shade. Height 600 mm–1.2 m (2–4 ft). Sow in March.*

There are also green-flowered tulips and 'Angel', a Double Early Viridiflora variety, is yellowish white with apple-green petals.

HARDY BORDER PLANTS

NAME AND HEIGHT	FLOWERS	SITE	NOTES
WHITE FLOWERS			
Convallaria majalis (lily-of-the-valley) 200 mm (8 in)	April–May	Part shade	Good for ground cover. Fragrant. Needs moisture
Helleborus niger (Christmas rose) 300 mm (1 ft)	Jan–March	Shade	Needs moist rich loam. Feed with manure in spring
Dianthus plumarius 'Mrs Sinkins' (pink) 300 mm (1 ft)	June–July	Sun	Needs well-drained soil

BULBS
WHITE FLOWERS

NAME AND HEIGHT	PLANT	FLOWERS	NOTES
Colchicum autumnale 'Album' (autumn crocus) 230 mm (9 in)	July	Sept	Full sun or light shade
Galanthus nivalis (snowdrop) 150 mm (6 in)	July–Aug	Jan	In grass or among shrubs
Leucojum vernum (snowflake) 450 mm (18 in)	Oct	April–May	Moist soil; part shade
Ornithogalum nutans (drooping star of Bethlehem) 250–350 mm (10–14 in)	March–April	June	Sun or part shade

FOLIAGE COLOURS

Coloured foliage – golden-yellow, copper, purple, red, silver and variegated – is a boon. Shrubs, border plants, annuals and climbers that possess it enrich the garden as much as colourful flowers.

If you are looking through the catalogues, cultivars called 'Aurea', 'Aureum' or 'Aureus' indicate that their leaves are golden (from Latin *aureus*, golden).

One of the finest is the full-moon maple, *Acer japonicum* 'Aureum'. This elegant, slow-growing tree is somewhat wind-frost-tender, so site it in a sheltered spot. *Berberis thunbergii* 'Aurea' almost dazzles with the intensity of its butter-yellow leaves. It makes a smallish bush and is best positioned well away from more robust shrubs that could smother it. Out of the sun, its leaves turn green, so keep it in an open site.

Heathers provide us with 'Gold Feather', 'Gold Haze' and 'Joy Vanstone' forms of *Calluna vulgaris*, commonly called ling. Though these flower in late summer, the beauty of their leaves is best appreciated in winter.

Golden privet (*Ligustrum ovalifolium* 'Aureum') is a neat shrub and good for hedging. If green-leaved shoots appear, cut them out to prevent them from dominating. One of the few golden-leaved shrubs to retain its colour in light shade is the mock orange, *Philadelphus coronarius* 'Aureus'. Cut this back each spring to enjoy a robust regrowth of handsome stems clad with extra large leaves. Another golden beauty is the elderberry, *Sambucus racemosa* 'Plumosa'. This must have a sunny spot or the gold will pale to green.

A dazzling display of primrose-yellow foliage is your reward for planting the 'Aureum' variety of the full-moon maple (Acer japonicum). Slow-growing and compact, it is ideal for the smaller garden. Plant in deep, rich, peaty soil in a site sheltered from icy winds.

Left *One of the most strikingly coloured barberries,* Berberis thunbergii *'Rose Glow' looks splendid on its own or associated with its golden-leaved cousin 'Aurea'. As a hedge, it stays low, about 600 mm (2 ft), and is easily trimmed.*

Two spectacular border perennials are *Valeriana phu* 'Aurea' and *Hosta fortunei* 'Aurea'. Both start life a brilliant golden yellow, commanding attention until mid-summer, when the leaves pale to lime-green.

Purple-leaved plants are indicated by the words 'Purpurea' or 'Purpureum' (from the old English for heraldic purple). A choice shrub for a tub or gap in the paving stones on a terrace or patio is the Japanese maple, *Acer palmatum* 'Dissectum Atropurpureum'. It grows very slowly and its intriguing umbrella habit draws admiring comments. A really first-class shrub is *Berberis × ottowensis* 'Purpurea' (syn. 'Superba'), whose yellow flowers and red berries complement the vinous purple of its leaves. Its cousin, *B. thunbergii* 'Atropurpurea Nana' (syn. 'Little Favourite'), makes a splendid feature for a rock garden.

Others to look out for – and remember, they make a perfect backcloth for red-flowered plants – are the filbert *Corylus maxima* 'Purpurea', smoke tree *Cotinus coggygria* 'Royal Purple', and blackthorn *Prunus spinosa* 'Purpurea'.

Cream or yellow variegated plants, mostly shrubs, are very appealing, and evergreens among them become a focus in winter. *Elaeagnus pungens* 'Maculata' is prized for its evergreen leaves which are brightened by a central splash of gold. *E. × ebbingei* 'Gilt Edge' is one of a number of varieties with green leaves fetchingly rimmed with gold.

Euonymus fortunei radicans 'Silver Queen's leaves are edged in creamy white, but in early spring the young leaves open a creamy yellow colour with a pale border. *E. japonicus* 'Ovatus Aureus', a cultivar of a popular hedging shrub for coastal gardens, has very attractive golden yellow variegation. *Hebe × franciscana* 'Variegata' is slightly less hardy than the hybrid type, but it will flourish in a sheltered corner, producing its creamy variegated leaves all year.

Among the hollies (Ilex), there are two excellent clones of *I. aquifolium*: the broad-leaved common form 'Argenteo-marginata' (silver variegation) and 'Golden Queen' (deep yellow). The pittosporums include some of the most beautiful evergreen shrubs; unfortunately, most of them are too tender to thrive outdoors in this country. Hardier than most is *P. tenuifolium*, which is well worth trying if you live in a warmer part of the south or west. Two cultivars with variegation are 'Silver Queen' (silvery white) and 'Variegatum' (creamy white). In both, the colours contrast strikingly with the black stems. *Weigela florida* is a very popular medium-sized shrub bearing pink, bell-shaped flowers in May and June. Its cultivar 'Variegata' has cream-edged leaves.

Below *Of all weigelas,* W. florida *'Variegata' is most suitable in a shrub or mixed border for breaking up hotter colours – reds, yellows and oranges. Its arching branches are decked with bloom from May to June and its creamy-yellow-rimmed leaves stay bright all summer.*

The first chill October nights transform the smoke tree (Cotinus coggygria) from plain green to glowing orange, best seen against a dark green backcloth. Purple-leaved varieties are also available.

COLOUR CHANGES

We all delight in the turn of green leaves of deciduous trees to glorious browns and golds in the autumn. One of the most interesting recent developments has been the introduction of ever-green shrub cultivars whose leaves change colour from season to season. The most striking of these are clones of *Calluna vulgaris*, the common heather of the English and Scottish countryside. Among the finest of these clones are 'Blazeaway', which is green in summer and rich red in winter; 'Golden Feather', light gold in summer, deeper gold in winter; 'Gold Haze', a 600 mm (2 ft) heather with bright yellow leaves; and 'Robert Chapman', pale gold in spring, orange in summer and red in winter.

COLOURED LEAVES

Gold, purple, silver or variegated leaved shrubs add interest for much of the year; evergreen kinds are specially useful in winter. All need an open sunny position or their rich hues will pale. They will thrive in ordinary soil fortified with manure and fertilizer

SHRUBS FOR FOLIAGE

NAME	HEIGHT
GOLDEN YELLOW	
Calluna vulgaris 'Gold Feather' (heather, ling)	230 mm (9 in)
Erica cinerea 'Golden Drop' (heath)	230 mm (9 in)
Lonicera nitida 'Baggesen's Gold' (honeysuckle)	1.5–2.1 m (5–7 ft)
Philadelphus coronarius 'Aureus' (mock orange)	1.8–2.4 m (6–8 ft)
Sambucus racemosa 'Plumosa Aurea' (elder)	1.8–2.7 m (6–9 ft)

NAME	HEIGHT
REDDISH PURPLE	
Berberis thunbergii 'Rose Glow' (barberry)	1.2–1.8 m (4–6 ft)
Cotinus coggygria 'Rubrifolius' (smoke-tree)	1.8–2.4 m (6–8 ft)
Photinia × fraseri 'Red Robin'	1.2–1.8 m (4–6 ft)
PURPLE	
Berberis thunbergii 'Atropurpurea'	1.2–1.8 m (4–6 ft)
Corylus maxima 'Purpurea' (hazel)	1.8–2.4 m (6–8 ft)
Weigela florida 'Foliis Purpureis'	1.8–2.4 m (6–8 ft)

Far left *Richly scented mock orange (Philadelphus) has a particularly showy member in P. coronarius 'Aureus'.*

Near left *The leaves of Photinia × fraseri 'Red Robin' open shining scarlet. Grown as a small tree or bush, it thrives in deep, rich soil sheltered from cold winds.*

NAME	HEIGHT
GREY/SILVER	
Artemisia 'Powis Castle' (lad's love)	900 mm–1.2 m (3–4 ft)
Buddleia fallowiana	1.8–2.7 m (6–9 ft)
Buddleia × 'Lochinch'	1.8–2.7 m (6–9 ft)
Calluna vulgaris 'Silver Queen' (heather)	200–300 mm (8–12 in)
Cotoneaster lacteus	1.8–2.4 m (6–8 ft)
Elaeagnus macrophylla	1.8–2.4 m (6–8 ft)
Hebe pinguifolia 'Pagei'	150–200 mm (6–8 in)
Hippophae rhamnoides (sea buckthorn)	1.8–2.7 m (6–9 ft)
Lavandula angustifolia	300 mm–1.2 m (1–4 ft)
Olearia × mollis	1.2–2.4 m (4–8 ft)
Perovskia atriplicifolia	600–900 mm (2–3 ft)
Potentilla arbuscula 'Beesii' (cinquefoil)	300–450 mm (1–1½ ft)
Potentilla fruticosa 'Mandschurica'	1.2–1.5 m (4–5 ft)
Santolina chamaecyparissus (cotton lavender)	600–750 mm (2–2½ ft)
Senecio × 'Sunshine'	660–900 mm (2–3 ft)

NAME	HEIGHT
VARIEGATED	
Aucuba japonica 'Crotonifolia' (spotted laurel)	2.1–2.7 m (7–9 ft)
Cornus alba 'Elegantissima' (dogwood)	1.5–2.1 m (5–7 ft)
Elaeagnus pungens 'Maculata'	1.5–2.1 m (5–7 ft)
Euonymus fortunei radicans 'Variegatus'	230–250 mm (9–10 in)
Griselinia littoralis 'Bantry Bay'	2.1–3 m (7–10 ft)
Ilex aquifolium 'Golden Queen' (holly)	3–4.5 m (12–15 ft)
Kerria japonica 'Variegata' (jew's mallow)	1.5–2.1 m (5–7 ft)
Pachysandra terminalis 'Variegata' (Japanese spurge)	150–230 mm (6–9 in)
Ruta graveolens 'Variegata' (rue)	300–600 mm (1–2 ft)
Viburnum tinus 'Variegata'	2–3 m (6½–10 ft)
Weigela florida 'Variegata' and 'Atropurpureum'	1.8–2.4 m (6–8 ft) / 1.8–2.4 m (6–8 ft)

Far left *Non-flowering Artemisia 'Powis Castle' develops a filigree of silvery leaves. Interplant it with yellow, blue, orange or red flowers.*

Near left *In autumn, winter and early spring, before much of the garden has awoken to the sun's warming rays, Elaeagnus pungens 'Maculata' delights with its vivid show of gold-splashed evergreen leaves.*

Red-berried elder (Sambucus racemosa 'Plumosa Aurea') *Shrub. Flowers in April; fruits in July. Ordinary soil; variety prefers sheltered, partly shaded site. Height 1.8–3 m (6–10 ft). Root hardwood cuttings in autumn.*

Scottish ling (Calluna vulgaris 'Golden Feather') *Golden summer foliage turns reddish orange in winter. Poor, well-drained acid soil; exposed, sunny site. Height 300 mm (1 ft). Root cuttings of new growth in August.*

Japanese maple (Acer palmatum 'Dissectum Atropurpureum') *Slow-growing tree. Leaves purple in summer, crimson in autumn. Moist, well-drained soil; light shade, shelter. Height 2 m (6½ ft).*

Elaeagnus × ebbingei 'Gilt Edge'. *Evergreen shrub. Gold-margined leaves; fragrant flowers in autumn. Well-drained, fertile soil; open, sunny site. Height 1.5 m (5 ft). Root cuttings in summer.*

Spotted laurel (Aucuba japonica 'Crotonifolia') *Evergreen shrub; male (non-berrying) form. Ordinary soil preferred; likes open, sunny site. Height 1.5–3 m (5–10 ft). Root cuttings in late summer.*

Senecio × 'Sunshine' *Evergreen shrub. Leaves felted with grey-white hairs; yellow flowers in July–August. Free-draining soil; full sun. Height 900 mm–1.2 m (3–4 ft). Take cuttings in late summer.*

ROSES
BUSH ROSES
Colourful, reliable, long-flowering and neat in growth, modern bush roses are especially suitable for smaller gardens. In flower June to October.

NAME	COLOUR	HEIGHT	NOTES
Allgold (cluster-flowered)	Yellow	600 mm (2 ft)	Small double flower, slightly scented; glossy foliage; wide-branching growth
Dearest (cluster-flowered)	Salmon pink	750 mm (2½ ft)	Fragrant, free-flowering; bushy growth; glossy, dark green foliage
Iceberg (cluster-flowered)	White	1.8 m (6 ft)	Large, open flower; vigorous and leafy growth
Lilli Marlene (cluster-flowered)	Crimson red	600 mm (2 ft)	Large semi-double flowers in clusters

NAME	COLOUR	HEIGHT	NOTES
Josephine Bruce (large-flowered)	Dark crimson	900 mm (3 ft)	Fragrant, double, dark velvet flower
Wendy Cussons (large-flowered)	Rosy red	900 mm (3 ft)	Fragrant; full flower; vigorous

OLD & MODERN SHRUB ROSES
Old shrub roses demand space and are somewhat prone to disease, but include some of the loveliest roses of all. The modern shrub roses are more reliable with neater habit. Flowering season June–October.

NAME	COLOUR	HEIGHT	NOTES
Cécile Brunner (China)	Shell pink	600 mm (2 ft)	Tiny shapely flowers, delicate form; free-flowering
Fantin Latour ('cabbage')	Pale pink	1.8 m (6 ft)	Lovely double flower; free-flowering
Frühlingsmorgen (modern shrub)	Pink, gold	1.8 m (6 ft)	Single open flowers, repeat flowering

NAME	COLOUR	HEIGHT	NOTES
Golden Wings (modern shrub)	Pale yellow	1.8 m (6 ft)	Fragrant, single flower; graceful and spreading habit
Madam Hardy (damask)	White	1.5 m (5 ft)	Perfect double flower, green centre; vigorous and leafy growth
Mme Pierre Oger (Bourbon)	Shell pink	1.5 m (5 ft)	Cup-shaped double flower; neat, upright habit
Nevada (modern shrub)	Creamy white	2 m (6½ ft)	Lovely open flower; wide-arching habit
Tuscany Superb (Gallica)	Crimson purple	1.5 m (5 ft)	Double, deep velvet flowers; wide arching habit
Canary Bird (species)	Clear yellow	2 m (6½ ft)	Single flowers; slender, arching branches

CLIMBING & RAMBLER ROSES

Climbers are best trained up walls, sheds, and pergolas. Ramblers, with more flexible stems are best for tumbling over structures.

NAME	COLOUR	HEIGHT	NOTES
Albéric Barbier (rambler)	Creamy white	7 m (23 ft)	Fragrant double flowers; dark foliage. Good screen
Albertine (rambler)	Copper pink	7 m (23 ft)	Clusters of loose double flowers; very vigorous
Climbing Etoile de Hollande (climber)	Dark red	6 m (20 ft)	Fragrant; will grow on north or east wall
Danse du Feu (perpetual climber)	Vivid red	3 m (10 ft)	Large double flower; free-flowering
Gloire de Dijon (climber)	Buff yellow	5 m (16½ ft)	Fragrant, free-flowering
Golden Showers (perpetual climber)	Golden yellow	2.4 m (8 ft)	Short climber; flowers all summer
Mme Alfred Carrière (climber)	White	5 m (16½ ft)	Small shapely flower; free-flowering, even on north wall

CLIMBING SHRUBS

All climbers need some vertical support. Self-clingers, like ivy and Virginia creeper, will adhere or hook themselves on to surfaces and do not need tying in. The rest need wires or trellis to guide and support the shoots.

NAME, HEIGHT	FLOWERS	COLOUR	SITE	NOTES
Actinidia kolomikta to 4 m (13 ft)	June	White	Sun or part shade	Heart-shaped leaves, cream and pink. May be slow to establish
Campsis grandiflora (trumpet vine) 3 m (10 ft)	Aug	Orange scarlet	Sun	Not fully hardy: needs warm sheltered wall. Large trumpet flowers
Clematis 'Jackmanii Superba' 4–6 m (13–20 ft)	June–Sept	Deep purple	Sun or part shade	Prune as above
Clematis montana 'Elizabeth' 7–10 m (23–33 ft)	May–June	Soft pink	Sun or part shade	Prune in June only if necessary. Well-drained soil
Hedera helix 'Goldheart' (ivy) 2–3 m (6½–10 ft)			Shade	Self-clinging; small leaf with gold centre
Hydrangea petiolaris (climbing hydrangea) 2–3 m (6½–10 ft)	June–July	White	Shade	Self-clinging
Jasminum nudiflorum (winter jasmine) to 3 m (10 ft)	Nov–March	Yellow	Sun or part shade	Arching growth; needs tying to support

Above *Heralding early summer with sumptuous single blooms, 'Nevada', a modern shrub rose, grows about 2 m (6 ft) high and wide and looks superb billowing over a sheltered patio or among the branches of an old, open tree.*

Left *Esteemed for its profusion of blooms on some of the longest, thorniest of climbing-rose stems, 'Albertine' enjoys three weeks of glory in late June and early July. Use it to camouflage an ugly garage wall, fence, or unshapely fruit tree.*

PLANTS FOR THE PATIO

The fact that patios are essentially hard-paved areas need place few restrictions on the range of plants you wish to choose to decorate the area. Large shrubs and even trees will grow happily in containers, and climbers can be trained up walls or pergolas and along overhead beams. In this chapter we look at some of the best plants for different sites on the patio.

Far right A massive wine jar plays host to Clematis macropetala *'Maidwell Hall'.*

CONTAINERS

Containers of all kinds – pots, tubs, troughs and home-built raised beds – are the basic furnishings of the patio, your outdoor room. With their help you are able to have colour all year round, arranging it in different ways according to your whim. There is no heavy digging to do; you will not even have to bend down if your containers are sited high enough; there is little or no weeding to worry about; and you are less troubled by weather conditions than in a conventional plot. You can suit yourself as far as soil is concerned, filling some containers with the acid kind for lime-hating plants such as rhododendrons and azaleas, and others with chalky soil, which such favourites as aster, clematis and lilac love. In short, you have the best of all gardening worlds.

You can also shift your garden around in any way you want, provided that you have made sure that your containers are movable. You can give them each a turn to have their fair share of the sun. You can tuck ones that have finished flowering behind the others, or use planted containers to hide an unattractive feature. Plan your containers for bold massed effect. It is more labour-saving to put several plants into one large container rather than have the same number singly in an array of pots. They grow better together, they need watering less frequently, and they make a greater visual impact: one large tub looks more impressive and takes up less space than half a dozen flower pots huddled together.

Right A tub crammed with a fine display of the 'Resisto Rose' variety of petunia.

TUBS, POTS AND TROUGHS

These are made in several different kinds of material and it is important to choose the material that suits both you and your garden. Plastic saves the most labour and it is usually cheapest, too. It is lightweight, colour-fast, and, unless it gets cracked or torn, will last for a long time, although it tends to get brittle after several years in the sunlight. Plants in such containers need watering less often than those in conventional clay pots, from which moisture evaporates through the walls. Plastic containers are now made in some attractive classic shapes; they range in appearance from imitation wood to plain white and some good colours, too. If you do not like the colours, it is easy to repaint plastic pots using acrylic-based paints. Glass-fibre containers are expensive, but should, if handled properly, last for a life-time. If you want a 'period' look for your pots, this is your best choice, as glass-fibre can be used to simulate any container material, from wood to lead.

Stone, artificial stone, and concrete containers look very attractive, but they are very heavy, so you should be sure where you want to site them before you plant them up. They are expensive, too, and tend to be fragile: they may crack in a heavy frost or crumble with age, so they should never be moved unless it is absolutely necessary to do so.

Terracotta pots, including the traditional flower pot, look and feel good, but they too are expensive and tend to break easily, and their plants need watering frequently. Plants grown in such containers are also more likely to have their roots affected by frost, so they need more attention, and it is a good idea to protect them in really cold weather. With all these drawbacks, however, terracotta pots are most people's favourite containers: plants somehow look *right* in them. Wooden containers are also very attractive, but they will deteriorate over a period of time, however thoroughly you paint them or treat them with preservative. Wood is invaluable for purpose-built-containers – a specially made box to fit an awkwardly shaped window-sill, for instance, or a wooden tub to fit over a manhole cover. Wooden tubs or half barrels are fairly heavy; they also lose water easily – in summer a tub on a hot patio may need watering two or even three times a day.

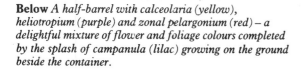

Below *A half-barrel with calceolaria (yellow), heliotropium (purple) and zonal pelargonium (red) – a delightful mixture of flower and foliage colours completed by the splash of campanula (lilac) growing on the ground beside the container.*

Above *A trough made of natural stone makes a fine container in formal gardens of older houses.*

HANGING BASKETS

The containers mentioned so far are placed on the patio floor. Hanging baskets are particularly useful because they create centres of interest at or above eye level. Half baskets can be hung on walls; full baskets can be suspended from wall brackets or from beams. But remember that when large baskets are filled they are heavy, so wall or beam fixings must be suitably strong.

Baskets should be lined with tightly-packed sphagnum moss, a cellulose liner or black polythene. If moss is used, a saucer should be placed on the layer of moss at the bottom to provide a reservoir of water – life-saving in hot weather. Watering can be a problem. Baskets dry out quickly when exposed to sun and wind, and need to be watered daily during the summer. It may be necessary to take the basket down once a week for a good soak; and a syringe with water each evening in hot weather will be appreciated.

Far right, above
Hanging baskets are useful and decorative spacesavers on a small patio. This one sports nasturtiums (orange), pelargoniums (red and white), and lobelias (pink).

Above *The window box at right (crowded with pelargoniums and lobelias) is fine for sash-windows sills. For outward-opening casement windows, however, something else is needed. One answer is a row of easily movable pots, as in the picture at left.*

CONVERSIONS AND HOME-MADES

If you want to get away from purpose-built containers and look for something interestingly unconventional in which to house your plants, the range is enormous. Anything from a cocoa tin to an old domestic cold-water tank can be used to hold plants. Surprisingly large trees can be grown on the patio in containers too – you could even have a mini-orchard provided you fed the fruit trees well.

There's no end to the items you can press into service: old kitchen coppers make very attractive plant containers, as do cisterns which can often be found abandoned on skips. Pots and pans that have outlived their usefulness make good portable containers and you can paint them in vivid colours or decorate them, narrow-boat style, in bright patterns. Canteen-size kettles make good plant holders, and so do outsize teapots. It pays to look around second-hand shops for items that are chipped or cracked and knocked down for a few pence which might make attractive plant holders.

Chimney pots are so well known now in their new guise as plant containers that you may have to pay over the odds for them. But if you are lucky enough to secure one, it is more sensible to sit a large flower-pot in the top of it, rather than fill the entire chimney pot with soil. If you want to mass a number of plants together, a small wooden wheelbarrow makes a good display piece, or an old tin hip bath. Even a dolls' pram can be used as a plant holder: give it a good coat of paint first and it should last several seasons. On the fun front, discarded wellies or climbing boots make amusing temporary homes for plants, such as spring bulbs, that are to sit on a window sill.

Old kitchen sinks make good troughs for small plants such as alpines. Stone sinks can be left as they are, but china ones look better if you give them a rough-cast treatment. Spread them first with an impact-bonding PVA glue (you will need rubber gloves for this job), then pat on a mixture of Portland cement, sand and peat, in proportions of 1:2½:1½, over the sides and

A section of a dead tree trunk makes a pleasantly informal plant container.

leave it to dry. Do not try to put on too much rough cast at a time. The best way is to build up the thickness of the coating by making several applications, allowing the rough cast to dry between each thickness. The same technique could be used for any ceramic object; an old, large mixing bowl, for instance, could very easily be turned into a rough-cast plant pot.

If cash is limited, you can save your money for the plants, rather than spend it on containers, by copying the French and Italians. Collect together the largest paint cans you can find and spray or paint them all the same colour with lacquer (dazzling turquoise blue looks particularly effective). Before you plant them up, make drainage holes in the bottom.

You may be lucky enough to lay your hands

on a cheap, large tub or a half-barrel to grow plants in. Strawberry barrels are well known, but there is no reason why you should not plant them up with flowers instead; they look particularly good if you mix bedding plants with trailers like sweet peas (*Lathyrus odoratus*) or nasturtiums (*Tropaeolum*). To plant up a barrel effectively, place a piece of drainpipe down over the centre as you fill it, and fill the pipe with gravel or small stones, pulling it up as you go. This gives the barrel a central draining system.

One of the best ways of getting the kind of container you want is to build a raised bed for your plants. You can then have exactly the right dimensions and, provided the soil is topped up from time to time with fertiliser, it is a permanent fixture. Small plants like alpines can be viewed more easily when raised above ground level. You can use a number of materials other than brick – stone, baulks of timber, or peat blocks. But if you use wood, it must first be treated with a non-toxic preservative.

The larger and higher the bed, the more secure the foundations will have to be. A low bed can just be constructed on the patio floor. The front wall should have a slight backward slope, to help to contain the earth inside. It must have drainage holes in it; insert pieces of tubing between courses of brick, stone, or timber near the bottom of the bed so that excess water can drip out.

The austere lines of Versailles tubs (here with petunias and lobelias) lend themselves to formal settings.

125

SMALL-SPACE EVERGREEN SHRUBS AND PERENNIALS

Acaena	Escallonia	Osmanthus
Arbutus	Eucalyptus	Pachysandra
Arundinaria	Eucryphia (some)	Pernettya
Aucuba	Euonymus (some)	Phlomis
Berberis (some)	Euphorbia (some)	Phormium
Bergenia (most)	× Fatshedera	Photinia
Buxus	Fatsia	Picea
Calluna	Festuca	Pieris
Camellia	Fremontodendron	Pyracantha
Ceanothus (some)	Garrya	Rhododendron
Chamaecyparis	Gaultheria	(many)
lawsoniana	Hebe	Rosmarinus
dwarf forms	Hedera	Ruscus
Choisya	Hypericum (some)	Ruta
Cistus	Iberis	Santolina
Convolvulus cneorum	Ilex	Sarcococca
Cotoneaster (some)	Juniperus	Senecio (most)
Cryptomeria	Kalmia (some)	Skimmia
× *Cupressocyparis*	Laurus	Taxus
leylandii	Leptospermum	Teucrium
'Castlewellan'	Ligustrum (some)	Thuja
Daboecia	Lonicera (some)	Thymus
Daphne (some)	*Magnolia grandiflora*	Trachycarpus
Elaeagnus	Mahonia	Viburnum (some)
Embothrium	Myrtus	Vinca
Erica	Olearia	Yucca

Above, right
Evergreen Fatsia japonica, *with its white October flowers, makes a good permanent resident in sun or shade.*

Right *Make a virtue of necessity by building a patio around an awkwardly sited tree. The speckled shade cast by its foliage will be a boon on hot summer days.*

DECORATIVE PLANTS

PERMANENT RESIDENTS

The long-term inhabitants of the patio need to be chosen with care, as they are to be planted in a small space – but that does not mean that they need to be dull. Evergreen, for instance, does not necessarily have to be green: there are many attractive shrubs and small trees whose foliage comes in golden or variegated versions; holly (*Ilex*) and box (*Buxus*) provide several examples. Some of the *Chamaecyparis* species (including the familiar Lawson's cypress) have dwarf varieties bearing gold, silvery blue, or purplish foliage; while some heathers (*Calluna*) are yellow all year round. Many of the hebes have leaves with white or cream edges, as does the variegated form of Japanese spurge (*Pachysandra terminalis*).

When you are looking through catalogues of shrubs and perennials, make a point of checking to see if there are variegated as well as plain versions of the plants you are interested in. Variegated or golden foliage looks particularly good if the patio is dark and shady, as it will tend to light it up. A good evergreen for shade, incidentally is the false castor-oil plant (*Fatsia japonica* 'Variegata') whose huge, glossy green leaves with white tips look very exotic. Resembling an indoor rather than an outdoor plant, it goes well with plants like the yucca if you are giving your patio a tropical look.

Rhododendrons and camellias, with their

elegant dark green leaves, are useful additions to the patio because of the shapely, vividly coloured flowers that they also bring. Rhododendrons, especially the smaller azalea forms, are a good choice because they are shallow rooting and therefore suitable for raised beds and tubs; but remember that rhododendrons must be planted in acid soil – they are lime-haters.

Having got your backdrop installed, there are a number of attractive perennials that can be put

in place as further furnishings to add interest all year round. Rosemary and lavender will add fragrance, and, like sage (*Salvia*) and thyme, are useful herbs to have around. Go for variety in colour and shape with your perennial plants – contrasting, for instance, the deep-cut silvery leaves of wormwood (*Artemisia absinthium*) with the round, golden-green leaves of lady's mantle (*Alchemilla mollis*) together with the sword-like spikes of New Zealand flax (*Phormium tenax*). You should aim at a mix of tall spiky and round hummocky plants, and a range of foliage colours from near golden yellow to the silver shades and blue-greens.

Make bulbs part of your overall scheme, for in a small space nothing gives better value for money year after year. Plant daffodils (*Narcissus*) tulips, and crocuses in clumps rather than strung out in rows: they look much more effective when massed together. And have at least one tub crammed with colour in this way in spring. If you have a raised bed or two, then consider growing the tiny species bulbs as well, they look wonderful mixed with alpines. Remember that you can have bulbs in flower in the autumn too, if you plant in early summer. The autumn crocus (*Colchicum*) has crocus-like flowers almost as big as those of tulips; they come up on bare stalks, however, so they need to be mixed in with something else – the silvery sea ragwort (*Senecio cineraria*) makes a particularly good foil for them (it is, however, not fully hardy and is usually treated as an annual). Later on the nerines, those beautiful pink 'lilies' from South Africa, will reward you with their delicate colour from early autumn almost up to Christmas.

Plants for shade

Acanthus
Aconitum
Anemone
Aquilegia
Astrantia
Aucuba
Begonia
Bergenia
Berberis
Camellia
Convallaria
Cotoneaster simonsii
Digitalis
Euonymus radicans
Forsythia
Galanthus
Helleborus
Hosta
Hydrangea
Hypericum
Impatiens
Kerria japonica 'Pleniflora'
Lilium
Lysimachia
Phlox
Primula
Pyracantha
Rhododendron (Azalea)
Ribes sanguineum
Saxifraga umbrosa
Skimmia japonica
Vinca
Viola

Plant	Planting time	Depth	Flowering time	Height
Acidanthera	May	75mm (3in)	July-Oct	450-600mm (18-24in)
Anemone ('De Caen' and 'St Brigid' strains)	Spring	50mm (2in)	June-Sept	200-300mm (8-12in)
Begonia	May	50mm (2in)	July-Oct	200-250mm (8-10in)
Brodiaea	March-April	75-100mm (3-4in)	June-July	400-500mm (16-20in)
Dahlia	After last frost	75-100mm (3-4in)	Aug-Oct	300-1500mm (1-5ft)
Freesia	From mid-Apr	50mm (2in)	July-Sept	200-250mm (8-10in)
Galtonia	Apr	100mm (4in)	July-Aug	900-1200mm (3-4ft)
Gladiolus:				
small-flowered	Apr-June	75mm (3in)	June-July	450mm (18in)
large-flowered	Apr-June	75mm (3in)	July-Sept	1.5m (5ft)
Hymenocallis	May-June	125-150mm (5-6in)	July-Aug	450mm (18in)
Lilium	Feb-Apr	100-125mm (4-5in)	June-Sept	600-1500mm (2-5ft)
Montbretia (syn. Crocosmia)	Apr-May	50mm (2in)	July-Sept	400mm (16in)
Ornithogalum	Mar-Apr	50mm (2in)	Aug-Oct	300-350mm (12-14in)
Oxalis	Apr-May	50mm (2in)	July-Sept	100-150mm (4-6in)
Ranunculus	Mar-May	50mm (2in)	June-Aug	250mm (10in)
Sparaxis	Apr	50mm (2in)	June-July	200mm (8in)
Sprekelia	Apr	100mm (4in)	June	450-600mm (18-24in)
Tigridia	Mar-Apr	75mm (3in)	July-Aug	400mm (16in)

Above, left *The vibrant colours of many azaleas deserve a special position on the patio.*

Left *A selection of summer-flowering bulbs. Use them with larger permanent residents to provide additional colour in tubs and troughs.*

The slower-growing climber wisteria (above) contrasts with aptly named mile-a-minute or Russian vine (right).

Climbers for the patio

Akebia
Campsis
Celastrus
Clematis
Cobaea
Eccremocarpus
Hedera
Hydrangea petiolaris
Ipomoea
Jasminum
Lathyrus
Lonicera
Parthenocissus
Passiflora
Polygonum
Rosa
Solanum
Tropaeolum
Wisteria

proposition for, say, a pergola where you want overhead leaves, and its long delicate racemes of white flowers hang down in an attractive way. It is a good idea to team it with a slower-growing, more attractive climber, such as a grape-vine or wisteria, provided you keep it under control. Two other rapid climbers to look for are varieties of *Clematis montana* and *Rosa filipes* 'Kiftsgate', a very vigorous rambler with huge trusses of white flowers that will eventually need checking.

Some climbers are self-supporting and do not need help in the form of netting or wires. Those valued mainly for foliage include common ivy, Boston ivy (*Parthenocissus tricuspidata* 'Veitchii') and Virginia creeper (*P. quinquefolia*). Climbing roses, on the whole, can look after themselves and just need fastening here and there against the wall. They make a marvellous show, but they should be sited with care in a very small space, as their thorns may become a nuisance.

Clematis and other 'softer' climbers, such as winter jasmine (*Jasminum nudiflorum*) and honeysuckle (*Lonicera*), need plenty of wire, netting or trellis to cling to and climb over and to protect them from strong winds. But they do tend to make fast growth and flower quickly and they do not need tying in. They can also be grown easily in pots, as can passion flower (*Passiflora caerulea*), which actually flowers better if it has some root restriction. If you are planning on climbers for pergolas and posts

CLIMBERS

You can almost double the potential growing space of your patio if you use the boundary walls in an imaginative way by planting them with climbers. Moreover, it's a good way to 'tie in' the walls of the house with the rest of the garden. Climbers can also be used to hide unsightly items like sheds, or to screen off the patio from the eyes of neighbours or from a view you would rather not see. The opportunities are endless. A climber can frame a window, or you can build a narrow trellis and grow climbers up it. Even a humble chain-link fence can have a climber, such as common ivy (*Hedera helix*), trained and tied to it so that it is completely covered and becomes a lush green 'wall'. If you have a wall or an unsightly feature that you want to cover rapidly, the fastest, most vigorous climber you are likely to come across is Russian vine (*Polygonum baldschuanicum*), which can cover 6m (20ft) of wall in the space of one season. However, the trouble is that once you have started it, it is difficult to get it to stop. It is deciduous, too, so you are left with bare branches in winter. But if judiciously clipped and pruned back, it quite quickly forms a thick network of stems which makes it an attractive

Wall plants for the patio

Abutilon
Berberis
Buddleia
Camellia
Ceanothus
Chaenomeles
Chimonanthus
Choisya
Cotoneaster
Cytisus
Forsythia
Garrya
Ilex
Kerria
Ligustrum
Magnolia
Pittosporum
Prunus
Pyracantha
Rhododendron
Symphoricarpos
Viburnum

Left *The Japanese climbing hydrangea* (H. petiolaris) *is another vigorous grower, especially on north-facing walls. Its creamy flowers come out in June.*

around a terrace, a grape-vine traditionally makes an attractive network of leaves under which to dine out or sit. The most vigorous variety to choose is *Vitis vinifera* 'Brandt', which has foliage that colours reddish purple in the autumn and succulent black grapes.

North walls can be a problem, but fortunately there are a number of attractive climbers that will cope with them, notably *Hydrangea petiolaris*. Wisteria will also take to a north wall happily, so will the Japanese honeysuckle (*Lonicera japonica*), which will give you perfume as well.

Then there is a number of free-standing shrubs that will grow anything up to 2.5m (8ft) high and can be used in place of climbers where the backdrop is not able to take them. The best known of these is the Leyland cypress (× *Cupressocyparis leylandii*), which makes a quick-growing hedge, especially in its 'Castlewellan' form. If you want a different effect, plant it in pairs and tie their tops together so that they bend to form a series of arches. Several of the free-standing shrubs that can be grown against a wall have attractive berries in the autumn. *Berberis darwinii*, for instance, and the somewhat smaller Oregon grape (*Mahonia aquifolium*) follow their bright yellow flowers in spring with dark purple berries; while species of *Cotoneaster*, which bear white or pink flowers in June, have rich red berries which stay on for most of the winter. The various firethorns (*Pyracantha*), too, have masses of red, orange, or yellow berries.

When buying climbers, bear in mind that container-grown plants can be put into the ground at any time of the year. Among bare-root climbers, most evergreens are planted in spring (late March or early April), while deciduous plants should be put in during their dormant period (between October and March).

Right *The 'Aurea' variety of Indian bean tree* (Catalpa bignonioides) *bears striking yellow, heart-shaped leaves.*

TREES

Trees, if you have the space for them, are a great asset in and around the patio because they provide shelter from the wind and from noise, and also help to give some degree of privacy. If you feel that an ugly building, say, or a pylon or telegraph pole at the end of the garden needs blotting from view, then a tree placed near the house will do so much better than one that is further away. But you must be careful not to shade the patio in doing so. Choose columnar trees like *Prunus* 'Amanogawa', one of the Japanese cherries, or the Dawyck beech (*Fagus sylvatica* 'Fastigiata'), both of which cast slender shadows.

Forest trees should be avoided because of their size, but in many cases smaller, fastigiate (columnar) forms of such trees have become available; they take little space and are well suited to most patios. Some of the fastigiate trees worth consideration are *Betula pendula* 'Fasti-giata', an erect form of silver birch; *Carpinus betulus* 'Columnaris', a slow-growing columnar form of common hornbeam, useful for a clay soil; *Crataegus monogyna* 'Stricta', an erect form *of common hawthorn; Quercus robur* 'Fastigiata' a form of common oak; and *Ginkgo biloba* 'Fastigiata' (a columnar form of maidenhair tree).

Two weeping trees that are deservedly popular are Young's weeping birch (*Betula pendula* 'Youngii') and the purple osier (*Salix purpurea*

'Pendula'), with its purple-tinted shoot tips. Another favourite tree for town is the Indian bean-tree (*Catalpa bignonioides*), its golden form *C. b.* 'Aurea' is especially attractive and slower growing, but is not so easy to find.

The Judas tree (*Cercis siliquastrun*), with rosy clusters of pea-shaped flowers borne on the naked branches in May has great charm. The magnolias are also highly desirable trees or large shrubs; most of them are deciduous, but *M. grandiflora* is an evergreen with huge, cream,

Right *Of the various magnolias, the slow-growing* M. stellata, *which rarely exceeds 3m (10ft) in height, is the best for associating with the patio. Its fragrant flowers appear in March and April.*

sweetly fragrant goblets, and makes a superb wall shrub; *M. stellata*, though deciduous, is the one magnolia that will not ultimately outgrow the patio confines. The *Prunus* genus provides many decorative forms of cherry, peach, almond and plum, all of which adapt to town conditions, with pretty flowers in spring or early summer. Choose one of the smaller species (or a small form of one of the others): many a suburban garden suffers from an ornamental cherry or almond tree that has outgrown its site.

Trees that are grown in troughs or tubs will not achieve the same heights as those in open ground as restriction of their roots tends to have a Bonsai effect on them. It is a good idea to choose a tub with a removable side panel (many cube-shaped 'Versailles' tubs have them). This will enable you to remove and renew the soil around the roots occasionally, which is beneficial if the tree has been *in situ* for some years.

PLANTS FOR MINI-POOLS

You will need plants to aerate your pool and also some to decorate it. If possible, instal plants around the pool as well as in it; this will help to 'soften' the edges and give it a well-established look in a very short time.

A pond up to 1.5 square metres (16 sq ft) in size needs to have at least five oxygenating plants in it to keep the water sweet and clean. Permanently submerged plants such as *Elodea* and *Myriophyllum* will do this job efficiently, as will water starwort (*Callitriche stagnalis*), which also keeps algae at bay. It needs planting in heavy soil at the bottom of the pool, where it spreads to form a mat.

Apart from the familiar and well-loved water lilies (*Nymphaea*), there are a number of flowers for small ponds: two of the best are the water-violet or featherfoil (*Hottonia palustris*) and the water-soldier (*Stratiotes aloides*), which looks just like the spider plant, sending out runners with mini-plants on the end. The water soldier normally floats just under the surface of the water but comes up to bloom, when it produces white flowers in June.

Marginal plants to fringe your pond come into two categories: those that need some depth of water – about 150-450mm (6-18in) – to the shallow marginals which just want to paddle in the water to a depth of 100mm (4in) at the most. The water hawthorn (*Aponogeton distachyus*), with its starry white flowers, cotton grass with its attractive tufts, and marsh marigold (*Caltha palustris*), with its round, golden flowerheads, are all good choices.

Above *A traditional favourite for ornamental ponds is the lovely water lily* (Nymphaea). *This is one of the N. × laydekeri hybrids, which are among the best for small pools.*

Left Iris laevigata *is one of the prettiest waterside plants, thriving in water up to 150mm (6in) deep.*

Deep Marginal Plants	**Shallow Marginal Plants**
Aponogeton distachyus (water hawthorn)	*Alisma plantago-aquatica*
Orontium aquaticum (golden club)	*Butomus umbellatus*
Villarsia hennettii	*Iris laevigata*
	Mentha aquatica (water mint)
	Myosotis scorpioides

Above *These violet flowers identify 'Dr Mules', one of the best of the popular aubrietas.*

Right *Ericas (heaths) make attractive low-growing subjects for borders, raised beds or containers. These two are varieties of bell heather (E. cinerea).*

PERMANENT PLANTS FOR TUBS AND SMALL BEDS

With the right perennial plants installed in them, to act as a backdrop for other flowers, your tubs and flower beds can be in use all year round on the patio.

Aubrieta Low-growing, hardy evergreens that prefer a limy soil but are easy to grow. The flowers, which appear from March to June, are usually in the pink-purple colour range. *A. aurea* has leaves tinged with gold.

Buxus sempervirens 'Suffruticosus' (box) makes a good evergreen mini-hedge or can be trained into topiary. It will take shade and will grow to a maximum of 600mm (24in). 'Aurea' is a golden-leaved, slightly larger form.

Convallaria (lily-of-the-valley) Plants that like partial shade, they spread quickly and need thinning out from time to time. The waxy white, bell-like flowers appear in April or May.

Cryptomeria japonica 'Elegans Compacta' is a miniature form of the Japanese cedar with blue-green leaves that turn red-bronze in winter. It rarely reaches more than about 750mm (30in) high and wide.

Elaeagnus pungens 'Maculata' is a slow-growing evergreen with foliage boldly marked in gold. A useful mini-bush for a tub or raised bed.

Erica carnea (syn. *E. herbacea*; winter heath) One of several ericas that tolerates alkaline soils, it flowers in winter from December on and may keep in bloom until May. It rarely grows above 300mm (12in) in height.

Hebe (veronica) species also make useful evergreen mini-bushes bearing white flowers in summer. *H.* 'Autumn Glory' has purplish green leaves, *H.* 'Pagei' has light green leaves and is the smallest version, reaching about 300mm (12in).

Hedera (ivy) makes a marvellous evergreen trailer, climber or ground cover plant in tubs and raised beds. Common ivy (*H. helix*) comes in many variegated forms too, notably 'Goldheart', which has small dark leaves with gold centres, and 'Glacier', with leaves variegated with silver grey, edged with white. *Juniperus communis* 'Compressa' is a dwarf juniper with attractive grey-green foliage which grows, very slowly, seldom more than 750mm (30in) high.

Lavandula angustifolia 'Munstead' A dwarf version of the traditional lavender which can be clipped to make an attractive edging or left as a small bush.

Lonicera nitida 'Baggesen's Gold' One of the evergreen honeysuckles, this useful plant has tiny golden leaves and can be clipped into topiary shapes if you wish.

Lysimachia nummularia (creeping jenny) A useful ground-covering plant which produces

Left *The 'Compressa' variety of common juniper (Juniperus communis) is no more than 600mm (2ft) high, and its columnar shape makes it an ideal subject for patio containers.*

Above *The lesser periwinkle (Vinca minor) makes a fine ground-cover plant. Its flowers bloom at intervals from spring to mid-autumn.*

yellow cup-shaped flowers in June and July. *Rosa* Miniature roses come now in many different forms – there are even climbing/trailing miniatures, none of which reach more than about 450mm (18in) high. If you plant these make sure that they are in a sunny position and that they have rich soil to grow in.

Saxifraga × urbium (London pride) Another useful inhabitant for a tub, this member of the saxifrage family prefers shade and produces masses of small pink flowers in early summer.

Senecio cineraria. Not always hardy in this country, it survives some winters in a sheltered spot and is invaluable for setting off colourful flowers late on. Its leaves, covered with woolly hairs, have an attractive silvery look and are deeply indented. It reaches a height of about 600mm (24in).

Vinca minor (lesser periwinkle) makes useful evergreen ground-cover for larger tubs and raised beds. It will also trail over the sides of containers. It has pretty blue cup-shaped flowers in summer and can be relied upon to spread to about 450mm (18in). Varieties are available, some with white or purple flowers; some with variegated foliage.

SHRUBS FOR TUBS

Always be generous with the depth of a container for a shrub or small tree if it is to stay there for any length of time. The plants will be less likely to dry out and will thrive given plenty of room. Remember that shrubs in tubs under the shade of trees or beside walls may not get their full share of rain, so check them and water them regularly.

Azaleas (Rhododendron) come in both evergreen and deciduous hybrids. Superb deciduous forms include the Ghent, Mollis and Knaphill hybrids; evergreens include the Kaempferi, Kurume and Vuyk groups. *Camellia × williamsii* 'Donation' has glossy evergreen foliage and large soft pink flowers resembling open roses. The Japanese quince (*Chaenomeles × superba*) makes a fine wall shrub. Several excellent varieties are available with spring flowers in shades of red, pink or white. Lawson's cypress (*Chamaecyparis lawsoniana*) makes a good tub conifer if you choose the right (slow-growing) cultivar. Names to look out for include 'Ellwood's Gold', with grey-blue foliage with yellow shoot-tips; and 'Minima Aurea', pyramid-shaped, which has branches edged with gold, and is excellent for a small container.

Deutzia × elegantissima, a most elegant hybrid, has scented, rose-tinted white flowers on arching branches; look for variety 'Rosealind'. *Elaeagnus pungens* 'Maculata', a dense, spreading evergreen, with silvery flowers in autumn, has variegated evergreen foliage splashed with yellow. *Escallonia* 'Donard Radiance' is a pretty shrub with attractive pink flowers in early summer and large, glossy leaves.

One of the finest of the camellias, the 'Donation' variety of C. × williamsii *will grow to a height of 2.5m (8¼ft), with flowers as much as 100mm (4in) across.*

Above *The Hortensia hydrangeas bear flower-heads that are more than 150mm (6in) in diameter.*

Left *The 'Rosealind' variety of* Deutzia × elegantissima *grows up to 1.5m (5ft) high and wide.*

Above *Hybrids of the pretty mock orange* (Philadelphus) *grow to 2m (6½ft); the delightfully fragrant flowers come out in June and July.*

Fuchsia are well-known patio plants, but unless you pick the hardy varieties the tub will have to overwinter indoors. Outdoor varieties include 'Alice Hoffman', Corallina', 'Mrs Popple', 'Tennessee Waltz'; 'Tom Thumb' is a good miniature. *Hydrangea macrophylla* produces large panicles of paper-like pink, blue or white flowers. Acid soil in the tub produces blue flowers; chalky soil produces pink ones. Some dwarf forms are available. The mock-orange (*Philadelphus*) is a pleasant shrub to have near the house; the white flowers are scented like orange-blossom. Good hybrids include 'Beau-clerk' (single flowers), 'Belle Etoile' (single), and 'Manteau d'Hermine' (double).

The modern compact rhododendron hybrids are fully hardy and most are not more than 1.2m (4ft) high and wide. Examples include 'Bluebird' (violet-blue flowers), 'Scarlet Wonder' (scarlet). Sweet-scented, grey-foliaged rosemary (*Rosmarinus officinalis*) is a useful evergreen to have around the patio, especially if you have installed a barbecue. The slow-growing yew (*Taxus baccata*) takes well to topiary – a bird, bear or other small beast would make an amusing decoration for the patio.

FLOWERS AND FOLIAGE FOR TUBS AND RAISED BEDS

Plants which give colour just where it is wanted are a valuable asset around the patio. So are those with leaves of an interesting shape or texture which act as a foil to summer bedding flowers and, in most cases, provide some interest all year round.

Acanthus (bear's breech) are attractive foliage plants with tall spikes of flowers varying from lavender to white. The dwarf varieties of yarrow (*Achillea*) are good for rockeries or containers. *A. chrysocoma* has woolly grey-green leaves and yellow flowers; *A. clavenae* has white daisy-like blooms. *Adonis amurensis* is a pretty, low-growing plant with bright yellow flowers in February-March and matt-green, fern-like foliage; it prefers a partially shaded situation and is good to underplant among taller plants.

Aethionema pulchellum is a compact plant with attractive dark pink flowers. Basically a rockery plant, it grows well in tubs and window-boxes. African lilies (*Agapanthus*) are showy specimen plants for tubs and small borders; they can also be grown in a box alongside a terrace. Choose the hardy *A. inapertus*, which has deep violet-blue flowers. *Agave* makes a marvellous foliage plant, especially if you want a tropical look in a tub or a border. *A. americana* 'Marginata' (syn. 'Variegata') has narrow sword-like leaves edged with gold; *A. victoriae-reginae* forms a pompon head like a cactus. They are not completely hardy and are best brought indoors during the winter.

Lady's mantle (*Alchemilla*) is another handsome foliage plant that is often used for flower arrangements and which looks good in a tub. *A. mollis* has star-shaped yellow-green flowers and will self-seed. *Allium giganteum* is a decorative form of onion which makes a good feature plant in a small bed. It forms deep lilac flower heads which can be dried for decoration indoors. The Peruvian lily (*Alstroemeria*) is a striking plant with flowers somewhere between those of orchids and gladioli in appearance. *A. aurantiaca* has flowers ranging from yellow to scarlet.

Alyssum is a reliable carpeting plant for tubs, dry-stone walls and rockeries. *A. argenteum* has bright yellow flowers; *A. maritimum* (strictly *Lobularia maritima*) has white or lilac flowers and is low-growing. The scarlet pimpernel

Left *On a fully paved patio a long, low trough can be planted up like a mixed border.*

Below *The* Agave victoriae-reginae, *one of the smaller of its kind, makes a fine specimen plant for the patio.*

(*Anagallis arvensis*) is a pretty, prostrate plant with small red flowers. It is an annual, but it will generally self-seed for the next year. *A. arvensis* 'Caerulea' is a form with dark blue flowers. The Japanese windflower (*Anemone × hybrida*) is an attractive large-flowered anemone which blooms from August to October. The variety 'Queen Charlotte' has attractive semi-double pink flowers.

There are many forms of chamomile (*Anthemis*), ranging from the carpeting (non-flowering) *Anthemis nobilis* 'Treneague' to the yellow or ox-eye chamomile (*A. tinctoria*). One of the most decorative varieties is *A. sancti-johannis*, with bright orange flowers. The columbine (*Aquilegia*) makes delicate, attractive flowers to grow in a small space. *A. longissima* has pretty yellow flowers on slender stems; *A. bertolonii* is a small Alpine version that looks, at a distance, rather like edelweiss; *A. vulgaris*, which comes in many colours, is the best-known columbine.

The thrifts (*Armeria*) are useful plants to edge a tub or go between paving stones. They produce hummocks of spiky grass-like leaves and pink flower heads. There are several different species, ranging from *A. caespitosa*, which grows only 50-75mm (2-3in) high, to *A. maritima* which can reach 300mm (12in). *Artemisia* are grown for their silvery white leaves; they are useful plants to mix with colourful annual flowers. *A. stelleriana* (dusty miller) has leaves that are almost white, and yellow flowers; *A. gnaphalodes* has woolly white leaves. *Asperula suberosa* is a small semi-training plant (a relative of sweet woodruff) that has a profusion of pretty pink flowers and white, hairy leaves.

Aster is a large genus, best known for the Michaelmas daisies. Asters have flowers in purples, blues, reds, and pinks. The smallest is *A. alpinus*, which has purple-blue flowers with orange-yellow centres. If growing true Michaelmas daisies (such as *A. novi-belgii*), pick a dwarf variety such as 'Audrey', 'Lady in Blue', or 'Professor Kippenburg'.

Begonias are a great standby for tubs, hanging baskets, and window-boxes. The fibrous-rooted *B. semperflorens* has small flowers in red, pink, or white, and leaves ranging from glossy green to bronze-purple. The tuberous-rooted begonias of the Pendula group (*B.* × *tuberhybrida*) make good trailers for hanging baskets; examples include 'Dawn' (yellow), 'Golden Shower', 'Lou Anne' (pink), and 'Red Cascade' (scarlet).

The pot marigold (*Calendula officinalis*) is the true marigold, with its double daisy-like flowers in bright orange (though you can also get versions with creamy, apricot, even pink flowers) and growing to a height of 500mm (20in) or more. 'Kelmscott Giant Orange' is a good one to choose; 'Pacific Beauty' will give you a mixture of colours. Their long flowering season lasts from the last days of spring to the first frosts of autumn.

Callirhoes are basically rock-garden plants; they are dwarf trailers with simple bowl-shaped, mauve-red flowers produced in mid-summer. *C. involucrata* is a good version to choose. Good dwarf annuals are available in bedding strains of the China aster (*Callistephus chinensis*). Of slightly larger forms, Lilliput Mixed, with flowers ranging from white to crimson, is particularly suitable for small tubs; it blooms from mid-summer to early autumn.

Indian shot (*Canna* × *generalis*) bears showy, tropical-looking flowers and makes a good specimen in tubs. Good cultivars are 'Orange Perfection' and 'President', which has bright scarlet flowers. Chionodoxas are good spring-flowering bulbs to go under permanent plantings in a tub, Glory-of-the-snow (*C. luciliae*) has light blue flowers with white centres. *C. sardensis* has deeper-blue flowers.

Chrysanthemums contribute a huge range of very reliable flowers for tubs and boxes. Look for the attractive alpine species, *C. alpinum*, for

very-small-scale planting; it rarely grows taller than 150mm (6in). It has white daisy-like flowers in July and August. *C. carinatum*, a North African annual, is much taller – up to 600mm (24in) – and has very colourful flowers over a longer season.

The hardy outdoor forms of the cyclamen, a very popular plant, are smaller and much more delicate-looking than indoor types. One of the best is *C. coum*, with pink flowers in winter.

Dahlias are available in a vast variety, ranging from those with pompon heads to simple versions almost like huge daisies. For small areas choose the dwarf varieties of bedding dahlias: a good example is 'Early Bird', which has semi-double flowers in pink, yellow, orange, and deep red. Pinks and carnations (*Dianthus*) are real cottage-garden flowers, including sweet william (*D. barbatus*). *D. alpinus*, which is basically a rock-garden plant, is useful if space is limited. Miniature versions of the so-called Modern pinks include 'Bombardier', which has red flowers, and 'Fay', which has mauve flowers.

Left *Glory-of-the-snow* (Chionodoxa) *makes a good underplanting bulb for tubs; its flowers come out in March to late April.*

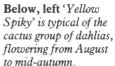

Below, left '*Yellow Spiky*' *is typical of the cactus group of dahlias, flowering from August to mid-autumn.*

Plants for sheltered spots

Agapanthus
Agave americana
Amaryllis belladonna
Ballota pseudodictamnus
Berberidopsis
Buddleia fallowiana
Callistemon
Calocephalus
Camellia sasanqua
Campsis
Centaurea gymnocarpa
Chrysanthemum ptarmacaefolium
Cistus
Clerodendron
Clianthus
Crinum
Convolvulus cneorum
Dimorphotheca
Gazania
Hebe hybrids
Helichrysum petiolatum
Indigofera
Jasminum officinalis
Lapageria
Mesembryanthemum
Mutisia
Nerine
Nerium oleander
Passiflora caerulea
Piptanthus
Senecio cineraria
Sparaxis
Teucrium fruticans
Tigridia
Tropaeolum tuberosum
Yucca

Above *Leopard's banes (this one is* Doronicum plantagineum*) grow to about 600mm (2ft) and flower in June.*

Leopard's banes (*Doronicum*) are daisy-like flowers which bloom early and, if dead-headed regularly, will often produce a second flush in the autumn. *D. columnae* has single golden yellow flowers. Fleabane (*Erigeron*) has daisy-like flowerheads in pinks, blues, and yellows. *E aureus* is typical and bears yellow flowers about 25mm (1in) across in June and July. The Californian poppy (*Eschscholzia californica*) produces masses of orange or yellow flowers. A good dwarf species is *E. caespitosa*.

Above *The annual and perennial forms of sea lavender (*Limonium*) flower in late summer to early autumn; the annuals, especially varieties of* L. sinuatum, *make good everlasting flowers.*

Crane's-bills (*Geranium*) are true geraniums – not to be confused with pelargoniums – and they too make good plants for a tub. They have pretty pink, white or blue flowers and lacy leaves. *G. dalmaticum* is an almost alpine species that makes a broad cushion of light pink flowers. Avens (*Geum*) are good in display beds or, in the case of alpine varieties, in small window-boxes and hanging baskets. *G. montanum* and *G. reptans* are excellent dwarf versions, their yellow flowers followed by interesting silvery seed heads.

Godetias are hardy annuals with double or single flowers. *G. grandiflora* is one of the most attractive, with rose-purple blooms; its cultivar 'Azalea-flowered Mixed' has frilled petals. St John's worts (*Hypericum*) are useful yellow flowers for a raised bed. Rose-of-Sharon (*H. calycinum*) is the most commonly planted species, but *H. patulum* 'Hidcote' is a more attractive plant if you have the space for it. St John's worts give berries and coloured foliage in the autumn. Candytufts (*Iberis*) are good plants for town gardens since they stand up well to atmospheric pollution. *I. amara* has pink-carmine flowers.

Statice, or sea lavenders (*Limonium*), make delightful, ideal 'everlasting' flowers when they have done their duty in summer. Attractive Mediterranean annuals, they come in many different colours. *L. sinuatum* and its cultivars are best if you want the dried flowers. Toadflaxes (*Linaria alpina*) make pretty plants to put among paving stones. They have purple snapdragon-like flowers.

Bells of Ireland (*Moluccella laevis*) is an unusual plant with curious green flowers that make an interesting effect if put in a tub. It looks good if mixed with white flowers; and the flower-heads can be dried for winter decoration. *Nemesia strumosa* is a useful half-hardy plant for a mixed display. Choose the cultivar 'Carnival Mixed', a dwarf version with flowers in various vivid colours. Poppies *(Papaver)* are excellent in raised beds and tubs, especially when mixed with plants with silvery foliage. If you are worried about height, choose the alpine poppy *(P. alpinum)*, which is available with flowers of white, yellow, red, and orange. The Iceland poppy *(P. nudicaule)* has flowers with petals like tissue paper and is particularly attractive.

Phlox drummondii is an annual with flowers of pink, purple, lavender, red, and white. *Salvia splendens* makes a good standby if you need a splash of colour. Its cultivar 'Blaze of Fire' has particularly brilliant flowers of bright scarlet. Lamb's tongue *(Stachys lanata)* is grown for its distinctive woolly foliage, which makes a good foil to colourful bedding plants. Its spikes of purple blooms open in midsummer. Speedwell *(Veronica)* includes a group of alpines useful as ground-cover plants, ranging from *V. cinerea*, with pink flowers, to the carpet-like bright-blue-flowered *V. filiformis*.

Left *Bells-of-Ireland* (Moluccella laevis) *has intriguing green flowers. Growing to a height of 600mm (2ft), it makes a good companion for white-flowered plants.*

Below *By contrast, the brilliant oriental poppy* (Papaver orientale), *a perennial, often looks best with foliage plants for company. It flowers in May-June.*

BEDDING PLANTS FOR BOXES, BASKETS & TUBS

Colour is what you want when choosing display plants for boxes and hanging baskets. Never be afraid to experiment: unusual combinations like hot oranges, reds and yellows can look quite spectacular; so can the cool colours, the blues mixed with green. Or, for a very sophisticated look, try a one-tone arrangement like white. Switch your colour schemes around from year to year to vary the look of your patio; co-ordinate coloured boxes to match your living-room curtains to add to the effect of an outdoor room.

Ageratum houstonianum is a fluffy blue, pink or white flower from Mexico. 'Blue Chip' and 'Fairy Pink' are long-flowering varieties. *Alyssum* perennials make good, compact flowers in almost all colours of the rainbow. Cut back well after flowering to keep them in shape. (The alyssum annuals are now classified under *Lobularia*.)

Snapdragons (*Antirrhinum*), notably the dwarf bedding varieties, are available in many colours. Planted out in May they will produce a succession of blooms throughout summer and into autumn. Another reliable, long-flowering

Two invaluable small-flowered trailers for hanging baskets are alyssums (here in white but available in pinks and purples) and lobelias (blue here but also common in light blue, red and mixtures).

Left *Another favourite container plant is the fibrous-rooted begonia* (B. semperflorens), *available in reds, pinks and whites. It flowers from June to October.*

Below *The slipper-flower* (Calceolaria integrifolia) *blooms from July to September. Slightly tender, it needs a sunny, sheltered spot.*

favourite *Begonia semperflorens* – the fibrous-rooted type – comes in many colours, from white through cream to deep reds and pinks, with leaves that are green or bronze.

Slipper-flowers (*Calceolaria*), often grown as indoor plants, have distinctive spotted, pouch-shaped flowers in reds and yellows. They can be planted out after the last frosts and will go on through the summer. The China aster (*Callistephus chinensis*) has many cultivars with flowers that vary from those looking like a daisy to complicated chrysanthemum-like blooms in pinks, blues, and white.

Star-of-Bethlehem (*Campanula isophylla*), a relative of the Canterbury bell, can be grown in a container in a warm, sheltered position, where it rewards you with heart-shaped leaves and starry, bell-like flowers over a long period from late spring to autumn.

The dwarf varieties of cockscomb (*Celosia argentea*) are best for patio plantings. Forms such as 'Golden Feather', 'Fiery Feather', 'Lilliput' Mixed', or 'Jewel Box' have plume-like flowers in reds and yellows and bloom throughout summer. Cornflowers (*Centaurea*) come in other shades than cornflower blue – deep scarlet, for instance. Cornflowers are best grown *in situ* from seed. Choose *C. imperialis* for good compact patio plants. A compact form of another traditional favourite is the Siberian wallflower (*Cheiranthus* × *allionii*). Two good varieties are 'Golden Queen' and 'Orange Queen'.

Right *Busy-lizzie* (Impatiens wallerana) *is one of the best and longest-flowering of the bedding plants, a particular favourite for hanging baskets. Many colours are available; this vermilion form is 'Blitz'.*

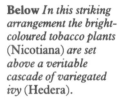

Below *In this striking arrangement the bright-coloured tobacco plants* (Nicotiana) *are set above a veritable cascade of variegated ivy* (Hedera).

Marguerite, or Paris daisy (*Chrysanthemum frutescens*), is a bushy perennial which produces abundant white daisies with yellow centres. An ideal plant to train as a flowering standard in an ornamental pot, if given plenty of sunlight it will bloom from spring to autumn.

Cinerarias (strictly *Senecio* species) are very popular bedding plants for window-boxes, pro-ducing masses of close-packed flowers in the spring. *Senecio cruentus* (syn. *Cineraria cruenta*) 'Gem Mixed' is a good variety, with flowers (some bicoloured) in pink, red, lilac and purple. Stocks (*Matthiola*) are cottage-garden flowers that thrive in boxes and baskets. The night-scented stock (*M. bicornis*), bears perfumed lavender flowers; other varieties come in pinks, blues and white. Plant it in pots or baskets near house windows to enjoy its lovely evening fragrance.

The Livingstone daisy (*Mesembryanthemum criniflorum*, syn. *Dorotheanthus bellidiformis*) is a tiny succulent plant that likes plenty of sun, and produces rich pink and orange flowers. *Nemesia strumosa*, a half-hardy annual, makes compact plants with large flowers in a variety of colours: 'Suttons Mixed' is in red-orange tones; 'Blue Gem' has blue flowers. Tobacco plants (*Nicotiana*) are grown as much for their fragrance as for their looks. Flowers come in white, sharp yellow-green, and reds.

Pelargoniums are great window-box and hanging-basket standbys. Choose the zonal varieties for height and the ivy-leaved varieties for climbers or trailers. Look out for scented-leaved varieties, too: their flowers are unremark-able, but the fine-toothed leaves are fragrant and attractive.

The petunia (*Petunia × hybrida*) is one of the showiest window-box plants with white, pink, red or blue flowers. It can be had in standard, dwarf, or trailing varieties and is very good for hanging baskets as well as for boxes. It blooms throughout the summer and on into September. The polyanthus, or polyantha primroses (*Primula*), are hardy perennials available in a variety of delightful colours that will light up the patio in late spring. They can be left as permanent occupants of pots and tubs provided that they are divided from time to time after flowering.

Salvia species are colourful plants with bright red spike-like flowers that are good for formal boxes. Mother-of-thousands (*Saxifraga stolonifera*, syn *S. sarmentosa*), often grown as a houseplant, can also be grown out of doors in summer. It is liked for its colourful leaves – green tinged with pink and silver, with plantlets on runners.

Among several types of marigold, choose the French form (*Tagetes patula*) if you want a low-growing plant; the African variety (*T. erecta*) is somewhat taller. Delicately scented, the African marigold has pompon blooms in pale yellows through to red; the French marigold has single or double flowers in the same colours.

Verbena peruviana, a low-growing perennial that needs shelter in the winter, bears brilliant scarlet, star-shaped flowers in great profusion in summer. Heartsease (*Viola tricolor*) is a pretty low-grower which comes in a wide variety of colours and blooms in mid-summer. *Zinnia elegans* resembles a chrysanthemum; the compact cultivar 'Lilliput', about 250mm (10in) tall, is the best form for boxes and baskets. Even smaller is 'Thumbelina', which rarely exceeds 150mm (6in). Both varieties have multi-coloured flowers that bloom from June to September.

Two other plants for a long-flowering season: petunias (here mainly reds, purple, lilac and white) and pelargoniums (pink, at top).

145

PART 3

GARDENING UNDER GLASS

A greenhouse greatly extends your year-round range of gardening activities. This section explains how to choose a greenhouse to suit your particular needs, what equipment you will require, and how to grow a variety of flowering and foliage plants, fruit and vegetables in it. The section includes detailed advice on plant propagation, combating pests and diseases, and devising programmes of activity enabling you to raise flowers and crops throughout the year.

GREENHOUSES AND CONSERVATORIES

The word 'greenhouse' describes a building used for a wide variety of horticultural purposes, including propagation, raising bedding plants, producing food crops, protecting tender plants over winter, and cultivating ornamentals. The word 'conservatory' on the other hand defines a place where decorative plants are displayed to please the eye.

Most conservatories are designed to be attractive structurally, both inside and out, and to be pleasant places where people can sit and relax. Ideally, they should be attached to a dwelling with a communicating door for easy access. They generally take the form of a lean-to. However, an ordinary free-standing greenhouse can be used instead in many cases.

Both greenhouses and conservatories can give enormous pleasure, and a greenhouse can also be a sound financial investment, soon paying back its cost in the form of produce. The weather protection it provides enables a vast range of plants from all over the world to be grown. Greenhouse gardening is a fascinating hobby that can be enjoyed all year round by both young and old.

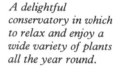

A delightful conservatory in which to relax and enjoy a wide variety of plants all the year round.

A well-organized greenhouse is a source of both profit and pleasure.

TEMPERATURES

Much can be done without any artificial heating whatsoever. The protection from weather extremes that an unheated greenhouse gives is adequate for many plants and a glass structure traps enough free solar radiation to be warmer than outside for most of the winter. Providing enough heat to keep conditions frost free greatly widens your scope, and a minimum of about 4–7°C (40–45°F), 'cool house' temperatures, enables many subtropical plants to be grown. Temperatures above this can become rather expensive to maintain and are best provided for only small compartments, such as propagators, when required. Most of the plants dealt with in this book do not need high temperatures and are within the growing ability of most people.

SIZE AND STRUCTURE

Many people prefer to buy a prefabricated structure rather than build their own. Unless you are reasonably skilled in construction, this is by far the wisest procedure. There are now many types, sizes, and shapes available in a selection of materials. So it should not be difficult to suit individual requirements. The most popular size for a practical home greenhouse is about 3m × 2.4m (10ft × 8ft). However, if you can meet the expense, it may be worth buying something a bit larger, particularly if you do not plan to heat it; many almost hardy plants can become very large and will soon cry out for space. If you do plan to heat it, estimate the cost of fuel before buying. Some greenhouse designs can be extended by simply adding extra units as required. This is a feature to look out for when buying. Partitions with communicating doors can also be fitted to some. This means you can, for example, heat only a small section for greater economy, or provide a special environment for a particular group of plants.

Always buy from a reputable and, preferably, long-established firm. There are plenty of cheap greenhouses on the market, but they are likely to be a very poor investment. It is advisable to consult your local authority regarding planning permission before buying. This is particularly important if the structure is to be attached to a dwelling; there may be building regulations to comply with and often a low rate will be demanded. For small greenhouses, especially if they can be described as portable – that is, easily taken down and re-erected – there is rarely any regulation or rate requirement. Also check whether buildings erected on ground that is not your freehold become the legal property of the landlord.

GREENHOUSE DESIGN

Greenhouses come in a great many shapes and sizes, all with their own advantages and disadvantages. If you are thinking about buying one, it is a good idea to become familiar with the main types available, so that you end up with one that meets your requirements.

TRADITIONAL

This is the 'barn' or 'tent' shape. It forms a square or rectangle, with vertical sides and has a span roof with a central ridge. This design is still the most practical and allows the maximum utilization of available space. In some examples the ridge can be set off-centre to meet site requirements. This is usually known as three-quarter span. Nowadays it is not a common feature.

The roof should always have a good slope to shed any collected dirt, dead leaves and snow, for example. This applies to all greenhouse designs.

TUNNEL

This design is technically called 'curvilinear' and, with the exception of those made of plastic, is built of six or more panes of glass set in a continuous curve to give a 'tunnel' shape. For reasons described under Dutch light, this model allows excellent light entry, but suffers from the same disadvantages regarding lack of headroom and poor use of space.

CIRCULAR

These structures have at least six sides arranged to form a circle. They are by no means new – the shape was a favourite in Victorian times for conservatories. They were usually highly ornamental and there are models available today that will create the same atmosphere. A small circular greenhouse could be of special benefit to a disabled person, since most of it is easily accessible without much physical movement.

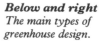

Below and right
The main types of greenhouse design.

Traditional

Dutch light

Plastic Tunnel

Circular

DUTCH LIGHT

This design has sloping sides. The idea is to set the glass as near as possible at right angles to the sun's rays so that light has a minimum thickness of glass to travel through and there is consequently minimum absorption. A pane of glass can absorb up to 20 per cent of light passing through it, even though it appears perfectly transparent to the eye. The Dutch light shape is of particular use to those growing winter crops, as the slightly increased light levels may give earlier maturation. However, sloping sides can be a nuisance: they make working close to the sides inconvenient and reduce headroom, and it may not be so easy to fit in taller plants or make as much use of the floor area as in traditional houses. Certainly, designs with sides set at a great angle should be viewed very critically.

Slanting sides can give greater stability to a structure, and this design should be given special consideration where the site is very windy or exposed to gales.

To the professional grower, the term 'Dutch light' also means a framed glass unit of specific size, used to make up frames or other structures. They are rarely employed by home gardeners.

DOME

The dome shape is a fairly recent introduction. It is made up of many triangular panes of glass supported by a strong metal framework. The effect is quite striking and futuristic. Light entry is excellent and the same advantages and disadvantages described under Dutch light apply. Better headroom around the sides can be obtained by mounting a dome on a low base wall. Domes make delightful conservatories and sun traps, but it's doubtful whether there's much point in using them for down-to-earth plant growing.

HIGH SOUTH WALL

This is another new introduction. It consists of two slanting sides of different heights, with a sloping roof between them. The taller of the sides is intended to face south or the direction with most light. Whether this has any advantage over conventional shapes is a matter of opinion.

LEAN-TO

This is a popular design with numerous special applications, and it's a favourite for conservatories, garden rooms, and sun rooms. It's also particularly suited to the cultivation of crops such as grapes and other fruits which can be trained against the rear wall. Lean-tos are usually set against brick walls at the side of a house or garage, but in some cases a tall weather-proof boarded fence would suffice. There is also a model which is half greenhouse and half timber garden shed. When set against a substantial wall, the greenhouse stays warmer overnight. Lean-tos are always the cheapest design to heat artificially.

Lean-tos can incorporate Dutch light sloping sides and such features as curved shapes and base walls. The type of environment offered by a lean-to, regarding light and warmth, depends on orientation (see page 153). Lean-to home extensions are rarely suitable as conservatories.

Dome

Lean-to

High south wall

Base wall

BASE WALL OR GLASS TO GROUND

Some greenhouse designs have timber-board or brick bases. Various forms of composition sheeting are also used, but asbestos is becoming less favoured for safety reasons. Base walls help to conserve warmth when a greenhouse is heated, but they obstruct sunlight and cut off a free supply of solar heat. A base-walled greenhouse is known as a 'plant house' and is usually fitted with staging to about the height of the wall for convenient working with potted plants. Space under the staging can be employed for those plants demanding less light. There are also designs with only partial base walling, the side admitting most light being left glass to ground. Some manufacturers produce models with removable base panels. These can be clipped on in the winter to conserve heat and removed in the summer months. Generally, a glass-to-ground house is the most versatile because of the amount of light admitted. It is easy to provide shade when wanted but no simple matter artificially to match the intensity of daylight. When a framework is designed to fit on to a brick or concrete base wall, it is best to have the base built by a professional bricklayer unless you are reasonably skilled.

SPECIAL DESIGNS

For some groups of plants, and for certain growing purposes, special designs of greenhouse are available. Some of the designs already mentioned would be suitable for some of these purposes. A glass-to-ground house is ideal for cacti and other light lovers, such as tomato plants and carnations. For perpetual flowering carnations, special carnation houses are made which give plenty of light, adequate height, and efficient ventilation. Base-wall greenhouses can be kept warmer and are hence suited to all particularly tender subjects, such as orchids and tropical pot plants. They are also useful for propagation needing moderate

warmth. Designs with a base wall fitted with staging on one side, and glass-to-ground on the other, to accommodate tall light lovers, such as tomatoes, allow a wide range of plants to be grown happily in the same greenhouse. For alpines there are special greenhouses with plenty of ventilation and high staging to bring the dainty plants nearer the eye. These examples emphasize the importance of deciding what to grow before choosing a greenhouse. However, a purpose-designed greenhouse is not usually necessary. For example, various orchids, alpines, and other specialist plants will normally be quite happy in a mixed greenhouse if treated with reasonable care.

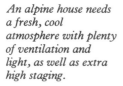

An alpine house needs a fresh, cool atmosphere with plenty of ventilation and light, as well as extra high staging.

CONSERVATORY DESIGN

Many of the basic comments made about greenhouse design also apply to conservatories. It has been pointed out that the lean-to is the favourite shape. If it can be sited where there is a direct communicating door giving easy access, a conservatory becomes almost an extension of the house. A design to blend architecturally with the dwelling is usually desirable. There are firms that can make reproduction ornamental structures if this would be more fitting.

Many ordinary 'greenhouse' lean-tos can be used as conservatories. Some people try to convert garden-room or home-extension buildings to conservatory use. But many of these have flattish roofs made of plastic which tend to collect dirt, dead leaves and the like, and need constant cleaning. They also exclude too much light, which limits the range of plants you can grow successfully.

If your house is a bungalow, be careful to check that any prefabricated structure you propose to buy is not too tall. The choice is often limited by the height of the house.

Lean-tos, designed for conservatory use, often have extra-wide sliding doors, allowing easy access to the garden. This is useful if you intend bringing in garden furniture or using the space as a patio extension. Some designs have partial or complete double glazing, others have curved glass pane eaves, an attractive feature which is now becoming popular. Structures with *toughened* glass are also available. This would be a wise choice where there are small children or elderly or infirm people. Where a conservatory is to be used for sitting out, as a place of relaxation, a design with a base wall may be preferred as it gives more privacy. The best conservatory design for a particular site is also, to some extent, governed by the direction in which it is to face (see page 9).

CHOICE OF SITE

GREENHOUSE ORIENTATION

A square or rectangular greenhouse is best sited with its ridge, or length, running as near as possible from east to west. This gives maximum entry of sunlight in winter, when the sun is low in the sky, and hence maximum solar heat. In summer it is only necessary to shade the south side.

LEAN-TO AND CONSERVATORY ORIENTATION

The environment in a lean-to is greatly influenced by the direction it faces. A southern aspect gives the warmest and brightest conditions. In summer, shade must be given, or the greenhouse used for only warmth- and sun-loving plants. A north-facing lean-to tends to be chilly in winter, and is generally shady, but provides perfect conditions for most popular decorative plants, which prefer cool conditions. An eastern aspect warms up rapidly as the sun rises. A westerly facing lean-to gives warm conditions overnight. How a lean-to is used, therefore, obviously depends on orientation, and common sense should be applied in making the best use of the environment provided.

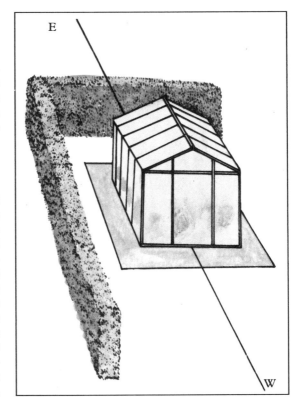

A rectangular greenhouse should be sited with the roof ridge running east-west and be sheltered from prevailing wind.

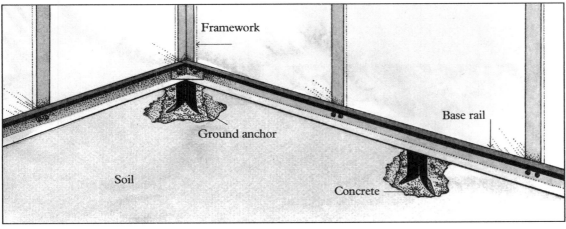

Ground-anchor system of foundation, in which alloy anchors bolted to the frame are concreted into the ground.

FOUNDATIONS

Suppliers of greenhouses usually recommend the most suitable form of foundation. When special kerbing is offered, this is a wise purchase. The ground must always be firm and level. Some modern alloy structures use a ground-anchor system. The frame is erected on firm level ground, and holes about the size of a bucket are dug at intervals around the base of the frame. Alloy anchors are then bolted on so that they drop down into the holes, which are then filled with concrete. This is the method most people find easiest to carry out. Another simple way to make a foundation for a *small* greenhouse, is to dig a trench about 150mm (6in) deep and 150mm (6in) wide to match the base size, and then fill it with a rather liquid concrete mix, which will find its own level.

It is worth taking trouble over constructing a sound foundation. If there is movement or subsidence after erection the glass may crack and the entire structure may have to be re-erected.

THE SITE

In a small garden there may be little choice of site for the greenhouse. For the convenience of running services, such as water, electricity or gas, a site near the dwelling house is desirable. An open, bright position should be chosen whenever possible. Avoid close proximity to large trees, especially evergreens. However, a wall, fence, or hedge, on the side of the prevailing wind and distant enough not to cast shade, makes a useful windbreak. Avoid wet and waterlogged ground, and places where frost is known to form.

STRUCTURAL MATERIALS

GLASS VERSUS PLASTIC

There is no doubt that, at present, glass is the best choice if a permanent long-lasting greenhouse is wanted. Glass has excellent solar heat trapping properties. You do not need to know much about the technicalities to appreciate this. Go into a glass greenhouse on a bright day when it's freezing outside and you will immediately feel the difference. In plastic structures the temperature can fluctuate widely with changes in weather conditions. With glass it's usually possible to maintain a steadier environment, and any artificial warmth provided is more easily retained.

Although some of the more rigid plastics are fairly long lived, none is as permanent as glass. Plastics have a tendency to become brittle with age, warp or crack, and some lose transparency or become tinted. Many plastics also look less aesthetically pleasing – they do not have that sparkling clarity. Plastics are also very soft compared with glass and soon scratch or become abraded by wind blown grit. Once dirt becomes ingrained, cleaning is difficult or impossible. There are a number of different types of plastic now used as glass substitutes. The best are, however, quite expensive.

A problem that arises with plastic is condensation. Water collects in droplets on a plastic surface and does not form a transparent film as it does on glass. The droplets may cut down light entry and raise humidity excessively. They can coalesce, producing annoying drips. Corrugated plastic roofs are particularly troublesome in this way. Despite this criticism, plastics do have their place and when used with common sense can be a better choice than glass in some cases.

An important property of plastic is safety. It may be a wise choice where there are small children or elderly people around or where structures are at risk from vandals. Plastics can also be used to partially 'glaze' a structure. They should be fitted where glass is most likely to break.

Plastic's lightness makes it easy to move and it is therefore useful in places such as a vegetable plot, where the entire structure can be moved as part of an annual crop rotation. Polythene houses are particularly useful in this respect. They are also convenient for crops that need little more than protection from the weather, or temporary accommodation.

Polythene and other plastics used for growing, must be of the ultra-violet light inhibited kind. This ensures maximum life when the plastic is exposed to sunlight. The letters 'U.V.I.' are what to look for. Even so, polythene is relatively short lived and must be replaced every two to three years. The best models are designed so that a new polythene cover can easily be slipped over a sturdy metal or timber frame.

Below A light, easily portable and storable plastic greenhouse fitted on a sturdy frame.

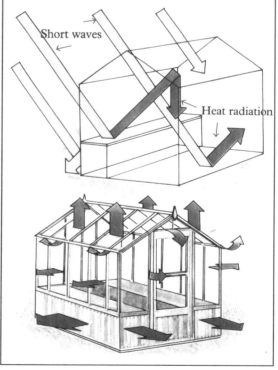

Top Solar heat. Glass admits short waves; these change to heat radiation which is trapped.
Bottom Heat escape. Arrow size reflects rate.

TIMBER FRAMEWORK

Timber is the traditional material and has been used for many years, but it has numerous disadvantages, such as its liability to rot or warp in a warm, damp greenhouse environment. However, timber has attractions: it's easy to work with, it's easily adapted and has a pleasing appearance. Its durability and the maintenance it needs depend on the quality and type of wood.

So-called western red cedar is reasonably priced, pleasing to the eye and remarkably resistant to rot, although *not* immune, as is sometimes suggested. It's advisable to have the framework chemically treated by the supplier before purchase, either with an anti-rot preparation or water repellant. All timber frames will need periodic painting or treating with preservative to keep them in good condition. For large greenhouses this can be inconvenient, expensive and time consuming. Be careful to use preservatives that are harmless to plants. *Never* use creosote.

Most traditional timber frames need linseed oil putty for glazing, although some special glazing mastics, which never set really hard, are to be preferred (see below). In some models the glazing bars are slotted and the glass merely slides in with no need of putty. This system produces a surprisingly watertight fit.

METAL FRAMEWORK

Metal greenhouses are often said to be 'cold' when compared with timber. It is true that metal is a much better heat conductor than timber but, since it's stronger, much less of it is necessary and more solar energy is therefore admitted. In fact, there is usually little thermal difference between timber and metal constructions except in houses with base walls, where there are large areas of unlagged metal. This should be strictly avoided. Large metal surfaces conduct away much valuable heat and become 'refrigerating' plates in frosty weather.

Although galvanized steel is sometimes employed, especially for the frames of polythene houses, the preference these days is for aluminium alloy. This material is extremely strong, and produces a framework that is light and easily transported. Erection is quick and simple, and dismantling, should the structure require removal at any time, is also easy. Aluminium alloy will not corrode, rust, rot, warp, or suffer attack by boring insects. It needs the minimum of maintenance and should retain its strength and quality for more than a lifetime.

If you don't care for the metallic appearance of alloy, you could buy a model in one of the newer white, green or bronze finishes. These look particularly good in conservatories. Unadorned metal will eventually form a dull grey coating that will protect the metal from further decay.

A timber-framed greenhouse of good quality wood can last well for many years but it will need some regular maintenance to keep it in good condition.

GLAZING

Glass should be of good quality and clear. For most general purpose glazing, it should be about 3mm thick (24oz/sq ft), but for some purposes it should be thicker or toughened, particularly where there is a greater need for safety, such as in conservatories. Where curved eaves are fitted, they should preferably be made from glass rather than plastic, although this is more expensive.

With a metal framework, linseed oil putty should *not* be used. A mastic that never sets hard, and hence allows expansion and contraction with temperature changes, should be employed, otherwise the glass is likely to crack. Many metal-framework houses now have glazing systems involving clips, strips, and plastic cushioning.

When glazing with putty or mastic, you need only bed the glass – do not put putty or mastic on top of the glazing bars as is done in domestic glazing. Also, you only need about 10mm (0.4in) of overlap between the panes. An excessive overlap collects dirt and algae.

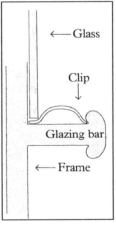

A cross-section of one patent glazing system.

FEATURES TO LOOK FOR WHEN CHOOSING A GREENHOUSE OR CONSERVATORY

General strength and rigidity of frame
Strong ridge bar
Plenty of ventilators
Built-in guttering
Sliding doors
Good foundations – either kerbing or the ground-anchor system
Provision for the addition of an extension or partition
Well-fitting doors and vents – no gaps that might admit draughts
The roof, especially that of a lean-to, should have a moderately steep slope
Lean-tos designed for bungalows should be of the correct height

EQUIPPING THE GREENHOUSE

Before a greenhouse is ready for use, a certain amount of basic equipment, such as ventilators and staging, has to be fitted. It is also worth thinking about automatic watering, and, if the greenhouse is to be used for raising tender plants, some form of heating.

VENTILATORS

The provision of ventilators is a matter that should be checked at the time of buying a greenhouse or conservatory; some suppliers consider them as extras. Most alloy greenhouses can be fitted with as many ventilators as you like. The basic number is usually included in the price. Always make sure that you have enough to ventilate the interior freely. It is better to have more than necessary; you do not have to open them all together, and a good distribution around the structure allows you to use them according to wind direction. The average 2.5 × 3m (8 × 10ft) greenhouse has at least two ventilators, one on the roof and one at the side; the number should be increased in proportion.

The conventional hinged ventilator with a stay

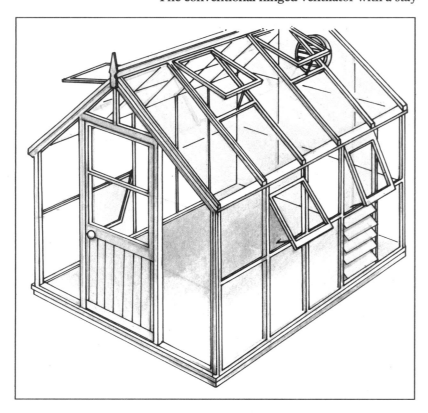

The ventilation system should be adjustable to give the optimum effect in all weather conditions. Automatic systems are also available.

bar is still used in most timber houses, but some designs incorporate sliding vents. Alloy structures are now being increasingly fitted with louvred vents but make sure these are tight fitting.

Ideally, the greenhouse ventilation system should be installed so that the roof ventilator is positioned as high up as possible, and the side ventilators are at ground level. This allows warm air to flow out freely at the top while cool air is drawn in from below. However, when there is staging or base walls, the vents are normally positioned just above them.

DOORS

Sliding doors are now often fitted to both timber and alloy structures, but the design of some leaves much to be desired. Metal doors can freeze up in winter and some have gaps which let in draughts. Doorways should be wide enough to allow free access for wheelbarrows or, in the case of conservatories, to admit plants in large pots or even garden furniture. Larger structures often have double doors. Sliding doors can be used as extra ventilators, since they are more easily adjusted than the hinged type. Where there are children, doors should be lockable for their safety.

GUTTERING

This is a highly desirable feature, since the constant shedding of rainwater around the perimeter of a greenhouse or conservatory can, in some cases, cause subsidence of the foundations because of the solvent action on the soil. The water can also seep inside, causing cold damp conditions. Many alloy structures are now equipped with built-in guttering, but, if not, plastic guttering is easy to fit to any type. The rainwater should be led away to a proper soakaway at a convenient distance from the greenhouse or conservatory or collected in a butt. This water can *not* be used for greenhouse irrigation. Today, we grow our plants in special composts which are clean and relatively sterile and to use rainwater collected from roofs is utter folly. It's a 'soup' of weed seeds, slimes, algae, pests, and diseases. Roofs can also collect weedkiller drift, which, even in trace amounts, can ruin greenhouse crops. (See page 163).

STAGING AND SHELVING

To make the most of space, some staging (benching) and shelving is needed. Sometimes this is at least partly supplied with a greenhouse and is included in the price, but it may be considered as an 'extra'. Timber greenhouses are often equipped with conventional slatted wooden staging. Alloy structures have metal supports topped with a variety of materials, including stout wire mesh on which pot plants are stood. In both cases shelving is generally of similar construction. Check that staging is strong enough to take a reasonable weight and that the greenhouse framework is similarly strong enough to support shelving laden with pots.

Staging should be covered with a layer of fine shingle or similar material to retain moisture during the summer months. This helps to maintain the right level of atmospheric humidity (see page 163). Slatted or mesh-topped staging will consequently have to be covered with polythene or some other suitable material to prevent the shingle falling through. Instead of shingle, capillary matting (see page 160) is often substituted. This holds moisture well and can be managed much more easily. In winter, it's desirable that any moisture-holding covering be removed to give dryer air conditions and encourage good air circulation. Slatted or mesh-topped staging can at this time be particularly beneficial.

Often it is useful to set staging along just one of the sides. A popular position is along the north side, leaving the south side free for tall plants. In many cases, modern staging is designed to be portable, and may also be adjustable for height and adaptable into different shapes and configurations. It is also available in tiered or stepped forms, for displaying plants in a conservatory, for example.

FRAMES

These are very useful adjuncts to the greenhouse, where they can relieve space for growing on the shorter plants. They can be used for the more hardy plants and for hardening off bedding plants (see page 195). Frames can be economically warmed with electric warming cables (page 159) and can be used inside the greenhouse for raising the temperature of a limited area. They make excellent large propagators treated in this fashion.

Whether they are used outdoors or in the greenhouse they are best situated with a northerly aspect, where they get little direct sunshine.

A frame, whether cold or heated, can be very useful both inside and outside the greenhouse. Many modern frames have all glass sides.

Above *Conventional slatted wooden staging and shelving. The staging should be covered in summer to help maintain the level of humidity.*

SERVICES

Electricity, water, and natural gas are all very useful in the greenhouse. In all cases the work of installation should be done in consultation with the authorities concerned and by professional contractors. Electricity is very useful for operating gadgets as well as for lighting and may be used for heating. Special fittings designed for safety in damp greenhouse conditions are available. A nearby supply of clean mains water, which can be used for automatic watering if desired, is also worthwhile. Natural gas is now becoming an important fuel for greenhouse heating.

CONSERVATION AND COST

The cost of raising the temperature of an average-sized greenhouse or conservatory to somewhere between frost free and 10°C (50°F) should not be prohibitively expensive. There are many ways in which heating costs can be kept to a minimum. A bright site will ensure maximum free solar heat. Shelter from excessive wind also cuts heat loss. It's essential to eliminate all sources of draught, such as gaps in the structure, ill fitting doors, vents, and glass. Except in some conservatory designs, double glazing is either very expensive or impractical for certain technical reasons. Lining with polythene is a simple and inexpensive way to achieve insulation that is almost as good. Clear polythene film, or preferably 'bubble' plastic which is sold specially for the purpose, will prevent at least 40 to 50 per cent of heat loss. It must be put up so that it encloses about 20 to 30mm (0.75 to 1.2in) of static air between the glass and the plastic. Special devices are available for fitting the plastic to metal framework, but on timber houses drawing pins can be used.

ASSESSING HEAT REQUIREMENTS

When installing heating equipment bear in mind that it must have a heat output to match heat loss when outside conditions are coldest. This can be roughly calculated from the size of the structure, the type and surface area of construction materials used, the minimum interior temperature desired, and the lowest outside temperature expected. Given these figures, suppliers of greenhouse heaters will recommend equipment with the most suitable rating in terms of British thermal units per hour, or wattage, in the case of electricity. It is most unwise to buy heaters without making this check first.

ELECTRICAL HEATING

This used to be considered expensive, but it must be remembered that there is virtually no waste and it involves the minimum of attention, and there is absolutely no contamination of the greenhouse atmosphere, which means ventilation, and therefore loss of heat, can be reduced considerably. Non-flued paraffin- and gas-heaters sometimes produce fumes, and there is always condensation and excessive humidity owing to the water vapour produced on the combustion of fuel. With these heaters, some ventilation must be constantly provided, to keep the air fresh and admit oxygen for the fuel's combustion. This means some waste of heat is inevitable, and therefore the fuel does not work out as cheap as might be supposed.

Electric fan heaters are very popular and give excellent distribution of warmed air. However, be sure to install a model in which the fan *and* the heater are both controlled by the thermostat. Models in which the fan runs all the time and only

*Electrical heaters suitable for the greenhouse: tubular heaters (**top left**); soil-warming cables (**bottom left**); fan heater (**below**).*

---

the heater is thermostatically controlled are available, but in these the air continues to circulate after it has been warmed and consequently cools down more quickly. These systems are more expensive to run, but lining the greenhouse as described (see page 158) will reduce heat loss.

Tubular heaters are also favourites. They are best distributed evenly around the greenhouse and not banked all in one place. They are better positioned near the central pathway on both sides, than close to the greenhouse sides.

Convector heaters give moderate circulation of warmed air in the same way as fan heaters. Surprisingly, they are not often installed, but are nevertheless a good buy.

Warming cables have many uses. They can be used in beds or on limited areas of the staging to provide economical localized warmth. They are invaluable for gentle forcing of winter vegetable crops, and they can be used in frames or cases to warm small areas to a higher temperature than the greenhouse generally. This is especially useful for propagation. For the home greenhouse, special warming cables are sold. These should be used strictly according to the manufacturer's recommendations.

Only electrical heaters specially designed for use in the greenhouse should be used. Domestic equipment can be extremely dangerous in damp conditions and must not be used.

GAS HEATING

Piped natural gas is probably the cheapest fuel at present, and bottled gas the most expensive. Both can be used as fuel in the special greenhouse gas heaters that are now available. A high degree of thermostatic control is attainable with gas appliances, thus reducing heat waste. However, constant ventilation is essential. When the heater is not in operation and if weather permits the greenhouse should be freely ventilated.

PARAFFIN HEATING

The wick-type paraffin heater was at one time widely employed, but it is not easily controlled thermostatically and the fuel is expensive. Considerable waste is inevitable unless one is constantly at hand to adjust the wick according to weather conditions. Even so, this form is so reliable that it is a good idea to have an appliance at hand in case of an emergency, such as a breakdown in the main heating system or an exceptionally cold spell of weather.

If used as the main source of heat, the remarks made for gas regarding ventilation apply. Condensation is often excessive. Make sure you buy a properly designed greenhouse heater with adequate heat output. Check also that the BThU/hr rating is satisfactory. This is most important, since heaters are often purchased with outputs that are far too low. Gadgets for automatically topping up oil reservoirs are available, and these cut the chore of filling. The best type of greenhouse paraffin heater is a blue-flame type with a circular wick. It gives efficient combustion and is less liable to produce smells and fumes, provided you learn how to light the burner properly and obey the maker's instructions.

PIPED HOT WATER AND CONSERVATORY HEATING

Hot water pipes were often used at one time. They operate more efficiently where higher temperatures are required. They can be fuelled by solid fuel, oil, or gas. In conservatories or lean-tos, hot water heating can sometimes be run in from a domestic central heating system. It is essential, however, to consult a heating engineer beforehand to make certain the system can be extended.

Pipe heating is not now commonly employed for the average small home greenhouse. Even so, a modern boiler and equipment are much easier to install and operate than earlier types.

*Gas heater (**far left**) and paraffin heater (**left**), both designed for greenhouse use. Some constant ventilation is essential if either is used.*

Capillary matting is an excellent base for an automatic watering system. It absorbs and holds an amazing amount of water.

AUTOMATION

Thermostatic heating control is an important feature and should always be looked for, when buying equipment; the more accurate the thermostat the better.

There is now much automatic watering equipment on the market. One of the best systems employs special capillary matting which is kept constantly moist. This is spread over the staging and the plant pots are pressed on to it, uncrocked (see page 157), so that moisture can pass into the potting compost from the matting. Various trickle irrigation, overhead misting and spraying systems are also available but have more restricted, and sometimes specialized, applications. Generally, automatic watering is well worth considering, especially if you have to leave the greenhouse or conservatory unattended for long periods.

Ventilation can also be efficiently controlled by special greenhouse extractor fans operated by a thermostat. They should be of the type designed to prevent back draught. The size of fan, and the volume of air moved, depends on greenhouse size. Consult the supplier before buying and installing. Because fan-ventilated greenhouses are liable to dry out very quickly, some form of automatic watering or humidity control is a wise addition.

For the ordinary home greenhouse, automatic ventilator operators, controlled by temperature change, can be simply fitted. They need no electricity and require little attention. They are now very popular.

Automatic shading can be achieved using motor-operated blinds controlled by photo-electric cells. Unfortunately, this system is extremely expensive and is only used for special purposes.

GROUND SOIL, BEDS, FLOORS AND PATHS

SOIL SICKNESS

Crop rotation and the reasons for it are familiar to most schoolchildren. It is a practice followed by most outdoor gardeners – yet it is often promptly forgotten in the greenhouse. For the average small non-commercial greenhouse it's best not to use the ground soil for growing. Reasonably good results may be obtained for about two years or so, but after that what is known as soil sickness nearly always sets in. This condition produces serious plant deterioration due to a build up of excess unbalanced fertilizers, waste biochemical products from plant roots, and possibly pests and diseases. Under the cover of a greenhouse, where the soil is unexposed to weathering, 'sickness' soon becomes a problem, even if some crop rotation is carried out. Flooding the soil each year to wash out salts, sterilizing, or changing the soil, can help to overcome the trouble. But these measures are inconvenient, laborious, and rarely entirely satisfactory.

It is wise, therefore, to ignore the ground soil and grow everything in a suitable compost.

GREENHOUSE FLOORS AND PATHS

When the ground soil is not used for growing, a greenhouse can be erected almost anywhere on a sound flat surface. Concrete, asphalt, paving slabs, and the like make suitable floors. However, if there is no drainage, water may collect in puddles when the greenhouse is damped down (see page 163). Where a greenhouse is erected on soil, as is usually the case in the average garden, a simple effective floor can be made by levelling and firming the ground, and then strewing it with clean shingle or gravel, as used on driveways. This holds plenty of moisture during summer and will maintain atmospheric humidity without puddling. It is cheap and reasonably attractive.

Most small greenhouses are given a central path but, in houses more than 3m (10ft) wide, there is usually room for an additional central run of staging with a path on both sides.

CONSERVATORY FLOORS

Most people prefer a conservatory floor to be decorative or at least to be in keeping with the surroundings. Whatever is used should be unaffected by water, although, in conservatories, damping down is done with more care and discretion. Vinyl flooring, as used in domestic kitchens (but not cushion backed) lasts well provided it's put down on a perfectly smooth surface. Special self-levelling surface mixes for application to concrete bases are available. Ceramic floor tiles can be used, but plastic flooring tiles are liable to lift if water gets under them.

BEDS

Where beds or borders are wanted in greenhouses or conservatories, dig trenches of the required size and depth and remove the soil. Line the trenches with polythene sheeting. Make slits at intervals for drainage and fill with a suitable compost (see page 162). Raised beds or borders can be made similarly by draping polythene over a frame of boards of the required height. The polythene isolates the compost from the ground soil so that it cannot become contaminated, and the more restricted volume of compost is easier to replace. It is also easier to maintain a better fertilizer balance. Electric warming cables can be used in the beds to provide localized warmth. Beds and borders such as these can be filled with peat for the display of ornamentals. The plants are left in their pots and plunged to just over their rims. This also allows plants to be easily changed about according to the season. You should always try to arrange them in an attractive way, especially when using the beds and borders for display. Raised beds could be of special benefit to some disabled people.

Right top *It is best not to use ground soil in the greenhouse. A bed should consist of a polythene-lined trench filled with suitable compost.*
Bottom *Slatted exterior blinds are best for shading.*

SHADING

Nearly all greenhouses need shading at one time or another. An unshaded structure in a bright position can become so hot in summer that all the plants will be severely damaged or even killed. Blinds and special paints for application to the exterior glass are employed. The former can be expensive but are usually preferred for conservatories. For this purpose, slatted exterior blinds are best. Flimsy blinds of plastic or textile are liable to blow away in a strong wind. Interior blinds may give protection from direct sun scorch, but do little to keep down temperature.

Shading paints can be difficult to apply and to remove. However, a recently introduced electrostatic type, sold under the name Coolglass, is much easier to handle. It is a powder and mixes instantly with water. It can be sprayed or brushed on and is quite fast, even in torrential rain; yet it wipes off easily with a dry duster.

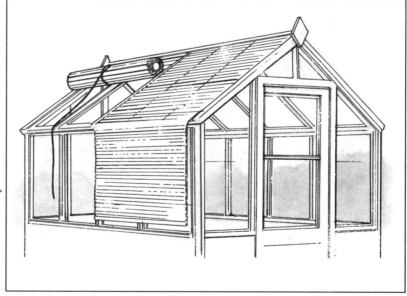

THERMOMETER

To help maintain the correct temperature in a greenhouse, a maximum and minimum thermometer should be installed. This type of thermometer has indicators which record the lowest and highest temperatures reached since the thermometer was last set. This is useful to show the temperature range in your absence. There are various designs. It is a small item – but a vital piece of equipment for proper management of greenhouse temperature. If you have separate sections, each needs its own thermometer.

161

FLOWERING AND FOLIAGE PLANTS

It is vital to choose plants that are suitable for growing in the temperature and light conditions of your greenhouse or conservatory. If you do not mix plants with very different requirements, for example, succulents, which need plenty of light, and ferns, which need shade and moisture, you will obtain far better results. It may, however, be possible to suit individual needs to some extent by putting plants which require shade under staging, for instance.

Buy plants only from reputable suppliers. Make sure they are healthy and correctly identified and labelled. There are specialist nurseries for some types of plants but many others can be grown successfully and cheaply from seed (see page 194).

COMPOSTS
Never use garden soil for pot work nor, in most cases, the greenhouse ground soil (see page 160). The use of unsterilized garden soil and crude fertilizers, such as animal manures, is inviting failure and disappointment; all manner of pests and diseases can be introduced.

There are a number of proprietary seed and potting composts available from which to choose. These are mostly peat based, are free from pests, disease and weed seed, and have an ideal fertilizer balance. The John Innes composts, which are loam based, are also a good buy provided they are made exactly to the original formulae set by the John Innes Horticultural Institute.

When a lot of compost is needed, it is cheaper to make up a peat and grit mix yourself and add a ready-mixed fertilizer concentrate, available with full instructions from garden shops. Such DIY composts can be made up with very little effort in a few minutes. The John Innes composts have more complicated ingredients, including special loam, and DIY preparation is, therefore, not often attempted.

POTS AND POTTING
Plastic pots are now widely used. They are lightweight, easy to store and clean, and retain moisture better than clay so the compost does not dry out so quickly. Clay pots, being porous, are a better choice when plants need to be plunged in a moisture-retaining material (see page 161).

Pot sizes mentioned in the text are all average. When potting most decorative plants, use a pot just large enough to take the plant comfortably. As it grows, the plant needs to be potted-on. This means transferring it into successively larger pots as the roots fill the existing one. Tap the plant out of the container, if there's a mass of tangled roots encircling the pot, the plant is 'pot bound' and should be put into a slightly larger container with fresh compost. This ensures that the roots always have a supply of 'sweet' compost with the right balance of nutrients. Exceptions to this treatment are plants known to be fast growers and vigorous. These, which include certain vegetable crops, can be given larger pots in the early stages.

Obviously, after a time, plants cannot be potted-on any further. If they are perennial, they can simply be repotted. This means removing the plant from its pot, carefully reducing the size of the root ball, teasing away old roots and compost, and potting back into the same sized pot with fresh compost. You should do this just before the plant is expected to make new growth.

When potting on, pass the fingers of one hand, palm down, around the base of the plant, turn the pot upside down and tap the pot then gently pull it away.

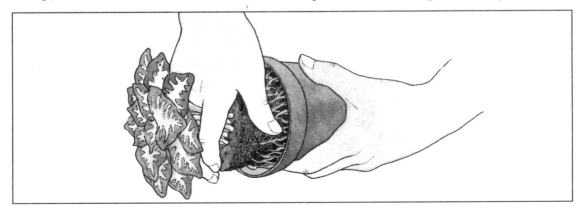

Another method for plants in final pots is to top dress. This means removing the upper layers of compost and replacing them with fresh. Alternatively, mix in some balanced fertilizer at the top of the pot. Nowadays, the excellent systemic and foliar feeds available make the feeding of estab-lished plants easier and top dressing less important than it used to be.

When potting, always leave a space between the surface of the compost and the top of the pot. This is the watering space. It assures water penetration and helps to assess the amount needed.

When repotting a mature plant, reduce the size of the root ball before potting back in the same size pot with fresh compost.

CULTURAL CARE

DAMPING DOWN
This entails sprinkling water over as much of the floor and staging as is convenient. Evaporation of the water then causes cooling and increases humidity which growing plants like. A moist atmosphere also means that they need less frequent watering. Damping down must not be done in winter. The air then should be kept on the dry side since too much humidity encourages moulds and mildews when conditions are cool.

WATERING
Always use *clean* water. Rainwater collected from roofs and stored in dirty butts should never be used as it is likely to be contaminated. Most plants will be far healthier with tap water. In areas where this is 'hard', plants disliking lime can be watered with clean rainwater collected in bowls. However, it is doubtful if this is really necessary provided that such plants are grown in special lime-free 'ericaceous' composts, which are available from garden shops.

The best general rule for watering plants is to keep the roots constantly moist. It is vital to avoid absolute dryness or waterlogging. Water must also be given according to a plant's needs and not in standard doses. When plants are dormant, as in winter, little if any water is required. Wet conditions then will lead to rotting and possibly to cold damage. In summer, however, water may be needed frequently: vigorous plants may require watering several times a day.

In general, plants need more water when conditions are warm and bright than when they are cold and dull. The best time to water is in the morning. Erratic watering leads to wilting and bud, flower or leaf shedding. Overwatering is often indicated by a sickly appearance, poor growth and yellowish foliage.

FEEDING
The rules given for watering also apply to feeding. Feed according to a plant's needs and vigour. When a suitable potting compost is used, feeding is not necessary until the plant is in the final pot. Feeding can be done with proprietary feeds which contain the nutrients in the correct, scientifically balanced proportions. These should be used according to the instructions on the label. Using DIY mixes, hit and miss fertilizers, or crude manures is most unwise. Overfeeding is harmful and you should never exceed the recommended doses. Frequent feeding with weak solutions gives the best results. Do not feed when the roots are dry. Foliar feeds, which are sprayed onto the leaves, can give a quick improvement. Some contain plant vitamins and hormones.

TEMPERATURE CONTROL
Make every effort to ensure that the temperature does not fall below the minimum required by your plants in winter. Thermostatic control of artifical heating usually makes management easy. In summer, conditions must not be allowed to become too hot. Damping down, shading with a white compound (such as Coolglass) and careful use of ventilators enables temperature adjustment. Excessive heat can prevent some plants from flowering. Erratic temperature changes lead to bud shedding and physiological problems.

Abutilon

GROWING FROM SEED

The cheapest way to acquire plants is to grow them from seed. Look through the catalogues from the leading seed firms and you will find an exciting and extensive range to choose from. There are always lots of seed novelties on offer as well as the more popular bedding plants, many of which make fine pot plants.

Some people think that starting from seed is a slow and difficult way to begin. This is not true, and if you follow the techniques given in chapter 5 success can be assured.

PLANTS TO GROW FROM SEED

Plant	Description/Cultural Hints	Final Pot Size	Min. Temp.	Germination Temp.
Abutilon	<u>Indian mallow</u>. The hybrids have a neat habit with large cup-shaped, veined and richly coloured flowers in the same year as sowing; flowers in winter if frost free. Grow the hybrid 'bella'.	130mm	5°C	16–18°C
Asparagus sprengeri	Foliage plant with trailing stems of fine needles; good for hanging baskets. *A. plumosus* has very fine needles and a spreading habit. It is popularly called the asparagus fern. Easy to grow.	180mm	5°C	18–21°C
Begonia	The fibrous-rooted bedding begonias make fine pot plants, with masses of flowers in many colours and glossy attractive foliage. They may also flower in winter, given a bright position.	130–180mm	10°C	18–21°C
Browallia	Sow the dwarf variety 'Troll' in March to give masses of blue or white cup-shaped flowers in autumn and winter. Discard after flowering.	130mm	10°C	18–21°C
Calceolaria	<u>Slipper flower</u>. A great favourite with a profusion of pouch-shaped flowers in dramatic colours, often speckled. Sow May to June for Christmas-to-spring bloom. F1 hybrids bloom earliest. Keep frost free over winter.	130mm	5°C	16–18°C
Capsicum	Ornamental shrub bearing orange to red berries, usually elongate in shape, between summer and Christmas. Easy to grow. Discard when berries shrivel.	100mm	5°C	18–24°C
Catharanthus rosea (Vinca)	Dainty evergreen shrubby perennial with eyed flowers in white to carmine. Dislikes chill.	130mm	10°C	16–18°C
Cineraria	Very popular neat plant smothered with daisy-like flowers in rich colours, often zoned with white. Can be grown with calceolarias.	130mm	5°C	16–18°C
Coleus	Beautifully coloured foliage plants; now available in many forms including miniatures. Sow February to March for summer/autumn display. Not worth trying to save over winter.	100–130mm	5°C	16–18°C
Cuphea ignea	<u>Mexican cigar plant</u>. Sow February/March. Neat bushy plant smothered with small red tubular flowers from summer to autumn. Discard after flowering.	130mm	5°C	18–21°C
Cyclamen	Popular winter-flowering plant with shuttlecock-shaped flowers. Takes about 14 months to flower from seed; sow November and maintain a steady temperature.	130mm	10°C	16–18°C
Eucalyptus	*E. citriodora*, with lemon-scented, spear-shaped foliage is best for pot cultivation. This species dislikes chill. Can be grown in 130mm pot for several years.	130mm	10°C	18–24°C
Exacum affine	Short, compact plant with small purplish flowers. It is grown mainly for its scent, but note not all varieties are fragrant. Sow February/March for late summer/autumn bloom. Grow several seedlings in a 10cm pot. Discard after flowering.	130mm	5°C	18–21°C
Fatsia japonica	Foliage plant with large glossy palmate leaves. Good for cold conditons. Will eventually grow very large; can then be put outdoors.	180mm	5°C	18–24°C

Calceolaria

Exacum affine

PLANTS TO GROW FROM SEED

Plant	Description/Cultural Hints	Final Pot Size	Min. Temp.	Germina-tion Temp.
Geranium	Popular name for zonal pelargoniums. Several excellent hybrids can be grown from seed. F1 hybrids are especially recommended. Sow January/February for flowering the following summer. Plants can be saved and propagated from cuttings. See page 30.	130mm	5°C	22–23°C
Gerbera	Grow the variety 'Happipot' which has a dwarf habit and large daisy-like flowers in lovely colours. Sow February/March for summer/autumn bloom.	150mm	5°C	18–21°C
Grevillea robusta	A graceful foliage plant with 'ferny' foliage. Excellent for cool conservatories. Pot into a lime-free (ericaceous) compost. Can become rather large after a few years.	170mm	5°C	18–24°C
Heliotropium peruvianum	Heliotrope. Shrubby plant with wrinkled mid- to dark-green leaves; sometimes known as cherry pie. The variety 'Marine' has flattish heads of purplish flowers with powerful fragrance. Sow February/March for summer/autumn bloom. Cut back after flowering and save over winter in frost-free conditions.	130mm	5°C	18–21°C
Hibiscus	Grow the variety 'Southern Belle' which has exciting flowers the size of dinner plates, coloured white to carmine. Sow February/March for summer/autumn blooms. Discard after flowering.	250mm	5°C	18–21°C
Hypoestes phyllostachya	Polka-dot plant. Foliage plant with pink spots on olive-green, pink flushed foliage. Grow the variety 'Pink Splash'. Sow February/March for summer onwards. Pinch back frequently. Discard when plant becomes straggly.	100mm	5°C	18–21°C
Impatiens	Busy-lizzie. Extremely popular ornamental plant bearing a profusion of flowers in bright colours. Choose low compact varieties for pots. Sow March to bloom from summer onwards. Will flower in winter with moderate warmth. Sow afresh when plants deteriorate.	100–130mm	5°C	21–24°C
Ipomoea	Morning Glory. Annual climber with beautiful large convolvulous flowers. Variety 'Heavenly Blue' is a favourite; other colours are available. Climbs to 2.4m (8ft). Give a bright position.	180mm	5°C	20–24°C
Jacaranda mimosaefolia	Foliage plants with graceful 'ferny' appear-ance, ideal for conservatories. May become too high for limited space in a few years.	250mm	5°C	18–24°C
Lagerstroemia indica	Neat perennial shrub with unusual white, pink, or reddish flowers. Keep dryish after the leaves are shed in winter. Grow dwarf hybrids.	150mm	5°C	18–21°C
Lantana	Verbena-like flowers in various colours, changing as they age. Grow hybrids with neat shrubby habit.	150mm	5°C	21–24°C
Lobelia tenuoir	Large blue-flowered greenhouse annual lobelia. Dislikes chill. Put several seedlings to each 130mm pot.	Several seedlings per 130mm pot	5°C	16–18°C
Mimosa pudica	Sensitive Plant. A foliage plant with delicate foliage folding up when touched. Grow as an annual.	100–130mm	5°C	18–21°C
Nemesia	Dwarf garden hybrids, make good pot plants. The variety 'Fire King' has rich red shades.	Several seedlings per 130mm pot	5°C	16–18°C
Nierembergia	Low-growing perennial with campanula-like purplish flowers. Keep dryish after the leaves are shed in winter. Grow the variety 'Purple Robe'.	130mm	5°C	16–18°C

Heliotrope

Morning glory

Nemesia

Plumbago

African violet

Butterfly flower

PLANTS TO GROW FROM SEED

Plant	Description/Cultural Hints	Final Pot Size	Min. Temp.	Germination Temp.
Petunia	Most are suitable for hanging baskets; the double forms are useful for pots. Give a position in bright light or, under glass, flowering may be poor.	3–6 seedlings per 130–180mm pot	5°C	18–21°C
Phlox drummondii	Can be sown in autumn for early spring display as well as given usual half-hardy annual treatment. Grow the dwarf compact varieties.	3 seedlings per 130mm pot	5°C	16–18°C
Plumbago capensis	Attractive perennial wall shrub with beautiful blue phlox-like flowers. There is also a white form. Flowers two years after sowing. Size can be restricted by pruning back after flowering.	250mm	5°C	18–21°C
Polyanthus	Choice of many varieties; innumerable colours. Sow February/March for winter to spring flowering. Ideal for cold conditions.	130mm	5°C	16–18°C
Primula malacoides	Fairy Primula. Whorls of flowers in various colours, borne above a neat leaf rosette. Sow May for following spring bloom. This species does not cause skin rash like *P. obconica* and *P. praenitens*.	100–130mm	5°C	16–18°C
Ricinus	Caster oil plant. Annual foliage plant. Grow 'Impala' with rich maroon-tinted glossy foliage and reddish seed capsules. Sow February/March. The seeds are poisonous.	130mm	5°C	18–21°C
Saintpaulia	African Violet. Popular houseplant. Needs moderate steady warmth. Transfer indoors during winter. Grow F1 hybrids, such as 'Blue' and 'Pink Fairy Tale', which are vigorous and easier to manage. Sow February/March.	130mm	5°C	21–24°C
Salpiglossis	Glorious trumpet-flowered annuals with rich colours and exotic veining. Sow February/March. Pinch out seedlings to encourage bushy growth. Can also be sown autumn for flowering following early spring. Grow hybrids 'Splash' or 'Ingrid'.	1–3 seedlings per 130mm pot	5°C	18–21°C
Schefflera	There are several species of different heights. Large pale green, shiny palmate foliage with a tropical look. Good for the cool conservatory.	180mm	5°C	18–24°C
Schizanthus	Butterfly Flower. Dainty 'ferny' foliage and masses of pretty butterfly flowers with many colours and markings. Sow February/March for summer flowering. Giant hybrids can be sown in autumn for spring flowers. Pinch out seedlings of tall forms only to promote bushy growth. Keep frost free over winter. The dwarf varieties are easy to grow as annuals.	Several seedlings per 130mm pot	5°C	16–18°C
Solanum	Winter Cherry. Popular winter and Christmas pot plants with bright cherry-sized red berries. Sow February. Stand outside while flowering to set fruit. Plants can often be saved if cut back when berries shrivel.	100–130mm	5°C	18–24°C
Streptocarpus	Cape primrose. Profusion of trumpet flowers on wiry stems in delicate colours. Sow February to flower same year. Keep frost free and only slightly moist during winter.	130mm	5°C	18–24°C
Thunbergia alata	Black-eyed Susan. Dainty annual climber with orange, cream, or white flowers, often with a jet black 'eye'. Sow February/March to flower from summer onwards. Train up canes. Can also be used to trail from hanging baskets.	130–180mm	5°C	18–21°C

GROWING FROM BULBS, CORMS AND TUBERS

The word 'bulb' is often used by the layman to include corms, tubers, rhizomes, and similar items which are known as 'storage organs' by the botanist. These storage organs all contain food, which ensures the plant gets a good start in life. When you buy them, look for high quality, since their performance depends on how well they have been produced.

Always purchase from a reputable firm. Do not accept anything soft and spongy or showing signs of rot or mildew. Small size is also best avoided, since it may indicate that the organ is not developed enough to produce flowers.

COMPOST, POTTING AND GENERAL CULTURE

Always use a proper potting compost (see page 162). Choose a pot of suitable size for the particular bulb. Small bulbs can be grouped, large bulbs need individual pots. Most bulbs grown for the greenhouse can be potted shallowly with their tips protruding well above the compost surface. This gives plenty of room for the roots in the pot. Decorative bowls are popular for growing bulbs in, but take care as these may become waterlogged if there are no drainage holes.

Position the bulbs on a layer of moist compost.

HARDY AND TENDER GROUPS

Plant storage organs fall into two categories: hardy and tender. The treatment of each is quite different. The hardy group includes the popular, well-loved spring-flowering favourites such as daffodil, hyacinth and crocus. These are indispensable for unheated or cold conditions. The tender group includes many of the greenhouse 'exotics', for example, gloxinia, begonia, and hippeastrum, which require warmer conditions.

GROWING THE WINTER TO SPRING FLOWERING GROUP (Hardy)

The great majority of these should be potted from August to October. After potting they should be plunged in moist peat or grit, outdoors, to give about 150mm (6in) covering. The plunge must be kept moist but protected from rain to prevent waterlogging. On no account keep the containers in a warm place. Leave them in the plunge for about six to eight weeks. The bulbs should by then have made plenty of roots and can be brought into a cool greenhouse or conservatory and gradually introduced to full light. Too much warmth is harmful to this group and may cause weak, lanky growth and failure to flower.

GROWING THE SUMMER TO WINTER FLOWERING GROUP (Tender)

These are potted or started into growth in gentle warmth from early to late spring. Those storage organs without an obvious growing point, such as gloxinia and begonia, should be just covered with moist peat in a warm propagator. Inspect them daily and, as soon as you can see roots or shoots, pot into a suitable potting compost. Again they need only be potted at a shallow depth. Most of this group require a minimum temperature of about 10°C (50°F) and will grow faster if it is a few degrees higher. Keep the atmosphere moist and protect from direct sunlight.

TREATMENT AFTER FLOWERING

Plants of the hardy group can be put outdoors in any convenient place. Continue to water and feed them until the foliage dies down naturally, this is important to their flowering in future years. The bulbs often multiply and may need separating and repotting in the future.

The tender group should also be watered and fed until the foliage shows signs of deterioration, and then allowed to become dry. When dry, tip out of the pots, free from compost, remove stem and leaf vegetation, and store dry in clean sand in a frost-free place over winter. Delicate or brittle storage organs, such as some rhizomes and tubers, can be left in their pots, which should be turned on their sides until next repotted.

PREPARED BULBS

This term is used to describe bulbs and other storage organs that have been specially temperature treated to induce early or out-of-season flowering. The suppliers' instructions should be closely followed regarding cultivation and temperature. The temperature stated is sometimes initially rather high and may not be practical to attain in an ordinary greenhouse. The forcing can then be done in a warm room indoors. When approaching flowering, move the plants to the cooler conditions of a conservatory.

Anemone

Crocus

Gloxinia

COLOURFUL BULBS, CORMS AND TUBERS

Name	Storage Organ	Hardiness	Description/Cultural Hints	Planting Density
Achimenes	Catkin-like rhizome	Tender	Grow the named hybrids, some of which are ideal for hanging baskets; profusions of flowers in rich colours, late summer and autumn. Erect types need twiggy sticks for support. Likes moderate warmth, humidity, and slight shade.	5 per 130mm pot
Anemone	Small tuber	Hardy	The single-flowered De Caen and the double St Brigid are well known; wide range of glorious colours. Anemone blanda, with daisy-like flowers, can also be grown in pots.	5–7 per 180mm pot
Begonia	Tuber	Tender	Tuberous begonias are an important group. The giant-flowered types are most impressive. Remove the single female flowers, on each side of the large showy male flowers, as early as possible. The pendulous forms, with tassel blooms are wonderful for hanging baskets or pots. Give moderate shade.	Large flowered: 1 per 130mm pot Pendulous: 3 per basket
Bulbocodium vernum	Bulb	Hardy	Corms with crocus-like purplish flowers appearing very early in the year.	5–7 per 180mm pot
Chionodoxa luciliae	Bulb	Hardy	Beautiful blue starry flowers with white centres early in the year. *C. gigantea* has larger flowers. Excellent for a cold conservatory.	5–7 per 180mm pot
Crocus	Bulb	Hardy	These are favourites for pots or bowls in the cold conservatory. Choice named types are available for indoor culture; the extra-large-flowered forms are especially beautiful.	7 per 180mm pot
Cyclamen	Tuber	Tender	The tender cyclamen (not the hardy types) can be potted from July to August for flowering from winter to spring. Many fancy forms.	1 per 130mm pot
Erythronium	Bulb	Hardy	Some species have attractive variegated foliage and pendant starry flowers. Good for shaded positions.	5–7 per 180mm pot
Freesia	Corm	Tender	For best results purchase *named* types recommended for pot culture. Some, but not all, are fragrant. Will flower in winter if potted in summer.	7 per 130mm pot
Galanthus	Bulb	Hardy	This genus includes the well-loved snowdrop; there are also some especially choice large-flowered forms ideally suited to pots or bowls.	Plant generously
Gloriosa	Tuber	Tender	The glory lily. Tuberous climbers. The most frequently grown is *G. rothschildiana*, which has flowers like reflexed lilies, borne summer to autumn. Plant the tubers with the thick end just under the compost surface and the thin end protruding. Slightly poisonous: handle carefully.	1 per 180mm pot
Gloxinia	Corm	Tender	Clusters of huge trumpet flowers in rich colours and velvety green foliage. Flowers summer to autumn. The named hybrids are especially showy.	1 per 130mm pot

COLOURFUL BULBS, CORMS AND TUBERS

Name	Storage Organ	Hardiness	Description/Cultural Hints	Planting Density
Haemanthus	Bulb	Tender	The blood lily. One of the most spectacular species is *H. multiflorus*, which has enormous spherical, crimson flowers, shaped like dandelion clocks. It is grown like hippeastrum.	1 per 120mm pot
Hippeastrum	Bulb	Tender	Bears enormous trumpet flowers in various fine colours on a thick stalk. Foliage often comes after flowers in newly potted bulbs. Pot with the tip well above the compost surface. Do not dry off over winter – the bulb is *evergreen*. Often sold erroneously as amaryllis.	1 per 180mm pot
Hyacinth	Bulb	Hardy	One of the best-known pot plants. There are very many named cultivars and wide range of colours.	1 per 130mm pot 3 per 180mm pot
Lachenalia	Bulb	Tender	*Lachenalia bulbifera* (*L. pendula*) is beautiful in hanging baskets in the conservatory. *L. aloides* 'Nelsonii' has a more erect habit and is better for pots. The flowers are tubular, in shades of yellow and red. Bulbs are best potted during August for flowering about December. Keep cool but frost free.	5–7 per 130mm pot 14cm apart in hanging baskets
Lilium	Bulb	Hardy	Lilies make delightful conservatory plants and there are many kinds suited to pots. Bulbs can be obtained that flower from summer to autumn. Low-growing lilies, such as forms of *L. umbellatum*, are best for pots.	1 per 180mm pot
Muscari	Bulb	Hardy	Grape Hyacinth. Looks well grown in pots. White forms as well as blue are available, some are fragrant. The form *M. comosum plumosum* has flowers forming clusters of bluish filaments.	5 per 130mm pot
Narcissus	Bulb	Hardy	This group includes the daffodil. Dwarf species are charming for pots and bowls and are seen at their best with weather protection, as are double-flowered narcissi. The group is invaluable for cold conservatories.	5 per 180mm pot 8 per 250mm pot
Nerine	Bulb	Tender	Bears umbels of flowers, often with unusual colours and a glistening sheen. Pot in *August* for flowering autumn to early winter. Grow *only* the named varieties developed for pots.	1 per 130mm pot
Tulip	Bulb	Hardy	Choose carefully, not all do well in pots. Best are the early doubles which are short stemmed and strong with showy flowers. Some of the early singles are also good. 'Brilliant Star' is a favourite crimson red variety.	5 per 180mm pot 8 per 150mm pot
Vallota	Bulb	Tender	Scarborough lily. *V. speciosa* is usually grown. It should be treated like hippeastrum. A fine conservatory plant, with large scarlet trumpet flowers in autumn. Pot in August.	1 per 150mm pot

Hippeastrum

Lachenalia

Grape hyacinth

USEFUL FLOWERING PLANTS

Many pot plants can be bought from florist shops and large stores. Garden centres are another source. Those plants described as 'houseplants' are often excellent for the greenhouse and conservatory, frequently growing more vigorously there than in the house itself, which rarely provides a good environment for flowering plants. Most of these plants have been grown by rooting cuttings. You can often increase your stock in the same way once you have established them (see page 196).

Above Azalea *variety* 'Addy Wery' *is an evergreen which has glossy leaves and masses of glorious coral-red flowers.*

AZALEA (Rhododendron).

There are two kinds, one hardy and the other tender. The easiest to grow and also the best for greenhouses or conservatories are the hardy evergreen named types, often sold by nurseries and garden centres. Those sold by florists around Christmas are Indian azaleas (*Rhododendron simsii*) which are specially forced. They will not flower again at the same time of year if kept and must be overwintered in a greenhouse. During summer, azaleas can be stood outdoors in a shady place, but watering must not be forgotten. When potting, use an acid, ericaceous compost and, if possible, water with *clean* rainwater.

BELOPERONE

Shrimp plant is the name given to *B. guttata* because of the strange colour and appearance of the bracts around the flowers. When buying for the greenhouse, it is wise to remove the flowers and bracts that have already formed. This encourages the plant to grow larger and become more decorative. Shade is often recommended, but good light, even some direct sunlight, produces superior colouring. A minimum winter temperature of about 7°C (45°F) is needed.

CAMELLIA

It is not widely realized that these well-known evergreens make fine pot plants when young, and flower well. They make superb conservatory plants, especially where conditions tend to be chilly. With glass protection, blooming is early and the flowers are not ruined by weather as so often happens outdoors. Give an acid, ericaceous compost and water with *clean* rainwater if possible. Do not allow the pots to dry out at any time. This needs to be watched particularly if the plants are stood out for the summer.

CAMPANULA

C. isophylla is an old favourite for hanging baskets in conservatories. It forms an attractive cascade and becomes smothered with blue or white flowers from about July to Autumn. Sometimes leaf variegation occurs spontaneously. When this happens the shoot can be removed as a cutting and rooted. Cream and green variegated plants often have smaller flowers.

Below Italian bellflower, Campanula isophylla, *is one of the best summer-flowering, trailing plants.*

Glorious chrysanthemum blooms such as these last for several weeks.

CARNATIONS

With a little care you can grow exquisite carnations just like those sold by florists. These are called perpetual flowering (PF for short) because they continue to produce blooms for cutting almost the whole year round. A minimum winter temperature of about 7–10°C (45–50°F) is essential. Provided you have a greenhouse with plenty of light, they usually fit in well with other plants.

Buy named varieties of rooted cuttings from a specialist nursery in early spring. Not all are fragrant. For beginners the 'Sim' varieties are recommended. In recent years low-growing types have been introduced.

Grow the cuttings for a few weeks in small pots and then transfer to 180mm (7in) pots. Usually, young plants have already been 'stopped' by the nurseryman, if not, you should pinch out the tips. Also 'stop' the side shoots that form later, 'stopping' the fastest growing first. Do not 'stop' them all at once. This procedure is to encourage the growth of stems, all of which will bear one large bloom. The small buds that form from the stem or around the main bud (crown bud), must be removed carefully by bending them back. They usually snap off. This is to direct the plant's energy into development of the crown bud.

Special carnation feeds are sold, but a tomato feed will also give good results. The stems need careful support with canes or special wire carnation supports. It is inadvisable to keep plants for more than three years. Calyx splitting, which causes petals to bulge in one place and spoils the bloom, is a common problem. Avoiding wide temperature fluctuations and erratic watering and feeding will help prevent it.

CHRYSANTHEMUMS

These make wonderful conservatory plants. Certain types are also grown for cutting and can follow a tomato crop. When choosing, consult a descriptive catalogue from a specialist nursery since there are so many types. The catalogue will also give guidance regarding 'stopping' which is particularly important for the large-flowered types.

The large-flowered forms are classified according to flower character, for example, 'incurved' when petals turn inwards, and 'reflexed' when they turn outwards. The plants are grown from rooted cuttings. These can be bought in spring and put outdoors in large pots for the summer. They must be carefully staked to prevent wind damage. They need regular watering and feeding and should be 'stopped' at the recommended time. To obtain high quality blooms, allow only a few stems with one bud on each to develop. The large-flowered varieties also need disbudding to ensure the development of one huge bloom on each stem. Transfer the plants to the greenhouse in autumn for the final training and blooming.

Much easier are the Charm types which can be grown from seed. The rooted cuttings or seedlings must be 'stopped' but they can then be allowed to develop naturally. They first form a neat compact bush, then spread out, later becoming smothered with small 'daisy' blooms forming cushions of colour.

Some other chrysanthemums are also easy to grow from seed, notably the F1 and F2 hybrids. For example, 'Autumn Glory' and 'Petit Point' which are neat and compact. Korean hybrids are worth growing too.

CITRUS

Oranges, lemons, limes, grapefruits, and the like are often grown from 'pips'. The results can be disappointing and it is far better to buy named plant varieties or species from a specialist nursery. *Citrus mitis*, which is often sold as a houseplant, is very popular. It has fragrant, white, waxy star-shaped flowers, followed by small oranges the size of a walnut, which remain decorative for most of the year. Pot on when necessary into an acid, ericaceous compost and use *clean* rainwater if your tap water is 'hard'. It likes full sun and can be put outdoors in summer. A minimum winter temperature of 10°C (50°F) is necessary.

CLIVIA MINIATA

This is an impressive conservatory plant with strap-shaped foliage and enormous umbels of large orange flowers in spring. It need only be kept just frost free, but is severely damaged or killed if temperatures fall below freezing. It should be grown in large pots or small tubs and should be left undisturbed until it is seriously root bound. Avoid direct sun and in winter put in an unheated room and water sparingly.

Broom, Cytisus × racemosus, has arching sprays of fragrant yellow flowers from winter to late spring.

CYTISUS (brooms)

Two brooms are often sold as houseplants, genista (*C. canariensis*) and *C. × racemosus*. If given large pots they will grow to the height of a man. Restricting pot size and severe pruning can keep them more manageable. Genista has scented yellow flowers, spring to summer, and is evergreen. *C. × racemosus* has showy, yellow, scented flowers, winter to spring, and greyish-green foliage. Prune back after flowering and stand outdoors for the summer. Do not allow it to dry out at any time; give slight shade. Bring indoors in September and keep cool but frost free. Water liberally during flowering.

ERICA (bell heathers, or heaths)

From about Christmas time onwards, *Erica gracilis*, which has pink or white flowers and *E. hyemalis*, with pink tubular flowers, are sold by florists. These plants are usually forced for early bloom. After flowering, pot into an acid, ericaceous compost and stand outdoors during summer. Do not allow to dry out. Water with clean rainwater if necessary. Return to the greenhouse for winter. A minimum temperature about 7°C (45°F) is needed.

Fuchsia, variety 'Cascade', is one of very many named varieties of this popular pot plant.

FUCHSIAS

Fuchsias are among the most popular of all pot plants. The flowers have a particular fascination and the plants lend themselves to training in various shapes. There are now innumerable varieties and before making a choice it is best to obtain descriptive catalogues from specialist nurseries. The most convenient way to acquire plants is to buy rooted cuttings in spring, which will flower well the first year.

Training is done by pinching out the tips of shoots. This technique, known as 'stopping', causes several new shoots to grow, all of which will carry flowers in due course. It is important to remember to cease 'stopping' about eight weeks before you want the flowers. Some fuchsias are marvellous displayed in hanging baskets.

To train a standard, select a strong-rooted cutting. Do not 'stop' the tip of the cutting, but allow it to grow normally. Do pinch out *all* side shoots that may form, but not leaves growing from the stem. When the stem has reached the desired height, pinch out the tip. This causes many shoots to form below and these should be 'stopped' in turn, to produce a bushy 'head'. Leaves can then be removed from the supporting stem. A stout cane will be needed for support.

Fuchsias can be overwintered as long as they are kept frost free, but standards need warmer conditions to prevent die back. Shade them in summer and water well. Give good light in winter and water sparingly.

HYDRANGEA

This is a popular gift plant. After flowering cut off the heads and any straggly growth. Stand out-doors in a shady place with pots plunged. New shoots should form. Cut out the old stems (that produced flowers) just above the new ones. The new shoots should flower the following year. Water with clean rainwater if your tap water is 'hard'. Return to the greenhouse in autumn, but do not allow the temperature to rise much above 10°C (50°F) until February as this could inhibit flowering. The flowers will not have rich colour if the compost is alkaline. Use an acid, ericaceous compost for potting.

NERIUM (Oleander)

An ideal evergreen plant for the cool conservatory. Masses of flowers are produced from summer to autumn, in white, pink, and shades of carmine. The plants become untidy unless properly pruned. Shoots that form at the base of the flower trusses should be removed promptly, and in autumn, after flowering, the shoots of the previous year's development should be reduced to about a finger's length. This will encourage new growth from the base. Water well in summer and sparingly in winter. Keep frost free. Note that the sap is poisonous so handle with great care. It can be kept in 200mm (8in) pots for some years.

Hydrangeas last in flower for a very long time if kept cool, moist and shaded.

Oleander, Nerium oleander, *bears pretty, fragrant flowers in clusters above willow-like foliage.*

ORCHIDS

The great majority of orchids we cultivate are hybrids created by man. There are many that grow well alongside other plants in our greenhouses and conservatories – it is not essential to have special conditions. Some people think that orchids are difficult and expensive. This is just not true; they can be cheaper and easier than some other plants we grow.

Orchids do need a special compost of fibrous texture, but this is easy enough to obtain from nurseries specializing in the plants. Such nurseries are also the best source for the orchids themselves. Try to visit nurseries and choose your plants when most orchids are in flower, from winter to spring. Some large stores now also sell fine plants. Since the average home greenhouse or conservatory has a cool winter minimum, it's wise to select orchids accordingly. Undoubtedly top of the list should be the cymbidiums. These bear arching stems of typical orchid flowers with delightful colours and markings, and the blooms are amazingly long lasting. They do very well in a 'mixed' greenhouse. During summer they can be put in a bright position outside.

Many people find paphiopedilums fascinating because of their slipper shape and quaint markings. There are plain-leaved and mottled-leaved kinds; the former are usually better for cool conditions. Unlike most, these orchids do not have pseudobulbs, and they need more shade than cymbidiums. Cattleyas are very exotic and need a higher temperature, but they are compact, and perhaps just part of the greenhouse could be specially heated for them. You could also consider growing the beautiful odontoglossums, miltonias (pansy orchids), and some laelias and vandas.

Orchid growers will advise you on which plants are most suitable for the conditions you have. They will also probably have useful literature giving details of the best treatment for all the many, very varied orchid types available.

PELARGONIUMS

These rival fuchsias in popularity. There are a large number of named cultivars and when choosing you should consult a specialist catalogue.

The plant commonly called 'geranium' is, in fact, the **zonal** pelargonium. The named types now have considerable competition from the F1 hybrids which are easily grown from seed. Most of the group have zoned leaf markings. There are many colours, as well as doubles, semi-doubles, types with variously shaped petals and miniatures. Also some with beautiful leaf colouring and variegation.

The **regal** group have exceptionally showy flowers but these are not borne over such a long period. They are best kept in a greenhouse and can reach a considerable size after a few years. They are very impressive when in flower.

The **ivy-leaved** group are long flowering and particularly suitable for hanging-baskets. Use three or four plants per basket.

All these can be bought as rooted cuttings. 'Stopping' is important to prevent lanky, untidy development. Overwinter in the same conditions as fuchsias and be sure to ventilate freely when possible. Most pelargoniums need plenty of light, and moderate ventilation. Do not overwater.

Cymbidium is the best type of orchid for the beginner. It has all the exotic orchid qualities yet it is easy to grow.

Madagascar jasmine,
Stephanotis
floribunda, *so-called
because of the exquisite
but heavy scent of its
flowers.*

STEPHANOTIS FLORIBUNDA
(Madagascar jasmine)

An evergreen climber with waxy white tubular flowers having a powerful fragrance. Although it will often survive conditions little more than frost free, it really prefers moderate warmth and humidity. In good conditions it will climb up into the roof of a greenhouse. The stems should be trained on a support and cut back after flowering. Water well in summer and sparingly in winter. It likes a position of moderate light.

STRELITZIA REGINA
(Bird-of-paradise flower)

This is one of the most spectacular of all pot plants, the famous bird-of-paradise flower. It has bold, evergreen spear-shaped leaves and large flowers in orange and blue like an exotic bird's head. The flowers, produced twice a year in summer and at Christmas, are on tall stalks and last for several weeks. Although its appearance is exotic it is, in fact ideal for a frost-free conservatory and does not demand high temperatures, as is often stated. Give a position in good light, but shade from hot sun. Water well in summer and very sparingly in winter. A mature plant needs a 250mm (10in) pot or larger, and should be left until seriously pot bound. Large plants that have 'clumped' can be divided by cutting through the roots in spring. The roots should be separated so that each piece has a 'fan' of leaves. A young plant may take up to two years before it flowers.

TIBOUCHINA

The correct botanical name for this is *Tibouchina urvilleana*, but it's usually labelled *T. semidecandra*. It is a favourite conservatory perennial, bearing pansy-shaped violet-coloured flowers summer to autumn. Buy plants as rooted cuttings and pinch out the top and the tips of any laterals that form after potting. Pot in 180mm (7in) pots for flowering and give a cane for support. Water well in summer and sparingly in winter; cut back severely in late winter.

The Bird-of-Paradise Flower, Strelitzia reginae, *is actually a member of the banana family although, contrary to popular belief, it does not need hot conditions and is easy to grow.*

EASILY GROWN FOLIAGE PLANTS

ARAUCARIA HETEROPHYLLA

The Norfolk Island pine makes a splendid plant for a cool conservatory and can be kept in a 250mm (10in) pot for a long time. It has a form rather like a Christmas tree. It prefers slight shade and good ventilation. If the plants become too large or leggy, cut them back and use the cuttings for propagating new stock. Water well in summer and sparingly in winter. Keep frost free.

The Norfolk Island pine, Araucaria heterophylla, *a handsome plant.*

ASPIDISTRA

This plant is sometimes known humorously as the cast-iron plant because of its resistance to neglect. When looked after well, it can be quite handsome. The cream variegated form should be especially looked for. The plants do well in slight shade and their appearance can be greatly enhanced by treatment with a leaf-shine product. A minimum temperature of 7°C (45°F) is needed.

BEGONIA

There are many extremely beautiful foliage begonias. Most are liable to deteriorate at temperatures below about 10°C (50°F), and they like slight shade and moderate humidity in summer. *Begonia rex* is a favourite, with exotically marked and coloured leaves often splashed silver. The iron cross begonia (*B. masoniana*), so named because of the bold cross mark on its leaves, is also most attractive. Many begonias bear flowers as well as striking foliage, but only rarely can the flowers compete in catching the eye, as in *B. corallina* and *B. tiger*, for example.

BROMELIADS

This group of plants belongs to the pineapple family and is found in nature growing in moss or leaf debris, often above ground in tree branches or rocks. This indicates how they should be grown, that is, in a mossy, leafy compost. There are many bromeliads to choose from. A number produce exotic 'flowers' which are mostly composed of coloured bracts. The species with the more striking leaves may have the least interesting flowers. Most plants form a rosette of foliage with a central 'cup', called an 'urn'. Keep this topped up with water, otherwise water or spray sparingly from the top of the plant only. Most will survive a minimum temperature of about 10°C (50°F).

CALADIUM

This delightful plant is best bought in the form of a large tuber which can be started into growth in spring, in a warm propagator. Large handsome arrow-shaped leaves, veined and marked with various lovely colours, are soon produced. It loves warmth and humidity but is easily grown from tubers. When the foliage fades, let the pots become almost dry. Then store indoors over winter at a minimum temperature of 13°C (55°F).

CHLOROPHYTUM CAPENSE
(spider plant)

This is a very popular and adaptable plant. From a clump of arching foliage grow long stems bearing small white flowers followed by tiny plantlets. It makes a fine basket plant for the conservatory, given about 7°C (45°F) minimum temperature in winter.

CISSUS ANTARCTICA

This is a climber which, in greenhouse conditions, can reach the roof. It has pale green, spear-shaped leaves with toothed edges. Despite the name it needs a winter minimum of about 5°C (41°F). Watch out for aphid attack and red spider to which the plant is prone. Give an 180mm (7in) pot with good drainage. To encourage bushy growth pinch out the stem tips.

Blue Gum, Eucalyptus globulus, *has very attractive grey-blue-green juvenile foliage.*

EUCALYPTUS

Many species make fine foliage plants for the cool conservatory, but they can become very large. The blue gum (*Eucalyptus globulus*) is popular and is easy to grow from seed. Look out also for the dwarf golden gum (*E. exima nana*), the silver gum (*E. cordata*) and the alpine gum (*E. archeri*). Eucalypts have attractive juvenile leaves, which may be lost on maturity. Fortunately, new plants are usually easy to grow from seed. Many species produce the familiar eucalyptus aroma and will scent the greenhouse during periods of warm weather.

EUONYMUS

The attractive dwarf evergreen varieties are excellent foliage plants for cold conditions and deserve to be grown more often in conservatories. Especially recommended are *Euonymus japonica* 'Variegata' and 'Aurea', and *E. fortunei* 'Vegeta' and 'Silver Queen'. The variegated foliage looks its best during winter. They are generally slow growers, but 'Silver Queen' can grow tall if allowed.

Bromeliad, Neoregelia carolinae, *often called the nest plant because of the central cup.*

× FATSHEDERA

This bigeneric cross between *Fatsia* and *Hedera* has characteristics of both and is excellent for chilly places. The best form is 'Variegata' which has cream variegated, glossy ivy-like leaves, but needs to be kept frost free. It can be trained as a bush by pruning, or led up supports as a climber. Do not overwater.

FATSIA JAPONICA

Although this can be raised from seed (see page 194) the cream variegated form cannot. This is a desirable form but is not so hardy and is best kept frost free. Its foliage is a glossier, lighter green.

FERNS

There are very many ferns from which to choose, and a good selection is readily obtainable. Some recommended species are ribbon fern (*Pteris cretica*); ladder fern (*Nephrolepis exaltata*); holly fern (*Cyrtomium falcatum*), which has an unusual appearance; bird's nest fern (*Asplenium nidus*); and *Polypodium vulgare* in its choice forms. Most of the hardy garden ferns can be grown in pots but it's preferable to choose evergreen subjects. They usually do well in shaded places and are ideal in north-facing conservatories or under the staging.

Below *Bird's Nest Fern*, Asplenium nidus, *has large fronds with wavy edges and dark midribs.*

FICUS

The best-known species is the rubber plant (*Ficus elastica*). This, however, needs a minimum temperature of 10°C (50°F) to remain decorative. Relatively hardy and ideal for chilly conservatories are the mistletoe fig (*F. deltoidea*), which bears reddish to yellow berries all year round, and the creeping fig (*F. pumila*) which is a trailer but can also be grown up supports. In both, the foliage is small and dainty.

Above *The Canary Island ivy*, Hedera canariensis.

HEDERA (Ivy)

There are many ivies of variable appearance, leaf form and height size. All are useful for cold shady places. One of the most impressive is *Hedera canariensis* which has cream and two-tone-green variegation. This species is hardy, but will grow rampantly in warmth. Sudden wide temperature changes may, however, lead to leaf shedding. It will reach roof height if allowed.

MONSTERA DELICIOSA (Swiss cheese plant)

This well-known houseplant has leaves which are perforated when mature and lobed when young. It can grow to well over a man's height in good conditions and is happy in surprisingly small pots. It sends down long aerial roots to enter the compost and can survive almost freezing temperatures. If kept at above 13°C (55°F), it may produce arum-like flowers and elongate pineapple-like fruits.

Right *The Swiss Cheese plant*, Monstera deliciosa, *can grow very tall. Use a moss-covered stake for support and for moisture for aerial roots.*

Chamaerops humilis
*is a stately fan palm
which makes an ideal
specimen plant.*

PALMS

There are a number of hardy palms for gardens that can be grown in pots indoors and are ideal for chilly conservatories. For example, *Chamaerops humilis* and *Phoenix canariensis*, which is almost hardy. Several are sold as houseplants and grow very well in cool greenhouses or conservatories. The *Howeia* palms are especially good, but need 7°C (45°F) winter minimum. Palms seem to grow well in comparatively small pots. Water well in summer and sparingly in winter. Pot-on every two years at the most when young.

PELARGONIUM (Scented geranium)

This group of pelargoniums is noted for leaf fragrance and few have much in the way of showy flowers. They are named according to their scent. For example, nutmeg, lemon, orange, rose bowl, and peppermint. They can be grown much like other pelargoniums, in general, and have the same preferences for light and air. They are most desirable in conservatories, where they often scent the air when conditions are warm. Specialist pelargonium nurseries will have a good selection from which to choose.

Aluminium plant, Pilea cadieri, *is grown for the beauty of its silvery leaves.*

PILEA CADIEREI (aluminium plant)

There are a number of pileas, but this species is the most common and is easy to grow. Its attractive silvery foliage suggests its common name. It is neat and bushy in habit and is useful where space is limited. It can suffer from magnesium deficiency, causing leaf distortion and poor growth. Treat by adding a few crystals of Epsom salts from time to time.

SAXIFRAGA STOLONIFERA (mother of thousands)

This well-known pot plant has long runners carrying baby plants which can be detached and rooted. Look out for the superior variety 'Tricolor', which has roundish pinkish veined leaves. It is slower growing but very attractive. Keep frost free. It is very useful for wall pots, shelves and similar positions.

SOLEIROLIA SOLEIROLII (mind your own business)

So-called because of its creeping invasive habit, this plant is mat forming and therefore very useful for creating 'carpet' effects; it will grow over the surface of beds and pots to hide them and produce a natural effect. Do not allow it to dry out at any time. Winter at 5–7°C (41–45°F).

TOLMIEA MENZIESII (pick-a-back plant)

This plant is so called because of the little plantlets that form around the leaf edges. These can be detached and easily rooted. A creeping plant with prettily marked foliage. It produces spikes of pinky flowers in summer and is useful for shelves, hanging containers, edges of staging and similar positions; ideal for chilly conditions. There is a variegated form but it is not so hardy.

TRADESCANTIA

Tradescantia fluminensis, in its various forms, is a popular trailing houseplant. Its pretty markings and colours develop best if it is given good light and not overwatered. It is frequently confused with *Zebrina pendula*, which has leaves that are green and silver above, and purplish below. This plant does tolerate shade and will often grow under staging. Keep well pruned and propagate from cuttings.

Some saxifrage species can be grown in pots for their pretty flowers.

CACTI AND OTHER SUCCULENTS

There is a vast range of these attractive plants, and many can be grown successfully in a mixed greenhouse collection. With few exceptions they need a lot of light and make a good choice for such places as a south-facing conservatory. They can survive without water for quite a time and, therefore, are ideal if you are unable to give regular care. This obviously does not mean that they can be left without water indefinitely. During summer most need plenty of water but they should be left to rest on the dry side in winter. Many produce quite showy flowers. Make your choice from the following selection.

Peanut cactus, Chamaecereus silvestrii, *is easy to grow and can flower profusely.*

Left *Thread agave,* Agave filifera, *is a succulent, with thread-like filaments on its spiky leaves.*

CACTI AND SUCCULENTS

Plant	Category	Description
Agave	Succulent	Rosettes of long sword-like leaves, sometimes with cream striping.
Aloe	Succulent	Many have rosettes of spiny, attractively marked leaves and spikes of flowers.
Cephalocereus senilis	Cactus	Old man cactus. Cylindrical in appearance with dense coating of long grey hair.
Chamaecereus silvestrii	Cactus	Peanut cactus. Forms a mat of finger-like stems and produces brilliant scarlet, starry flowers.
Cotyledon	Succulent	Shrubby plants with attractively coloured foliage. Most have pendulous flowers.
Crassula	Succulent	A large group of variable shape and appearance, mostly very easy to grow. *C. argentia* is known as the jade plant.
Echinocactus grusonii	Cactus	A popular species with globular form, and spines, Slow growing, eventually becoming large.
Echinocereus	Cactus	Ribbed, free flowering and easy to grow.
Epiphyllums	Cactus	A group containing many named hybrids with enormous flowers, freely produced.
Euphorbia obesa	Succulent	Often called Turkish temple because of shape. Slow grower, eventually reaching the size of an orange. *E. milii* is also popular.
Kalanchoe	Succulent	Flaming Katy. Large range of hybrids, popularly grown from seed.
Lithops	Succulent	So-called living stones because of their pebble-like appearance. They have very showy flowers.
Mammillaria	Cactus	Globular in shape and spiny; encircled with delightful flowers.
Schlumbergera	Cactus	A popular group that includes the Christmas cactus, crab cactus and Easter cactus. All have attractive flowers.

FRUIT AND VEGETABLES

Growing food crops in the greenhouse can be very worthwhile financially. There are also other important benefits. You can be sure of a fresh supply that has excellent flavour and texture, is high in vitamins and conveniently at hand at any time. Useful food crops can be grown all year round and, with careful planning, you can usually fit them in with most of your favourite decorative plants, thus getting the best of both worlds.

For home greenhouse gardeners it is important, as we have already seen, to avoid using the ground soil for growing. You can grow most food crops in containers of some kind. Proprietary growing bags and growing boards, which swell up after the addition of water and are easier to transport, are very popular now. Since some crops need quite a large quantity of compost, DIY mixes of peat and grit, with added proprietary, premixed balanced fertilizers, can be made up for economy.

Most food crops require good light conditions. In gloom they may crop badly and have poor quality and flavour. Glass-to-ground greenhouses and those sited in open, light positions, usually give best results, especially for winter crops.

Even the most efficiently run greenhouses are liable to invasion by pests and diseases. If you use pesticides on food crops, make a special point of reading the labels carefully. Some are safer than others; some are too toxic and not suitable at all. The edible safety period for harvesting after treatment must be noted and followed exactly.

Most of the edible crops are cheaply raised from seed. The sowing technique is much the same as that for decorative plants (see page 194).

Electric soil-warming cables can be extremely useful in growing some crops. They are invaluable for warming frames in the greenhouse and for gently forcing winter and early salad crops. They can also be used to provide a little extra root warmth for various other crops so that you can enjoy them earlier.

AUBERGINE
This is grown in much the same way as the sweet pepper (see page 189), but it needs a strong cane to support the heavy fruits. Allow only two or three fruits to mature per plant; pick the others off as early as possible. The young plants can be 'stopped' to encourage short bushy growth but this delays cropping. The plants can grow to about 1m (3ft) without 'stopping'. Grow them in large pots or growing bags. The variety 'Early Purple' can be recommended. It is best to pick the ripe aubergines while the 'bloom' or shine is still on them because when this goes they begin to have a bitter flavour.

CABBAGE AND CAULIFLOWER
The cabbage varieties 'Hispi' and 'May Star' can be sown January/March for planting out later and harvesting from May onwards. Transfer seedlings, initially, to small pots for growing on. In very cold areas, autumn sow and plant out in early March.

Cauliflowers for starting under glass must be chosen carefully from those varieties sold for sowing in September and harvesting May/June. Winter cauliflower (curding broccoli) can be sown April/May for cropping January. There are both hardy and less hardy varieties. Select according to your greenhouse temperature. Keep plants in frames during the summer. When moved to the greenhouse, space them 450mm (18in) apart.

CAPE GOOSEBERRY

This plant is related to the garden ornamental Chinese lantern. In the greenhouse it is cultivated for the golden-yellow berries that develop inside the lantern-shaped husks. The berries are about the size of large cherries and golden yellow when ready to eat. They have a pleasant, refreshing flavour eaten raw and can also be cooked and used in preserves.

For greenhouse culture choose the variety 'Golden Berry'. Grow the plants at first in the same way as tomatoes (see page 190). Use the same size pots and place in a light position. The height to which they are grown can vary considerably. You can 'stop' the plants at an early stage to encourage bushy growth and to get more fruits, but avoid too much 'stopping' since it may delay fruiting. The main harvest should be about late summer.

The true Cape gooseberry is *Physalis peruviana* (*P. edulis*) but, as grown, other species may be involved.

Below *Cabbages raised from seed in the greenhouse are grown on in pots for planting out later.*

CLIMBING FRENCH BEAN

The ideal minimum temperature for this crop is about 13°C (55°F) – it's wise not to start it too early in the year. Late winter is probably the best time. Grow the plants in the same way as tomatoes (see page 190) and in the same position, spacing 350mm (14in) apart. Provide strings for the plants to climb up, and 'stop' the laterals and secondary laterals (side shoots) at the third joint. A recent new variety recommended for the greenhouse is 'Selka'. The crop should be mature by late spring. Gather at once for best flavour and clear the site which can then be used for tomatoes.

Above *French beans should be picked young. The pods should snap off the plant.*

Training and 'stopping' are essential for a good crop of high quality cucumbers.

few fruits, the plants can be trained up canes. Training properly on strings should ensure cropping over a long period.

For proper training it is best to set the growing containers at staging level. The roof above should be fitted with strings running lengthways about 200mm (8in) apart. At first, grow the plants as a single stem up the greenhouse side with canes for support. Remove all side shoots. When a plant reaches the roof, lead it under the strings. Laterals which then form should be led along the nearest string. By the time four leaves have formed, the female flowers should also have developed. Now 'stop' the shoot. Secondary laterals will now grow out and can be secured to a string and treated in a similar manner. The main stem should be 'stopped' when it has reached the uppermost string.

Keep the compost moist, but be very careful not to overwater. Wet conditions quickly cause deterioration, leaves go yellow and fruits start to rot, or drop while immature. The best quality is obtained when plants are grown so that the fruits form and mature quickly.

CUCUMBER

The home-grown cucumber can far excel the shop-bought product. The flavour, crispness, and digestibility of modern varieties are excellent and, nowadays, they are easy to grow; there are all-female varieties needing little attention to prevent pollination (see below), there are new pesticides available that do not harm the cucumber family in general. The crop can be grown alongside other plants including tomato. There is also often greater tolerance of low temperatures.

Ordinary varieties bear both male and female flowers and it is vital to prevent pollination of the females. Do this by promptly picking off the male flowers, which are the ones without tiny fruits attached. If pollination occurs, the fruits will go to seed, becoming club-shaped and sometimes bitter in taste. The 'all-female' varieties produce few, if any, male flowers and, although the seed is more expensive, the yield and flavour is usually far superior.

Sow the flattish seeds on their sides in small pots. Early March is a good sowing time. Germination occurs in a few days at about 18°C (64°F). Grow on in small pots in the same way as tomatoes (see page 190), subsequently planting into large pots or growing bags. If you want only a

FIG

Given a free root run, figs can become far too rampant and invasive for the home greenhouse, so it's wise to grow them in large free-standing pots or small tubs. This way the plants can be put outdoors in summer, which saves space and seems to improve the crop. However, some people do prefer to fan-train them against the wall of a lean-to, which should preferably be south facing. The most popular variety is 'Brown Turkey'. This is available, container grown, from garden centres.

The best planting time is spring. When the fruit is borne, 'stop' the fruit-bearing shoots about four leaves beyond, and allow only about three or four fruits per shoot to develop. The fruits are upright as they develop. When they hang down they are ripe and can be picked. Prune in spring, cutting out weak or excessive growth.

The fig 'Brown turkey' has medium-sized fruit.

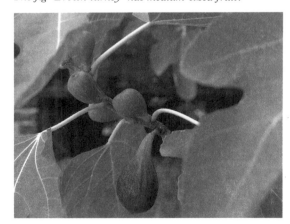

A grape vine should bear a good crop like this by its third year.

GRAPE

The grape vine is not a good companion for other plants. It does not want heat in winter and it can also severely cut out the light level. The best management can be given when the plant has a house to itself. Lean-tos make particularly good vineries.

The traditional way to grow the vines is to plant the roots outside the greenhouse, in a border running alongside. The stems, called 'rods', are then led through small holes made along the base and up inside the greenhouse. The roots can be put inside the greenhouse, but various troubles due to drying out and soil sickness are then liable to develop. Plant early in the year and then cut back the roots to about 450mm (18in). For the average greenhouse, allow two shoots to grow, leading them horizontally in opposite directions. The lateral shoots that grow from these can be trained vertically. Shoots from this upright growth should be stopped when 600mm (2ft) long, and cut back in winter. The main upright shoots should then be cut back too.

The side shoots must be fastened to wires in the second year and all laterals reduced to one or two buds in winter. A few bunches of grapes may appear in the second year, and the third year should bring a good crop. However, do not allow more than one bunch to form on each lateral. The bunches must be thinned. Do this with finely tipped scissors, without touching the grapes with your fingers as this spoils the 'bloom'.

No heating is necessary in winter but during flowering try to maintain a minimum temperature of 13°C (55°F). Efficient ventilation is essential to deter mildew, which is a common problem.

Although vines are now container grown and sold by garden centres, it's advisable to buy from a specialist grower who will also suggest suitable varieties.

Grape vines can be grown in pots. 'Royal Muscadine' and 'Black Hamburgh' have long been cultivated in this way. The vines are potted at Christmas and put outdoors at first. In late winter they are taken into the greenhouse where no heating is necessary. They are trained on a pair of vertical bamboos, up one and then down the other. Laterals must be thinned to about 300mm (12in) apart and 'stopped' two leaves from where a bunch of grapes develops. You receive only about six bunches per plant and the plants have to be discarded after three years.

185

Kiwi fruit grow only on a female plant but a male one is essential for pollination.

KIWI FRUIT

Also known as the Chinese gooseberry, this is becoming more widely available in fruit shops. It is a brownish, furry, elongate fruit about the size of a large egg, and is quite delicious. *Actinidia chinensis* makes a good wall shrub for a lean-to greenhouse or conservatory. Buy the plants from a specialist nursery in pairs – a male and a female. The former is needed for pollination and can be planted outside the greenhouse provided it's close by. Insects will then usually visit both plants, but to be sure of fruit, you can hand pollinate the creamy-yellow female flowers using fluffed-up cotton wool. Plants can also be grown in large pots. 'Stop' them when young to produce branching for wall training. Prune in February.

LETTUCE

This crop can be grown in the greenhouse for gathering from winter to spring. It is essential to choose suitable varieties (see below) since some are quite unsatisfactory for cultivation under glass.

Lettuce can be grown in troughs or trenches of specially prepared compost or in pots. Some people use ground soil but the crop is often then attacked by grey mould, which causes the plant to wilt or collapse.

Sow the seed as described on page 194. Prick out the seedlings into seed trays for growing-on and transfer them to permanent positions when large enough to handle. Give good light and ventilation.

The variety 'Kwiek' is suitable for a cold greenhouse, and should be sown in late summer to crop in winter. 'Kloek' can also be grown in cold conditions but should be sown in autumn for spring use. 'Sea Queen', which can be grown in either cool or cold conditions, is sown in late summer or winter for winter or spring cropping. 'Emerald' can be treated similarly. Sow 'May Queen' in autumn or spring in a cold or cool greenhouse for spring or summer cropping. 'Dandie', which is a fast maturing variety, can be sown in autumn to give you a good crop from late autumn onwards.

A bumper crop of greenhouse-grown lettuces.

'Early Sweet' is a large Cantaloupe melon, which can be grown like the Casaba type.

MELON

The best melons to grow in the greenhouse are the very large Casaba types. The small kinds, such as Musk or Cantaloupe, are more suitable for frame culture.

Treatment is the same as for cucumber in the early stages. The training is also similar, but differs in that the strings for support, which must be strong, should be spaced further apart, about 300mm (12in). The female flowers must be deliberately pollinated. Do this by removing a male flower, which is one with no swelling behind it on the stalk, and transferring the pollen directly to the female flowers, which have the swelling. Successful pollination is indicated by the swellings becoming larger and soon taking the form of tiny melons.

Melons need plenty of light and there is rarely need for shading. Allow only three to four fruits on each plant. When the fruit has matured, avoid excessive humidity and ventilate more freely than before. Owing to their weight, the fruit may need supporting with netting; you can improvise with string bags. Fruit is ripe when the opposite end from the stalk feels soft when you press it with a finger; and when it gives off a fruity aroma.

Recommended varieties are 'Superlative', 'Hero of Lockinge', and 'Emerald Gem'. The Cantaloupe melon, 'Early Sweet', is a vigorous F1 hybrid and larger than others of this kind. It can be grown like the Casabas. Of the Cantaloupes the variety 'No Name' is especially recommended for unheated frames. Sow and raise initially in the greenhouse.

MUSHROOM

The mushroom is the fungus *Psalliota campestris*. It is a useful crop for the understage area, if a temperature of about 10°C (50°F) minimum can be maintained. The area can be sectioned off and heated with soil warming cables for economy, if desired. Mushroom growing is normally an elaborate procedure requiring special composts and spawn. However, it is now made easy by the availability of ready-spawned 'buckets' stocked by most seedsmen. Full instructions, which are quite simple, are provided. You can obtain a constant supply of fresh, delicious mushrooms using this method, but they may not be cheap.

PEACH, NECTARINE, APRICOT

These, like the grape, are not generally suitable for growing in a mixed greenhouse collection. The ideal site for them is the rear wall of a south-facing lean-to. They are grown in much the same way as other wall-trained outdoor plants, except that hand pollination is usually required. This is simply done by brushing over the flowers lightly with a piece of fluffed-up cotton wool. Midday is the best time to do it.

If you grow them in the greenhouse, keep the atmosphere moderately humid by damping down, but do not spray the flowers with water. Apricots can be tricky and the flowers tend to drop if the temperature rises high and ventilation is inadequate. Contact a specialist nursery when buying the plants. Recently there have been new varieties introduced and also specially dwarfed forms, which are ideal for growing in pots or limited space.

Some old-established varieties are 'Lord Napier' and 'Early Rivers' (nectarine); 'Moorpark' (apricot); 'Hale's Early' and 'Duke of York' (peach).

Mushrooms can be grown easily in bags of ready-spawned compost under greenhouse staging.

SPROUTING SEEDS

Seed sprouts (salad sprouts), which include a variety of plants, have recently received much publicity because of their possible health-giving properties. In particular, they often have high vitamin and protein content and in some cases minerals too. They are delicious, and in winter, salad sprouts can be especially welcome. You can produce an edible crop within about one week.

Many seedsmen offer packets of seeds suitable for sprouting and supply full instructions. The best place to grow them is in a propagator. A temperature of about 20°C (68°F) is desirable, which can be attained in most simple propagating cases. The old favourite, mustard and cress, is included in this group. You can also sprout mung bean (*Phaseolus mungo*) well known because of its use in Chinese cooking, alfalfa (*Medicago sativa*) particularly valuable for winter salads, adzuki beans (*Phaseolus angularis*) with a nutty flavour, and fenugreek (*Trigonella foenum-graecum*).

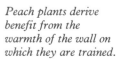

Peach plants derive benefit from the warmth of the wall on which they are trained.

SQUASHES

These include courgettes, marrows, and pump-kins. They are not usually cropped in the greenhouse, but the sowings and initial growing of the young plants can be made under glass to ensure earlier crops. Don't forget to harden off the young plants (see page 195) before putting them outdoors.

STRAWBERRY

These are really most suited to frames but a few pots can be grown in the greenhouse. They look good planted in special strawberry urns, which are available at most garden centres. Buy the plants freshly each year from a specialist grower who will have the fine modern varieties. Grow them on outdoors until early in the year. Pot up in an approved compost, one plant to each 130mm (5in) pot if desired. The best minimum temperature is 7°C (45°F). Hand pollinate by brushing over the flowers lightly with fluffed-up cotton wool.

Pumpkins, such as this variety, 'Patty Pan', can be started into growth in the greenhouse.

Strawberry plants can be decorative as well as useful in a greenhouse.

SWEET PEPPER

The correct common name for this plant is pimiento, but sometimes the incorrect name 'cap-sicum', suggesting a hot taste, is given. This crop is well worth growing particularly because it is expensive to buy yet quite easy to grow. The F1 hybrid varieties are especially recommended. Initially, treat in the same way as tomatoes (see page 190), sowing the seed at about the same time. Unlike tomatoes, rogueing is not necessary. Pot the young plants finally into 180mm (7in) pots. For some of the taller varieties a cane may be needed for support. From then on little attention, apart from watering, is necessary until the tiny fruits start to form. Depending on variety, you may need to thin these to prevent overcrowding, giving room for those left to develop properly. The fruits are ready to pick from summer on-wards. The green fruits ripen through yellow to red, even if picked at the green stage, provided they are stored in a warm place.

Sweet peppers can be picked and eaten when still green or left to ripen to red.

'Big boy' tomato has giant fruits which are firm with good flavour.

TOMATOES

The tomato is the most popular of all home greenhouse crops. Some people fit in a few pots here and there, others give it a large part of the greenhouse. Although the tomato is easy to grow, it can be affected by a variety of problems, but many can be avoided, as they generally arise when the crop is grown in the ground soil for several years. Excellent plants can be grown in large pots, growing bags or other containers. The system of ring culture (see opposite) also works well. The best position for the crop is one with good light. The south side of an east-west greenhouse is ideal.

There are now many seed varieties. 'Money-maker', is an old favourite but it has been largely replaced by 'Alicante'. Don't be afraid to be adventurous. A selection is given in the table.

Sow the seeds from late winter onwards, using the methods given on page 194. The ideal germination temperature is 16°C (61°F). Prick out the seedlings into 80–100mm (3–4in) pots of an approved potting compost and grow on until well rooted. The plants should then be 'rogued'. This means discarding any that are weak, stunted or distorted, or have pale-coloured or mottled foliage, and any that have a bushy or unusually vigorous habit. Such plants are liable to prove unproductive and may be affected by diseases.

When potting the plants into their final pots, try to use at least 250mm (10in) pots. Fibre disposable pots, usually about 230mm in diameter can also be used. If the pots are too small the roots suffer from erratic changes in water availability and temperature, which should be avoided. Use an approved compost and, when potting, leave a space between the compost surface and the top of the pot. This can be topped up with fresh compost as the plant develops and the compost shrinks.

The plants need strings (use rough string) or canes for support. Train them round these in a clockwise direction. It is essential, as a daily routine, to remove the side shoots that appear at the joints between the main stem and the leaves. To obtain a good set of fruit, distribute the pollen by tapping the plants or spraying with a mist of water when conditions are bright and warm. You can also spray with a hormone setting preparation.

When fruit is ripening, avoid temperatures over 27°C (81°F). With too much heat the red pigment does not form and you may get green rings, or greenish/yellowish blotches. An excellent shading product is found in Coolglass, which gives the right degree of shade for strong growth but does not cast gloom. Remove any foliage that has deteriorated, but avoid excessive defoliation as this weakens plants and can spoil the fruit flavour. Special high potassium tomato feeds are available which should be used according to the label instructions.

When plants reach the greenhouse roof, pinch out the growing tips. This allows the fruit on the plants to reach maturity and ripen before conditions become too cool. It is essential to avoid erratic changes of any kind. Keep the compost moist all the time. Feed often with weak feeds and try to prevent wide temperature fluctuations. If these points are ignored, flower shedding, immature fruit fall, blotchy ripening, split skins, sun scald, or dark-coloured rots at the stalk or flower end of the fruit may occur.

RING CULTURE

This is often used for tomato cultivation but can also be adapted for other similar crops, including aubergine, sweet pepper and cucumber. The plants are grown in bottomless rings. You can buy disposable fibre rings, about 230mm in diameter, made for the purpose. The procedure is as follows. Put down a layer of aggregate, such as clean shingle or, preferably, coarse peat on a strip of polythene to prevent contact with the greenhouse ground soil. The polythene should be slit for drainage here and there if necessary. The rings are then placed on the aggregate, which should be about 130mm (5in) thick, and filled with an approved potting compost, into which the tomatoes are planted. The compost must be kept moist until the roots of the plants have reached the aggregate layer. From then on, water is applied only to the aggregate layer, which is kept constantly moist. Moisture rises up into the compost from the aggregate by capillary action. Feeding with liquid feeds, however, is done via the compost in the rings. The lower roots of the plants are the 'drinking roots' and the upper ones are the 'feeders'. This method gives the plants a highly stable environment and lends itself well to automatic watering systems. It is particularly useful if you have to leave plants unattended for long periods. At the end of the season, discard the aggregate; use fresh material for the next crop to prevent pest and disease carry over.

'Tigerella' is an early tomato with yellow striped fruit.

'Yellow Perfection' is a tomato of fine quality and superb flavour.

RECOMMENDED TOMATO VARIETIES

Alicante	Good general quality and disease resistance.
Big boy	Huge fruits of fleshy texture. Excellent for slicing and for sandwiches.
Eurocross A	Similar to Moneymaker, but superior vigour and yield.
Growers pride F1	Recommended for beginners. Good early yield. Generally useful.
Mandel F1	Good disease resistance and generally useful. Dark red colour.
Odine F1	Short jointed and ideal for small greenhouses. Generally useful.
Tigerella	Fruit has yellow stripes. Excellent flavour. Early. Generally useful.
Vibelco	Said to be the most disease resistant of all varieties so far.
Yellow perfection	Golden yellow fruits of exceptional flavour and quality. Must be tried.

PROPAGATION

So that you can make the most of your greenhouse, it is a good idea to become familiar with the techniques used to propagate plants. Once you are proficient in using these you can increase your stock, decrease your expenditure and sometimes help to preserve plants already in your collection. Most forms of propagation are also fascinating and give pleasure in themselves.

Some plants are very easy to propagate, others very difficult. The easy ones tend to become far too numerous, so be wary of accepting all propagating material, such as cuttings, offered by friends. Never use plant material which is itself unhealthy or has been taken from a diseased or pest-infected plant. For propagation, only use the best in both general quality and health. Undesirable characteristics can be inherited as well as desirable ones, and certain diseases, such as virus infections, can also be passed on.

PROPAGATING EQUIPMENT

For the quick and efficient propagation of most greenhouse plants it is best to set aside a specific area. It will need to be warmed from underneath and have a transparent cover to retain heat and moisture while letting in light. You can make up such an area yourself by laying electric warming cables over a part of the staging, covering it with sand, then enclosing it with transparent plastic sheeting or a glass frame. The suppliers of warming cables give recommendations for their use in propagation. As a rough guide, a 120–150 watt cable will heat a space about 1.5m × 600mm (5ft × 2ft). It can be thermostatically controlled. Other forms of electric greenhouse heater, such as tubes (see page 159), can be used, either controlled manually or thermostatically. A paraffin lamp is another possible heat source.

You may prefer to buy a ready-made propagator. These are available with electric or paraffin heaters. Electric ones are preferable, if you have the power supply, because they have a thermostat which makes them easy to control and set for different temperatures as required. For most greenhouse propagation, a range of temperature from little more than frost free, for hardy plants, to about 27°C (80°F), for sub-tropicals, is necessary. Many plants need a high temperature for propagation, higher than they normally require once established, so it's important to check that a propagator can give high temperatures when necessary.

The propagators available vary greatly in size, temperature range, and design. For the greenhouse, choose a covered design that has a variable temperature control and is of a suitable size for your requirements and the amount of space you have available. It is often useful to have room enough to keep plants in congenial warmth after propagation, until they become well established. Large enclosed propagators can be used as a permanent home for a small sub-tropical plant collection.

A mist propagation area, in which propagating material is coated with moisture by a central misting jet and warmed by warming cables.

USING A PROPAGATOR

A propagator should have a base of sand which is always kept moist. The moist sand distributes the warmth evenly and keeps the atmosphere in the propagator humid. Dry conditions must be avoided because propagating material, such as seeds and cuttings, can quickly become dehydrated and die before roots have a chance to form. A transparent cover is also desirable to retain moisture and warmth, particularly for plants needing higher temperatures. Light is another essential for much propagation, but you should avoid direct sunlight. Site the propagator or propagation area where there's slight shade. If necessary, shade an area of the greenhouse glass with white Coolglass. Excessively high temperatures can also cause severe damage, and it is important to remember that the temperature in the propagator is affected by the temperature of its surroundings.

The propagator comes into its own about late winter to spring, when it is used for such purposes as striking cuttings, seed germination, and starting tubers etc. into growth. During the rest of the year there is usually sufficient natural warmth for the types of plants then propagated.

A well-designed, electrically heated, covered propagator. The temperature can be varied and is controlled by a thermostat.

POTTING BENCH

This is an area of staging set aside for potting, seed sowing, preparation of cuttings, mixing composts and similar operations. A portable bench is a good idea. This can be simply made using a sheet of aluminium or zinc, which is available from most builders' merchants or DIY shops. Select the right size for the chosen section of your staging, then turn up the sides of the sheet to form a three-sided tray to fit the space exactly. Keep the surface clean and wipe down from time to time with disinfectant (see page 199).

A portable bench or tray provides a conveniently sized hygienic surface for potting and similar tasks.

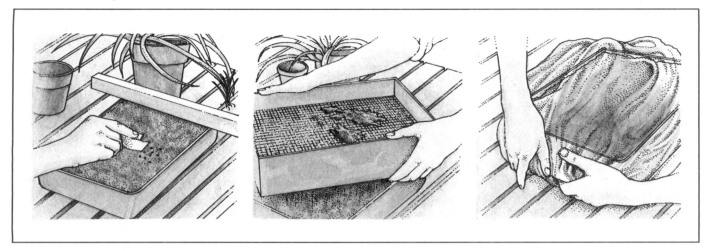

PROPAGATION FROM SEED

Seed is a cheap source of plants and, nowadays, is widely available from plants that grow all over the world.

Sometimes you can save seed from your own plants or from other growing sources. Seed from hybrids, however, particularly F1 hybrids, is usually unreliable. It may not yield plants true to type and should not be saved.

Seed should be ripe and reasonably fresh. Old seed generally germinates poorly. Sow as soon as possible after you get it or, if it has to be kept a while, store in a cool, dry place in the home. Do not leave packets in the damp and heat of a greenhouse. Most seed companies now supply seed in special sealed packs with controlled humidity. Seed will remain viable for a long time when kept in these packs but normal ageing begins once they have been opened.

To make tiny seed easier to handle, some varieties are pelleted with an inert material by the seedsmen. However, there is some difference of opinion about whether this is an advantage, since germination of this type is sometimes poor. To hasten germination, large seeds can be soaked in water overnight before sowing. Another common practice which is used particularly for tough or hard-coated seeds, is to slice off a tiny sliver of the outer coating with a razor blade, being very careful not to damage the interior.

Seed must be sown in proper seed compost to ensure success. You can use John Innes loam–based seed compost or any of the numerous proprietary peat-based seed composts now available. Another essential is general cleanliness. Keep the seed compost in closed plastic bags or containers when not in use. Make sure that the rectangular plastic seed trays in which you put the seed compost are kept clean, as well as the plastic pots which are used for sowing some larger types of seed. Fill the tray or pot by lightly pressing the compost into it to about 1cm ($\frac{1}{2}$ inch) below the

When sowing seed, tap it from the packet with the forefinger. A sieve can be used to riddle compost over very fine seed. Finally, cover the tray with polythene to help retain moisture.

rim. Then level off the surface and firm it down with your hand. Before you begin sowing, label each container. It is a good idea to put the date as well as the name of the seeds. Be sure to use a waterproof pencil.

The compost must be made moist before sowing; it should be neither dry nor waterlogged. Sow thinly to make pricking out easy. Very fine seed should not be covered with compost after sowing. Otherwise the rule is to cover the seed with a depth of compost roughly equal to its own diameter. The best way to sow is to tap the seed from the packet with your forefinger while moving your hand over the surface. To aid even distribution of very fine seed when sowing, mix the seed with a little silver sand. Large seed can be sown with the fingers or a pair of tweezers. If there is a lot of seed in a packet, there is no need to sow it all at once. Often sowings can be staggered over a couple of weeks or so. This will provide batches of plants in different stages of development, giving you longer flowering and cropping periods. After sowing, water-in the seed using a mist of water from a fine sprayer. The same technique should be used for subsequent waterings, and also, for watering the tiny seedlings when they show through. It is not a good idea to water by immersing the sowing containers in water, as is so often suggested, because this leaches out all the soluble fertilizers added to the seed compost. Overwatering must in fact be avoided since too much water can suffocate the seed – air must be able to penetrate for it to germinate. On the other hand, complete drying out once the seed has started to germinate is equally fatal.

GERMINATION AND AFTERCARE

After sowing, cover the seed container with a sheet of clean white paper, then lay a piece of glass on top or slide it into a polythene bag to help retain moisture; the paper prevents drips of condensation from saturating the compost surface and waterlogging the seed. Some greenhouse plant seed germinates best if exposed to a certain amount of light, which is all the more reason for not sowing too deeply. This is particularly worth doing with bromeliads, cacti and other succulents, calceolarias, rubber plants, gloxinias, lettuce, petunias, African violets and Cape primroses.

When the containers are put in a propagator be careful to check that the temperature is optimum for the seed type. Obviously, one must not try to germinate different types of seed with widely different temperature requirements at the same time. If the temperature is excessively high, although germination will be speeded up, pale, weak, lanky seedlings will be produced.

Most of the popular greenhouse-sown seed germinates in one to three weeks. Some may take considerably longer, so do be patient. As soon as germination is seen to be taking place, remove all covering. Pricking out and transferring to potting compost must be done as soon as the seedlings can be safely handled without damage. The sooner this is done after germination the less setback the seedling will suffer and the less likelihood there is of damaging the roots. The best tool for this job is a pair of long finely tipped tweezers but be careful not to actually grasp the seedlings with them. Just lift using the 'V' shape made by the tips of the tweezers. You can adjust the distance between the tips, according to seedling root size, by varying your finger pressure. Another popular tool for pricking out is a thin strip of wood or plastic with a 'V' notch cut at the end. If you need to handle a seedling with the fingers, lift it by one of the first formed 'seed leaves' and not by the stem. Replant the seedlings using a blunt-pointed dibber to make holes in the potting compost just large enough to take the roots easily.

The seedlings can be transferred to pots or to plastic seedling trays, depending on their further treatment. Many pot plants can initially be grown-on for a time in trays, which avoids the use of lots of small pots. To prevent damping-off (see page 200), water-in the seedlings with Cheshunt compound.

In the case of bedding plants, be particularly careful not to overcrowd seed trays. About 24 plants per tray is average. Seed, such as lobelia that yields crowds of minute seedlings, should be 'patched' out. This means lifting them in tiny groups and not attempting to separate out individual seedlings. The groups can be subsequently treated as a single plant and will grow as a clump perfectly well.

HARDENING-OFF

Before bedding plants are put out in permanent positions in the garden, they must be gradually acclimatized to full light conditions and low temperatures. If this is not done, and they are suddenly transferred from the warmth of the greenhouse, they will immediately become sickly and take a long time to start growing. Start hardening-off about two weeks before planting-out time which is roughly May–June, depending on area. If you are not sure about the timing, find out what the local parks or keen neighbouring gardeners do. The hardening-off procedure begins with moving the plants to the coolest part of the greenhouse, then, later, to closed unheated frames outside. Shade the frames from full sun at first but reduce the degree of shade or the period of shading each day. At the same time, give more and more ventilation until the plants are fully exposed. In the early stages, however, it may be necessary to close the frames at night if you think that there is any risk of frost.

Lift the seedling carefully from underneath when pricking out. Handle only the seed leaves.

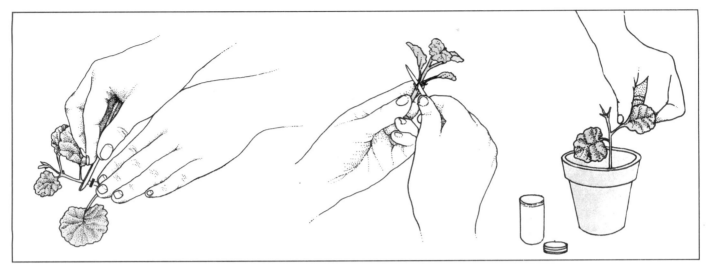

For a softwood cutting, cut off selected shoot with a sharp blade, pull away lower leaves and make a clean cut below nodes, dip stem in hormone rooting compound and insert in compost.

VEGETATIVE PROPAGATION

SOFTWOOD CUTTINGS

Cuttings taken from greenhouse plants are usually 'softwood', that is taken from soft immature growth. The best time to take cuttings is when the plants have just moved into their active growth period, as in spring. However, some cuttings can be taken in early autumn. Semi-hardwood and hardwood cuttings are cut from woody plants and shrubs. These can also be rooted in the greenhouse.

When taking cuttings, select small vigorous shoots – about a finger length is long enough. Use a sharp blade such as a razor, so not to bruise the tissue, and cut the shoot at the base of the stem, just below the point where the leaves are borne. The leaves, just above the cut, must then be pulled away. It is from this point that the roots will eventually emerge. The cutting is then inserted into a cutting compost consisting of a mixture of clean grit and peat. A proprietary cutting compost can also be used. Several cuttings may be inserted around the edge of a pot, but seed trays can be used instead if there are many cuttings to be rooted. Small bags, like mini growing bags, are available for rooting cuttings. Finally, put the cuttings where they will receive the correct amount of warmth and will not lose moisture during rooting. Covering the containers with clear sheet polythene or a polythene bag may be adequate, or use a covered propagator to provide extra warmth and maintain humidity.

You can dip the base of the cuttings in a hormone rooting preparation before insertion into the compost. This sometimes hastens rooting, and most of these preparations also contain a fungicide to prevent rotting. Some cuttings of greenhouse plants, such as nerium and tradescantia, root very easily just standing in water, for example. Others, such as camellia, take quite a time. The cuttings and the compost must not be allowed to dry out whilst rooting. The method known as 'mist propagation' automatically keeps cuttings sprayed with a fine mist of water to keep them at the point of maximum water uptake. Small units for this method are now available for the keen amateur. As soon as a reasonable root system has developed, the cuttings must be potted into a proper potting compost.

A very simple procedure for rooting cuttings without the aid of a propagator in summer and early autumn is to put a little cutting compost at the bottom of small polythene bags and insert the cuttings in this. The bags are then closed and hung up in the greenhouse. When rooting occurs it can be seen through the polythene.

LEAF CUTTINGS

This method can be used for a large number of favourite greenhouse plants, particularly for the gesneria and begonia families. It is especially applicable to plants with bold leaf veins. Leaf cuttings can be propagated in several ways. The simplest is to take a leaf and make slits with a razor blade in the veins at intervals on the undersurface. The leaf is then placed flat, slits downward, on the surface of some cutting compost. A few clean pebbles can be used, if necessary, to keep it flat and in close contact. Roots will grow from the slits and tiny plants form that can be separated and potted. Leaves can also be cut into small triangles with a vein at the apex of each triangle. The point with the vein is then inserted into the rooting compost in the same way as a stem cutting. If plants have elongate leaves these can usually be cut into sections, and each inserted in a similar manner. Some small-leaved plants, such as African violets and peperomias, can be propagated by merely detaching a leaf with a piece of stalk attached and inserting it as far as the top of the stalk in a rooting compost. Leaf cuttings usually need warmth, and the maintenance of humidity is essential.

DIVISION

This is the simplest and quickest way of propagation and can be done with any plants that form a clump of roots. First remove the plant from its pot, then, using a sharp knife, cut down through the clump to make several pieces. Pot each one in the usual manner. Division is best done with most plants just as growth is about to begin. Make sure the compost is moist, initially, but after potting be sparing with water until the plant is seen to be actively growing.

In the case of tuberous plants, division should be done after the tubers have started into growth, when well-defined shoots can be seen. Divide them up so that there's a shoot to each piece, then dust the cut surfaces with powdered charcoal to check sap loss before potting.

LAYERING

This method is used mainly for climbers and trailers but can sometimes be used for other plants if their stems are flexible enough. A length of stem is led into a pot of rooting compost so that a short portion is immersed. This is then weighted in position. You can either make a slit in the stem where it dips into the compost, or remove the leaves at that point, as with stem cuttings. When roots have formed, the stem is cut from the parent plant and potted into a potting compost.

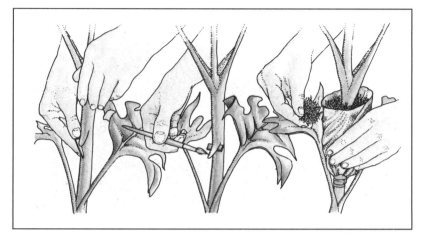

AIR LAYERING

This can be useful for plants that become 'leggy' and lose their lower leaves. It is most applicable for plants such as the rubber plant (*Ficus elastica*). First make a slit in the stem where a new root system is required and insert a tuft of peat dusted with a hormone powder. Then fasten a ball of moist peat and sphagnum moss around the slit, wrap it around with clear polythene sheeting and secure with string or florists' wire. When roots can be seen through the polythene, cut the stem just below the point from which they emerge and pot in the usual way. Moderate warmth over several weeks is essential for the success of this method, so it is best to start it during late spring.

When air layering, cut an upwards slit, insert a wedge of peat dusted with hormone powder and enclose with clear polythene containing moist peat and moss.

OFFSETS

Greenhouse bulbs and corms may produce small 'bulblets' around their sides as they reach maturity. These can be isolated and potted individually. Such small storage organs may take several years to become large enough to flower. Some rhizomes and tubers, such as achimenes and gloriosa, also reproduce themselves. The offspring can be separated during the dormant period and may flower well in the first year of potting.

Some plants, bromeliads, for example, send out shoots from the base which form into young plants. These can be carefully cut off close to the parent stem, which eventually dies, and potted separately.

Leaf cuttings: leaf with cut veins on underside and detached leaves with stalk in compost.

Separate offsets from the base of bulbous plants when repotting and pot these individually.

HYGIENE IN THE GREENHOUSE

A high standard of hygiene is essential to successful greenhouse horticulture. The congenial environment you provide for your plants is also one in which pests and diseases thrive and quickly multiply, spreading from plant to plant. The greenhouse structure and all equipment must, therefore, be kept clean, and sickly plants must be kept apart from healthy ones.

Crude animal manures, unsterilized leaf mould and garden soil must never be brought inside. Dirty rainwater collected from roofs is another source of infection. The dangers of using the ground soil have been explained (see page 160).

Pots, seed trays, and other similar equipment must be kept clean, and preferably sterilized before use each year. Seed and potting composts should be stored in clean plastic bags or lidded plastic bins to keep them free from contamination.

Cleaning the interior of the greenhouse is essential for combatting pests and diseases, while a clean exterior admits maximum light.

GREENHOUSE STERILIZATION

The term 'sterilization' does not have the same implications as it does when used to describe an operating theatre, for example. The aim in the greenhouse is to destroy as many as possible of the pests and diseases which might overwinter there. These are frequently found in the form of eggs or fungal spores. For the home gardener only a limited number of disinfectants are available, for safety reasons. The most widely used are those based on phenol. These are relatively safe, provided they are used strictly according to the instructions on the label.

The best time to disinfect and clean your greenhouse is when all plants can be removed, preferably before the main growing season begins. Autumn to late winter is often most convenient. You should start by washing down the entire interior structure, glass and frame, with a soft brush soaked with the manufacturer's recommended dilution of the disinfectant. Apply the solution generously and make sure it gets into cracks and joints, and into the 'T' slots of alloy structures. The floor and staging should be soaked too.

After this treatment, leave the house closed for a couple of days, then open vents and allow a few days for vapours to clear. Although there is usually a persistent odour, as long as all plants are container grown they can be moved back in without fear of damage. If the ground soil is treated, a longer period of time must elapse before it can be used for growing. A test can be made by sowing some cress seed in samples of the treated soil. If this germinates and grows normally, the soil is safe to use.

The phenolic disinfectants will clear algae, slimes and mosses. There is also a disinfectant called Algofen that can be used for this purpose during the growing period since it's safe with plants. It's excellent for keeping automatic watering systems and capillary matting, for example, algae free and hygienic. It can also be used on the surface of potting composts.

Don't use your greenhouse to store junk. Clutter will provide hiding places for pests and diseases and make cleaning difficult. Keep the exterior of the greenhouse crystal clear in winter to admit maximum light. Also, try to keep the surroundings weed free at all times, particularly because many weeds can be hosts for invasive pests, whitefly, for example.

PESTICIDES AND THEIR USE

The most important point before buying or using pesticides is to *read the label*. Then always follow the instructions exactly. Some pesticides damage certain plants and should not be used near them. With regard to food crops, there are usually restrictions on how soon they can be picked after spraying. Always avoid personal contact in any form. Never store pesticides in unlabelled containers or domestic bottles, and *keep them out of reach of children*.

Sprays are generally more effective than pesticidal dusts but the most efficient contact method is fumigation, either with 'smokes' or aerosols. Systemic pesticides are also extremely efficient since they are absorbed by the plant, making all parts poisonous to the pest. They remain active for a long time but they are not initially as fast acting as contact methods. Always make sure that the undersurfaces of leaves get thorough treatment, since this is usually where pests and diseases first congregate. It is wise to make routine inspections of your plants every few days. A small magnifying glass is helpful to spot minute pests such as red spider mite and mould or mildew spots in the early stages. Act immediately if trouble is suspected. Treatment is usually easier and more effective in the early stages.

Pay particular attention to the underside of the leaves when spraying with a pesticide.

Lighting the fuse of a cone fumigator. Check that no plants need to be removed before its use.

COMMON PESTS AND DISEASES

ANTS
When large numbers of ants invade the compost in pots they cause considerable root disturbance and severe plant wilting. They usually get in via the drainage holes. Several specific antkiller dusts are now available which are very effective.

APHIDS
Greenfly are the most common aphids in the greenhouse but others frequently find their way in too. Like a number of similar insects, they deposit a sticky secretion called 'honeydew' on which an unsightly blackish mould grows. There are many aphid killers on the market and you should choose according to the plants you are growing.

Spraying tomato plants. Leave for specified time before picking.

DAMPING-OFF
This is a problem affecting seedlings after pricking out, and is caused by several fungi. It is common when unsterilized composts, garden soil or crude manures are used, and where hygiene is poor. It causes the seedlings to topple over and shrivel. The trouble can spread very quickly unless immediately checked. You should water with Cheshunt compound, available from garden shops. It is advisable to do this as a routine preventive measure after all pricking out.

EARWIGS
The presence of this pest should be suspected if flower petals or leaves are being eaten away and left with tattered and ragged edges. Seedlings can also be attacked. Earwigs hide during daylight and become active at night so the damage may seem something of a mystery. Plants with large flowers, such as chrysanthemums, are very susceptible. Pots stuffed with straw and inverted on canes can be used to trap the earwigs. An effective chemical that is safe for most plants, including food crops, is permethrin.

GREY MOULD (Botrytis cinerea).
This mould always appears sooner or later, even in the best kept greenhouses. It attacks both living and dead plant tissues, forming a greyish-to-brownish furry covering. It is frequently seen on damaged tissue. If the mould is disturbed, a smoke-like cloud of spores is released which spreads the infection. Pelargoniums, lettuces, and chrysanthemum flowers are often affected. On tomatoes the fungus causes small whitish rings with a tiny central black speck on the fruits (ghost spotting). The fruit is, however, safe to eat. The fungus is encouraged by generally bad hygiene, poor ventilation and excessive humidity. Fortunately, TCNB fumigation and spraying with a mixture of benomyl and a foliar feed (a proprietary formulation is available) can both prevent and control the fungus. It's wise to use them as a preventive measure.

LEAFMINER
This pest particularly affects chrysanthemums, and sometimes polyanthus. It manifests itself as wandering brownish lines on the foliage, and a tiny burrowing grub is responsible. It can be prevented and controlled by spraying with permethrin, pirimphos-methyl, or gamma-HCH.

MEALY BUG
This appears as tiny scales with a mealy, whitish waxy covering. It is common on succulents and thick-leaved plants. Wipe off by hand when possible, using a tuft of cotton wool saturated in methylated spirit. Where infestation is considerable spray with pirimphos-methyl.

MOULDS AND MILDEWS

There is a wide variety of these fungi. Most of them form whitish-to-greyish velvety coatings on foliage, usually appearing at first as isolated patches. They are encouraged by poor ventilation, overcrowding and cold damp conditions. There are now a number of general-purpose fungicides available, including systemic types, which effectively control a wide spectrum of these fungi. The black sooty mould which grows on insect secretions is not in itself harmful, merely unsightly, but it could interfere with plant metabolism. It is best to wipe it off using cotton wool soaked in a weak solution of detergent in water.

RED SPIDER MITE

This can be a very serious pest if allowed to gain a hold. It usually appears during the summer months. Foliage may turn yellowish and plants become sickly for no apparent reason. A look at the undersurface of the leaves through a powerful lens will reveal tiny spider-like greyish-to-red mites and spherical whitish eggs. In severe attacks they may swarm and form an obvious web, by which time the plants are usually ruined and are best burnt. Sterilization helps to prevent the pest and kills overwintering eggs. Probably the best treatment and control is fumigation at seven-day intervals with a pirimphos-methyl smoke cone.

SCALE INSECTS

These are similar to mealy bugs in habit and they attack similar plants, but they appear as cream-to-brownish scales without the mealy coating. They often cause a sooty mould on foliage just below where they congregate. Treatment is the same as for mealy bug.

*Scale insects (**left**) and whitefly (**right**), two common pests which both cause sooty mould.*

SCIARID FLY MAGGOTS

These are tiny whitish-coloured maggots which attack roots and the base of plants and seedlings. They can do a surprisingly large amount of damage; wilting may be the first sign of their presence. They are the larvae of tiny flies, which may be noticed hovering nearby. Peat composts and damp conditions seem to encourage them. If possible, let pots become dryish and then water with pirimphos-methyl. The flies should be controlled by general fumigation with a general-purpose smoke cone.

SLUGS, SNAILS, WOODLICE

These common garden pests find their way into the greenhouse and cause severe damage. Just one snail or slug can eat a box of seedlings overnight. They hide during the day, under staging, for example. There are a number of baits available. The miniature pellets are particularly useful in the greenhouse. Woodlice eat roots and seedlings but are easily controlled with antkiller dusts.

THRIPS

These minute insects produce whitish patches surrounded by black specks on leaves. To confirm their presence, place white paper under the plant and shake the foliage. Wriggling insects will fall and show up clearly. Use a general systemic insecticide.

VIRUS DISEASES

Symptoms include yellowing and mottling of foliage, distortion, stunting, striping of flower colours, and general unsatisfactory growth. They can be spread by insects, pruning and cutting tools, and by handling. Plants should be burnt and not used for propagation. There's no cure.

WHITEFLY

This is a tiny fly with whitish triangular wings. It usually occurs in considerable numbers and, like aphids, causes sooty mould. Weeds around the greenhouse can harbour whitefly. Fumigate with special whitefly smoke cones.

PART 4

THE GARDENING YEAR

A work-planner (and memory-jogger) for the main gardening tasks in spring, summer, autumn and winter, this section provides schedules for sowing, planting, feeding, harvesting, pruning, weed-control, lawn maintenance and repair and much else in the flower garden, vegetable plot and fruit-growing area. Each seasonal chapter includes a perennial 'diary' in which you can make note of particular jobs that need to be attended to in your garden at that time every year.

SPRING

Spring is the busiest time of the year in the garden. Sowing and planting, of many plants, are in full swing. But beware of the weather. Mild spells will encourage early growth and germination, which could be knocked back by a sudden cold snap. At this time of the year cloches and frames are invaluable.

MARCH

ORNAMENTAL GARDEN

If the soil is sufficiently dry make a start in sowing hardy annuals.

Gladiolus corms and ranunculus tubers can be planted if soil conditions are suitable; so, too, can hardy herbaceous perennials.

Dormant dahlia tubers can be planted at the end of the month.

Evergreen shrubs can be planted at the end of the month.

Roses should be pruned just as they are starting into growth.

Carry out lawn repairs before mowing starts.

Sow summer bedding plants in the greenhouse.

Prune shrubs that flower on new wood.

UTILITY GARDEN

Apply and hoe-in a general-purpose fertilizer around all fruits. Give them a mulch, too.

As soon as the soil is in a suitable state, make a start with vegetable sowings.

Potatoes are planted at the end of the month.

If you have spring cabbages, give them a feed of high-nitrogen fertilizer to boost growth.

If the vegetable plot is still wet, put some cloches in place to help it dry out before sowing.

APRIL

ORNAMENTAL GARDEN

Sow hardy annuals outdoors and summer bedding plants under glass.

Continue to plant gladioli, dahlia tubers, herbaceous plants, summer-flowering bulbs, evergreen shrubs and conifers.

Continue with weed control; weeds will be in full growth by now.

There is still time to carry out lawn repairs and this is a good time to sow a new lawn, apply lawn fertilizer, moss killer and weedkiller.

Liquid feed spring bulbs after flowering.

Apply mulches around all permanent plants.

Lawn mowing starts in earnest this month.

UTILITY GARDEN

Spray fruits as necessary to control pests and diseases, but not when in flower.

Continue with vegetable sowings of all kinds.

Sow tomatoes in a greenhouse.

Thin out vegetables sown last month.

Earth up potatoes and plant maincrop varieties.

Support peas and tall broad beans.

MAY

ORNAMENTAL GARDEN

At the end of May plant summer bedding plants in tubs and prepared flower beds.

Sow seeds of hardy herbaceous perennials, trees and shrubs, rock plants, spring bedding plants and summer-flowering biennials for next year.

Discard spring bedding plants after flowering. Spring bulbs can be lifted and 'heeled-in' a spare piece of ground until the foliage has died down.

Chrysanthemum and dahlia plants can be set out (dahlias at the end of May).

Thin out hardy annuals if necessary.

Make a start on hedge trimming.

Water the lawn well in dry periods.

UTILITY GARDEN

Plant out tomatoes at the end of May.

Continue with vegetable sowings, including sprouting broccoli, cucumbers, kale, marrows and swedes.

Hoe regularly and water well in dry periods.

Keep an eye open for pests and diseases.

Plant tomatoes, capsicums, aubergines and cucumbers, in the greenhouse.

Daffodils and other bulbs light up the garden in spring.

SPRING DIARY

Use this space to write down the particular jobs that recur in your garden every spring.

MARCH

ORNAMENTAL GARDEN

SOW_____
_____
_____

PLANT_____
_____
_____

FEED_____
_____

PRUNE_____
_____

CONTROL PESTS ON_____
_____

OTHER TASKS_____
_____
_____
_____

UTILITY GARDEN

SOW_____
_____
_____

PLANT_____
_____
_____

FEED_____
_____

PRUNE_____
_____

CONTROL PESTS ON_____
_____

OTHER TASKS_____

APRIL

ORNAMENTAL GARDEN

SOW_____
_____
_____

PLANT_____
_____
_____

FEED_____
_____

PRUNE_____
_____

CONTROL PESTS ON_____
_____

OTHER TASKS_____
_____
_____
_____

UTILITY GARDEN

SOW_____
_____
_____

PLANT_____
_____
_____

FEED_____
_____

PRUNE_____
_____

CONTROL PESTS ON_____
_____

OTHER TASKS_____

MAY

ORNAMENTAL GARDEN

SOW_____
_____
_____

PLANT_____
_____
_____

FEED_____
_____

PRUNE_____
_____

CONTROL PESTS ON_____
_____

OTHER TASKS_____
_____
_____
_____

UTILITY GARDEN

SOW_____
_____
_____

PLANT_____
_____
_____

FEED_____
_____

PRUNE_____
_____

CONTROL PESTS ON_____
_____

OTHER TASKS_____

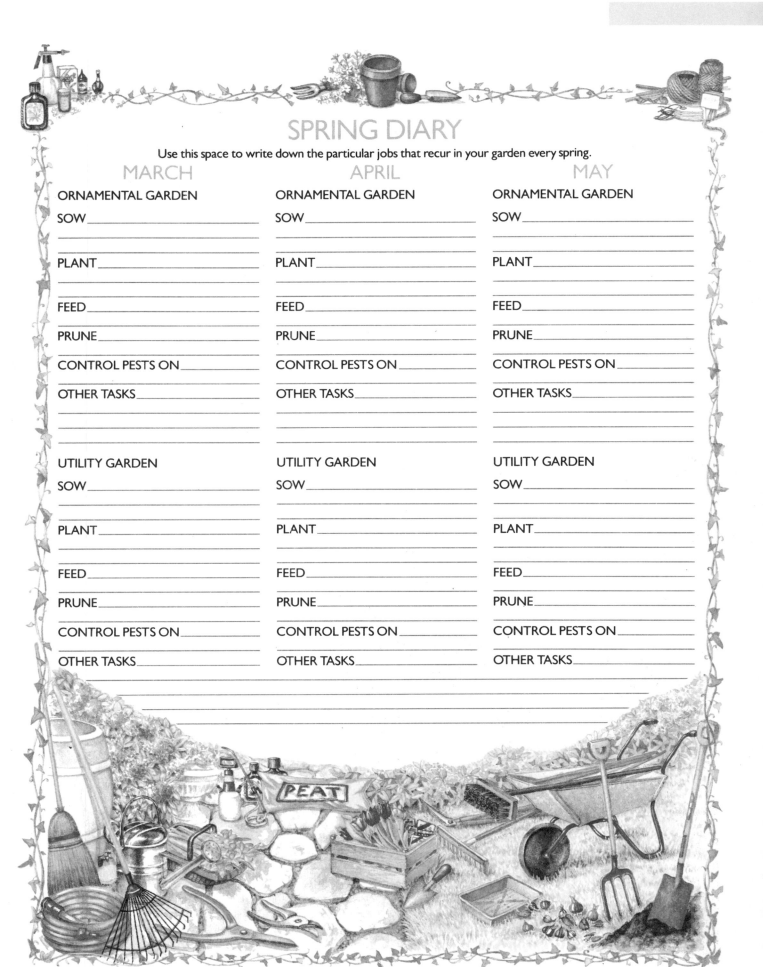

PLANT IT NOW

Plants which grow from bulbs, corms and tubers provide an easy means of filling the garden with colour. One can virtually guarantee they will grow and produce plenty of blooms.

All need plenty of sun and a reasonably fertile, well-drained soil, which can be improved before planting by digging in peat and adding a slow-release fertilizer.

SUMMER-FLOWERING BULBS
Dahlia, a range of subjects from dwarf bedding varieties to giants over 1.2m (4ft) tall. A vast range of colours is available. Plant 100-150mm (4-6in) deep and 450-900mm (18-36in) apart.
Begonia, invaluable for troughs, tubs and summer bedding. Grows 150-250mm (6-10in) in height, bearing brilliantly coloured flowers.
Gladiolus, handsome spikes of flowers in many colours. They are ideal for cutting. Plant 100mm (4in) deep and 150-200mm (6-8in) apart.
Anemone 'De Caen' and 'St Brigid' varieties are available in various colours. Plant 50-75mm (2-3in) deep and 150mm (6in) apart each way.
Galtonia candicans, the white summer hyacinth. Plant 150mm (6in) deep and 300mm (12in) apart.
Ranunculus, good cut flowers in a variety of colours. Plant 50-75mm (2-3in) deep and 100-150mm (4-6in) apart.
Tigridia, the brightly coloured tiger flower. Plant 75mm (3in) deep and 150mm (6in) apart.

PERENNIAL BORDER PLANTS
Otherwise known as herbaceous plants, these are excellent value for money as they live for many years if well looked after. Prepare the ground as for bulbs.

Most need a sunny spot. Popular plants are achilleas, aquilegia, asters or Michaelmas daisies (autumn flowering), Chinese lanterns, coreopsis, delphiniums, erigerons, gaillardias, geums, gypsophila, heleniums, irises, lupins, oriental poppies, phlox, pyrethrum, rudbeckias, scabious and solidago (golden rod).

For shade try alchemilla, dicentra, epimediums, hardy geraniums, hemerocallis (day lilies), hostas (plantain lilies), and tradescantia.

Planting is easy if you buy plants in containers from a garden centre – take out a hole slightly larger than the rootball and of such a depth that the 'crowns' of the plants (where the stems join the roots) are at soil level. Firm in well and keep watered in dry spells.

HARDY ANNUALS
These provide a cheap and very colourful display in summer. Seeds are sown in spring, ideally in bold patches – one for each variety.

Pick a spot in full sun for best results. Before sowing, mark out the patches and then in each one make shallow parallel furrows with a pointed stick, about 150mm (6in) apart, in which to sow the seeds. The top ten:

1. Alyssum – white or pink flowers, for edging
2. Calendula (pot marigold) – orange, yellow flowers
3. Candytuft – dwarf, mixed colours
4. Clarkia – tall, double flowers, mixture of colours
5. Cornflower – tall or dwarf, blue flowers
6. Eschscholzia – dwarf, bright poppy flowers
7. Godetia – tall or dwarf, poppy-like blooms
8. Larkspur – tall, annual delphinium, many colours
9. Nasturtium – dwarf or climbing, brilliantly coloured
10. Nigella – medium grower, ferny foliage, mixture of colours

Heleniums make tall, colourful hardy perennials. This one, H. autumnale 'Baudirektor Linne', grows 1.2m (4ft) tall and flowers in August and September.

EVERGREEN SHRUBS AND TREES

Evergreen shrubs, trees and conifers can be planted in spring as well as autumn. They are supplied in containers so all you need do is take out an adequate planting hole for the rootball, and ensure its top is slightly below soil level when planting.

PLANTING TIPS

Add a proprietary evergreen, planting mixture to the planting hole, and to the backfilling soil.
Keep well watered throughout the spring and summer if the weather is dry.
For the first six weeks after planting, spray the foliage daily with plain water (unless it is raining). Alternatively, use a proprietary anti-transpirant spray, available from garden centres (see also pages 244-5).

SOWING TENDER BEDDING PLANTS

If you have a heated greenhouse, try raising your own summer bedding plants such as French and African marigolds (*Tagetes*), busy-lizzie (*Impatiens*), monkey-flower (*Mimulus*), zinnias, petu-

Left Pot marigolds (Calendula), *in shades from pale yellow to vivid reddish orange, are among the most popular hardy annuals and make good cut flowers.*

nias, ageratum, alyssum (*Lobularia*), tobacco plant (*Nicotiana*), verbena, and *Phlox drummondii*. These are the easy ones.

You should use a heated propagating case, as the seeds need a temperature of 18-21°C (65-70°F) to germinate.

Above *The summer hyacinth* (Galtonia candicans) *is a native of southern Africa. Its beautiful pendent flowers are borne in summer and autumn.*

Left 'St Brigid' *is a beautiful double variety of* Anemone coronaria.

PRUNE IT RIGHT

ROSES

Roses need annual pruning to:

Encourage growth of new shoots

Shape and restrict size

Control habit

Ensure plenty of flowers

Maintain a healthy youthfulness by encouraging basal growth.

With the exception of ramblers, most roses are pruned in March when the sap is just beginning to rise. Ramblers are pruned later in the year, after flowering.

Use very sharp secateurs when pruning to ensure you make clean and not ragged cuts. Always cut immediately above a growth bud that is facing outwards, away from the centre of the bush. The cut should be made at an angle, away from the bud.

The first stage in pruning is to go over the plants and remove ruthlessly any diseased or damaged wood. Then cut away any dead wood, and any stems which are rubbing, or crossing the centre of the bush. Very thin or weak shoots should be cut out. You will now be left with only strong healthy shoots, which in turn must be pruned as shown in the illustrations.

Hybrid tea or large-flowered roses are pruned hard back to encourage new shoots to grow from the base of the plant. Do not cut back into old wood, rather, only into wood produced during the previous year and which still has dormant

Hybrid tea roses are pruned hard. Cut back each stem to an outward-facing bud.

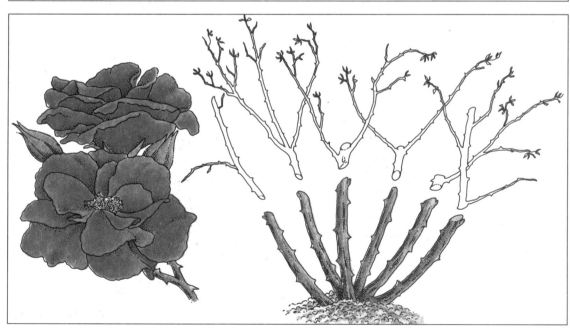

Floribunda roses make more shapely plants if cut back less severely. Always try to keep the centre open.

buds. Cut back to leave two or three buds on
each stem.

Floribunda or cluster-flowered roses do not have
to be pruned back quite so severely as hybrid
teas. Cut back the stems to leave five or six
growth buds.

Standard roses. A standard or half standard
rose, whether a hybrid tea or floribunda variety,
is pruned in the same way as the ordinary bush
form. Indeed, a standard is simply a bush on a
tall stem. In general, try to ensure all cut-back
stems are of the same length to give a symmetrical head to the plant. Weeping standards are
rambler roses grafted, normally, onto 1.8-2.1m
(6-7ft) stems, and are pruned accordingly. (See
also page 237.)

Climbing roses. Prune climbing roses by cutting
back some side shoots to six or seven buds, and
others, the weaker ones, to two or three buds,
leaving the main stems unpruned. The only
exception is where the main stems have dead or
frosted tips.

SHRUBS

Several popular garden shrubs should be pruned
in March to ensure plenty of new growth and
flowers. These are the shrubs that flower on
wood produced in the current year. A good
example is the butterfly bush (*Buddleia davidii*).

The previous year's stems are cut back almost
to the base, to leave one or two growth buds.
Other shrubs pruned in this way are hardy
fuchsias, deciduous ceanothus, caryopteris,
Hydrangea paniculata and tamarix. Shrubs
which are grown for the beauty of their bark are
also pruned in March in the same way. Examples are red- and yellow-stemmed dogwoods or
cornus, and the red-stemmed willows.

Some shrubs which bloom in early spring are
pruned immediately after flowering. The main
example is forsythia. The oldest stems are
pruned hard back every year.

Winter-flowering heathers can be given a light
trim with garden shears after flowering to
remove the dead flower heads. On no account,
though, cut into the old wood.

Some clematis can be pruned in March,
particularly *C.* × 'Jackmanii Superba' and other
hybrids that bloom late – from July onwards –
on the current season's stems. Cut back the
previous summer's growth to within a few buds
of the base. The winter jasmine (*Jasminum
nudiflorum*) is pruned as soon as it has finished
flowering by cutting back hard all the side
shoots which have flowered, leaving the main
stems. Some of the very old main stems can be
thinned out if growth is becoming congested.

Left *Weeping
standards differ from
standard roses in being
grafted rambling roses.
Cut out all shoots that
have flowered, and
keep the head open and
well balanced.*

Below *Climbing roses
should be pruned by
cutting out old,
unproductive wood and
shortening side shoots to
two or three buds.*

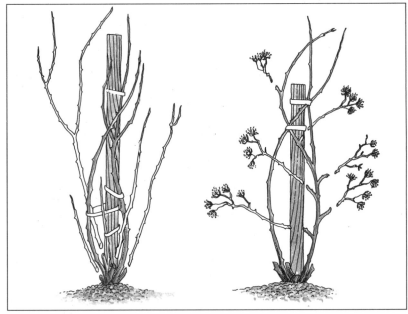

Left *Summer-
flowering shrubs, such
as caryopteris, bloom
on wood produced
earlier in the same
season. They should be
pruned hard back each
spring.*

PLANTS FROM SEED

Buying plants from garden centres and nurseries is not exactly a cheap exercise, although, to be fair, most offer good value for money, especially long-term plants such as hardy herbaceous perennials, trees, shrubs, and alpines or rock plants.

But have you ever considered raising any of these from seeds? It is quite easy and works out a lot cheaper. Take a look through any good seed catalogue and you will find a wide selection of these plants. Spring is the time to sow them, and sowing can take place out of doors.

Seed bed preparation must be done thoroughly. Remove all weeds during digging and incorporate a little general-purpose fertilizer a few weeks before sowing. Break down the soil into a fine tilth and incorporate peat, especially if the soil is heavy or inclined to dry out rapidly. The seed bed should be in a sunny part of the garden.

Sowing is best done in drills or shallow furrows taken out with a draw hoe or a pointed stick – use a garden line to ensure straight rows. Do not sow too deeply (check with the seed packet) and be sure to water the ground well after sowing.

Spring bedding plants can be raised in the same way and are generally sown in May to flower the following year. Try subjects like forget-me-nots (*Myosotis*), wallflowers (*Cheiranthus*) and double daisies (*Bellis*). Biennials for early summer flowering can be sown in May, too: sweet williams (*Dianthus barbatus*), Canterbury bells (*Campanula medium*) and foxgloves (*Digitalis*).

Transplanting is necessary to give the young plants more room to grow. They are transferred to a nursery bed prepared in the same way as the seed bed. Seedlings of perennials, rock plants, spring bedding plants and biennials are transplanted when they are 50-75mm (2-3in) high. Seedlings of trees and shrubs are best left until the following autumn.

Set the plants in rows about 300mm (12in) apart, with about 150mm (6in) between the plants.

In the autumn the perennials, rock plants, spring bedding and biennials can be moved to their final positions in the flower garden. Trees and shrubs can be moved to their final sites as soon as you consider they are large enough. They are best moved in autumn or early spring.

VEGETABLES

Spring is the main season for sowing vegetables. Many people make the mistake of carrying out one large annual sowing of individual vegetables such as carrots and beetroot, which become old and tasteless before they can all be used. It is far better to make small repeated sowings throughout the season (successional sowings), a practice assisted by catch cropping – sowing crops that mature quickly between rows of those that occupy land for a long time.

Globe beetroots and short-rooted carrots can be sown at intervals until the end of July. Peas can be sown at intervals until the third week in July using first early dwarf varieties such as 'Kelvedon Wonder'.

Dwarf French beans can be sown in May, but if a second sowing is made about mid-July beans will be available until the first frosts.

Salad crops such as endive and lettuce can be sown now, but further sowings can be made after earlier subjects have been cleared. Salad onions such as 'White Lisbon' can be sown in small batches from April until late August.

Radishes can be sown in succession in between other crops or in odd corners as long as there is full light and the soil is in good condition. Winter spinach and spinach beet may also be sown in summer. Turnips can also be catch cropped and are greatly appreciated from early autumn onwards, when many vegetables are becoming scarce.

The secret of successful catch cropping and successional sowings (which are intensive forms of cultivation) is to prepare the soil well and ensure it is highly fertile. Vegetables should be regularly fed and kept well watered.

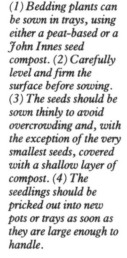

(1) Bedding plants can be sown in trays, using either a peat-based or a John Innes seed compost. (2) Carefully level and firm the surface before sowing. (3) The seeds should be sown thinly to avoid overcrowding and, with the exception of the very smallest seeds, covered with a shallow layer of compost. (4) The seedlings should be pricked out into new pots or trays as soon as they are large enough to handle.

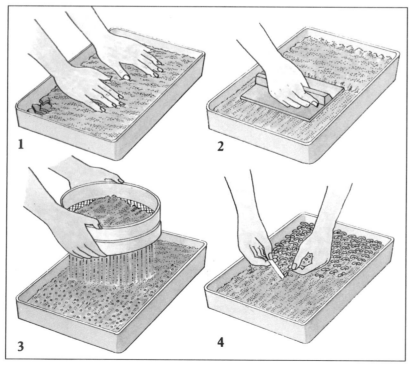

Sowing, Planting and Harvesting

Crop	Month J F M A M J J A S O N D	Rows	Plants
Beans, broad		60cm*	20 × 20cm
Beans, dwarf		45cm	25cm
Beans, runner		1·5m	25cm
Beetroot		30cm	12cm
Broccoli, sprouting		60cm	45cm
Brussels sprouts		75cm	70cm
Cabbage, spring sown		50cm	22/44cm
Cabbage, summer sown		50cm	40cm
Cabbage, savoy		60cm	50cm
Carrot		30cm	10cm
Cauliflower		60cm	45/60cm
Celery		1·2m**	20cm
Cucumber		90cm	60cm
Kale		60cm	60cm
Leek		30cm	20cm
Lettuce		30cm	22cm
Marrow		90cm	60cm
Onion, bulb		30/45cm	12cm
Onion, spring or salad		30cm	2cm
Onion, sets		30cm	12cm
Parsnip		45cm	20cm
Peas, round seeded		60cm***	5cm
Peas, wrinkled		1·2m	5cm
Radish		25cm	1cm
Shallots		30cm	15cm
Spinach, summer		30cm	25cm
Spinach, winter		30cm	25cm
Spinach, perpetual		30cm	25cm
Swede		45cm	25cm
Sweet corn		75cm	45cm
Tomato		60cm	45cm
Turnip		35cm	12cm

Key

= Outdoor sowing   * = Distance between double rows

= Indoor sowing   ** = Self-blanch type only needs 25cm

= Harvest   *** = Narrow space is for dwarf varieties

SUMMER

Summer is a time to relax and enjoy the fruits of your labours. The main worries are watering and pest control. It is all too easy to allow plants, particularly if they are in tubs, to dry out in hot weather. Make a regular point of checking the garden, especially the vegetables, for signs of disease and insect damage.

JUNE

ORNAMENTAL GARDEN

Plant out summer bedding plants.
Prune shrubs after flowering.
Apply fertilizers to all established plants.
Keep an eye open for pests and diseases and spray as soon as they are noticed.
Remove dead flower-heads.
Take softwood cuttings of shrubs and perennials.
Thin out hardy annuals.
Provide support for plants.
Plant out dahlias and fuchsias.
Lift and store spring-flowering bulbs.

UTILITY GARDEN

Protect strawberries from slugs – put down slug pellets.
Spray fruit and vegetables against pests and diseases.
Plant out tender vegetables such as tomatoes, marrows, sweet corn and celery.
Continue sowing green vegetables and salad crops, plus roots such as carrots, swedes, turnips and radishes.
Provide support for peas and beans.
Sow runner and French beans.

JULY

ORNAMENTAL GARDEN

Trim hedges as necessary.
Continue dead-heading, feeding, and pest and disease control.
Lift and divide bearded irises.
Continue shrub pruning as necessary, after flowering.
Lawns might benefit from another feed.

UTILITY GARDEN

Continue feeding and spraying against pests and diseases.
Protect fruits from birds by draping netting over the bushes.
Remove old leaves, and unwanted runners, from strawberries.
Make sowings of spring cabbage, turnips, carrots, lettuces, winter radishes, beetroots, early peas and winter spinach.

AUGUST

ORNAMENTAL GARDEN

Plant autumn-flowering bulbs.
Propagate plants from semi-ripe cuttings.
Continue dead-heading, and pest and disease control. Continue feeding, too, if you feel plants need a boost.
Continue hedge trimming.

UTILITY GARDEN

Plant strawberries, either in a bed in the open ground, or in strawberry containers.
Prune raspberries as soon as the fruits have been picked. Cut out old fruited stems to ground level.
Lift onions and shallots, dry off and store.
Sow spring cabbage, winter spinach and salad crops.
Cut and dry herbs for winter use.
Continue with feeding, and pest and disease control.

Left *A perennial flower border in full bloom is one of the joys of summer. No matter how variable the colours, they never seem to clash.*

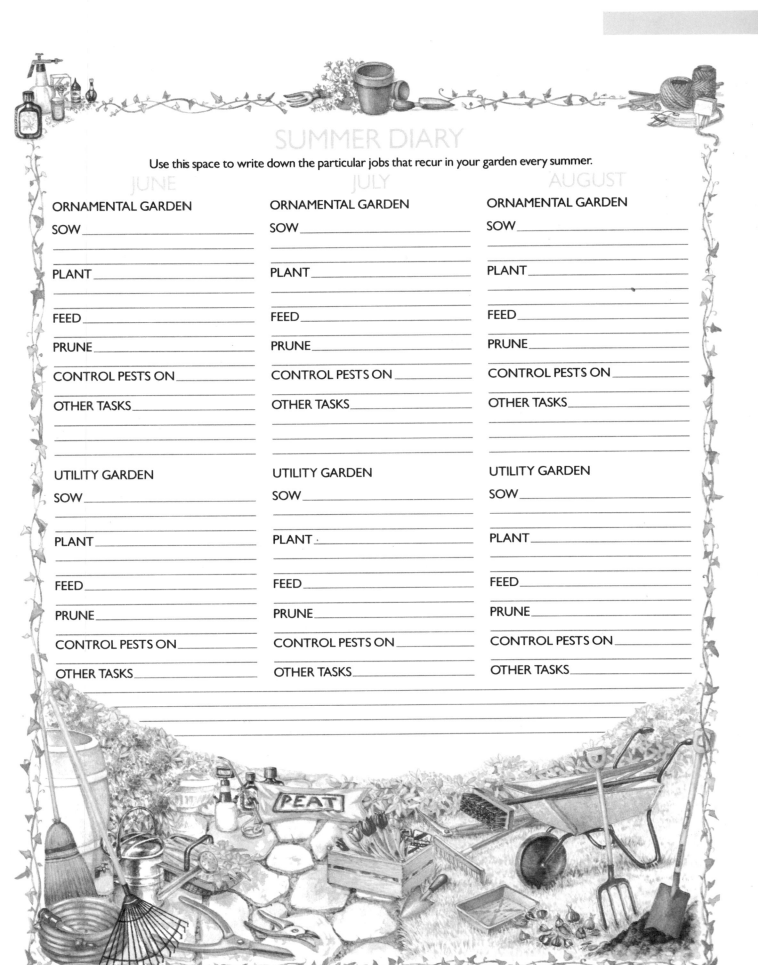

SUMMER DIARY

Use this space to write down the particular jobs that recur in your garden every summer.

JUNE

ORNAMENTAL GARDEN

SOW _____

_____

PLANT _____

_____

FEED _____

PRUNE _____

CONTROL PESTS ON _____

OTHER TASKS _____

_____

_____

_____

UTILITY GARDEN

SOW _____

_____

PLANT _____

_____

FEED _____

PRUNE _____

CONTROL PESTS ON _____

OTHER TASKS _____

JULY

ORNAMENTAL GARDEN

SOW _____

_____

PLANT _____

_____

FEED _____

PRUNE _____

CONTROL PESTS ON _____

OTHER TASKS _____

_____

_____

UTILITY GARDEN

SOW _____

_____

PLANT _____

_____

FEED _____

PRUNE _____

CONTROL PESTS ON _____

OTHER TASKS _____

AUGUST

ORNAMENTAL GARDEN

SOW _____

_____

PLANT _____

_____

FEED _____

PRUNE _____

CONTROL PESTS ON _____

OTHER TASKS _____

_____

_____

_____

UTILITY GARDEN

SOW _____

_____

PLANT _____

_____

FEED _____

PRUNE _____

CONTROL PESTS ON _____

OTHER TASKS _____

PEAT

WISE BUYS

Most people today buy plants from garden centres or high-street chain stores.

The beauty of a garden centre is that plants are sold in containers and so can be planted at virtually any time of year, provided they are hardy and the soil is in suitable condition. Plants can be bought in full flower and planted immediately you get them home. An advantage of the garden centre over the chain store is that one has a much wider choice of plants. Usually, if you are unable to obtain the variety you want, there is a good chance that the garden centre will have another, very similar.

Very often, plants offered by chain stores are prepacked with roots wrapped in polythene to keep them moist.

RECOGNIZING QUALITY
The majority of garden centres sell good quality plants, and the plants are well cared for while they are waiting to be sold. Even so, it pays to inspect plants carefully before buying, just as you would with any item that you buy in a shop.

The following guide will help you to select quality plants:

Make sure that plants, such as shrubs, trees, roses, conifers, perennials, and so on, are not loose in their containers. This would indicate they had not long been potted, and would therefore not transplant well when you got them home.

Ideally, there should be a little root showing through the bottom of the container to indicate that the plant is well established.

Ensure the compost in the container is moist. If plants have been allowed to dry out their growth may have been checked and they may later lose their leaves.

Ensure there are no weeds or moss growing on the compost surface.

It goes without saying that plants should be completely free from pests and diseases.

Growth generally should be sturdy – not thin, weak and lanky.

Foliage should be healthy – not showing brown marks, spots or other discoloration. It should not be yellowing, nor have brown edges.

Similar comments apply to spring and summer bedding plants. Summer bedding plants should be just coming into flower when they are offered for sale – with one or two blooms open and a number of flower buds to follow. The plants should be sturdy and short jointed, particularly subjects such as geraniums and fuchsias.

Summer bedding plants should have been well hardened off (acclimatized to outdoor conditions) before they are offered for sale. It is not too easy to tell if this has been done, but if the plants look very sappy, soft and lush, then suspect that they have just come out of a warm greenhouse, in which case they would receive a check to growth if planted straight away in the open ground. Plants such as these are best avoided.

Alpines – most of the above comments apply to alpines and rock plants. Many are offered just as they are coming into flower and can be planted even when in full bloom if grown in containers such as pots.

When buying prepacked plants from a chain store – shrubs, roses or perennials, for instance – it is more difficult to inspect them closely.

Try to find out how long they have been on the shelves. They can, of course, deteriorate if kept for too long. Ideally, they should be bought as soon as possible after they have been delivered to the garden centre.

WHEN YOU GET THEM HOME . . .
Hardy plants should be planted immediately if the soil is not too wet or frozen. However, if they are in containers they can be kept that way for as long as necessary. But do keep them watered.

If you cannot plant prepacked plants immediately, they can be kept in a cool garage or shed for up to a week. Unwrap the tops to prevent condensation, but keep the roots wrapped to ensure they do not dry out. If you find you cannot plant them for several weeks, they should be heeled in, in a spare piece of ground. Choose a sheltered, shady spot. They will then remain in good condition for several weeks.

Summer bedding plants are tender and must not be planted out until all danger of frost is over. The usual planting times are late May and early June. If you buy them before, keep the plants in a cold frame to give them frost protection. Don't forget to water them regularly, and they will undoubtedly benefit from weekly liquid feeding.

Right When buying plants in a garden centre always make sure that the subjects you choose are in tip-top condition. Look out for tell-tale signs of age or neglect and never buy anything that looks as if it has suffered from pest damage or disease.

PLANT IT NOW

SUMMER BEDDING PLANTS

Summer bedding plants (the half-hardy annuals and perennials) are planted out when all danger of frost is over. This may be late May in the south, but is generally considered to be early June in colder, northern counties. If you are in any doubt it is better to delay planting for a week or so – the first week of June should be safe enough anywhere in the country.

We have already considered these plants for containers, but many people like to plant them in special beds, generally of formal shape, perhaps around the house or patio. They can also be planted around permanent features such as shrubs.

The site should be sunny for most bedding plants, but impatiens (or busy-lizzie), mimulus, fibrous-rooted begonias (*Begonia semperflorens*) and bush fuchsias will flower well enough in light shade.

The bed should be dug over beforehand, broken down, firmed and levelled, and a general-purpose fertilizer worked in several days before planting.

A bedding scheme traditionally consists of the following elements: an edging of a low-growing plant such as lobelia, alyssum, ageratum or dwarf French marigolds and a main 'carpet' of plants, which could consist of just one type of plant, say salvias, geraniums (pelargoniums), antirrhinums, dwarf bedding dahlias, African marigolds, petunias, and so on. Alternatively, you could mix together several different kinds, aiming for pleasant colour harmonies or contrasts. The main carpet could again be formed of low or dwarf plants, a little taller than the edging. However, this gives a flat-looking scheme. So to provide height some taller 'dot' plants could be introduced at random over the bed. Dot plants could be standard or half-standard fuchsias, geraniums or heliotropes; or foliage plants such as *Abutilon striatum* 'Thompsonii', *Eucalyptus globulus* or cannas (Indian shot). The latter do flower in a good summer.

As for colour combinations, you might like to get away from this traditional red, white and blue theme formed of an edging of lobelia and white alyssum, and a carpet of red salvias or geraniums. Here are a few alternative suggestions:

An edging of mauve or blue ageratum, a carpet of pink fibrous-rooted begonias, mixed with violet *Verbena venosa*, and dot plants of bush or standard fuchsias.

A carpet of orange-red geraniums, interplanted with blue or purple petunias, and dot plants of standard geraniums also in orangy red. (There's no need always to have an edging.)

A carpet of scarlet salvias, with *Verbena rigida*, an edging of mauve ageratum, and dot plants of silver-leaved *Senecio maritimus*.

A carpet of blue petunias and yellow antirrhinums, and dot plants of tall yellow African marigolds.

AUTUMN-FLOWERING BULBS

Many people plant spring-flowering bulbs and perhaps some of the better-known summer-flowering kinds, but autumn-flowering bulbs seem to be somewhat neglected by all but the

Orange-red geraniums, some grown as standards, are interplanted with purple petunias. This summer bedding scheme produces an intensely coloured, long-lasting display.

most enthusiastic gardeners. Yet they are just as easy to grow, and bring a welcome splash of colour to the garden, combining beautifully with shrubs and other plants noted for their autumn leaf colour and berries. Some suggestions:

Amaryllis belladonna produces deep pink trumpet-shaped flowers on 450mm (18in) high stems in early autumn. It needs a warm sunny position with well-drained soil. Plant 100mm (4in) deep and 300mm (12in) apart in August.

Colchicum speciosum is a crocus-like plant with mauve flowers; it grows about 200mm (8in) high. It will thrive in sun or partial shade and likes well-drained soil. Plant in July or August, 75mm (3in) deep and 150mm (6in) apart.

Crocus speciosus is an autumn-flowering species, with lilac-blue flowers. Provide it with a sunny position in well-drained soil; plant in July, 75mm (3in) deep and 75mm apart.

Cyclamen hederifolium (C. neapolitanum) is a hardy miniature cyclamen whose flowers vary from mauve to pale pink. It grows about 100mm (4in) high. Provide with a cool shady spot and plant during August, about 25mm (1in) deep and 75mm (3in) apart. It is best to use pot-grown plants, as they establish better.

Nerine bowdenii is the Diamond lily. It has heads of pink flowers on 45mm (18in) tall stems. Plant in a sunny, well-drained spot, in August, 75mm (3in) deep and 100mm (4in) apart.

Sternbergia lutea is a crocus-like bulb with bright yellow flowers. Plant the bulbs 100mm (4in) deep and 150mm (6in) apart in August. Choose a warm, sunny, well-drained site.

Scarlet salvias inter-planted with Verbena rigida *and* Senecio maritimus, *as dot plants, provide a display of widely varying texture and colour. An edging of mauve ageratum completes the scheme.*

A dazzling effect is produced by mixing African marigolds, yellow antirrhinums, and blue petunias.

PRUNE IT RIGHT

SHRUBS

Some shrubs are pruned in the spring, but others are pruned in summer, immediately after flowering. These include types which bloom in the early summer on shoots formed the previous year. If they are pruned as soon as flowering is over, they will have a chance to make plenty of new shoots in the growing season, and these will produce blooms the following year.

Shrubs which need pruning now include philadelphus (mock orange), kerria or Jew's mallow, the brooms (*Cytisus*), deutzias, weigelas and several spiraeas, such as *S. thunbergii*, *S. arguta* and *S. prunifolia* 'Plena'.

The pruning technique is simple: the shoots or stems that produced blooms are cut back to just above young shoots which are developing lower down the plant.

A word about brooms. Be careful not to cut into the old wood because the plants may die. Just remove the tops of the shoots carrying the dead flowers.

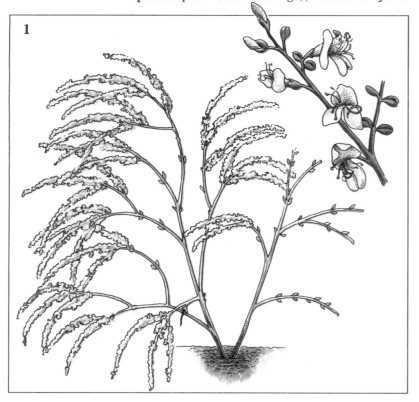

Above left and right *Broom* (Cytisus) *(1) and mock orange* (Philadelphus) *(2) should be pruned in summer after flowering. Take care that brooms are not cut back into old wood, as they cannot regenerate from woody growth.*

Left *Wisteria (3) is a vigorous and invasive climber. If not pruned, it will soon reach the height of a house.*

REMOVING SUCKERS

At this time of year some shrubs and trees that have been budded or grafted onto a rootstock throw up vigorous shoots from the roots, known as suckers. Roses, lilacs and rhododendrons are examples of plants that may 'sucker'. Suckers should be pulled out at their point of origin, which entails carefully digging down to the roots of the plant. If the suckers are not removed they will eventually 'swamp' the plant.

CLIMBERS

Wisteria needs to be pruned in July or August. It forms a framework of old stems from which new shoots are produced each year. These shoots can become very long and must be reduced in length during the summer to prevent them from turning into a tangled mass of growth. Cut them back to within five or six buds of their base. In the winter they should be cut back again – to within about 25mm (1in) of the old stems.

Another popular climber, *Clematis montana*, and its varieties can be pruned in summer by cutting back the side shoots on the main stems almost to their base. If they get out of hand, they can be cut back severely as they start into growth in spring; the flowers for that season will, however, be lost.

HEDGES

Hedges are trimmed during the summer, but some need more attention than others.

Formal hedges of privet will need clipping at least once a month to keep them looking neat and tidy. The Chinese honeysuckle (*Lonicera nitida*) is also a fast grower, but not quite as vigorous as privet. It will, perhaps, need two or three trims during the growing season.

Most other formal hedges need clipping only once a year. This is usually done in August. Examples include the Leyland cypress (× *Cupressocyparis leylandii*), the Lawson cypress (*Chamaecyparis lawsoniana*), the yew (*Taxus baccata*), holly (*Ilex aquifolium*), box (*Buxus sempervirens*), beech (*Fagus sylvatica*), hornbeam (*Carpinus betulus*), and laurel (*Prunus laurocerasus*). Box may need to be trimmed more often.

Informal hedges – those grown for their flowers and/or berries – need little or no trimming apart from shortening overlong shoots that may be spoiling the overall shape of the hedge. This should be done immediately after flowering.

Dwarf lavender hedges are grown informally and all you need to do with these is trim off the dead flower heads towards the end of the summer. Do not cut into the old wood.

Most hedges can be clipped with a pair of garden shears, or with an electric hedge trimmer if you want to speed up the job. An electric trimmer does not make quite such as good a job, though, as a pair of really sharp shears. It is inclined to leave ragged cuts.

Hedges with large leaves, such as the laurel, should not be cut with shears or an electric trimmer. These tools cut the leaves in half, which looks unsightly, especially when the cut edges turn brown. Instead, cut each shoot with a pair of secateurs. Of course, this is time-consuming and laborious, but it results in a much better appearance. Informal hedges should also be trimmed, if necessary, with a pair of secateurs to keep their irregular appearance.

Below *Beech makes an attractive formal hedge. It will retain its leaves over winter if pruned in August.*

Bottom *Lavender is a popular plant for informal hedges. It should be clipped after flowering.*

FEEDING AND PEST CONTROL

FLOWERS

Most flowers, including herbaceous perennials, dahlias, chrysanthemums, gladioli, roses and summer bedding plants, benefit from feeding during the summer, when they are in full growth, to ensure plenty of blooms.

A top dressing of dry general-purpose fertilizer, or flower-garden fertilizer, can be applied and lightly forked into the soil. A fertilizer which is high in potash will ensure even better results, as this food is responsible for flower production in plants.

If growth and flowering seem to be very poor, try, instead, a liquid fertilizer, which is quicker acting, perhaps even combined with a foliar feed, which is applied to the leaves. Special foliar fertilizers are available from garden centres: they are quickly absorbed by the leaves and so the plants can make use of the foods straight away.

There are fertilizers specially made for particular plants, having the right balance of plant foods, such as nitrogen, phosphorus and potash. For instance, both rose fertilizers and chrysanthemum fertilizers are readily available.

Never feed plants if the soil is dry and they are suffering from lack of water. Give them a good watering first and allow them time to fully absorb it before applying the fertilizer. A good plan is to water in the evening, and feed the following day.

Flower pests

There are several major pests and diseases which appear in the summer in the flower garden. Keep an eye open for the following, and spray the plants as soon as they are noticed:

Aphids (greenfly and blackfly) suck plant sap. Spray with pirimicarb rather than general insecticides such as dimethoate or fenitrothion.
Earwigs can be recognized by their rear 'pincers'. They eat the petals of flowers, such as dahlias. Spray with gamma-HCH or fenitrothion.
Leaf hoppers cause mottling of leaves, especially roses. Spray with fenitrothion.
Slugs and snails eat the soft growth of many plants. Put down slug pellets.
Caterpillars eat the foliage of a wide range of plants; spray with pirimiphos-methyl.
Black spot is a major disease of roses. It appears as dark spots on the leaves; spray with thiophanate-methyl.
Powdery mildew appears as a white powdery coating on leaves of many plants, including roses; spray with benomyl.
Rose rust shows itself as rust-coloured spots on the leaves of roses; spray with copper compound or mancozeb.

There are now available proprietary rose pesticides containing both insecticides and fungicides, to control all the major pests and diseases of roses. These save buying a variety of chemicals.

Black spot

Aphids (blackfly)

Powdery mildew

FRUITS

Apply a general-purpose fertilizer, such as Growmore, in spring or early summer. Alternatively, you could apply a dressing of sulphate of ammonia at 28g per m² (1oz per yd²) and sulphate of potash at the same rate. Lightly hoe them into the soil surface.

If the leaves become yellowish between the veins, the plants might be suffering from a deficiency of magnesium. In this case water the soil around them with a solution of Epsom salts (magnesium sulphate) and spray the leaves with it, too. Raspberries are especially prone to magnesium deficiency.

Fruit pests

There are several pests and diseases to watch out for:

Woolly aphids, which are similar to ordinary aphids, but are covered in white wool. Spray with fenitrothion.

Capsid bugs. The adult phase damages the leaves. Spray with fenitrothion.

Raspberry beetle. The white grubs eat fruits plus those of blackberries and loganberries. Spray with fenitrothion or derris immediately after flowering, and repeat two weeks later.

Sawflies. The caterpillars severely damage leaves. Spray with pirimiphos-methyl.

Powdery mildew. (See flower pests, above.)

VEGETABLES

All vegetables benefit from a top dressing of general-purpose fertilizer, such as Growmore, in the summer. As for flowers, use a liquid fertilizer if growth seems particularly slow or poor. Use one with a particularly high nitrogen content for leaf vegetables such as cabbages and spinach. For tomatoes, capsicums and aubergines, use a proprietary liquid tomato fertilizer.

Vegetable pests

The following pests and diseases may be a problem:

Cabbage root fly. The maggots eat roots. Treat soil with bromophos.

Carrot fly. The maggots eat roots. Treat soil with bromophos.

Cabbage white butterfly. The caterpillars eat foliage. Spray with carbaryl or rotenone.

Club root attacks the roots of the cabbage tribe, causing swollen roots and stunted growth. Dip the roots in a proprietary club-root dip before planting.

Flea beetle produces small holes in leaves. Spray with gamma-HCH.

Potato blight. The foliage turns black and tubers rot; it also attacks tomatoes. Spray with a copper compound or mancozeb.

See also the charts on pages 296-7.

Woolly aphids

Carrot fly

Sawfly damage

Club root

TIDY UP

DEAD-HEADING FLOWERS

It pays to remove the dead flower heads from some plants before they set seeds, so that they are able to devote all their energy to making new growth, instead of wasting it on seed production.

Rhododendrons and azaleas, especially, greatly benefit from dead-heading. The dead blooms should be very carefully twisted off. Be careful not to damage the new growth buds immediately below them.

Also, dead-head your lilacs. This is most easily done with a pair of secateurs, again being careful not to damage buds below. Any brooms which have now finished flowering can be treated in the same way. Make sure you do not cut into the old wood; just remove the parts carrying the dead blooms.

Some plants are best treated by lightly trimming with a pair of garden shears. Heathers and lavender come into this category. With both of these do make sure you do not cut into old wood. The flowers of lavender, of course, can be cut before they are over, and dried if desired.

Dead-heading also encourages some plants to produce more flowers. This certainly applies to roses. Cut off the dead blooms with secateurs, together with a length of the flower stalk down to buds or new growth which are forming below. These will then develop and produce more blooms.

All summer bedding plants should be regularly dead-headed. This is normally a weekly task when they are in full flower and will ensure plenty more blooms follow.

It is worth doing the same with hardy annuals, although not all will produce more flowers. The same comments apply to hardy herbaceous plants: some will produce a second flush of blooms if dead-headed, while others will not. In any event, it's advisable to remove dead flowers for the sake of tidiness. With herbaceous plants, just remove the old flowers, not the complete stem. This is done in the autumn when the stems die down.

PLANT SUPPORTS

Rain and summer gales can flatten some plants if they are not provided with adequate support. Herbaceous plants with tall thin stems, such as Michaelmas daisies or asters, certainly need supporting. Twiggy hazel sticks could be inserted between and around the plants before they make too much growth. They should be slightly shorter than the ultimate height of the plants. The stems will then grow up through the sticks and hide them.

Another way of supporting herbaceous plants is to insert three canes around each clump and encircle the stems with loops of garden twine at different levels. There are also available proprietary metal supports which encircle the stems and hold them in. These can be used year after year, and come in various sizes and heights.

Herbaceous plants such as delphiniums, which have only a few tall thick stems, can have each stem supported by a bamboo cane, placed at the back so that it does not show. Tie in the stem with soft green garden string, but not too tightly or it will cut in.

Hardy annuals with thin floppy stems also

Dead-heading will extend the life of many summer bedding plants

need supports. Again, twiggy hazel sticks can be used. Insert them before the plants make too much growth.

Gladiolus spikes will need supporting with individual canes, as for delphiniums, and canes make ideal supports for chrysanthemums. Tall dahlias need something stronger – there are available special wooden dahlia stakes, about 25mm (1in) square. Use one or more per plant and tie the stems loosely with soft garden string.

LIFTING BULBS

Spring-flowering bulbs do not need lifting unless you require the bed for some other purpose, such as summer bedding. If you have to lift the plants before the leaves die down, heel in the bulbs in a spare piece of ground. You may find you need to lift clumps of established bulbs after some years, as they have become overcrowded and congested. Do this when the leaves have completely died down.

Once the leaves have turned brown, bulbs can be lifted and stored until planting time. First remove the dead foliage, then lay out the bulbs in single layers in trays to dry off, choosing a warm, dry, airy place, such as a greenhouse or cold frame. When dry, rub off any adhering soil, and store them in the trays in cool, airy, dry conditions until planting in the autumn. It is important to make sure that the bulbs remain dry during storage as even a little moisture between the scales could lead to mildew and decay. However, warm dry atmospheres should be avoided, as these will lead to desiccation.

Once lifted, bulbs should be stripped of any dead foliage and loose skins. The roots can be trimmed once the bulb is completely dry. The bulbs are then stored in trays, in single layers, or in paper bags with air holes.

NEW FROM OLD

SEED COLLECTION

Growing from seed is one of the major methods of raising new plants, and is very often a cheap one, particularly if you save your own.

It is best to collect seeds only from plants that are true species: those that have been found in the wild and have been unaltered by man. The resultant seedlings will then be true to type, that is, will be virtually identical to the parent plants. If you collect and sow seeds from highly bred plants – hybrids and cultivated varieties (cultivars) – such as roses or dahlias, the resultant seedlings will be very mixed and many will not have the same characteristics as the parent plants. Many will, in fact, be inferior.

There are sure to be many plants in your garden or greenhouse from which you can collect seeds: trees, shrubs, conifers, climbers, herbaceous plants, alpines, bulbs, hardy annuals, and greenhouse shrubs and perennials are all possibilities.

Collect the seeds when they are fully ripe but before they are shed by the plants. The main periods for seed collecting are summer and autumn.

Many plants produce seeds in dry pods and capsules which change colour as the seeds ripen, generally from green to brown or black. The pods and capsules usually split open to release the ripe seeds, so collect them just before this happens. Many plants such as hollies and cotoneasters produce their seeds within berries and fruits which generally turn red or orange as the seeds within ripen.

Collect the seeds on a warm, dry day. Seeds which are in dry pods and capsules should be dried off for several weeks in a warm, sunny, dry, airy place, such as a greenhouse or a windowsill, indoors. Spread out the pods and capsules in a single layer on sheets of newspaper, perhaps in seed trays.

Once dry, the seeds should be separated from the pods and capsules. You may have to crush them if they have not split open and released the

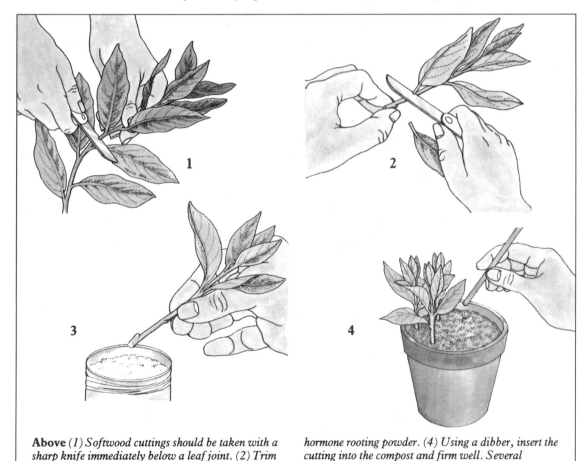

Above (1) Softwood cuttings should be taken with a sharp knife immediately below a leaf joint. (2) Trim off the lower leaves and (3) dip the cutting into hormone rooting powder. (4) Using a dibber, insert the cutting into the compost and firm well. Several cuttings can be placed around the edge of a pot.

seeds. Rub the seeds between your hands. The resultant mixture of seeds and debris (chaff) should be separated by gently blowing on it – the lighter debris will be blown away, leaving the seeds for you to collect.

The seeds should now be placed in paper envelopes, labelled and stored for the winter indoors. They must have cool, dry, frost-proof conditions.

Berries are not dried and stored by the above method, but are placed in single layers in moist sand. Use tins with drainage holes, and stand them in a shady, cold spot out of doors. For some seed this period of chilling is necessary to break their dormancy. The mixture of seeds and sand can be sown in spring.

CUTTINGS

Many hardy and tender plants are propagated from cuttings – prepared shoots which are encouraged to form roots. There are several different types of cutting:

Softwood cuttings are prepared from soft side shoots in the spring or early summer. Many shrubs, herbaceous plants such as delphiniums and chrysanthemums, alpines and greenhouse plants can be propagated in this way. Start by removing some shoots from the plant you wish to propagate and then, with a sharp knife, cut the stem immediately below a leaf joint or node. In general, you should have cuttings of between 75mm and 100mm (3-4in) in length. Cut off the leaves from the lower half of each and dip the base in hormone rooting powder. Insert the cuttings in a mixture of equal parts peat and coarse sand up to the level of their lowest leaves. Water in and place in a warm environment – ideally in an electrically heated propagating case inside a greenhouse or on a windowsill indoors. Some windowsill models are inexpensive and very cheap to run.

Semi-ripe cuttings are prepared and potted up in the same way as softwood cuttings. The shoots used are hard and woody at the base but still soft and green at the top. Semi-ripe cuttings can, if desired, also be rooted in a cold frame. In which case they are taken later in the year, in late summer or early autumn. Many shrubs can be propagated by this method, including evergreens, such as rosemary, and also conifers. Geraniums (*Pelargonium*), too, are raised from semi-ripe cuttings.

Hardwood cuttings of deciduous shrubs are taken once the leaves have fallen, the cuttings being then completely hard and woody. This is a useful method for propagating black and red currants, gooseberries, privet for hedging, and shrubby dogwoods, or cornus, as well as many other deciduous shrubs.

Cut shoots of the current year's growth into 150-200mm (6-8in) lengths. With gooseberries and red currants, cut out all buds except the top three or four. Insert the cuttings in the open ground, in a sheltered, well-drained spot, at a depth equal to two-thirds of their length, after treating with hormone rooting powder. Leave them for a year, by which time they should be well rooted.

DIVISION

This is a popular and easy method of propagating hardy herbaceous perennials, such as helenium, Michaelmas daisy and rudbeckia, as well as some shrubs and mat-forming alpines. It is best done in early spring or autumn.

Lift the plants with a fork, shake off the soil, and split either by hand or with garden forks, as shown in the illustration below, into a number of smaller pieces. Discard the centre of each clump as it will be the oldest part of the plant and will be declining in vigour. Save only the young, vigorous outer portions. Replant immediately. Herbaceous plants benefit from dividing every three or four years to keep them young, vigorous and free-flowering.

Herbaceous perennials can be divided by inserting garden forks into the clump and prising apart.

AUTUMN

Autumn is a lovely time of the year in the garden. The leaves begin to colour and the fruits to ripen. When the frosts begin to strike and the foliage to die back, one automatically thinks of next year; there are bulbs to plant and new shrubs to establish.

SEPTEMBER

ORNAMENTAL GARDEN

Plant spring bulbs, spring bedding plants and summer-flowering biennials.

Sow some of the tougher hardy annuals for an early show.

Rake, spike, top-dress and feed the lawn.

Lift and store frost-tender plants.

Prune rambler roses.

Plant ornamental containers with plants for winter/spring interest.

As herbaceous plants die down, cut down the stems to soil level.

Pull up and discard summer bedding plants when the display is over, plus hardy annuals.

Make final trimming of hedges, if they need it.

Good month to sow grass seed.

UTILITY GARDEN

Prune trained forms of fruit trees.

Lift and store maincrop carrots, beetroots and potatoes.

Plant spring cabbages.

Pick any green tomatoes and ripen them indoors.

Clear tomato plants from the greenhouse at the end of the month and bring in chrysanthemums in pots for autumn flowering.

Sow greenhouse lettuce for winter salads.

OCTOBER

ORNAMENTAL GARDEN

Apply timber preservative or paint to fences and gates, plus garden buildings.

Clear out bases of hedges, removing all rubbish and weeds.

Start making a compost heap with garden rubbish.

Protect newly planted evergreen shrubs and conifers from cold winds by erecting a screen.

Continue planting spring-flowering bulbs and spring bedding plants.

Continue cutting down herbaceous plants as they die back.

Continue dead-heading roses if they are still flowering.

Give lawns a final mowing if still growing.

Carry out turfing this month.

UTILITY GARDEN

Start digging the vegetable garden after clearing away old crops.

Prune soft fruits such as raspberries, black currants and blackberries.

New fruits can be planted in well-prepared soil.

Finish lifting maincrop vegetables, such as carrots, beetroots and potatoes, and store for winter use.

Pick and store apples and pears.

NOVEMBER

ORNAMENTAL GARDEN

Prune deciduous trees.

This is a good time to plant lily bulbs. A shrub border makes a good site, if it's well drained.

Plant deciduous trees and shrubs, plus climbers and roses.

Make sure tree ties are secure and climbers are well tied in so that they withstand winter gales.

Regularly check any tender plants and bulbs in store to ensure they are not drying out or rotting.

UTILITY GARDEN

Prune fruit trees such as apples and pears.

Check fruit in store and remove any that is starting to rot.

Plant new fruit trees and bushes.

Sow broad beans under cloches.

Continue with the digging.

The glowing tints of trees in autumn bring a wonderful blaze of colour to the garden.

AUTUMN DIARY

Use this space to write down the particular jobs that recur in your garden every autumn.

SEPTEMBER

ORNAMENTAL GARDEN

SOW_____
_____
_____

PLANT_____
_____

FEED_____

PRUNE_____

CONTROL PESTS ON_____

OTHER TASKS_____
_____
_____
_____

UTILITY GARDEN

SOW_____
_____
_____

PLANT_____
_____

FEED_____

PRUNE_____

CONTROL PESTS ON_____

OTHER TASKS_____

OCTOBER

ORNAMENTAL GARDEN

SOW_____
_____
_____

PLANT_____
_____

FEED_____

PRUNE_____

CONTROL PESTS ON_____

OTHER TASKS_____
_____
_____
_____

UTILITY GARDEN

SOW_____
_____
_____

PLANT_____
_____

FEED_____

PRUNE_____

CONTROL PESTS ON_____

OTHER TASKS_____

NOVEMBER

ORNAMENTAL GARDEN

SOW_____
_____
_____

PLANT_____
_____

FEED_____

PRUNE_____

CONTROL PESTS ON_____

OTHER TASKS_____
_____
_____
_____

UTILITY GARDEN

SOW_____
_____
_____

PLANT_____
_____

FEED_____

PRUNE_____

CONTROL PESTS ON_____

OTHER TASKS_____

_____
_____
_____
_____

ALL-ROUND MAINTENANCE

TIMBER PRESERVATION

Before the winter sets in make sure timber fences, gates, trellis panels, sheds and summer-houses are protected from the elements. If moisture penetrates timber, it will soon rot.

All of the items mentioned can be treated with timber preservative, instead of paint, so that the natural wood shows through. In the garden I would strongly recommend that you only use a horticultural timber preservative which will not harm nearby plants, for instance climbers growing up trellis. However, if there are no plants near by, creosote can be used, but do bear in mind that timber so treated can later give off fumes in warm weather that can damage nearby plants.

Several companies now supply timber preservatives for garden use and the latest are water soluble, strange though it may seem, so brushes and hands are easily cleaned. Probably the most popular preservative colour for the garden is red cedar. All timber can be treated with this, not just cedarwood. You may on the other hand prefer dark oak, or perhaps chestnut. All are natural colours which will blend into any garden.

How often you need to treat timber depends largely on exposure to the elements. But on average I would suggest treatment every two years. Do not wait until the fence, gate, shed, or whatever, looks unsightly.

Apply timber preservative only when the wood is dry, first cleaning it, if necessary, by brushing with a stiff brush to remove algae (green growth), dust and general grime. If you accidentally splash plants with preservative, wash it off immediately with water.

Of course, you may prefer to paint your timber items. Ranch-type fencing and picket fencing look particularly good painted white. Old paintwork should be rubbed down well with glasspaper and old flaking paint removed. If you expose the bare wood, retouch with priming paint, then apply an undercoat, followed by a finishing coat.

If you have some bare wood to paint, you might like to try the new microporous paints. When dry, the paint forms a film with tiny pores (or holes) in it which allows moisture to escape instead of remaining trapped, as happens with ordinary paint, causing rot to set in and the paint to blister and crack. With microporous paint you don't have these problems.

WROUGHT-IRONWORK

Wrought-iron gates, panels in walls, or railings need to be painted regularly to prevent them rusting. You can use ordinary black (or white) gloss paint over an undercoat, or you might like to try a paint with a hammered enamel finish. You only need apply one thick coat of this, even if the surface is rusty. Not much preparation is needed either: simply rub off the loose rust with a wire brush.

BRICK WALLS

If the mortar bonding between bricks starts to crumble and fall out, it must be replaced or the wall will quickly deteriorate, because rain and frost will penetrate.

Chisel out the old crumbling mortar to a depth of about 12mm (½in) and refill. Use a builder's trowel for this, and a mortar mix consisting of one part cement and six parts builder's sand. The idea is for the 'pointing', as it is called, to deflect rainwater, so make sure that the mortar is smoothed off.

HEDGE MAINTENANCE

All too often, established hedges receive no attention other than clipping in summer. Many of them would be better if weeds and any rubbish were cleared away from their bases in the autumn. Obstructions at the base can exclude light, so causing the lower shoots of the hedge to die off. This, of course, results in a bare base. If there is any dead material, cut it out to live healthy wood, or back to the main stems. It will help to give a scattering of bonemeal, lightly pricking it into the soil surface in the autumn. Apply a band about 450mm (18in) wide on each side of the hedge.

Stains are now available that will produce a range of colours on bare wood. Here 'light oak' has been used on the garden shed and 'red cedar' on the fence.

The wrought-iron moon gate gives the garden beyond an intriguing fairy-tale appearance.

Below (*1*) *To point a wall, first fill the vertical joints and finish them in a 'V' shape. (2) Next point the horizontal joints, giving the mortar a slight downward slope, and allowing it to overlap the lower edge. (3) Now trim off the excess mortar with the point of the trowel.*

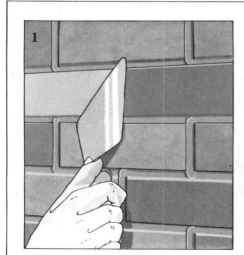

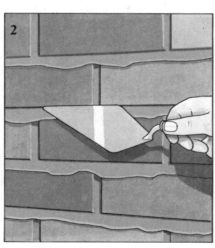

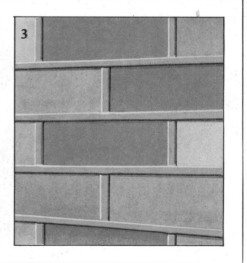

PLANT IT NOW

SPRING-FLOWERING BULBS

September is the main month for planting spring-flowering bulbs, although some, particularly tulips, can be planted as late as November.

Daffodils (narcissi) should be the first to go in and certainly should be planted by the end of September. Tall, large-flowered daffodils, such as 'Cheerfulness' and 'Unsurpassable', look superb naturalized in a lawn around a specimen tree, say, or on a grassy bank or even in drifts among shrubs in a border.

Do not forget the miniature daffodils, either, such as the hoop petticoat (*Narcissus bulbocodium*), which is ideal for the rock garden or the front of a small border. You may also like to try the following garden varieties: 'Tête-à-tête', 'Small Fry', 'Jack Snipe' and 'Little Gem'.

Tulips are better suited to more formal beds and borders, and look good intermixed with spring bedding plants such as wallflowers. Species tulips, such as *Tulipa greigii*, *T. kaufmanniana* and *T. tarda*, which are dwarf species, are ideally suited to the rock garden and containers, such as window boxes.

The hyacinths are also formal-looking and again are best mass planted in beds or containers, perhaps with spring bedding plants.

Crocuses are best mass planted at the front of a border, on rock gardens or in short grass. Varieties of the very small species crocuses, such as *Crocus chrysanthus*, are best for rock gardens.

If bulbs are planted with care and imagination, they will give a beautiful informal display in the following spring.

There is a wide range of other miniature bulbs, such as grape hyacinth (*Muscari*), glory of the snow (*Chionodoxa*), squills (*Scilla*), snake's head fritillary (*Fritillaria*), snowdrops (*Galanthus*), and winter aconites (*Eranthis*). They have several uses, such as mass planting at the front of shrub borders, or on rock gardens.

Most bulbs need full sun and well-drained soil, but daffodils will take partial shade, and so too will snowdrops.

All miniature bulbs are planted about 75mm (3in) deep and 75-100mm (3-4in) apart each way. The larger daffodils are planted 150mm (6in) deep and a similar distance apart, while large tulips and hyacinths should be set 100-125mm (4-5in) deep and 150mm (6in) apart.

If you have a lot of bulbs to plant consider using a bulb planter which takes out a neat core of soil; you place the bulb in the hole and return the core of soil. This technique is ideal for planting bulbs in grass, too. Otherwise take out planting holes with a hand trowel.

SPRING BEDDING

Also planted in the autumn are spring bedding plants such as forget-me-nots (*Myosotis*), wallflowers (*Cheiranthus*), double daisies (*Bellis*), polyanthus, and winter-flowering pansies. You can either plant them in bold groups at the front of mixed borders, or give them their own special beds, perhaps mixing them with spring bulbs

such as tulips and hyacinths. In this instance plant the bulbs first, followed by the bedding plants: the bulbs are planted deeper than the bedding plants and will not be damaged this way.

The majority of plants are spaced about 150-200mm (6-8in) apart each way, but the larger wallflowers may need a spacing of 300mm (12in).

Spring bedding plants are ideal for containers such as window boxes and tubs. Some will happily flower in shade, particularly polyanthus and forget-me-nots.

Biennials for early summer flowering, such as foxgloves, Canterbury bells (*Campanula medium*) and sweet williams (*Dianthus barbatus*), are planted in autumn.

HARDY ANNUALS

The tougher hardy annuals can be sown in early autumn to make them flower earlier the following year. It should be said, though, that this is not always successful, particularly in cold northern counties. And if we get a very severe winter the tiny plants may be killed. It is essential to sow them in really well-drained soil, in a sunny sheltered spot. They could be covered with cloches during the winter.

Try the following plants: sweet alyssum, calendula (pot marigold), cornflower, *Convolvulus tricolor*, *Eschscholzia californica*, gilia, godetia, annual gypsophila, candytuft, larkspur, *Limnanthes douglasii*, nigella, Shirley poppies, sweet peas and Virginia stocks.

Below *Bulbs can be naturalized in grass. Single bulbs can be planted by removing a plug of turf, inserting the bulb and then replacing the soil. Groups can be naturalized either by peeling back a square of turf or by removing the whole piece and inserting the bulbs. Replace the turf after the bulbs have been positioned.*

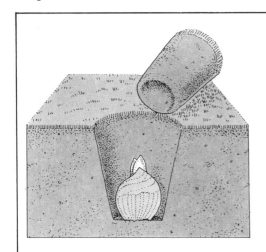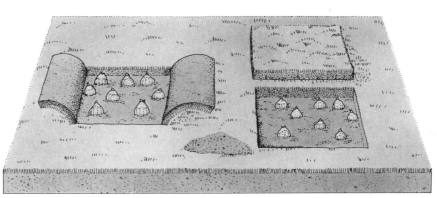

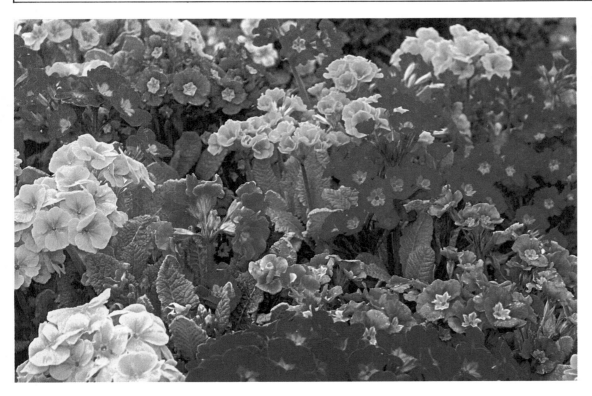

Left *Polyanthus* (Primula) *for spring bedding are available in a wide variety of brilliant colours.*

MAKE A COMPOST HEAP

Garden compost is bulky organic matter and the next best thing to (perhaps even as good as) farmyard manure for improving the soil.

Compost is decomposed garden rubbish and if well made is a medium or deep brown, crumbly, slightly moist, sweet-smelling material, with none of the original rubbish identifiable.

Garden compost is added to the trenches produced when digging and should be used when preparing both the vegetable and ornamental garden for either sowing or planting. It helps to retain moisture in dry periods, opens up heavy clay soils and assists in drainage, and provides plant foods.

Use garden compost also for mulching, in both the ornamental and utility parts of the garden.

Garden compost can be made at any time, as rubbish becomes available, and most people steadily build up a heap over the year. Most rubbish is collected in autumn during the 'big clean-up', so this is as good a time as any to start making a compost heap.

HOW TO MAKE A COMPOST HEAP

Use only soft garden rubbish for compost making: soft hedge clippings, lawn mowings, old bedding plants, leaves and old vegetables are ideal. Do not put perennial weeds on the heap or any annual weeds which have set seeds. Do not try to rot down woody rubbish such as shrub prunings. These are best burnt.

You will need something to contain the heap, either a proprietary bin or a homemade one, such as a timber or wire-netting enclosure.

A compost heap should be sited in a sheltered, shady part of the garden, for hot sun can dry it out too much and the rubbish will not rot. On the other hand, do not let the heap become excessively wet or you will end up with a soggy mess. Cover it with a sheet of polythene to keep off the rain, unless you are using a proprietary container with a lid.

The illustration shows how a compost heap is built up in layers. The roughage at the bottom is to ensure good drainage and air circulation. Air is important to help decomposition. Alternate layers of a fertilizer, such as sulphate of ammonia, and ground limestone should be added between the layers. Alternatively, use a proprietary compost accelerator. Both of these speed up decomposition. The ground limestone is to prevent very acid conditions, and to ensure a 'sweet' end product. If you use a proprietary compost accelerator there is no need for limestone.

How long will it be before the compost is ready to use? This depends on temperature. Decomposition is quickest in warm conditions, so if the heap is built in the spring or summer, it may be ready to use in three or four months. However, if it is built in autumn or winter it may take at least six months for the materials to rot down completely. It is a case of inspecting the heap regularly.

If you have a lot of garden rubbish, it is a good idea to have two heaps going – one ready for use and the other in the process of decomposition. In this way you will always have a supply.

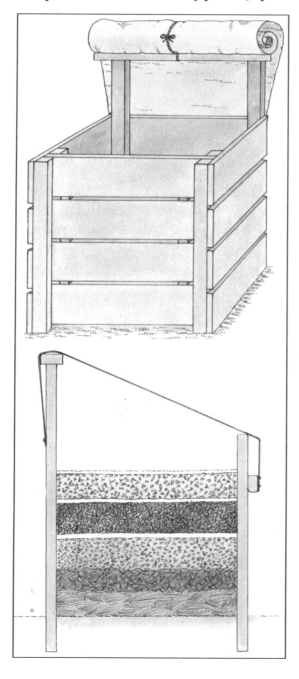

Compost bins are easily constructed from spare pieces of timber. The cover protects the compost from becoming saturated in wet weather. The compost is built up in layers. Fertilizer and ground limestone are added alternately between quantities of garden waste. Rough material is placed at the bottom to provide drainage.

Left *The compost heap can be screened off from the rest of the garden with fencing panels or lattice work.*

Below *When ready for use, the compost should be fibrous, crumbly and sweet-smelling. It is ideal for mulching shrubs and other permanent plants.*

PREPARE THE VEGETABLE GARDEN

Autumn is the time for digging the vegetable garden, before the bad weather sets in. Aim to complete it by Christmas at the latest as generally after that the ground is too wet or hard to dig. The soil should be left rough over the winter for the weather to break it down, so that by the spring the soil can be easily worked and you will be able to prepare seed beds and planting sites in no time at all.

A vegetable plot is best double dug (to two depths of the spade) about every three years, as this creates a good depth of loose soil in which plants can easily root, and ensures good drainage by breaking up any hard soil lower down. In the intervening years carry out single digging (to the depth of the spade).

Bulky organic matter, such as garden compost, well-rotted farmyard manure, mushroom compost, spent hops, leafmould, peat or shredded bark, should be added to part of the vegetable plot every year while digging, perhaps in conjunction with a crop rotation system (see pages 32-3).

THE DEEP BED SYSTEM
A system of vegetable growing which is becoming increasingly popular, especially in small gardens, is the deep bed system. Basically it involves dividing the vegetable plot into 1.2m (4ft) wide parallel beds, with 300-450mm (12-18in) wide paths between them. The beds are initially prepared by double digging and the addition of organic matter, so that they are raised about 100-150mm (4-6in) above normal soil level, greatly assisting drainage. As with traditional cultivation methods the beds should

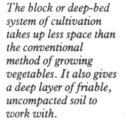

The block or deep-bed system of cultivation takes up less space than the conventional method of growing vegetables. It also gives a deep layer of friable, uncompacted soil to work with.

then be double-dug every three years, and single-dug in the intervening years.

The crops are grown in blocks or broad bands across the bed: they take up less space than traditional long rows and therefore it is possible to grow more plants in the available space. You do not tread on the beds except when digging, but work from the paths, so you always have a good depth of loose, easily worked soil in which to sow and plant.

DOUBLE DIGGING

The plot is best divided into 1.2m (4ft) wide strips for double digging (whether or not it is laid out as deep beds). You then dig down one strip, turn round and work back up the other, and so on, until the plot has been dug.

Start at the end of one strip by taking out a 600mm (2ft) wide trench across it, the depth of the spade. Place the soil near to where the last trench will fall, and use it to fill the final trench.

Get into the trench and break up the soil in the bottom to the depth of the spade or fork. Then spread a layer of organic matter over the bottom. A quarter of a barrowload is about right for a trench 1.2m (4ft) long.

Now take out the second trench, immediately behind the first, again 600mm (2ft) wide, and throw the soil forwards into the first one, at the same time turning it over to bury any weeds. (If there are perennial weeds in the soil remove them, complete with roots.) Again get into the trench, break up the soil to a spade's depth and add organic matter. Proceed in this way until the bed or plot has been dug.

SINGLE DIGGING

This is much easier and quicker than double digging. Again you will find it more convenient to divide the plot into strips. This time start by taking out a trench 300mm (12in) wide and depositing the soil near to where the final trench will be. Next, add a layer of organic matter. Then, 150mm (6in) back from the first trench, dig a second trench, throwing the soil forwards into the first one, at the same time turning it over. Add organic matter. Proceed like this until the bed or plot has been dug.

SOIL CONDITIONERS

After digging you may wish to apply a soil conditioner, particularly if your soil is 'difficult', for instance heavy clay. Horticultural gypsum can be used. Sprinkle over the dug ground and leave for the winter. It will help to break down the soil and take the stickiness out of it, making it easier to cultivate in the spring. There are lots of proprietary soil conditioners available, too. Some are based on seaweed. A good garden centre will stock a range of them.

Left *Border spades and forks are smaller than those used for digging open ground.*

LIME

Most vegetables like a neutral soil (neither very limy nor very acid), so do not add lime haphazardly. It's best to carry out a soil test first. If lime is needed, use hydrated lime. But do not apply it at the same time as manure. If you are manuring in the autumn, apply lime in the spring.

Below *Double digging and (lower drawing) single digging. Double digging involves digging soil to spade depth, then breaking up the underlying soil to a further spade depth. Soil removed from one trench is replaced by that dug from the next. Single digging involves working the soil only to a single spade depth.*

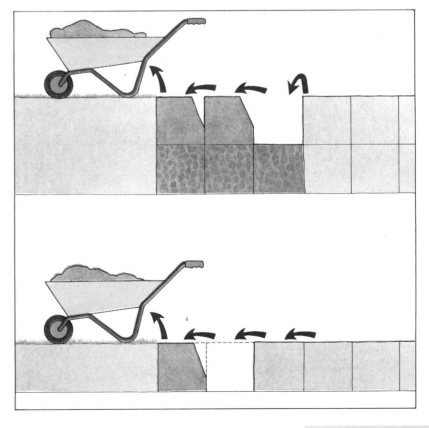

PRUNE IT RIGHT

TRAINED FRUIT TREES
As most people these days have small gardens, fruit trees are invariably trained as flat shapes against walls, fences or supports of posts and wires, so they take up little space. There are several recognized methods.

CORDONS
Apples and pears can be grown as cordons – single-stemmed trees with fruiting spurs, planted at an angle of 45 degrees in a straight row. These dwarf trees are convenient to look after; the fruit is easily picked, and spraying and pruning can be carried out without the aid of a ladder. They should be pruned in summer as well as autumn. Summer pruning consists of cutting back lateral or side shoots to four leaves, and any sub-laterals (secondary side shoots) to one leaf. Any further shoots growing in that year from laterals that have been pruned should be shortened again in September or October to one leaf. As the main stem grows, tie it to the wires. When it grows above the support, cut it back in spring.

ESPALIERS
Apples and pears can also be grown as espaliers.

Autumn pruning of cordons (upper picture) involves shortening any shoots that have grown in the summer from the laterals. Espaliers (lower picture) are treated similarly, with each horizontal branch being treated as a cordon.

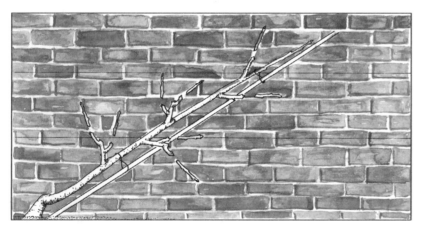

The tree consists of a central stem with pairs of branches on either side, spaced about 450mm (18in) apart. Trees are normally bought with the first pair of branches already formed. As the stem grows, you train further pairs of branches until the required height is reached. Pruning is the same as for cordons, that is, each branch can be considered as a cordon for pruning purposes.

FANS
These are popular for peaches and cherries grown against walls or fences. If a three-year-old tree is bought, it will already have its main framework of branches. Cut these back in late winter after planting to leave about 600mm (2ft) of last year's wood. Cut back to a cluster of three buds. This will produce shoots that can be tied in.

When the tree has filled its allotted space, concentrate on pruning for fruit production. Allow the end bud on each of the leading branches to grow out and tie it in. Rub out buds that are growing directly towards or away from the wall or fence. Select shoots growing from the top side and the bottom of the main branches and space these about 100mm (4in) apart, rubbing out others or pinching them back to two leaves. Allow the selected shoots to grow to 450mm (18in) and then pinch them back. Tie in these shoots at the end of the summer or in early autumn and they will produce fruit next year. Each year, train a new shoot arising from near the base of each lateral to replace it when the lateral is cut out after fruiting.

SOFT FRUITS
Blackberries and loganberries: prune as soon as the fruit has been gathered. Cut down to ground level the old stems which have carried the fruit. Tie in the new shoots, spacing them out evenly. These will produce fruits the following year.
Raspberries: prune as for blackberries, cutting out completely all old shoots which have carried fruit, leaving and tying in the young ones. In spring, cut back the tips to around 150mm (6in) above the top wire. Autumn-fruiting raspberries should be pruned before coming into growth in spring by cutting down to ground level.
Black currants: prune after fruiting. With varieties that produce lots of new shoots from soil level, cut away much of the old fruited wood. The young shoots will bear next year's crop. Varieties which produce side shoots from the stems are pruned differently: the wood that has carried the fruit is cut back to new side shoots.
Gooseberries: cooking varieties need up to

one-third of the oldest wood removed in autumn or winter, plus half of the new growth produced at the ends of the remaining stems. Dessert gooseberries are also pruned in autumn or winter: cut back by half the new growth on the leading shoots. Older bushes can be pruned harder, by two-thirds.

RAMBLER ROSES

These roses, unlike the climbers, have only one flowering period per year, and this is usually over by the middle of August. As soon as flowering is over, cut out to ground level all the old stems which carried flowers. Tie in the new ones that will produce blooms next year.

DECIDUOUS TREES

Most ornamental trees do not need much in the way of pruning. However, do remove any dead wood or branches, cutting back to either a branch or the trunk. Do not leave snags, as these will rot back and affect healthy wood.

If two branches are crossing over each other and rubbing, remove one of them. Most trees should have a reasonably open centre, so any branches growing in to the centre are best cut out. Any pruning cuts over 25mm (1in) in diameter should be 'painted' with a proprietary pruning compound to prevent water and diseases entering the wounds.

Above *The cordon method of growing fruit trees is very economical in the use of space.*

Left *Fan-trained trees, such as sweet cherry, should be pruned earlier in the season (upper drawing) by removing overcrowded branches and cutting back the laterals to five leaves. Later (lower drawing), cut back the laterals to three buds.*

HARDY FEATURES

No doubt your ornamental pots, tubs and window boxes have been filled with colourful summer bedding plants over the summer, but now that the display is over do consider planting something for winter and/or spring interest.

TEMPORARY PLANTS

Many people will replace their summer displays with spring bedding plants which, although they make a beautiful show for several months, are, like summer bedding, temporary features, discarded after flowering. The choice will be from forget-me-nots, double daisies, wallflowers, polyanthus and winter-flowering pansies (which also continue into spring). If you want to plant bulbs with them, choose hyacinths, which go very well with polyanthus, or dwarf tulips, which can be underplanted with forget-me-nots or dwarf wallflowers.

PERMANENT PLANTS

Instead of planting twice yearly why not consider permanent plants for some of your containers? These will provide some greenery all the year round, which can be topped up with seasonal colour.

A particularly pleasing scheme, perhaps for a window box, could be produced from the blue-green dwarf conifers, *Chamaecyparis lawsoniana* 'Minima Glauca' or *Juniperus communis* 'Compressa', with golden or lighter-coloured evergreen plants such as the golden ivy, *Hedera helix* 'Buttercup', cascading over the edge – a beautiful arrangement for winter.

Other plants suitable for tubs and window boxes include:

Aubrieta. Low-growing hardy evergreens that prefer a limy soil but are easy to grow. The flowers, which appear from March to June, are usually in the pink-purple colour range.

***Buxus sempervirens* 'Suffruticosa'.** The dwarf box makes a good evergreen edging to a box, and it will take shade.

Convallaria. Lily-of-the-valley also likes partial shade and is a good companion for box. It spreads quickly and the waxy, white, bell-like flowers appear in April or May.

Erica carnea (syn. *E. herbacea*). There are many varieties of winter-flowering heath, which can have flowers in white or shades of pink and red. It never exceeds more than 300mm (12in) in height. It makes an ideal companion for dwarf conifers. Plant at the edge of the container.

***Hebe pinguifolia* 'Pagei'**, a dwarf shrubby veronica with grey leaves and white flowers in summer. It is useful for winter foliage colour.

Hedera. The many varieties of the common ivy are ideal for planting at the edges of containers. Some have green leaves, while others are golden, or variegated green and white.

Lavandula. Dwarf lavenders, with their grey evergreen foliage, give winter interest and make a nice foil for spring-flowering bulbs.

Lysimachia nummularia 'Aurea' is a trailing plant with golden foliage, suitable for the edges of containers.

***Saxifraga* × *urbium*.** London pride is the most familiar member of the large saxifrage family. It prefers shade and produces masses of small pink flowers in late spring or early summer. The evergreen foliage is useful for winter effect, especially that of the golden-variegated variety.

***Senecio compactus*.** A small evergreen shrub with silver-grey foliage. In a hard winter it may be damaged or killed, as it's not one of the hardest plants. It can reach a height of 900mm (36in) so may need clipping.

***Vinca minor*.** The lesser periwinkle is a useful evergreen trailing plant for boxes, tubs and hanging baskets. It has bright blue flowers in spring or summer.

Right *Variegated ivy* (Hedera) *makes an excellent permanent resident for containers, trailing over the sides and providing a delightful setting for colourful flowers.*

Opposite page *Ericas add splashes of pink or white to the garden from late autumn to late spring.*

WINTER

Winter dormancy allows us to move plants that cannot be disturbed at other times of the year. We must, however, take care that the soil is not waterlogged or frozen. At these times it is better to leave the garden alone and catch up with maintenance instead.

DECEMBER

ORNAMENTAL GARDEN

Plant deciduous shrubs, trees, climbers and roses.
Erect training systems for ornamental climbers.
Clean, oil and store away garden tools, tidily.
Clean and prepare the lawnmower for winter storage.
Dig vacant beds and borders, and apply manure or compost.
Continue to tidy up the garden.

UTILITY GARDEN

Put up training systems for fruits.
Check all stored fruits.
Spray fruit trees and bushes with tar-oil winter wash to kill eggs of pests.
Continue to plant new fruit trees and bushes.
Check vegetables in store.
Aim to finish digging the vegetable plot.

JANUARY

ORNAMENTAL GARDEN

Plan some new features during this quiet time.
Stock up with insecticides and fungicides.
Order seeds from catalogues.
Check all plant supports; check tree ties.
Remove snow from evergreen shrubs, conifers and hedges.
Refirm any plants partially lifted by frost (this applies especially to spring bedding plants).

UTILITY GARDEN

Plan the vegetable garden, decide what you want to grow and order seeds.
Inspect root vegetables in store.
Lift parsnips and leeks as needed.
Inspect fruits in store.
Continue spraying fruit trees and bushes with tar-oil winter wash.

FEBRUARY

ORNAMENTAL GARDEN

Deciduous shrubs, trees, climbers and roses can still be planted if the ground is not too wet, or frozen.
Plant anemone corms under cloches.
Lift and divide snowdrops after flowering.
Check trees and shrubs for dead wood, and prune out if necessary.
Prune climbers such as large-flowered clematis, wisteria and ornamental grape vines.

UTILITY GARDEN

Complete the planting of fruit trees and bushes.
Spray peaches against leaf-curl disease.
Broad beans and early peas can be sown if the soil is not wet.
Plant shallots and onion sets if the ground is in a suitable state.
Seed potatoes should be sprouted in light, in a frost-proof place.

Left *Snowdrops signal the end of winter. They look wonderful when naturalized in grass or planted in a woodland garden.*

WINTER DIARY

Use this space to write down the particular jobs that recur in your garden every winter.

DECEMBER

ORNAMENTAL GARDEN
SOW _____

_____

PLANT _____

_____

FEED _____

PRUNE _____

CONTROL PESTS ON _____

OTHER TASKS _____

_____

_____

_____

UTILITY GARDEN
SOW _____

_____

PLANT _____

_____

FEED _____

PRUNE _____

CONTROL PESTS ON _____

OTHER TASKS _____

JANUARY

ORNAMENTAL GARDEN
SOW _____

_____

PLANT _____

_____

FEED _____

PRUNE _____

CONTROL PESTS ON _____

OTHER TASKS _____

_____

_____

_____

UTILITY GARDEN
SOW _____

_____

PLANT _____

_____

FEED _____

PRUNE _____

CONTROL PESTS ON _____

OTHER TASKS _____

FEBRUARY

ORNAMENTAL GARDEN
SOW _____

_____

PLANT _____

_____

FEED _____

PRUNE _____

CONTROL PESTS ON _____

OTHER TASKS _____

_____

_____

_____

UTILITY GARDEN
SOW _____

_____

PLANT _____

_____

FEED _____

PRUNE _____

CONTROL PESTS ON _____

OTHER TASKS _____

PEAT

PLANNING NEW FEATURES

Winter is probably the best time to sit down and plan new features; at this time there is not a great deal to do in the garden and so we should have some time to think of ways of making it more attractive and interesting.

Basically, there are two ways of planning a complete garden, or even small features: either the shapes can be drawn to scale on paper or, if you are not this way inclined, they can be marked out on the ground, perhaps using a length of hosepipe or rope, or by trickling sand along the ground. Positions for any large plants, such as trees, shrubs and conifers, can be marked with canes, which are easily moved around until you are satisfied you have found the right position.

Although there are really no hard and fast rules in garden planning, it should be said that all too often people go for square shapes which do nothing to enhance the design. So often one finds a small garden with a rectangular lawn and straight borders on either side, and maybe a straight path down the middle. Such an approach is very unexciting and makes the garden look even smaller.

If you are starting from scratch, or if you want to completely redesign an existing garden, then I would suggest you start with the lawn. This could be of an informal, irregular shape, with bold, sweeping, curving edges. In most gardens the edges of the lawn dictate the shape of the flower beds, so with this approach you will also have irregularly shaped borders, with curving edges. Do not make the curves too tight, or it will make mowing difficult. Aim for gentle curves.

If you would like a garden path, perhaps this could follow one of the curving lawn edges. If not, consider using stepping stones across the lawn – not in a straight line but again gently curving or winding.

Even in a small garden you should try to create elements of surprise – you should not see the whole of the garden in one glance. This is easily achieved by erecting some timber trellis screens, about 1.8m (6ft) high, and growing climbers on them.

Even the patio for sitting and entertaining need not be square or rectangular, and with a wide range of paving stones available in all shapes and sizes, you can make virtually any shape desired. A patio, however, needs to be in a

A curved lawn edge brings character to a garden, producing more interesting shapes for borders.

gravel area? Lay pea shingle to a depth of 25mm (1in) on well-rammed soil. You can grow plants in a gravel area, such as the exotic-looking phormiums, commonly known as New Zealand flax, which have attractive coloured leaves, plus ornamental grasses and yuccas. Or you may prefer to plant mat-forming rock plants.

Focal points are needed to lead the eye to particular parts of the garden, so creating an illusion of space; for instance, a statue or an urn at the far end of the lawn, or at the end of a path would do the trick. Small ornamental trees can also be used as focal points. Suitable species are the silvery willow-leaved pear (*Pyrus salicifolia* 'Pendula'), and the false acacia (*Robinia pseudoacacia* 'Frisia'), which has golden foliage.

Herbs are very popular today, so why not consider growing them in their own special garden? This can consist of a number of small beds with paths between them, perhaps formed of paving slabs or gravel. Such a garden would be a nice feature to have alongside a patio, and could even be an extension of it, for remember that herbs need very sunny conditions.

Likewise, pools are currently enjoying great popularity and are fortunately very easily constructed, either by sinking a prefabricated fibreglass unit into the ground, or by lining a prepared hole with a butyl-rubber pool liner. Try making a pool actually in the patio.

Above left *Gravel beds are excellent for growing the smallest alpine plants. If the beds are raised, they are easier to look after, and the plants are more easily seen.*

Above right *Trees and shrubs have been planted between the brick paving to produce an attractive informal effect.*

Left *This wonderful herb garden could be easily scaled down to suit the suburban gardener's needs.*

very sunny position, usually near to the house.

To make the patio 'cosy', and to protect it from cold winds, you could erect a screen on one or two sides – again using timber trellis panels – or, more expensively, build a screen-block wall.

A large area of paving can be a bit monotonous, so why not have part of the patio as a

243

PLANT IT NOW

Provided the soil is not very wet or frozen, deciduous shrubs, trees and roses can be planted in the winter. If conditions are very bad, though, bare-rooted plants should be heeled in, in a spare piece of ground, sheltered from the weather. Dig a trench, lay the plants at an angle with their roots in the trench, and cover the roots with soil, firming only moderately. If the plants are in containers, stand them in a sheltered spot and ensure the compost does not dry out.

SHRUBS

When planting shrubs, don't make your choice haphazardly but plan for year-round colour. You will need shrubs for spring flowering, such as forsythia and flowering currant (*Ribes*); for summer flowers, such as mock orange (*Philadelphus*) and butterfly bush (*Buddleia*); for autumn interest, such as berberis and cotoneasters which produce berries, and the smoke bush (*Cotinus coggygria*), which has attractive leaf colour; in winter shrubs such as the witch hazel (*Hamamelis*), which has yellow flowers, and the shrubby dogwoods (*Cornus*), with red or yellow stems, will provide colour.

Whether planting shrubs, trees or roses,

Spring-flowering shrubs, such as philadelphus, can be planted in the winter when the weather will allow.

prepare the ground thoroughly by double digging and adding garden compost or well-rotted manure to each trench. If planting bare-rooted shrubs, take out a planting hole sufficiently large to take the full spread of the roots – there should be no roots turning up at the ends. The hole should be of sufficient depth so that, after planting, the shrub is at the same depth as it was in the nursery. This depth is indicated by the soil mark at the base of the stem. To ensure that you are planting at the correct depth, place a straight-edged board across the hole before filling in with soil and get the soil mark level with this. Then gradually return fine soil over the roots, while at the same time gently shaking the shrub up and down to work the soil well between them. Add a little more soil and firm well by treading all round with your heels. Continue adding soil and firming until the hole is filled, and finish off by firming all round.

If your soil is very poor, or even if it is of average quality, consider using a proprietary planting mixture when planting shrubs. It should also be used for trees and roses. The mixture is basically peat with fertilizers added and gives the plant a good start. Work it into the bottom of the planting hole, and mix plenty with the soil that is to be returned to the hole.

Containerized shrubs are perhaps easier to plant. Carefully remove the shrub from its container, so that you do not disturb the rootball, and place it in a hole slightly wider than the rootball. Fill in the space with fine soil, working it well down and again firming with your heels as you proceed. The top of the rootball should be slightly below soil level – about 12mm (½in) would be ideal.

TREES

There are plenty of excellent small trees available, such as the golden-leaved *Robinia pseudoacacia* 'Frisia', the yellow-foliaged *Gleditsia triacanthos* 'Sunburst', the silvery *Pyrus salicifolia* 'Pendula', the spring-flowering columnar cherry, *Prunus* 'Amanogawa', and the *Sorbus* 'Joseph Rock', which provides autumn berries and leaf colour.

Plant trees as you would shrubs but stake them for the first year or two after planting. The stake should be inserted when the tree is in the hole, but before the soil is returned. Use a stout tree stake, about 75mm (3in) in diameter, and of sufficient length that it can be driven 450mm (18in) into the ground, and the top is just below the lowest branch of the tree. The stake should be about 25mm (1in) from the trunk of the tree.

If you are planting a containerized tree with a

large rootball, you will not be able to position the stake as close as this to the trunk. Instead, use two stakes, one on either side of the rootball, and join them together at the top with a cross-piece of timber.

After planting, tie the tree to the stake with proprietary plastic buckle-type tree ties. With a single stake you will need one at the top and another half-way down. With the double-stake method, use one tie, securing it to the cross-bar. When using these ties ensure there is a plastic buffer (supplied with the tie) between trunk and stake, and do them up really tightly. They should be checked, and loosened if necessary, as the trunk thickens.

ROSES

These are planted in the same way as shrubs. Ensure the budding union (the swollen part at the base of the stem, from which the branches grow) is just above soil level.

The more formal roses, such as the hybrid teas (large-flowered) and floribundas (cluster-flowered), look better in beds on their own. Ideally, one variety should be planted per bed, although most people will include several varieties due to lack of space in the garden. The more informal shrub roses are ideal for adding colour to a shrub or mixed border.

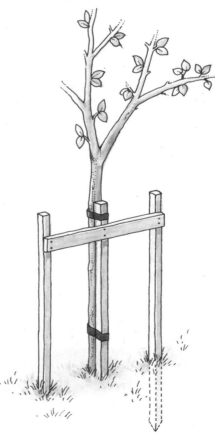

Above *Roses can be planted bare-rooted in the early winter.*

Left and below *Trees should be fixed to stakes with buckle-type tree ties. For extra support the stake can be nailed to a cross piece supported by two bracing struts. If the tree is containerized, the middle stake is omitted and the tree tied to the cross-piece.*

TRAINING SYSTEMS

Full use should be made of vertical space in the garden by growing trained forms of fruit and ornamental climbers. There are various supporting systems that can be easily erected.

FRUITS

Trained tree fruits, in such forms as cordons, espaliers and fans; and cane fruits, such as raspberries, blackberries and loganberries, can be trained flat on a system of posts and wires, set in a straight line, perhaps alongside a garden path or around the vegetable plot.

You will need stout timber posts, about 75mm (3in) in diameter, and they should be well treated with wood preservative. The ends can be soaked in preservative overnight, as they are most vulnerable to rot.

Climbing roses are wonderfully effective on the walls of old houses. This one is 'Mme Alfred Carrière'.

The easiest way to insert posts is to use steel post supports which are driven into the ground, each post then being inserted in the square 'cup' at the top. Posts should be at least 1.8m (6ft) high for all fruits, and ideally 2.1 or 2.4m (7 or 8ft) high. Set them about 2.4m (8ft) apart. Each end post should be braced with a diagonal timber strut inserted well into the soil. Heavy duty galvanized horizontal wires are then stapled to the posts, and to ensure they are really tight use a straining bolt at the end of each one.

Wires for espaliers and fans should be spaced no more than 450mm (18in) apart. For cordons and the cane fruits you need only three wires: one at the top and the other two equally spaced below.

Trained fruit trees and cane fruits can also be grown against free-standing trellis screens and the stems or branches tied directly to the trelliswork.

They can also be grown against walls and fences, but in this instance you will need to fix some horizontal wires at distances apart as described above. They should be about 25-38mm (1-1½in) away from the wall to allow air to circulate behind the plants. Fix the wires with vine eyes (available for either timber or masonry in good garden centres). Again use straining bolts to get them really tight.

ORNAMENTAL CLIMBERS

There are several ways of supporting climbers: on free-standing trellis screens as for fruits: on screen-block walls; and on fences or solid walls fitted with horizontal wires as described above. As an alternative to wires, ready-made trellis panels should likewise be fixed a little distance from the wall or fence using suitable brackets. Trellis panels come in timber, plastic, or plastic-coated steel. The last two are available in various colours, such as white, green or brown. Timber trellis should be either treated with a coloured or clear horticultural wood preservative, or painted. It looks good either white or pale grey.

An arch, over a path or gate, for instance, makes an attractive support for climbers and can be bought ready made or in kit form. Some are timber, others are plastic-coated steel.

A wooden pergola could perhaps be built at home if you are handy with a saw and hammer. They always look good built over a pathway, or over a patio where they will provide shade in summer. If it is to cover a patio, try growing a hardy grape vine over it, such as *Vitis* 'Brandt'. A wisteria or laburnum also looks good trained over a pergola.

Incidentally, the uprights for the pergola can

A wooden pergola is not difficult to construct; western red cedar would be a suitable choice of timber. A different climber could be planted at each pair of posts to provide colour all the year.

Below *Delicate mauve flowers and attractively shaped and coloured leaflets make wisteria one of the loveliest climbers for a house wall or pergola. It grows fast and needs plenty of support.*

be supported with steel post supports as mentioned above. Use sturdy timber, say 75mm (3in) square. It looks most natural when treated with a coloured horticultural wood preservative, perhaps red cedar or dark oak.

Don't forget that climbers can also be grown up well-established trees, or through large shrubs. This is a particularly good way of growing clematis.

If you want to grow a climber in a flower border, perhaps a climbing or rambling rose, insert a stout fencing post about 1.8m (6ft) high, again using a metal post support. Tie the stems in to the post with garden string or twine.

THE TOP TEN CLIMBING PLANTS

Clematis. Large-flowered hybrids, such as the purple 'Jackmanii Superba'.

Hedera canariensis 'Gloire de Marengo'. Variegated Canary Island ivy. Cream, grey and green variegated evergreen foliage.

Hydrangea petiolaris. Climbing hydrangea, deciduous, white flowers, summer.

Jasminum nudiflorum. Winter-flowering jasmine, yellow flowers, deciduous.

Jasminum officinale. Common white jasmine, summer flowering, deciduous.

Lonicera periclymenum 'Belgica'. Early Dutch honeysuckle, reddish and yellowish flowers, early summer, deciduous.

Passiflora caerulea. Blue passion flower, summer, evergreen.

Rosa. Climbing and rambling roses, summer. 'Golden Showers' a very popular less-vigorous type; 'Mme Alfred Carrière' is more vigorous.

Vitis 'Brandt'. Hardy grape vine, black fruits, deciduous.

Wisteria floribunda 'Macrobotrys'. Lilac-blue flowers, spring, deciduous.

TOOL MAINTENANCE

Time spent in the winter cleaning and organizing your equipment will pay handsome dividends in terms of time saved during the busier gardening months.

Garden tools are expensive but will last for many years if looked after. Clean them thoroughly after use and store them tidily.

HAND TOOLS
Digging and soil-cultivating tools – tools such as spades, forks, hoes, rakes, cultivators, hand forks and trowels, etc., should be washed free of soil after use (even stainless-steel versions), dried thoroughly and the metal parts wiped with an oily rag to cover them with a thin film of oil. This will prevent rusting and make them easier to use. Stainless-steel tools do not need oiling.
Pruning tools – secateurs, garden shears, edging shears, pruning saws and knives should be cleaned to remove plant sap. This can be done with steel wool and methylated spirits. Again,

when dry, rub the blades with an oily rag. All moving parts (e.g. the pivots of shears) should also be oiled, using an oil can. Flush out the pivots with oil to make sure there is no grit between the blades as this can cause damage.

MOWER MAINTENANCE
Cylinder mowers normally have some simple means of adjusting the moving blades in relation to the fixed blades and regular attention is necessary to ensure good cutting, so check the method of adjustment in the mower handbook. (Do not confuse this with the separate adjustment for height of cut.)

Sharpening is needed every year. Put this in hand during the winter as you may have to wait for a while in the spring, when many people

have their mowers serviced. Rotary cutters can be sharpened with a broad file (in the case of steel types only), or, in other cases, by turning the angle of the circular or triangular blades.

Drain the sump of a petrol mower each spring and fill with fresh oil. Lubricate oiling points regularly, not forgetting the control cables and levers. Store mowers in a dry shed during the winter after thoroughly cleaning and greasing.

Check electric cables each spring for signs of damage or perishing and check plug connections. Employ a professional if any damage or faults are observed. Keep batteries topped up, and recharge after mowing. Recharge once a month during the winter.

Wipe the rollers and blades clean after use, and lubricate regularly at the points recommended by the manufacturer.

ORGANIZING AN ORDERLY SHED
You will need a good dry shed for storing garden tools and the lawn mower. But do not just pile tools into it haphazardly; they should be hung up tidily and in some sort of order so that they can be selected quickly and easily.

There are available garden tool racks in many designs for hanging most kinds of tools. Or you could make your own from lengths of timber and suitable hooks.

I much prefer to group tools together so that I know where everything is. For instance, all the soil-cultivating tools – the fork, spade, hoes, rake, hand fork and trowel, cultivator, and so on – could be kept in one place. In another corner arrange the pruning and cutting tools – shears, lawn edgers, secateurs, electric hedge trimmer and pruning saws. Very small tools such as knives, and dibbers, used in the greenhouse for transplanting seedlings, I prefer to keep in a wooden box, together with the pruning gloves, which are so easily mislaid.

STORING CHEMICALS
Garden chemicals, such as weedkillers, insecticides and fungicides, must be kept in a safe place, well out of reach of children. Again the garden shed is suitable, but try to obtain a small lockable cupboard and place it high up in the shed. Alternatively, place chemicals on a high shelf to make sure children cannot reach them. In the interests of security and also to ensure children do not injure themselves, fit a secure lock to the shed door and when not in use keep the shed locked.

PESTS AND DISEASES
In the spring we will need to start spraying to control pests and diseases, so now is a good time to check your pesticide supply and stock up if necessary. Do check through the tables (page 296-7) to find out what chemicals are needed – you will find that some control a wide range of pests and diseases, so there is no need to buy all those recommended. It is best to buy those which control as wide a range as possible. Do try to buy systemic insecticides (such as dimethoate) and fungicides (such as benomyl), for these are absorbed by the plants and are not washed off the leaves by rain, as is the case with ordinary pesticides.

BENEFICIAL INSECTS
Not all insects that you see on your plants are harmful. Indeed some are decidedly beneficial and should not be eradicated. Examples are bumblebees and honeybees, which pollinate the flowers of fruits and so ensure bumper crops; wasps; beetles, including the violet ground beetle; ladybirds, which prey on aphids; green lacewings, which also prey on aphids; and ichneumon wasps, which prey on caterpillars. As a general rule do not spray plants when they are in flower as you will kill pollinating insects such as bees.

USING CHEMICALS
The chemicals mentioned in the tables (pages 296-8) are safe if used in accordance with the manufacturers' instructions. Remember:

Read the label carefully – all of it!

Certain chemicals may damage particular groups of plants (see labels).

Mixing stronger solutions will not increase the potency but may damage plants.

Always dispose of unused spray solutions safely – flush down an outside sink or drain, or pour into a hole in the soil in a spare corner of the garden, and then fill it in.

Do not spray in strong sunshine as this may damage the plants.

Use dusts when the morning dew is still on the leaves – powder will adhere more readily.

PART 5

QUESTIONS AND ANSWERS

This easy-reference section answers questions on all aspects of gardening, from hardy annuals to hedges and trees, rock gardens to roses, loganberries to lawns, and propagation to pests and diseases. Together with advice on selecting varieties for the ornamental and vegetable gardens, it offers some handy hints on how to stock a children's corner, a flower-arranger's border, and other areas singled out for special treatment.

FLOWERS
PERENNIALS

Q

What is an herbaceous perennial?

A

Below *A traditional herbaceous border. Although at their best in midsummer, such borders can be planned to provide pockets of colour in the garden all through the year.*

This is a plant that each year develops stems, leaves and flowers, and dies down to a crown of dormant buds at soil-level in autumn. The plant is perpetuated from season to season by its roots which are hardy enough to survive the winter in a dormant state.

Q

What is a mixed border?

A

This is when many different types of plants are grown in the same border to achieve a variety of effects and a maximum display of colour throughout the year. The plants can include narrow and upright conifers to bring height and coloured foliage the year through, flowering trees and shrubs to give seasonal interest, variegated trees and shrubs for year-round interest, or spring and summer attraction from deciduous types. Herbaceous plants play an important role and help to create interest before the more permanent residents such as trees and shrubs are fully established. And more short-lived plants such as annuals, which grow, flower and die in one year, and biennials, which flower and die in their second year, fill in bare areas that inevitably occur in all borders. Bulbs bring extra bright spots of colour.

Q

I have only a small border for herbaceous plants. Is it better to plant just one specimen of each type I wish to grow, or to plant several of each type and therefore not have such a wide selection?

A

Herbaceous plants are best seen in bold groupings rather than dotted singly here and there. Set them in clusters of three of a kind, as odd numbered arrangements are easier to arrange and look more attractive in a border than twos or fours which can look awkward.

When preparing and planting the border, first sketch it on graph paper. Transfer the shapes on the plan to the prepared border, using a trickle of sharp sand to indicate the outlines. The positions of the plants within these shapes can be indicated with small sticks. This ensures that the finished border will be evenly planted, and not appear sparse or congested at one end.

Q

I have a narrow border against a wall and wish to have an early-flowering herbaceous plant interplanted with tulips and daffodils so that it becomes a 'little-effort' flower bed. What do you suggest?

A

Choose plants with slender stems 'lightly clad' with smallish leaves that will not smother the daffodils and tulips. One of the most suitable is *Doronicum plantagineum*. There are several varieties to choose from, including 'Miss Mason' at 450 mm (1½ ft) high and with bright yellow flowers, 'Harpur Crewe' with golden-yellow flowers, and 'Spring Beauty' at 380 mm (15 inches) high with double, deep yellow flowers. Others include *Dicentra* 'Pearl Drops', 300 mm (1 ft), and *Dicentra spectabilis* 'Alba', 450 mm (1½ ft), both of which have arching sprays of white locket-like flowers; *Helleborus foetidus*, 450 mm (1½ ft), valued for its handsome, figured leaves and intriguing, nodding, greenish flowers; *Helleborus orientalis*, 300 mm (1 ft), whose saucer-shaped blooms range from greenish-white to plum and pink; and *Euphorbia griffithii* 'Fireglow', 600 mm (2 ft), a spreading beauty with fiery red heads that contrast effectively with daffodils. All bloom in early spring.

Q

I am planning an herbaceous border and would like to know which plants need staking and which do not. Advice, please.

A

Those which do need staking to avoid wind bending and breaking shoots include *Achillea* 'Gold Plate', delphiniums, the taller herbaceous geraniums such as *Geranium psilostemon* and Oriental Poppies.

The art of staking is to make the supports invisible. Pushing twiggy sticks into the soil while the plants are quite small so that the foliage grows and hides them is the best method. A few plants, such as delphiniums with tall stems, are best supported with strong bamboo canes and green string. Enclose clumps with three or four stout canes inserted securely, sloping slightly outwards, and linked with two tiers of soft string. Alternatively use stakes which are hooked together to enclose shoots. By

INCREASING HERBACEOUS PLANTS

Q

What is the easiest way to increase herbaceous plants?

A

During autumn or spring – the latter in cold areas – dig around large and established clumps and lift them on to the surface. Insert two garden forks back to back in the clump and lever it apart. Replant only young pieces from around the outside of the clump, and discard the old central part.

Border perennials with long tap roots (single tapering carrot-like roots), such as Bleeding Heart (*Dicentra spectabilis*), anchusa, Oriental Poppy and gypsophila, may also be increased from root cuttings. These are 75–100 mm (3–4 inch) vertical root sections, sliced off level at the top and sloping at the bottom, so you know which is which and don't make the mistake of planting them upside down. They are taken in autumn and planted vertically in deep pots of gritty potting compost with their tops just beneath the surface. Overwintered in a cold frame, new growth appears the following spring.

Border Phlox (*Phlox paniculata*) is also increased from root cuttings when stem eelworm has infested the plant and curled its leaves. The pest remains in the stem, never travelling to the roots, so these stay healthy. In this instance 50–75 mm (2–3 inch) long sections of the thread-like roots are laid flat in a pot of soil and covered to a depth of 12 mm (½ inch). If these are taken in the autumn and overwintered in a cold frame, new plants appear the next spring.

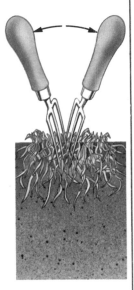

Above *Dividing an herbaceous plant. Push two forks, back to back, into the crown of the plant and force the forks apart. The size of the forks used depends on the size of the clump to be divided.*

the way, fewer and fewer herbaceous plants need supporting as plant breeders develop stronger and lower growing forms that need less attention.

Self-supporting candidates for an herbaceous border have an altogether more robust constitution, with flower stems that flex but do not break in gusty weather. Good examples are purple and white flowered Bear's Breech (*Acanthus spinosus*), rose, pink and white varieties of *Anemone hupehensis*, silver-leaved *Artemisia lactiflora*, mauve-blue *Aster frikartii*, Red Hot Poker (kniphofia), Border Phlox in many colours including red, orange, pink and white, pinkish-red sidalcea, orange-red crocosmias and architectural-leaved rodgersias and phormiums.

HARDY & HALF-HARDY ANNUALS

Q

What is the difference between a half-hardy annual and a hardy annual?

A

Both grow, flower and die within the year, but a half-hardy annual is frost-tender so it is raised in heat in late winter and early spring and planted out in late May or early June when nights are no longer frosty. Examples are zinnias, petunias, heliotrope and lobelia.

Hardy annuals have a tougher nature and are sown outdoors in late March or April to flower freely throughout the summer. Included among them are Marigolds (*Calendula*), Candytuft, Clarkia and Californian Poppy (*Eschscholzia*).

Most half-hardy annuals may be sown directly where they will flower, in late May. They will bloom much later than early spring-raised plants but yield a welcome bonus of colour in late summer. In warmer, south-western parts of the country many half-hardy annuals can be sown where they will flower, in April or May.

Below Lobelia erinus, *grown as a half-hardy annual, is often used in bedding schemes.*

Q

What are biennials and how are they grown?

A

These are plants that are sown one year to flower the following one, then die. The seeds are sown in a seedbed during early summer, germinated and grown into young plants, then transferred to their flowering positions in autumn. In extremely cold areas, cover them with cloches in winter. Remove the cloches in spring and set the plants in their flowering positions.

Q

How can I prevent my annual seeds being raked up by birds as soon as they are sown?

A

There are two easy methods of protecting your seeds. After they have been sown place brushwood over them, removing the sticks as soon as the seeds show signs of life. Alternatively, you could use a chemical bird deterrent.

Stretching black cotton over the whole bed is sometimes recommended, but it can cripple birds if it becomes entangled with their feet.

Incidentally, if sowing annuals on sloping ground, prevent erosion in wet weather by covering the sown area with fine plastic-covered mesh netting. Remove the netting as soon as seedlings push through the soil.

Q

I have several flower beds under my windows. Please suggest a range of seed-raised plants for both spring and summer fragrance.

A

Annuals and biennials are ideal for this purpose, and there is a wide range to choose from.
Wallflower (*Cheiranthus cheiri*)
  Height: 200–600 mm (8–24 inches)
          (range of heights)
  Spread: 250–380 mm (10–15 inches)
          (range of spreads)

A hardy perennial grown as a hardy biennial, and one of the most popular late spring-flowering plants. The colour range is extensive, including white, pink, red, yellow and orange.

Sweet William (*Dianthus barbatus*)
Height: 300–450 mm (1–1½ ft)
Spread: 300–380 mm (12–15 inches)
A perennial usually grown as a hardy biennial. The range of colours is extensive, and flowers appear during June and July.

Candytuft (*Iberis umbellata*)
Height: 150–300 mm (6–12 inches)
Spread: 250–300 mm (10–12 inches)
A hardy annual with clusters of purple, rose-red and white flowers 50 mm (2 inches) wide from June to September.

Virginian Stock (*Malcolmia maritima*)
Height: 200–250 mm (8–10 inches)
Spread: 150–200 mm (6–8 inches)
A hardy annual – ideal for sowing in combination with the Night-scented Stock – with flowers in a range of colours from May to August. They flower about four weeks after being sown.

Night-scented Stock (*Matthiola bicornis*)
Height: 300–380 mm (12–15 inches)
Spread: 200–250 mm (8–10 inches)
A hardy annual, known for its spikes of lilac-coloured fragrant flowers during July and August. As its common name suggests, it smells sweetest in the evenings.

Above *Sweet William* (Dianthus barbatus) *is a popular choice for flower beds, combining bright colours with exquisite fragrance.*

ANNUALS FOR SHADE

Q

My neighbour's new fence shades my annual border for part of the day. Which annuals are suited for such a position?

A

Try any of the following biennials:
Canterbury Bell (*Campanula medium*) (*pictured left*) 'Bells of Holland' in blue, mauve, rose and white, 380 mm (15 inches).
Foxglove (*Digitalis purpurea*) 'Suttons Excelsior Hybrids', colours range from cream through pink to purple, 1·5 m (5 ft).
Forget-me-not (*Myosotis sylvatica*) 'Royal Blue', intense rich blue flowers, 300 mm (1 ft); 'Carmine King', pure carmine flowers, 200 mm (8 inches).
Pansy (*Viola × wittrockiana*) F1 hybrids include 'Imperial Orange Prince', orange with a dark blotch; 'Azure Blue', clear blue with yellow eye; and 'Universal Mixture' representing twelve distinct colours. The F1 hybrids grow to 150–230 mm (6–9 inches).

BULBS, CORMS & TUBERS

Q

I would like to grow daffodils in an area of short grass. Can you recommend some eye-catching varieties?

A

There are many to choose from, but some of the finest are the trumpet varieties: golden-yellow 'Dutch Master', 'Golden Harvest', yellow and white 'Queen of Bicolours' and ice-white 'Mount Hood'. All grow to around 450 mm (1½ ft) tall.

Among the short-cupped forms are orange and white 'Margaret Mitchell' and 'La Riante', the latter growing to 350 mm (14 inches), the former to 425 mm (17 inches) tall.

Especially appealing are the split corona (orchid flowering) varieties in which the trumpet (corona) has been bred to lie flat on the perianth (outer ring of petals) and cover it for more than two thirds.

Dwarf forms have some exciting contenders and the Hoop Petticoat Daffodil (*Narcissus bulbocodium*) is a 100–150 mm (4–6 inch) delight. Its 25 mm (1 inch) wide yellow 'crinolines' appear in February and March. Another neat performer is *N. cyclamineus*. Growing to 200 mm (8 inches), this small golden daffodil is distinguished by its tubular trumpet being offset by attractively reflexed petals. It also flowers in very early spring. But it is important to remember that these small daffodils only naturalize well in short, fine grass.

Q

Apart from naturalizing bulbs in grass, how else can you feature them to enhance the garden?

A

For formal arrangements, you could interplant hyacinths with their stiff, soldier-like stance to contrast effectively with the globular heads of tulips.

Blue-flowered muscari look magnificent lighting up the ground beneath a beech hedge still in its russet-brown leaved winter garb.

Golden-flowered daffodils look resplendent against a red brick wall.

Double early tulips in pink, red or white create an eye-catching feature planted in troughs or windowboxes; white, blue and yellow crocuses peeping from the cups of a strawberry barrel make an attractive terrace or patio feature. Botanical tulips – *Tulipa chrysantha* in red and yellow; *T. eichleri* in scarlet, and golden *T. batalinii* are ideal for illuminating pockets in a rock garden.

Winter Aconites (*Eranthis hyemalis*) display their shining, golden cup-like flowers at the same time as *Iris histrioides* 'Major' sports its rich blue flowers and each complements the other.

Another winning combination is achieved by interplanting pale blue *Crocus tomasinianus* with nodding, white-flowered snowdrops, both of which flower during February and March.

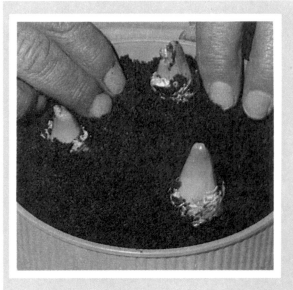

PLANTING HYACINTHS

Q

When planting hyacinths in bowls, should I cover the tops of the bulbs with bulb fibre or leave them uncovered?

A

It is essential to leave the tips exposed. Place bulb fibre in the base of the pot and work evenly around the bulbs. Do not pack the fibre too firmly or the roots will force up the bulbs. Bring the fibre to 12 mm (½ inch) below the rim of the container, leaving the tips uncovered.

Remember, when interposing one colour with another, it should either blend or contrast. Clashes are best avoided, as are greatly varying heights; beware of foliage which differs widely so one plant dominates with its wide spreading leaves, while the other's slender delicate leaves are swamped and beware also of flowering times which fail to coincide.

Q

What should I do when the foliage on my bulbs dies down?

A

The leaves are best left alone to die down naturally, returning the food value in them to the bulbs. Often the long leaves of daffodils can be a problem. These are often doubled back and held in position with an elastic-band but this is not good practice as it restricts the flow of sap to the bulb.

It is better to be patient until six weeks have elapsed after flowering. The leaves can then be cut off without impairing next year's crop of flowers.

Q

I would like to plant my large wooden tub with a blue-flowered plant that blossoms in summer. It's for a sun-drenched patio. What do you suggest?

A

For a strong impact choose *Agapanthus* 'Headbourne Hybrids'. They form a large clump and require a warm position. These plants look especially effective when set against a white wall. Although of the lily family, the agapanthus is often included in herbaceous catalogues. It grows some 750 mm (2½ ft) tall and its handsome rush-like foliage complements impressive stems topped with large almost globular heads of deep blue, trumpet-shaped flowers in July and August.

Hydrangeas form a dominant display and are especially useful for creating late summer colour. Choose *Hydrangea macrophylla* and use one of the large-flowered mop-headed hortensia types. To ensure blue varieties remain blue, the compost must be either neutral or slightly acid. In alkaline (chalky) composts almost all the blue varieties turn pink or reddish-purple.

Above *The graceful erythronium, which flourishes in slightly shaded positions.*

Q

I have a patch of semi-woodland and would like to grow some shade-lovers to carpet the ground. What do you recommend?

A

Choice bulbs that enjoy cool, moist soil and dappled shade include the violet, pink and white Dog's Tooth Violet (*Erythronium dens-canis*), its cousin the white American Trout Lily (*E. revolutum*) and the yellow *E. tuolumnense*. These flower in March.

Wind Flowers (anemones), blooming in early spring, love deep, leafy soil and *Anemone blanda* 'Atrocoerulea' in rich blue and the extraordinary cerise and white-zoned *A. blanda* 'Radar' should colonize well.

Primroses and hellebores revel in light shade, and finest among the latter are *Helleborus orientalis* in rich wine colours and white, and *H. atrorubens*, valued for its deep plum-coloured blooms. *Helleborus orientalis* flowers during February and March, while *H. atrorubens* creates colour from January to March or April.

257

SHRUBS

Q

How and when do I prune my Butterfly Bush?

A

This hardy deciduous shrub (*Buddleia davidii*), which attracts butterflies, is a vigorous plant which produces its handsome, tapering blooms mainly during July and August. These are borne on wood produced the same year, so you should prune the shrub in spring before new leaves develop, cutting back all growths produced during the previous year to within 50 mm (2 inches) of the old wood. This keeps the bush low, with plenty of flowers.

Right Chimonanthus praecox, *a shrub with strongly fragrant flowers.*

Q

Please suggest a late-flowering, hardy shrub.

A

A good choice would be the deciduous July to October flowering *Hibiscus syriacus*. It displays beautiful 75 mm (3 inch) wide flowers with pronounced central bosses. It grows 1·6–2·4 m (6–8 ft) high and 1·2–1·8 m (4–6 ft) wide. A wide range of varieties is available, including 'Blue Bird' (mid-blue, with large red centres), 'Woodbridge' (rose-pink), and 'Snowdrift' (white).

Below Hibiscus syriacus *bears large hollyhock-like flowers from July to October.*

Q

I want to form a winter-flowering shrub garden with scented flowers. What do you suggest?

A

You can choose from the following selection:
Lonicera × purpusii
  Height: 1·5–1·8 m (5–6 ft)
  Spread: 1·5–1·8 m (5–6 ft)
This deciduous shrub, known as the winter-flowering honeysuckle, bears lemon-scented, 12–18 mm (½–¾ inch) long, creamy-white flowers from December to March.
Viburnum farreri (**syn. *V. fragrans***)
  Height: 2·7–3·5 m (9–12 ft)
  Spread: 2·4–3 m (8–10 ft)
A deciduous shrub with richly-scented, pink-tinged, white flowers in pendant clusters on bare stems from November to March.
Viburnum × burkwoodii
  Height: 1·8–2·4 m (6–8 ft)
  Spread: 2·1–3 m (7–10 ft)
A beautiful evergreen shrub with sweetly-scented, waxy, white flowers that are pink when in bud.
Chimonanthus praecox (**syn. *C. fragrans***)
  Height: 1·8–2·4 m (6–8 ft)
  Spread: 1·5–2·1 m (5–7 ft)
This is the well-known winter sweet, a deciduous shrub with cup-shaped flowers, bearing yellow outer petals and short, purple inner ones from December to February. It looks particularly effective when trained against a wall, perhaps creating colour outside your lounge.

GOLDEN BORDER SHRUBS

I am planning a golden border. Can you recommend a few golden-leaved shrubs that I can use to bring height and focal points to the border?

There are many you can choose from; some are evergreen and variegated, others are deciduous. The following ones are very reliable as well as attractive:

Elaeagnus pungens 'Maculata'
   Height: 1·8–3 m (6–10 ft)
   Spread: 2·4–3 m (8–10 ft)
A distinctive, slow-growing, evergreen shrub with leathery leaves appearing to have been splashed with gold.

Philadelphus coronarius 'Aureus'
   Height: 1·8–2·4 m (6–8 ft)
   Spread: 1·5–2·1 m (5–7 ft)
A deciduous shrub with a bush nature and bright golden-yellow leaves. Incidentally, it is particularly useful as it does well in dry soils and semi-shade.

Sambucus racemosa 'Plumosa Aurea'
   Height: 2·1–3 m (7–10 ft)
   Spread: 1·8–2·4 m (6–8 ft)
A beautiful, slow-growing, deciduous shrub with finely-cut golden leaves. The whole plant has a somewhat wispy and feathery appearance that adds to its attractiveness. It looks especially effective at the back of a border, creating a colour contrast for dark-coloured plants.

Above Elaeagnus pungens '*Maculata*'. *Being evergreen, this shrub enlivens the garden all year round with its gold-splashed foliage.*

I want to brighten my garden in autumn and winter with a few berried shrubs. Have you any suggestions?

Fortunately, there are many to choose from. In some cases, you will need to have both male and female plants present before berries are produced. In other cases, both sexes exist on one plant, enabling it to produce berries on its own. Plants to try include:

Aucuba japonica 'Picturata'
   Height: 1·8–3 m (6–10 ft)
   Spread: 1·5–2·4 m (5–8 ft)
A rounded, evergreen shrub with leathery, shiny golden leaves rimmed with green. Round, bright scarlet berries are borne on female plants from autumn to spring.

Checkerberry, Partridge-berry, Winter-green (*Gaultheria procumbens*)
   Height: 100–150 mm (4–6 inches)
   Spread: 900 mm–1·5 m (3–5 ft)
A soil-hugging, evergreen shrub with shiny, dark green leaves and bright red, round berries in autumn and throughout winter.

Sea Buckthorn (*Hippophae rhamnoides*)
   Height: 1·8–2·7 m (6–9 ft)
   Spread: 1·8–2·4 m (6–8 ft)
A hardy, deciduous, bushy shrub, mainly grown for its round, bright orange berries during autumn and winter. They are clustered thickly around the shoots.

Skimmia × 'Foremanii'
   Height: 900 mm–1·2 m (3–4 ft)
   Spread: 900 mm–1·2 m (3–4 ft)
A beautiful, slow-growing, hardy evergreen shrub which displays fragrant star-like, creamy-white flowers and bright red berries throughout the winter months.

Snowberry (*Symphoricarpos albus*)
   Height: 1·5–1·8 m (5–6 ft)
   Spread: 1·5–2·1 m (5–7 ft)
A well-known, hardy, deciduous shrub with pink urn-shaped flowers during summer, followed by white, round berries throughout late autumn and into winter. This shrub is superb for scrambling and peeping over a low brick wall, and looks extremely striking in a front garden.

CLIMBERS & TRAILERS

Q

What is the Woodbine?

A

This is the common name for *Lonicera pericly-menum*, also known as Honeysuckle, a climber that grows to 6 m (20 ft) high, with terminal whorls of flowers from July to August. 'Belgica', the Early Dutch Honeysuckle, displays purple-red and yellow flowers during May and June; 'Serotina', the Late Dutch Honeysuckle, has red-purple flowers from July to October.

Below *Flowers of the Woodbine or Early Dutch Honeysuckle* (Lonicera periclymenum 'Belgica') *are fragrant as well as colourful.*

Q

I have a large blank wall I would like to cover with a handsome-leaved climber, ideally one with variegated leaves. What do you suggest?

A

There are several in which the leaf's green area is attractively blotched, mottled or rimmed with silver, white, pink or gold. Take your pick from *Actinidia kolomikta*, a tricoloured beauty with green leaves tipped white and pink; *Lonicera japonica* 'Aureo-reticulata', whose leaves are netted with striking yellow veins; *Trachelospermum jasminoides* 'Variegatum', in which they are edged and splashed with white; *Hedera* 'Gold-heart', green, centrally splashed with gold; *Hedera colchica* 'Dentata Variegata', rimmed with creamy white.

Q

Can you tell me why my Passion Flower has not produced new shoots this spring?

A

Passiflora caerulea is not fully hardy in all areas and, to be reliable, needs a south or west-facing wall in the South or West of the country. Cold and especially wet soil during severe winters cause death to the plant. If you are in a cold area replant with a variegated ivy.

Q

I have a trellis on a warm wall near to my back door and would like to plant a scented climber. What do you suggest?

A

The Common White Jasmine, *Jasminum officinale*, is vigorous, often rising to 7·5 m (25 ft), and displays clusters of pure white flowers from June to October.

Abeliophyllum distichum, with its star-shaped, white flowers in late winter, is a delight. It is a deciduous shrub, growing only to 900 mm (3 ft) high, with the flowers borne on bare stems.

Q

I would like to grow a climber up a wall which is three storeys high and would appreciate advice on the choice available.

A

You need a self-clinging climber for an area of that size, as it would be difficult to erect a trellis or wires over it. A suitable vigorous climber is *Parthenocissus quinquefolia*, the true Virginia Creeper. It is more or less self-clinging and reaches 12–18 m (40–60 ft) high, revealing leaves which turn brilliant crimson in autumn.

Slightly less vigorous, *Parthenocissus tricuspidata* at 9–12 m (30–40 ft) is the Boston Ivy with rich scarlet and crimson autumn leaves.

The Chinese Virginia Creeper (*Parthenocissus henryana*) rises to 7·5 m (25 ft) and displays brilliant red leaves in autumn.

Many of the ivies (hedera) are also suitable. The golden variegated types, such as large-leaved *Hedera colchica* 'Dentata Aurea', although more attractive than the all-green ones, are slightly slower growing.

Q

Can you suggest climbers with handsome leaves to cover my trelliswork? They must create a dense, peep-proof screen.

A

Humulus lupulus 'Aureus', the golden-leaved form of the hop, is superb for this position. It is a herbaceous climber and each year develops a fresh screen of three to five-lobed, soft-yellow leaves. When grown over trelliswork it soon develops a complete overhead canopy of leaves.

Another suitable climber is *Actinidia kolomikta*, whose leaves open green then assume cream and pink variegation. It is a robust climber and needs plenty of room.

Evergreens to suit your purpose include Canary Island Ivy (*Hedera canariensis* 'Variegata') also known as Gloire de Marengo, whose olive-green leaves are fetchingly edged with silver and cream, and *Trachelospermum jasminoides*, which, in addition to its richly scented, white flowers, has narrowly oval, polished green leaves. Many of the Honeysuckles, such as the Early and Late Dutch forms, will create a dense screen at eye-height, but often become bare of foliage at their bases.

Left *The Chinese Virginia Creeper* (Parthenocissus henryana), *a self-clinging climber prized for its autumn coloration.*

SCENTED ROSES FOR PERGOLAS
Choose rambler types:
'Albéric Barbier' Height: 7·5 m (25 ft) Creamy-white flowers, yellow buds.
'Albertine' Height: 5·4 m (18 ft) Salmon buds opening to coppery-pink.
'Easlea's Golden Rambler' Height: 3·5 m (12 ft) Butter-yellow flowers, splashed red.
'Emily Gray' Height: 3 m (10 ft) Buff-yellow fading to pale yellow.
'Veilchenblau' Height: 3.5 m (12 ft) Violet-mauve with white centres.

Q

My neighbour's garage is an eye-sore. Is there a climber that would quickly camouflage it?

A

The fastest-growing climber is the Mile-a-Minute *Fallopia baldschuanicum* (better known as *Polygonum baldschuanicum*). It is also known as the Russian Vine. From July to October it displays masses of frothy-headed white flowers. It often grows 3–4·5 m (10–15 ft) a year, ultimately to a height of 10·5–12 m (35–40 ft) although unless given a tree to climb in, it seldom reaches this height, tending to spread sideways instead.

Q

I have a cold, north-facing garage that I want to brighten up. How do you suggest I do this?

A

Several wall shrubs are suitable, such as the Firethorn *Pyracantha* × 'Orange Glow', *Cotoneaster horizontalis* and Flowering Quince (chaenomeles). Climbers to choose from include the Winter-flowering Jasmine (*Jasminum nudiflorum*) and the Climbing Hydrangea (*Hydrangea petiolaris*). Many members of the ivy (hedera) family are tough enough to be used.

The small-leaved types are better if a path is close to the garage, as the large-leaved types spread out considerably.

SOIL TYPES

Q

How do you tell a sandy soil from a clay type?

A

This is easily done by taking a handful of soil and rubbing it between your thumb and forefinger, If, as it passes between these fingers, it produces a smooth, shiny surface you can be sure that the soil holds more clay than sand. If, however, the surface is pitted and rough the sample contains more sand than clay. In practice you will be able to identify clay soils easily by their stickiness and difficulty to cultivate. Clay soils retain plant foods better than light soils, but because they are wet and cold they will not produce early crops.

Q

Can I improve heavy clay soil which is sticky in winter and dries out in lumps in summer?

A

Improve it by forking in all the rotted organic manure or garden compost you can muster, and sprinkling it with 100 g (4 oz) per sq. yd. of ground lime or gypsum each autumn. But don't add the manure and lime together, or there may be chemical reaction and a loss of valuable nitrogen from the soil.

It would also pay to top-dress (i.e. sprinkle the surface of) the soil with a seaweed soil conditioner, which physically splits up the sticky clay 'plates'. Repeat this treatment annually.

SHRUBS FOR DRY SOIL

Q

Please suggest a few shrubs which will grow well in dry soil in full sun.

A

Take your pick from the following selection:
Caryopterris × *clandonensis* **'Kew Blue'**: deep blue flowers from August to October; reaches 1 m (3 ft) in height.
Cistus × *crispus* **'Sunset'**: cerise flowers July to October; 750 mm (2½ ft) high and wide.
Cytisus praecox **'Allgold'**: deep yellow flowers on arching sprays in May; grows 1.5 m (5 ft) high and wide.
Genista lydia: wiry, arching green stems massed with tiny, butter-yellow flowers from May to June; 750 mm (2½ ft) high and wide.
Hebe **'Midsummer Beauty'**: lavender-purple flowers in tapering spires, July to August; 1.2 m (4 ft) high.
Hypericum patulum **'Hidcote'**: golden yellow, saucer-shaped flowers from June to September; 1.5 m (5 ft) high.
Phlomis fruticosa: Bright yellow flowers borne in tiered clusters round the stems, from June to July; 750 mm (2½ ft) high.
Salvia officinalis **'Icterina'**: handsome greyish green and yellow variegated leaves; 600 mm (2 ft) high. Makes a spreading bush.
Santolina virens: hummocks of bright green, thread-like foliage; lemon-yellow flowers in summer; 450 mm (1½ ft) high.
Senecio **'Sunshine'** (formerly greyi): valued for its silvery-grey leaves and yellow flowers in summer: 900 mm (3 ft) high.
Spartium junceum: honey-scented, golden-yellow flowers borne freely on grass-like stems July to September; 2.5 m (8 ft) high.

Right Hebe 'Midsummer Beauty', a pretty shrub for a dry, sunny position.

Q

Are there any flowering shrubs that will thrive in acid soil?

A

Enkianthus campanulatus
   Height: 2·1–2·4 m (7–8 ft)
   Spread: 1·8–2·1 m (6–7 ft)
A hardy, deciduous shrub with leaves that turn brilliant red in autumn, and which displays bell-shaped, creamy-yellow flowers with red veins during late spring and early summer.

Fothergilla monticola
   Height: 1·8–2·4 m (6–8 ft)
   Spread: 1·5–2·1 m (5–7 ft)
A hardy, deciduous shrub, with good autumn foliage in shades of orange and red, and sweetly-scented, creamy-white flowers that closely resemble small bottle-brushes.

Calico Bush (*Kalmia latifolia*)
   Height: 1·8–2·4 m (6–8 ft)
   Spread: 1·8–2·1 m (6–7 ft)
A hardy, evergreen shrub, with leathery leaves and 75–100 mm (3–4 inch) wide clusters of small, bright pink flowers during June.

Common Camellia (*Camellia japonica*)
   Height: 1·8–3 m (6–10 ft)
   Spread: 1·8–2·4 m (6–8 ft)
This is the well-known evergreen shrub that bears 75–130 mm (3–5 inch) wide flowers in colours from white to red and purple in late winter and spring. Many named forms are available in a range of flower shapes.

Q

My soil is light, sandy, and well drained. Which bulbs would do well there?

A

There are several to choose from, including pink to white *Crinum × powellii*, flowering from July to September; Star of Bethlehem (*Ornithogalum umbellatum*), a carpeter for lightly shaded spots with branching heads of starry white blooms in May; Harlequin Flower (*Sparaxis tricolor*), valued for its small branching stems topped with red, yellow, purple and white blooms from May to June; and the Peacock Flower (*Tigridia pavonia*), magnificent with yellow, pink or white three-petalled blooms with distinctive centres.

COLOUR ALL YEAR ROUND

JAPANESE CHERRIES FOR SPRING COLOUR

Prunus 'Fugenzo': Double rose-pink flowers in drooping clusters.

Prunus 'Hokusai': Semi-double pale-pink flowers.

Prunus 'Ichiyo': Double shell-pink flowers, frilled at their edges in long-stalked clusters.

Prunus 'Jo-nioi': Beautifully scented white flowers.

Prunus 'Ojochin': Pale pink flowers in long-stalked clusters.

Below *The autumn-flowering bulb* Nerine bowdenii *makes a delightful show.*

Q

I find bulbs very reliable in my garden. Please suggest some for late summer and autumn colour.

A

There is a wide range to choose from, including *Acidanthera bicolor*, which is hardy outside only in the mildest climates and which displays fragrant, star-shaped flowers during August and September. *Amaryllis belladonna* is another tender bulb, with 100–130 mm (4–5 inch) wide, trumpet-shaped, pale pink flowers during September and October.

Colchicum autumnale is easy to grow and displays white or rose-pink flowers during autumn. *Nerine bowdenii* has 100–150 mm (4–6 inch) wide heads of pink flowers from September to November, and *Sternbergia lutea* displays 50 mm (2 inch) long, shining yellow flowers during September and October.

Q

I have a garden pond in an informal setting and want to plant shrubs around it that have coloured stems in winter. Please suggest some plants for this purpose.

A

Many of the Dogwoods are suitable, such as *Cornus alba* with mid-green leaves turning orange and red in autumn, followed by beautiful deep red stems during winter. *Cornus alba* 'Westonbirt' has brilliant sealing wax red stems in winter, while 'Sibirica' reveals crimson shoots. For yellow shoots choose *Salix alba* 'Vitellina', and for bright orange shoots try *Salix alba* 'Chermesina'.

Q

My garden is usually bare of colour in winter. Please suggest trees which have colourful bark during this dull season.

A

Some of the best known ones include:
Paperbark Maple (*Acer griseum*)
   Height: 3–4·5 m (10–15 ft)
   Spread: 1·8–2·4 m (6–8 ft)
Orange-brown old bark peeling to reveal cinnamon-coloured new bark.
Snake-bark Maple/Mousewood (*Acer pensylvanicum*)
   Height: 5·4–6 m (18–20 ft)
   Spread: 3–3·5 m (10–12 ft)
Bark develops silvery-white stripes.
White-barked Himalayan Birch (*Betula jacquemontii*)
   Height: 6–7·5 m (20–25 ft)
   Spread: 4·5–5·4 m (15–18 ft)
Superb birch, with beautiful white peeling bark.
Himalayan Birch (*Betula utilis*)
   Height: 6–7·5 m (20–25 ft)
   Spread: 4·5–5·4 m (15–18 ft)
Magnificent grey-white bark which contrasts with the peeling cinnamon-brown branches.
Prunus serrula
   Height: 6–7·5 m (20–25 ft)
   Spread: 4·5–5·4 m (15–18 ft)
Beautiful shiny bark, which peels in strips to reveal reddish-brown bark beneath.

Q

I want to plant a tree with colourful fruits during autumn and into early winter. Have you any suggestions?

A

Malus 'Golden Hornet' is certainly one of the best types you could choose, with masses of bright yellow, almost conical fruits that persist into December. It is a medium-sized tree, rising to 4·5–5·4 m (15–18 ft) with a spread of 3–4·5 m (10–15 ft).

Malus 'Red Sentinel' has glossy, bright red fruits that persist even longer, into early spring. It is slightly smaller, with a height of 3–4·5 m (10–15 ft) and width of 2·4–3·5 m (8–12 ft).

Many sorbus species produce superb fruits, such as *S. aucuparia* 'Sheerwater Seedling' with spectacular orange-red berries, *S. aucuparia* 'Xanthocarpa' with bright yellow berries, and *S.* 'Embley' with magnificent, glistening, orange-red berries. And for small, rosy-red berries that turn first pink then blush white, choose the dainty *Sorbus vilmorinii*.

Q

One of my greatest joys is watching spring arrive in the garden. I have plenty of spring bulbs and now wish to plant a spring-flowering tree to harmonize with them. What do you recommend?

A

Some of the best spring trees are the flowering cherries. Perhaps *Prunus subhirtella* 'Pendula Rosea', the weeping spring cherry, is one of the best known early-flowering ornamental trees. It displays a mushroom-habit with flowers rich pink in bud, opening to pinkish-white. The weeping branches tend to fuse with daffodils planted underneath.

For a very small garden Cheal's Weeping Cherry, with a height of 4·5–6 m (15–20 ft) and spread of 4·5–5·4 m (15–18 ft) is superb. The arching and pendulous branches bear double pink flowers in March or April.

Even smaller is *Prunus triloba* with a height and spread of 3–3·5 m (10–12 ft) and 25 mm (1 inch) wide, clear pink flowers during late March and into April.

Right *A stunning display of spring colour.*

THE DIFFICULT GARDEN

Q

Each year a neighbouring tree gets larger and casts more shade over an area of my garden. Please suggest a few evergreen shrubs that I can grow there.

A

Below Pachysandra terminalis *'Variegata', an attractive evergreen shrub which does well in shade.*

You could choose from any of the following, although eventually the site may be so dark that you will have to discuss the tree's removal with your neighbour.

Arctostaphylos uva-ursi: creeping shrub with white, pink-tinged flowers.
Aucuba japonica: valued for its evergreen, often golden-speckled, leaves and red fruits.
Common Box (*Buxus sempervirens*): neat evergreen leaves and an ability to thrive in quite gloomy places.
Elaeagnus, especially *E. × ebbingei*: fast growing with silvery undersides to the leaves.
Fatsia japonica: white bobble flowers in winter and handsome fingered leaves.
Oregon Grape (*Mahonia aquifolium*): golden yellow flowers followed by clusters of blue-black, grape-like fruits.
Pachysandra terminalis: creeping carpeter a few inches high with leaves clustered at stem ends. *P. terminalis* 'Variegata' is the most distinctive form.
Sarcococca confusa: very fragrant small white flowers in winter, evergreen leaves.
Skimmia japonica 'Foremanii': white flowers in summer followed by abundance of scarlet fruits.
Snowberry (*Symphoricarpos*): pinkish-white, urn-shaped flowers give rise to polystyrene-textured white or purple-pink berries.
Vaccinium vitis-idae: good carpeter with white tinged-pink flowers followed by red fruit.

Each autumn, be sure to remove fallen leaves from on top of these plants, especially the lower-growing types.

Q

Can you suggest a tree I could plant as a focal point from my kitchen window? The soil is poor – infilling deposited by the builders.

A

Several trees could do well there, and become established quickly. These include *Acer platanoides* 'Drummondii', with its white-edged leaves, *Acer pseudoplatanus* 'Worlei' with yellow leaves from spring until mid-summer, and *Betula pendula*, the beautiful Silver Birch, so useful when planting in a grouping. This tree looks especially effective in a lawn setting with small crocuses growing around it. The silver bark is a further attraction, looking particularly dramatic in winter.

The Swedish cut-leaved birch, *Betula dalecarlica*, is an especially attractive form, with pendulous branches down to soil-level. It also has attractive bark.

PLANTS FOR THE COAST

Q

We have just retired to the coast, and the few plants we took with us are being scorched by the salt spray in the wind. What plants do you suggest we try?

A

The first job is to establish a salt-resistant screen around your garden. For this purpose, try the conifers × *Cupressocyparis leylandii*, *Cupressus macrocarpa* or *Cupressus arizonica*, all of which are useful for shelterbelts.

Behind this screen shrubs can be planted, such as *Elaeagnus ebbingei*, pink or red-flowered escallonia, orange-berried *Hippophae rhamnoides* (the Sea Buckthorn), molten gold flowered *Ulex europaeus* (Gorse), silver-tasselled *Garrya elliptica* and white flowered, red, orange or yellow-berried pyracantha.

There are, of course, many others such as pink-flowered, feathery-leaved *Tamarix gallica*; white-flowered *Hebe brachysiphon*; and *Euonymus japonicus*, a glossy, leathery-leaved stalwart that happily takes a salty battering.

Right Pyracantha atalantioides '*Aurea*'.

Q

I live in a town and my front garden often suffers damage as it is next to a main thoroughfare. Are there any shrubs that have natural defences against ill-use?

A

What you need are prickly plants. There are several to choose from, including coral-red berried *Berberis* × *rubrostilla* (deciduous), orange-flowered *Berberis* × *stenophylla* (evergreen), pink, red or white-flowered chaenomeles (deciduous) or *Elaeagnus angustifolia* (deciduous). You could also try orange-fruited *Hippophae rhamnoides* (deciduous), double golden yellow *Ulex europaeus* 'Plenus' (evergreen) or yucca (evergreen), a beauty with an impressive spire of white lily-like flowers. Pernettya is a very hardy evergreen and soon forms a dense wiry thicket. *Pernettya mucronata* 'Alba' produces clusters of white fruits.

Q

The traffic on the road outside my house has increased considerably in recent years, with the ensuing noise reaching a near intolerable level. Are hedges any use in reducing noise?

A

Yes, they can be of great help. Evergreen coniferous hedges are best for absorbing the noise. If the size of your garden allows it, set the plants in two rows, either making a very thick single hedge or two rows several feet apart. The rapid-growing × *Cupressocyparis leylandii* is often too large, but *Thuya plicata* planted 600–750 mm (2–2½ ft) apart makes a good screen for small gardens.

An alternative method is to use the combination of a wooden fence (up to 1·8 m (6 ft)) with a line of conifers behind it. Plant the conifers about 900 mm (3 ft) away from the fence to leave plenty of space for their development.

CONIFERS FOR WET GARDENS

The Swamp Cypress or Bald Cypress (*Taxodium distichum*) does well in wet soils or those that are permanently moist. Grows 7·5–10·5 m (25–35 ft) high, and is ideal as a specimen on a wet lawn.

The Dawn Redwood (*Metasequoia glyptostroboides*) rises to 9–13·5 m (30–45 ft) and is ideal for planting in a group at the side of a large pond.

The Sitka Spruce (*Picea sitchensis*) is larger and grows up to 18 m (60 ft) and is best featured as a specimen conifer in a large, wet lawn.

THE ROCK GARDEN

Above Erinus alpinus, *an ideal plant for rock gardens and dry walls.*

ROCK GARDEN SHRUBS
Garland Flower (*Daphne cneorum*)
  Height: 300 mm (1 ft)
  Spread: 600 mm (2 ft)
Carpeting evergreen with neat, small leaves interspersed in May and June with clusters of richly scented, rose-pink flowers.
Rock Rose (*Helianthemum nummularium*)
  Height: 150–200 mm (6–8 inches)
  Spread: 600–900 mm (2–3 ft)
Ground-hugging evergreen ideal for sprawling over outcrops. Massed display of 15–25 mm (½–1 inch) wide, saucer-shaped flowers in many hues during May and June.
***Spiraea nipponica* 'Snowmound'**
  Height: 300 mm (1 ft)
  Spread: 600 mm (2 ft)
Enchanting hummocks of green foliage dotted with white, green-centred flowers in June.

Q

My garden is small, without a slope. Is it still possible to grow rock garden plants?

A

The essential elements for a successful rock garden are an open site, preferably facing south or west, no trees which will cast their leaves over the plants in autumn, and good drainage. Even without the benefit of a slope, rock garden plants can still be grown in a raised bed. Use plenty of clean rubble to form a freely-draining base, placing weed-free soil over this. Pieces of natural stone can be positioned in the soil to appear like natural rock outcrops. The natural rock strata should be aligned at all times.

Q

I have a dry stone wall. Which plants would thrive there to provide early summer colour?

A

There are several to choose from, including:
***Aethionema* × 'Warley Rose'**
  Height: 100–150 mm (4–6 inches)
  Spread: 300–380 mm (12–15 inches)
A beautiful hybrid with narrow, grey-green leaves and 50–75 mm (2–3 inch) long spike of deep rose flowers during spring.
Arenaria montana
  Height: 100–150 mm (4–6 inches)
  Spread: 380–450 mm (15–18 inches)
Glistening, white, saucer-shaped flowers amid mid- to dark-green leaves in early summer.
Asperula lilaciflora caespitosa
  Height: 50–75 mm (2–3 inches)
  Spread: 100–150 mm (4–6 inches)
A neat carpeter, with deep carmine, tubular flowers during early summer.
Erinus alpinus
  Height: 75 mm (3 inches)
  Spread: 130–150 mm (5–6 inches)
A low, tufted plant with bright pink, star-shaped flowers from spring to late summer.
Geranium cinereum subcaulescens
  Height: 100–150 mm (4–6 inches)
  Spread: 300–380 mm (12–15 inches)
An alpine geranium with crimson-magenta 25 mm (1 inch) wide flowers in early summer.

YELLOW DISPLAY

Q

Can you suggest a small, yellow-flowered shrub for the top of my rock garden?

A

There are several members of the broom family to choose from, but the one perhaps best suited to a small rock garden is *Cytisus × kewensis* at 300–600 mm (1–2 ft) high and 750–900 mm (2½–3 ft) wide. During May it develops a stunning array of pea-shaped, pale yellow flowers. Other choices include *Genista pilosa*, 450 mm (1½ ft) high and 600–750 mm (2–2½ ft) wide. During May and June it produces a mass of small, yellow, pea-like flowers amid tangled shoots. The form 'Prostrata' is often grown, and this seldom rises above 75–100 mm (3–4 inches) with a spread up to 1·2 m (4 ft).

Genista sagittalis, 100–150 mm (4–6 inches) high and 450–600 mm (1½–2 ft) wide, is an interesting miniature broom, now correctly

Left Cytisus × kewensis, *an excellent rock garden shrub, which displays masses of creamy-yellow flowers.*

known as *Chamaespartium sagittale*, but seldom listed under this name. The small, yellow, pea-like flowers appear in summer. It is a good ground cover shrub, or for trailing and scrambling over rocks.

Q

Can you recommend an upright water plant with flowers and variegated foliage for the edge of my pond?

A

You could not do better than *Iris laevigata* 'Variegata'. It grows to 450–600 mm (1½–2 ft) high, with a spread of 250–380 mm (10–15 inches). Position it in water up to 150 mm (6 inches) deep, or in moist soil at the pond's edges. Its upright, sword-like, stiff leaves display silver-striped, vertical bands. Soft-blue, iris-like flowers are borne at the tops of stems during early June. Other suitable plants include:

Iris pseudacorus
  Height: 900 mm–1·2 m (3–4 ft)
  Spread: 450–600 mm (1½–2 ft)
A hardy water iris, suitable for water depths up to 380 mm (15 inches), with upright, sword-like, blue-green leaves. Yellow, iris-like, flowers are borne five or more at the tops of stems during early June. A variegated form is also available.

Scirpus tabernaemontanus 'Zebrinus'
  Height: 300–750 mm (1–2½ ft)
  Spread: 300–380 mm (12–15 inches)

An eye-catching, herbaceous perennial, ideal for water up to 150 mm (6 inches) deep. Its tubular, upright leaves are banded white and green, somewhat resembling porcupine quills.

Q

I have inherited a pile of sandstone and Westmorland limestone in my new garden. I intend to form two rock gardens. Any tips on using the stone would be welcome.

A

The sandstone should always be laid with the strata (the layers which form the stone) arranged horizontally. Position the individual pieces so that they either butt up to one another or overlap slightly. This helps to prevent soil erosion. They can then be formed into a series of terraces.

The Westmorland limestone, however, is more difficult to use, and should be laid with the largest surface area to the ground. Position the pieces to form a series of irregular small terraces. They are fitted together like a jig-saw puzzle, with as little space as possible between the joins. Small, low-growing plants can then be planted between them.

THE FLOWER ARRANGER'S GARDEN

BULBS FOR CUT FLOWERS

Acidanthera bicolor 'Murielae': scented, white, purple-centred, starry flowers in August.

Daffodils (*Narcissus*): especially fine are the scented bunch-flowered varieties such as white, yellow-centred 'Grand Primo Citroniere', 'Paper White Grandiflora' and golden 'Grand Soleil d'Or'.

Gladiolus: spikes of red, pink, blue, orange, yellow trumpet blooms from July to September. Harlequin flower (Sparaxis): choice combinations of flower colours: pink, red, orange and white with contrasting bronzy red or yellow centres.

Iris: Dutch and Spanish hybrids in white, yellow, blue and purple and English hybrids in white, blue, pink or purple, June to July.

Lilium: Mid-Century Hybrids, especially lemon-yellow 'Destiny' and nasturtium-red 'Enchantment'.

Tulips (*Tulipa*): scented varieties such as golden 'Bellona' and golden orange 'De Wet' and the long lasting, soft orange and purple-flame 'Princess Irene' bring colour to early spring.

Right Cosmos bipannatus (Cosmea) 'Gloria', a good flower for cutting and arranging.

Q

I am an avid flower arranger and would appreciate your suggestions for flowers suitable for cutting and displaying in the home.

A

There are many that produce superb flowers and last a long time when cut. The list below gives a selection of hardy annuals which make attractive arrangements.

Love-lies-bleeding (*Amaranthus caudatus*)
'Crimson' and 'Viridis' are varieties prized for their scarlet and green pendant tassels; both grow to a height of 750 mm (2½ ft).

Pot Marigold/English Marigold (*Calendula officinalis*)
'Orange Gitana'. Superb, compact plant with fully double orange blooms, 300 mm (1 ft) high.

Clarkia (*Clarkia elegans*)
'Brilliant Mixture' comes in soft hues of salmon, scarlet, purple and orange and white; 600 mm (2 ft) high.

Coreopsis (*Calliopsis*)
'Dwarf Mixed' produces an abundance of golden-yellow, maroon or crimson flowers, 300 mm (1 ft) high.

Cosmos (*Cosmos bipinnatus* (*Cosmea*))
'Gloria'. Valued for its very large, rose-pink blooms, up to 900 mm (3 ft) high.

Godetia grandiflora **'Sybil Sherwood'**, in salmon-pink or orange with a white rim, grows just 300 mm (1 ft) high.

Love-in-a-mist (*Nigella damascena*)
'Persian Jewels', white, pink, rose-red, mauve and purple, 450 mm (18 inches) high.

Black-eyed Susan (*Rudbeckia hirta*)
'Goldilocks'. Double and semi-double, rich golden-yellow flowers contrasting with central black cone. Branches freely, 450–600 mm (1½–2 ft) high. (Also known as Coneflower.)

Sweet Scabious (*Scabiosa atropurpurea*)
'Paper Moon'. Lavender flowers give way to intriguing papery spheres of blue-centred miniature shuttlecocks, 900 mm (3 ft) high.

Zinnia elegans (Half-hardy annual)
Chartreuse-green 'Envy' has superb semi-double and double blooms, 500 mm (20 inches).

Q

My neighbour has some very decorative silvery and feathery plumes at the tops of long, stiff stems. What are they?

A

This is the Pampas Grass (*Cortaderia selloana*) from Argentina. It is a member of the grass family, best planted as a specimen at the edge of an informal pond or in a lawn. It grows 1·8–2·7 m (6–9 ft) high and forms a clump 1·5–1·8 m (5–6 ft) wide. The long stems can be cut off in autumn and placed in a large, firmly-based container on the floor. The plume-like heads dry and last a long time.

Incidentally, Pampas Grass looks magnificent during winter when covered with frost and with low winter light falling on the plumes. For this reason set it in an open position, which is not continually shaded.

Left *Love-in-a-Mist*
(Nigella damascena
'*Persian Jewels*') *looks
stunning both in the
garden and the home.*

Q

I have a border of herbaceous perennials for cutting, and would now like to grow a few shrubs that will provide foliage for background colour. What do you suggest?

A

There are several to choose from, such as *Lonicera nitida* 'Baggesen's Gold' with small, golden-coloured leaves, *Philadelphus coronarius* 'Aureus' with soft yellow leaves, and the golden privet, again with gold leaves. For silver foliage *Artemesia arborescens* is superb, and *Eucalyptus gunnii* has blue-tinged silvery foliage. For really stunning, dark plum-purple foliage choose *Cotinus coggygria* 'Foliis Purpureis'. *Cotinus coggygria* 'Royal Red' is equally fine.

ORNAMENTAL GRASSES FOR CUTTING FOR HOME DECORATION

HARDY ANNUAL GRASSES
Pearl Grass (*Briza maxima*)
   Height: 450 mm (1½ ft)
   Spread: 300 mm (1 ft)
Long, nodding spikes of green and white flowers.
Hordeum jubatum
   Height: 450 mm (1½ ft)
   Spread: 300 mm (1 ft)
Long-haired, silky, barley-like tassels.
Lagurus ovatus
   Height: 450 mm (1½ ft)
   Spread: 300 mm (1 ft)
Woolly plumes borne on long stems.
Setaria italica
   Height: 450 mm (1½ ft)
   Spread: 300 mm (1 ft)
Nodding, large, graceful flower heads.

HERBACEOUS GRASSES
Pennisetum alopecuroides
   Height: 900 mm (3 ft)
   Spread: 450 mm (1½ ft)
A long-lived grass, with feathery, tawny-yellow plumes during September and October.
Pennisetum orientale
   Height: 300 mm (1 ft)
   Spread: 300 mm (1 ft)
Poker-like flower spires from July to October.
Stipa gigantea
   Height: 900 mm (3 ft)
   Spread: 450 mm (1½ ft)
Dense clumps of grey-green leaves.

Q

I am planning a herbaceous border. Please suggest a few plants that would provide flowers for cutting. And if any are suitable for drying, please indicate this.

A

The following plants will provide colour for the home: yellow-flowered *Achillea filipendulina* 'Gold Plate' (suitable for drying), pink, apricot and orange alstroemeria, white papery-flowered anaphalis (suitable for drying), primrose yellow, daisy-flowered anthemis, blue, red and pink aster, blue-flowered catananche (suitable for drying), pinkish-rose centaurea, blue delphinium, yellow doronicum, globe-headed blue echinops (suitable for drying), silvery-blue-flowered eryngium (suitable for drying), bronzy red helenium, blue-flowered limonium (suitable for drying), pink, scarlet or violet-purple monarda, pink, red or white phlox, pink physostegia, red and pink pyrethrum, golden rudbeckia, blue scabiosa, rose-pink solidago and golden-yellow trollius.

VEGETABLES
PLANNING A KITCHEN GARDEN

Q

I have soil-tested my new allotment and find that it has a pH of 6·5–7·5. What crops will grow best in it?

A

It is slightly on the alkaline (limy) side so parsnips and legumes including runner beans, broad beans and French beans will excel. So, too, will members of the cabbage family, which includes swedes and turnips. Carrots and lettuce grow well, too. But you may find that your soil's chalk content 'locks up' essential iron needed to produce the green colouring matter in the leaf, and in some instances leaves may be chlorotic, that is, yellowish with bright green veins. Overcome this problem by feeding with Sequestrene and adding bulky organic manure in autumn. Feed also with an acid-based nitrogenous fertilizer such as sulphate of ammonia.

Potatoes and rhubarb dislike limy conditions. If you would like to grow them, manure liberally and avoid using alkaline-based fertilizers.

Several years ago it was customary for many gardeners to scatter lime liberally over their soil every year, irrespective of the acidity or alkalinity of their soil. Nowadays, with the help of an inexpensive soil-testing kit, the correct amount of lime can be applied – if it is needed.

Q

My cabbages are growing lushly, with huge leaves, and are riddled with pests and diseases. How can I overcome this?

A

It is probable that your crop is suffering from too much nitrogen fertilizer which promotes soft growth vulnerable to attack by all kinds of garden troubles. For good growth, phosphate and potash also need to be present in balanced proportions. Carry out a soil test and apply a balanced compound fertilizer to ensure good growth in future crops.

CROP ROTATION

Q

What is crop rotation?

A

This is the rotation of certain types of vegetables on a piece of land, so that the same crops are not grown continuously in one position. Certain vegetables need different soil preparation and fertilizer and manure treatments from other vegetables. Also, growing a particular crop on the same piece of land year after year encourages the build up of soil pests and diseases.

Plants can be grouped in three broad types – *seed and stem crops* (group A), *root crops* (group B) and *greens* (group C). The vegetable plot can be divided into three equal parts and within each part over a three-year period a different type of vegetable can be grown.

	PLOT 1	PLOT 2	PLOT 3
YEAR 1	A	B	C
YEAR 2	B	C	A
YEAR 3	C	A	B

GROUP A	GROUP B	GROUP C
Bean crops	Beetroot	Broccoli
Cucumbers	Carrots	Brussels
Celery	Parsnips	sprouts
Leeks	Potatoes	Cabbages
Lettuce	Swedes	Cauliflowers
Marrows		Turnips
Onions		
Peas		
Shallots		
Spinach		
Sweetcorn		

GROWING BAGS

I only have a patio on which to grow plants. Is it possible to grow vegetables in growing bags?

A

Yes indeed. Growing bags are ideal for raising a range of vegetables on your patio. Do not try to grow deep-rooted vegetables, such as parsnips and swedes in growing bags. Rather, concentrate on salad crops such as lettuces, spring onions, cucumbers and tomatoes. You might also like to try dwarf beans.

Q

What do the initials N P K mean?

A

These stand for the major foods required by plants. N means *nitrogen*, P stands for *phosphate* and K for *potassium*, better known as potash. For strong growth, it is essential that these chemicals are present in the correct amounts to suit the particular crop and its stage of development. For instance, during their early stages tomato plants require more nitrogen than the other major foods so that they can develop plenty of leaves and shoots. But later, when the fruits are ripening, more potash is needed.

Q

I've heard that mulching benefits growth. What is a mulch and how do I use it?

A

A mulch can be organic – old manure, well rotted garden compost, grass cuttings, straw, peat or pulverized bark – or plastic. Its purpose is to conserve soil moisture in droughty spells in summer, keep down weeds and warm the soil to encourage early growth. Organic mulches also feed plants and are usually much more pleasant to look at than plastic types, and are, therefore, preferred by many gardeners.

However, if you choose to use a plastic mulch, use black plastic as it excludes light, thereby keeping down weeds, and absorbs sun heat to keep soil warm but moist, and speeds rapid growth. Unroll the black plastic between the rows and, to anchor it, sprinkle earth over the edges where they butt up to the plants.

When using black plastic mulches, scatter slug bait liberally before positioning the plastic, as the dark, warmth and moisture create an ideal environment for the creatures.

When mulching roses with organic material such as crumbly, decayed manure, in early spring, wait until the soil is free from frost and warmed by the sun.

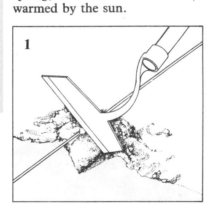

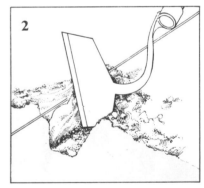

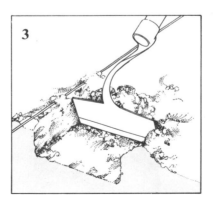

MAKING SEED DRILLS
Several different types of seed drills are used, depending on the seeds to be sown in them. For instance, a V-drill (1) formed with the edge of a draw hoe is ideal for small seeds. A narrow flat-bottomed drill (2) is suitable for potatoes and a wide-bottomed drill (3) is ideal for seeds such as peas.

SPECIFIC VEGETABLES

Q

How should runner beans be supported?

A

Several methods can be used. Traditionally, bean poles are used but these are often difficult to obtain. Strong netting stretched between two stout posts is a useful method if you wish to grow the beans across the width of your plot. Alternatively, a wig-wam formed of canes or a may-pole arrangement of strings are useful when positioning the beans in small plots or awkward-shaped corners.

Try to position your runner beans within range of a hose pipe, as these vegetables need plenty of water.

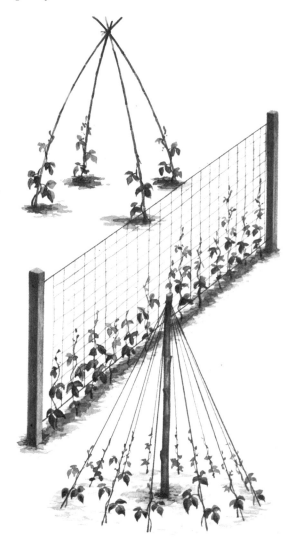

3 methods of supporting runner beans:
Top *A cane wig-wam.*
Middle *Netting stretched between two posts.*
Bottom *A maypole arrangement of strings.*

Q

I saw a lettuce in a greengrocer shop which had many small leaves, and did not form a heart like most types. What is it and when should I sow seeds?

A

It is a leaf type, and most probably the variety 'Salad Bowl', which produces a mass of small leaves within fifty days of being sown. From April to mid-May sow seeds thinly and 12 mm (½ inch) deep in drills spaced 130–150 mm (5–6 inches) apart.

Being somewhat ornamental it can be used to edge a flower border. Leaves are gathered regularly and many more sprout to replace them.

Q

I would like to grow asparagus. What is the best method?

A

The first step is to choose a high-yielding variety such as 'Lorella', which has thick, milky, green-tipped stems.

Select a patch of well-manured soil and top-dress with 50 g (2 oz) per sq. yd. of bonemeal and the same of superphosphate plus 25 g (1 oz) per sq. yd. of sulphate of potash.

Set the roots, which are long and spidery, on a rounded ridge of soil in a trench so the crowns (top, budded portion) are 100 mm (4 inches) below the surface. Space crowns 300 mm (1 ft) apart in three rows 300 mm (1 ft) apart. Then divide the three-row section with a 750 mm (2½ ft) path.

To help plants become well established, do not cut any spears in the first season after planting. In subsequent seasons, start cutting when spears are 150 mm (6 inches) above the soil. Cease harvesting in late June to allow ferny leaves to develop and strengthen growth for the next year.

Feed with 100 g (4 oz) dressing of balanced fertilizer each spring and follow with a thick mulch of old manure or well rotted garden compost.

In autumn, the ferny leaves turn brown and should be cut back to soil level.

POLLINATING MARROWS

Q

Is it necessary to hand-pollinate marrows?

A

Pollination usually takes place on its own with help from visiting insects, but during cold weather, or early in the year, hand-pollination may be necessary. The female flowers – those appearing to be sitting on small marrows – need to have a male flower, when it is releasing pollen, dusted over them.

During prolonged cold weather it may be necessary to repeat this hand-pollinating several times, until the weather improves and the insects return.

Q

How many bunches should I allow to form on my outdoor tomatoes before nipping out their tops and stopping them?

A

Allow four bunches, or trusses, to develop. As soon as the fruits on the fourth truss are swelling, either cut off or bend and snap the leading shoot, two leaves above the top truss.

Q

Is it necessary to cut off the tops of leeks before they are planted?

A

Yes, as it helps the newly-planted seedlings to become established quickly. Also, trim off about one-third of the roots to ensure that the young plant rests on the bottom of the hole which should be 230–300 mm (9–12 inches) deep. A thorough watering at that stage settles the plant in the hole. Do not pack the holes with soil as the plants need room to swell.

If the soil becomes dry during subsequent weeks, water the plants. This will eventually return soil to the hole and help to settle it around the roots.

Q

In previous years I've noticed birds tugging at my onion sets. Many are completely displaced. How can I prevent this?

A

Simple – cut off the wispy tops which protrude through the soil, attracting the birds. Use sharp scissors to snip off the tops, then set them with their tips slightly above the surface. Use a trowel to plant them 100–150 mm (4–6 inches) apart in rows 300 mm (1 ft) apart.

To discourage birds, it may be necessary to cover onions initially with wire-netting formed into tunnels. As soon as the onion sets have become well rooted the wire can be removed. Incidentally, frost can also lift the soil and make the sets loose. If this happens replant them immediately, firming the soil around them.

Below left *When planting leeks, do not firm the soil, but water in so the growing plant can swell more easily.*

Below right *Snip off the top of onion sets to prevent birds pulling at them when nest-building.*

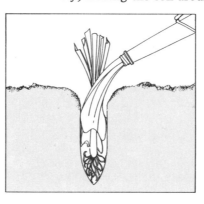

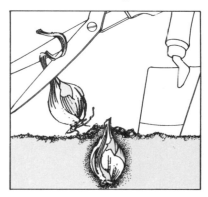

SPECIFIC VEGETABLES

Q

I would like to grow an early crop of potatoes and would appreciate your advice.

A

Start with a 'first early' variety such as 'Dunluce', 'Foremost' or 'Maris Bard'. Sprout the tubers by setting them eye-end uppermost in seed trays or egg cartons, in a light, warm place. (The temperature should not be over 13–16°C (55–60°F) or the shoots will grow spindly.)

When the soil is fit to cultivate in March or early April take out drills 150 mm (6 inches) deep and 600 mm (2 ft) apart and space the tubers 375 mm (15 inches) apart with their shoots uppermost. If the soil is poor, sprinkle a thin layer of processed manure along the bottom of the drill before setting tubers in position. Cover with soil.

When shoots push through the soil, earth up the rows, i.e. use a swan-necked hoe to ridge the soil up round the plants, to protect the frost-tender leaves. Another earthing-up when a further 150 mm (6 inches) of growth is made will ensure that developing tubers remain below the soil and stay blanched and edible.

Scatter fertilizer at 100 g (4 oz) per sq.yd. along the rows to speed development when the leaves are 300 mm (1 ft) or so above the soil in mid-June. Water freely in dry weather.

Another method of growing early potatoes is to plant two or three seed potatoes that already have sprouts (small shoots) growing from them in a large pot or box. Cover them with cloches (see pages 46–47), with extra protection from sacking whenever frost threatens.

ONIONS AND LEEKS

Q

How are large onions harvested to ensure they are fully ripe and will last a long time in store?

A

During late August or early September, bend the tops so that the rows are bent alternately to the left and right, so that you can walk between the rows. Use a fork to break the roots, still leaving the bulbs in rows to assist ripening. Make sure the base plate (bottom of the bulb) faces upwards to be ripened by the sun. Ideally, cover bulbs if rain threatens, to prevent them splitting and growing out from the base.

Q

Is there any special way to lift leeks from the soil? I don't want to damage them.

A

Use a strong garden fork, taking care not to damage the blanched stems. Although a hand can be placed on the stem, do not pull the plant up by this as it can quickly be damaged.

Using a strong garden fork, insert this well down beside the leek stem. Then, gently holding the green shaft, taking care not to wrench at it, for it will break, lever up on the fork and prise out the plant.

Is it essential to use a dibber to plant cabbages and other brassicas?

No, using a trowel is an alternative method, but a dibber does enable each plant to be set firmly in the soil. Push the dibber well into the soil, place the young plant in position – with the part where the leaves join the stem just above soil-level – and then use the dibber to lever soil against the roots. A test to ensure it is planted firmly is to try to pull off a leaf. If the leaf breaks then the plant has been set firmly in the soil.

My neighbour always nips out the tips of his broad bean plants. Is this essential?

It looks a destructive practice, but it has two vital effects on the plants. Firstly, it reduces the danger from Black Bean Aphids that enjoy sucking sap from the soft tips. Secondly, it encourages a more uniform development of pods on the plant. It is best done when the plants are in full flower, removing the top 100–150 mm (4–6 inches) of each shoot, when on each stem 4 clusters, or trusses, of pods have formed.

   If the tips are already infested with Black Bean Aphids, they are best put in an incinerator immediately. To prevent the aphids escaping, first put the tips in a plastic bag.

Is it essential to grow celery in trenches?

Many years ago this was essential, but now there are several superb so-called 'self-blanching' varieties that can be grown on the flat. The plants are set close together, so that each excludes light from its neighbour. (Growing celery in full light will result in stringy, less succulent growth.) Pieces of boarding around the outside will prevent light reaching plants at the perimeter. Suitable varieties include 'Lathom Self-Blanching' and 'Golden Self-Blanching'.

Friends tell me I should grow my sweetcorn in blocks rather than rows. Why is this?

Because sweetcorn is pollinated by wind it is essential that the plants are set in blocks of plants rather than long single rows. Then the chance is very much greater of the female, tassel-like flowers receiving pollen.

I am keen to grow exhibition parsnips. Can you give me any tips?

Get the best roots by using a crowbar to form holes up to 900 mm (3 ft) deep and 380 mm (15 inches) apart. Fill with sifted soil or old potting compost laced with a balanced fertilizer mixture. Choose a sunny site.

   'Tender and True' and 'Cobham Improved Marrow' are excellent exhibition varieties, having long tapering roots.

   In March, or as soon as the soil is warming nicely, sow three seeds per hole, thinning to the strongest when three or four leaves have formed.

   Water freely in dry spells, keep weeded and top-dress with a high-potash fertilizer in mid-May and mid-July. Stop the top of the root, where it joins the leaf stalks, from splitting by covering with a thick layer of peat.

   Guard against Celery Fly, which also attacks parsnips, by spraying with a permethrin-based insecticide in early June and repeat two or three times at 10 day intervals.

   Lift the roots carefully, excavating soil from around them so as not to break the much prized taper acclaimed by the judges.

Above left *Use a dibber to plant cabbages, levering the dibber to firm the soil against the roots.*

Above right *Test cabbage to see that it is firmly planted – a small portion of the leaf should tear away without shifting the plant.*

277

THE HERB GARDEN

Q

What is the best aspect for a herb garden?

A

Preferably, choose a border relatively close to your house, which is sunny, well-drained and facing south. Light shade for part of the day is acceptable to many herbs. Interestingly, a poor soil, which is somewhat short of nutrients, promotes stronger flavour and scents.

Q

Last year my parsley failed to germinate. Have you any idea what I may have done wrong?

A

Parsley is difficult to germinate if the soil dries out. In fact, in extremely dry years it may not germinate at all. During this coming year, sow seeds in drills that have had a drop of water trickled into their bases. After sowing, cover the seeds with dry soil. This will help to retain moisture around the seeds.

Q

Is it possible to grow a bay tree in a container, as I only have a small terraced garden?

A

Bay trees grow particularly well in large tubs, and are especially eye-catching when a pair of them are positioned either side of a doorway. Painting the container white makes the effect even more stunning. Protect them from cold winds which often damage the leaves.

If you live in an area with a high winter rainfall, it may be necessary to cover the soil in the pot with a piece of polythene or two tiles. The easiest method involves using the polythene, tying it around the pot with strong string or wire. If the compost in the pot is allowed to become saturated, there is a chance that the entire root ball will freeze, causing damage to the roots.

Q

What herbs can I grow from seeds each year?

A

There are many superb sorts that can be raised from seeds each year, such as:

Basil (*Ocimum basilicum*). A half-hardy annual, growing 600–900 mm (2–3 ft) high with fleshy stems and thick leaves 75 mm (3 inches) long, and with a strong smell of cloves. Delicious in cooked tomato dishes.

Borage (*Borago officinalis*). An annual, rising 450–600 mm (1½–2 ft) high. It is a plant with bristly and hairy leaves and beautiful, bright blue, star-like flowers borne in clusters. Chopped leaves flavour salads and wine cups.

Sweet Marjoram (*Origanum majorana*). A perennial usually treated as an annual. It grows 200–250 mm (8–10 inches) high (more when grown as a perennial), with grey-green leaves and white flowers in July. Use to enrich meat, fish and tomato dishes. Good in salads, too.

Parsley (*Pelroselinum crispum*). A biennial, often treated as an annual, and growing 150–200 mm (6–8 inches) high. Its curled and deeply-divided leaves are well known. Garnish for fish and meat dishes. Nourishing when used in soups and stews.

Below *Borage is an attractive plant which is easy to grow.*

Q

Can any herbs be picked fresh in winter?

A

There are several to choose from, such as Chervil (*Anthriscus cerefolium*) which is sown during August and September and will withstand most winters outside. As a substitute for chives you could grow either Welsh onions or perennial onions. Raise the Welsh onions from seed or by dividing old lumps in spring or autumn. It is possible to use both the leaves and the bulbs. Perennial onions, which look like pale chives, must be raised by division. Parsley can be sown during July for a winter supply, but it tends to be cut back by cold weather unless protected with cloches (see pages 46–47).

Other evergreen herbs are Thyme, Rosemary, Pot Marjoram and Winter Savory. These, as well as chervil, fare better if given the protection of frames or cloches during winter.

Q

I have a small round border previously used for roses. Can I convert this successfully into a herb garden? And which plants do you suggest I grow?

A

A small round bed of herbs can look very attractive and provide a wide range of culinary herbs. You will need to section off the bed; small pebbles or narrow edging blocks can be used for this purpose.

Invasive plants, such as mint, are best left in their pots; bury them so that the rims are 50 mm (2 inches) above the soil's surface.

To prevent the herbs spilling over into another section, trim them each year.

In the plot above, clockwise from the top are: a bay tree, rosemary, tarragon, chives, chervil, sage, thyme (lemon and common), parsley, marjoram, angelica, applemint and spearmint.

FRAMES & CLOCHES

COLD FRAMES

Q

I have an old-fashioned wooden-sided garden frame in my new garden. Can you please tell me what I can use it for?

A

During spring you will find the frame useful for raising early crops of lettuce, radish, or carrots. Also, you could raise seedlings in it.

In summer the frame is ideal for growing melons or cucumbers, which can be trained horizontally. Because of the limited amount of light this type of frame admits, it is not suitable for winter crops, but it can be used for over-wintering seedlings of summer cauliflowers, lettuces, and autumn-sown varieties of onions. In addition, it can be used for forcing chicory or blanching endives.

Frames are available in a wide variety of styles and sizes. The traditional wooden-box type is generally the cheapest and remains as useful as any. Some versions have asbestos sides. The modern glass-sided design with a span roof is useful for light-demanding winter crops such as lettuce.

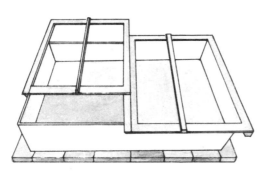

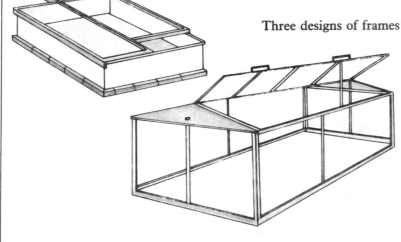

Three designs of frames

Q

How do cloches differ from cold frames?

A

Cloches are usually formed of glass or plastic and are about 450 mm (1½ ft) long and designed to cover part of a row of vegetables or soft fruit, usually strawberries. By putting several cloches end-to-end a row can be completely covered. Cold frames, however, are permanent fixtures formed of large sheets of glass set in a wooden surround. The frame rests on a framework of back and side boards, so the area is covered by glass and protected on all sides by wood.

Although cloches can be used for some of the same purposes as frames, their primary use is for extending the growing season of food crops in the garden. Under the protective covering of cloches, vegetable seedlings can be sown earlier and the plants will grow more rapidly.

Q

My outdoor tomatoes often do not ripen. Are cloches of any use in speeding up the process?

A

Yes. About mid-September cut down the tomatoes from their supports and lay them in a line on a bed of straw. Cloches can now be placed over them. Continue to water the plants, taking care not to splash the fruits.

Q

Can plastic cloches be used to produce early strawberries?

A

Plastic cloches are certainly useful as they are ideal for providing protection from cold winds. However, on spring nights when the temperature falls rapidly, the temperature under the cloches may be lower than that outside and this may damage early flowers and so kill the crop. Under these conditions spread sacks over the cloches, removing them during the day.

FRENCH BEANS

Q

How can I use cloches to produce early crops of dwarf French beans?

A

During early spring prepare a strip of soil for planting and place cloches over it to warm up the earth. In early April sow seeds under the cloches. The crop will be ready during late June. Remember, that for successful and quick germination of bean seeds the soil needs to be at least 10°C (50°F). Cold and wet soils encourage the seeds to rot. In cold areas wait until late April or early May before sowing seeds. Always choose a sunny but sheltered position.

Q

Are plastic cloches better than glass ones?

A

Glass transmits light more easily than plastic, and conserves heat better, especially at night. However, plastic is more durable and does not break so easily as glass. If you have inquisitive or energetic children it might be better to use plastic. However, plastic cloches are more likely to be blown away during fierce winds. If you do buy plastic types, ensure they have been treated with ultra-violet inhibitors as they last longer.

Q

What are polythene tunnels and what are their advantages?

A

Polythene tunnels are formed of polythene sheeting stretched over wire hoops to form a tunnel. Further wire hoops are used to prevent the plastic sheeting blowing away. Polythene tunnels are used widely in commercial horticulture. They are far cheaper than greenhouses, need no foundations and are quickly erected. They can also be moved from one place to another quite easily. The polythene transmits light and retains heat, enabling the tunnels to be used in the same way as cloches, The crops are ventilated either by leaving the ends of the tunnel open or by rolling up the polythene from one of the sides.

However, one of the disadvantages of polythene tunnels is that they are not very durable. The polythene can easily be torn and then has to be replaced.

Left *The traditional glass barn cloche, ideal for advancing early crops.*

Above *Corrugated rigid plastic tunnel cloches are easier to handle than polythene and longer-lasting, but much more expensive initially.*

FRUIT
FRUIT TREES

Q

I want to plant a plum that is suitable for dessert and culinary purposes.

A

You could not do better than 'Victoria'. It is self-fertile, so you do not need to plant other plum varieties close by. It produces heavy crops of large, oval, bright red fruits during late August. The plums are sometimes speckled with darker dots, and may have a golden-yellow flush.

Below *Plum 'Victoria', which has an excellent flavour.*

Q

As I do not have anywhere to store apples, please suggest a variety I can eat as soon as it is picked.

A

The variety 'James Grieve', with a rich, juicy flavour, is superb straight from the tree. It is dependable and crops heavily, with oval or irregularly-shaped fruits which have a red flush over-laying a pale yellow colour. Its one drawback is that it bruises easily – so take care when picking.

It does, however, need a pollinating partner to ensure regular crops. Choose from crisp and juicy, October to November ripening 'Jester', and orange-red-skinned 'Jupiter', a firm, juicy variety which is ready for picking from October to November.

Q

For some years now my apple tree has made strong shoots and few flowers, hence few fruits. How can I encourage it to crop well and regularly again?

A

Curb excessive shoot growth and stimulate the development of fruit spurs – which bear flowers, then apples – by root pruning and bark ringing.

Root pruning is done in winter. Take out a trench around the tree some 900 mm (3 ft) from the trunk and cut through all roots. This will encourage fine, feeding roots to form and will slow down leaf growth. Anchor the tree against high winds by fixing three guy lines to it.

Bark ringing is carried out in May, when the tree is in flower. Make two cuts 5 mm (¼ inch) apart round the trunk and peel off the bark between them. Seal the wound with waterproof tape to exclude air and speed healing. In autumn, when the cut has callused over, remove the tape.

In a year or two this treatment will result in plenty of flowers and good crops most years.

Q

What are the best rootstocks for apples, bearing in mind that I do not want a large tree?

A

There are many rootstocks used for apples, but only dwarf or semi-dwarf ones are suitable for the amateur. The dwarf ones are Malling 27 (M27), giving a tree up to 1·2 m (4 ft) high, Malling No 9 (M IX), producing growth up to 2·4 m (8 ft) high, and Malling 26 (M26). Semi-dwarfing ones are M VII and MM106 which impart much stronger growth, up to 3·5–4·5 m (12–15 ft).

The wisdom of selecting a dwarf rootstock can often be seen when visiting old orchards, where many of the fruits are too high to be picked.

Q

Please suggest several pear varieties which are ready at different times so that I can eat these fruits over a long period.

A

Pears are available for eating from September to January. Two September varieties are 'William's Bon Chrétien', a heavy and reliable cropper with juicy and sweet fruits, and 'Bristol Cross' which is ready in October as well as September and bears good flavoured juicy fruits; some people prefer it to 'Conference'. For November 'Doyenné du Comice' is superb, being the finest flavoured pear, while the well-known 'Winter Nelis' can be eaten right through from November to January.

TRAINING FRUIT TREES

Q

I have a west-facing closely-boarded fence and would like to grow fruit trees along it. What form of tree should I plant?

A

It is certainly possible to train fruit trees to grow along a fence or wall and there are many advantages in doing so, the greatest being that space is used economically, an important consideration in small gardens. The small size of trees grown in this way makes them easy to look after; the fruit can be picked effortlessly and pruning can be carried out without a ladder. The trees provide as much fruit as larger ones and in a much shorter time. There are various methods of training fruit trees.

Cordons are trained on a single stem tied to wires and are grown at an angle along a wall, fence or series of wires strained between posts.

An **espalier** is another form of tree with restricted growth. A central stem is trained vertically while tiers of horizontal branches are tied to wires. Building up the framework of an espalier takes time and skill, but the end result justifies the effort involved.

Cordons and espaliers are particularly suitable for growing apples. Peaches, nectarines and cherries can be trained in a fan-shape, with branches radiating out in the style of a fan.

Left *Cordons trained at an oblique angle.*

Below *A mature fruiting espalier.*

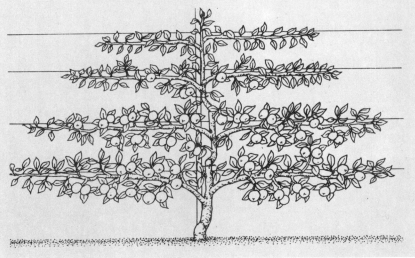

SOFT FRUIT

Q

How does the pruning of blackcurrants and redcurrants differ?

A

These fruits require totally different treatments; blackcurrants are grown as 'stooled' plants with the majority of new shoots arising from soil-level, whereas redcurrants are grown on a 'leg' with a permanent framework of shoots.

After blackcurrants have fruited and the crop has been picked, cut out all fruited wood to within 25 mm (1 inch) of soil-level.

It is essential that weak twigs and damaged or diseased wood are also cut out, together with any particularly low branches from which the blackcurrants may rub on the ground and become damaged.

With redcurrants, when the framework has been established, all that is needed is to cut back the growth produced that year to 25 mm (1 inch) of where it originated. The oldest dark wood can be cut back hard and new shoots from low down should be trained in to take its place.

Far right *Cordon-trained gooseberry bushes take up little space and are useful in small gardens.*

Below *Protect strawberry fruits by laying straw.*

Q

Please suggest several raspberry varieties that are suitable for freezing and for desserts.

A

There are several you could consider, such as 'Glen Clova' with medium to large fruits from July to August, 'Lloyd George' with large dark-ish red fruits during July, 'Malling Jewel' with bright red berries becoming darker as they open, during July and August, and 'Norfolk Giant' with heavy and regular crops of bright red, conical berries during August.

Q

Is there an alpine strawberry suitable for jam-making?

A

Yes. These runnerless alpine strawberries are long-cropping and ideal for dessert use as well as for making preserves. 'Baron Solemacher' and 'Alexandria' are ideal varieties, with fruits from June to October.

Q

Every year my strawberries are spoilt because heavy thunderstorms splash mud onto the fruits. Is there anything I can do to avoid this happening?

A

You can either spread straw between the rows and under the plants when the fruits are starting to form, or grow the plants in small holes cut in black polythene. Or buy special discs that are easily slipped round the crowns.

As well as heavy rain storms, birds can be a problem with strawberries – and, indeed, other fruits. For this reason it is worth considering covering the fruits with loose netting stretched over a low framework, or building a special wire-netting fruit cage. Many home gardeners do find it a permanent solution as birds can destroy buds as well as fruits.

Q

I have a small garden and wish to grow gooseberries. Is this possible?

A

Yes, but you may have to grow them as cordons, trained up a series of wire supports. Plant them in a good sunny position sheltered from cold winds and late-spring frosts. When gooseberries are grown as cordons they require special pruning in midsummer. Remove all surplus shoots and shorten side shoots to five leaves from the old wood to form fruiting spurs.

Q

Is there such a thing as a thornless loganberry? I am fed up with being scratched by thorns!

A

The variety 'LY 654,' which produces red berries, is well worth trying. It is excellent for cooking or bottling, with berries during July and August.

RASPBERRIES

Q

Is it essential to have a series of wires up which raspberries can be trained?

A

Yes, as some means of support is necessary to prevent the canes from snapping in the wind and to make it easy to pick the fruit. The easiest method is to erect posts at each end of the rows, stretching two strands of wire between them, the lowest being about 450 mm (18 inches) above the ground, and the second being 1·5 m (5 ft) above the ground. If the canes are not very strong, use more wires and space them about 300 mm (12 inches) apart. These canes support the young canes that develop each year as well as the canes made the previous year.

Raspberry canes bear fruits during their second year. Once picking has finished, cut out all fruited canes, tying in the new canes to replace them. Allow four or five new canes to each stool, removing all others, particularly those which are weak or small. Always keep the crop well picked, as over-ripe fruit left on the canes is liable to attack from mildew and other fungus disorders.

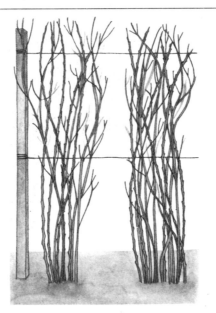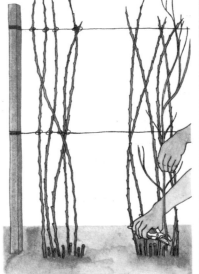

Above *Training and pruning raspberry canes.*

HEDGES AND TREES
HEDGES

Q

I live in a coastal area and want to plant a fast-growing coniferous hedge. What do you suggest?

A

The well-known Leyland Cypress × *Cupressocyparis leylandii* is widely planted in seaside gardens. It is the fastest growing hedge, but reaches a considerable size, up to 15 m (50 ft) in twenty or so years and eventually much higher. Set the plants about 750 mm (2½ ft) apart. If it is intended to form a shelter belt, set the plants in a staggered row, with the plants 1 m (3½ ft) apart. The golden form 'Castlewellan' displays brightly-coloured foliage and is ideal where a shorter hedge is needed. Set these plants 600 mm (2 ft) apart. Plant in September–November and keep watered if the weather is dry.

Below Lonicera nitida *'Baggesen's Gold', a superb golden-leaved hedge, which brightens any garden.*

Q

Is it better to have a hedge with slightly inward sloping sides, than vertical?

A

Yes, as this shape helps to prevent the base becoming straggly and allows more light and air to reach the base. Another advantage of trimming hedges this way is that they are less likely to become damaged by heavy snow falls.

Q

I have recently moved to an old house with a natural stone path down the centre of the garden. I want to plant a low, flowering hedge along either side of it. Is there a particular plant which will suit this purpose?

A

A plant which will harmonize with an old path in a cottage-garden setting is *Lavandula nana atropurpurea* (syn. *L.* 'Hidcote'). This is a compact and low-growing lavender, which achieves a height and width of 450–600 mm (1½–2 ft). It displays deep purple-blue flowers from July to September. The plants should be set 300 mm (1 ft) apart.

Q

I want to plant a small, golden-leaved hedge with an informal outline. What do you suggest?

A

Lonicera nitida 'Baggesen's Gold' is a superb form, with golden leaves. It is best when left unclipped with a somewhat unkempt outline. It does best in full sun, where the good light brings alive the foliage. It grows to about 1·5–1·8 m (5–6 ft) high and 750–900 mm (2½–3 ft) wide. The plants should be set 300 mm (1 ft) apart.

My wife yearns for a sweetly-scented old-fashioned rose hedge. Can you help?

The long flowering period and the sweetly-scented, semi-double, rich creamy-pink flowers of the Hybrid Musk 'Penelope' make it ideal as a hedge. Set the plants 750–900 mm (2½–3 ft) apart. This rose will form a hedge 1·5–1·8 m (5–6 ft) high and 1·2–1·5 m (4–5 ft) wide.

Another Hybrid Musk Rose to consider is 'Cornelia', which, with its coppery-apricot, scented blooms, also makes a lovely hedge. If the site is sunny these hedges will flower well and bloom throughout the summer.

Q

In my previous garden all of the hedges I planted eventually developed bare areas at their bases. I want to avoid this happening in my new garden. What should I do?

A

These bare bases occur because the plants were not properly pruned during their early months after being planted. During the first year it is essential to encourage plants to produce plenty of shoots from around their bases by pruning them as soon as they are planted.

Deciduous (leaf-shedding) kinds, such as beech, hornbeam and hawthorn, are cut back by a third to a half. This not only encourages bushiness, but reduces the amount of growth buffetted by winds that would otherwise loosen the plants in the soil. It also reduces the possibility of damage from heavy falls of snow during the first winter after planting.

Slow-growing evergreens which include Box (*Buxus sempervirens*) can be lightly tipped back after planting, but conifers should not be touched. However, formal evergreen hedging plants such as Privet and *Lonicera nitida* will need cutting back by one-third or half if the bases are to be kept full of growth and not to become bare during later years.

In old and neglected gardens hedges are often the first plants to get out of hand. There are then two solutions – first to cut the hedge hard back to see if it will create fresh shoots from ground level; and if not to dig it up, revitalize the soil and plant a fresh one.

Above Hybrid musk rose 'Penelope' makes an attractive, informal hedge that is colourful throughout the summer.

FLOWERING HEDGES

Berberis × *stenophylla*
An oustanding evergreen shrub with arching sprays of yellow flowers during May and June. Set the plants 600 mm (2 ft) apart. Clip the hedge after flowering, when it can be contained to 1·5–2·1 m (5–7 ft) high and 1–1·2 m (3½–4 ft wide. Suitable only for large gardens.

Escallonia 'Slieve Donard'
A beautiful evergreen shrub with an arching habit and large arrangements of apple-blossom-pink flowers in June on the previous season's wood. Set the plants 750 mm (2½ ft) apart. As a hedge it can be restricted to 1·5–1·8 m (5–6 ft) high and 900 mm–1 m (3–3½ ft) wide.

Pyracantha rogersiana
An evergreen, erect, dense shrub with white flowers and masses of red berries. Set the plants 500 mm (20 inches) apart. When grown as a hedge it can be contained to a height of 1·2–1·8 m (4–6 ft) and a width of 900 mm (3 ft).

Rosmarinus officinalis 'Jessop's Upright'
A delightful, erect, evergreen shrub with light mauve flowers mainly during spring. Set the plants 600 mm (2 ft) apart. It forms a hedge 1·2–1·8 m (4–6 ft) high and 900 mm (3 ft) wide.

Rhododendron luteum
A sprawling, deciduous shrub, ideal for an informal hedge in a wild garden. Its honey-suckle-like, scented, yellow flowers appear in June. Set the plants 750 mm (2½ ft) apart. It grows to 1·8–2·4 m (6–8 ft) high and 1·5–1·8 m (5–6 ft) wide.

TREES

Above *The spectacular Magnolia × soulangiana.*

Q

Please recommend a small magnolia.

A

One of the most spectacular forms is *Magnolia × soulangiana*. It displays white, chalice-shaped flowers 130–150 mm (5–6 inches) across, stained light purple at their bases during April. After twenty years it reaches 3·5–4·5 m (12–15 ft) tall and 3·5–5·4 m (12–18 ft) wide. The form 'Lennei' has rose-purple flowers.

Magnolia stellata is another small magnolia, rising to 2·4–3 m (8–10 ft) high and with a spread of 2·4–3·5 m (8–12 ft). It is frequently known as the Star Magnolia, producing white, star-like 75–100 mm (3–4 inch) wide flowers during March and April. The form 'Rosea' displays pink-flushed flowers, deep pink when in bud.

Q

At the bottom of my garden I want to plant a tree that develops rich autumn colours in its foliage. Have you any suggestions?

A

Perhaps the best known tree for vivid fiery tints is the Sweet Gum (*Liquidambar styraciflua*). It eventually develops into a large tree, but only reaches 5·4–6 m (18–20 ft) after twenty or so years. Its deeply-lobed leaves become brilliant scarlet and orange in October and November before falling.

Other superb autumn-colour trees include carmine, orange and reddish-hued *Parrotia persica* and *Cercidiphyllum japonicum* and flame-tinted *Nyssa sylvatica*.

Shrubs with autumn colouring include reddish orange-leaved *Fothergilla monticola*, golden-yellow tinted *Hamamelis mollis* 'Pallida', glowing, red-hued *Rhus typhina* and many of the small acers.

Q

Please suggest some trees with attractive leaves in purple, cream or yellow.

A

Some of the finest purples can be found amongst the following trees: purple beech *Fagus sylvatica* 'Purpurea', a magnificent and large tree; Pissard's Purple Plum (*Prunus cerasifera* 'Atropurpurea') which is more suitable for a small garden; *Acer platanoides* 'Goldsworth Purple,' and *Acer platanoides* 'Crimson King', resplendent with deep purple-crimson foliage.

Choice golden-leaved trees are *Robinia pseudoacacia* 'Frisia', a delight with ferny leaves on elegant branches, and *Gleditsia triacanthos* 'Sunburst', which is similar in appearance but with more glossy golden leaflets. Again, its shoots have a light, arching habit and it is possible to underplant with shade-loving border perennials.

Acer negundo 'Variegatum' has claim to fame with its creamy-white margined leaves and white bloomed new shoots. But it can revert, so green-leaved stems must be removed the moment they appear.

Q

Can you recommend a tree for a very small front garden?

A

The Japanese Cherry *Prunus* 'Amanogawa' is ideal for a restricted area. It presents a narrow, columnar shape covered in April and May with semi-double, slightly fragrant, soft pink flowers. After twenty or so years, it reaches 5·4–6 m (18–20 ft) high with a spread of 1·5–1·8 m (5–6 ft). In its early years it is quite slim.

For a flowering cherry with a shrub-like habit, the Dwarf Russian Almond (*Prunus tenella* 'Fire Hill') is worth considering. It forms an attractive mound 900 mm–1.2 m high and wide. During mid-spring it reveals 12–18mm (½–¾ inch) wide bright rose-crimson flowers along the stiff stems. It is an ideal shrub for a narrow border, but make sure you position it in good light and where the soil is well drained.

Q

What is the Golden Rain Tree?

A

There are, in fact, two trees known by this common name. One is *Koelreuteria paniculata* from Asia, which displays yellow flowers in loose, large, terminal clusters during July. The other tree is the well-known Laburnum with its pendulous clusters of yellow flowers which bloom during May and June.

Q

My local park has an Indian Bean Tree. I am told that there is a golden-leaved and smaller form, suitable for small gardens. Is this so?

A

The golden-leaved Indian Bean Tree is *Catalpa bignonioides* 'Aurea' and is, indeed, ideal for small gardens. It is deciduous and slow-growing, with large, heart-shaped, yellow leaves. During July it displays white flowers with yellow and purple markings. Try to position it so that the foliage is colour contrasted against darker leaved plants or even blue sky.

FLOWERING TREES FOR SMALL GARDENS

Shad Bush (*Amelanchier lamarckii*)
Height: 3–4·5 m (10–15 ft)
Spread: 3–3·5 m (10–12 ft)
A stunningly attractive deciduous tree with a profusion of star-shaped, white flowers in spring. Rich-coloured leaves in autumn.

Golden Rain Tree (*Laburnum* × *vossii*)
Height: 4·5–6 m (15–20 ft)
Spread: 3–3·5 m (10–12 ft)
A well-known tree, sometimes planted as a street tree, with spectacular pendulous bunches of pea-shaped, yellow flowers during May and June.

Flowering Crab (*Malus* × *lemoinei*)
Height: 4·5–6 m (15–20 ft)
Spread: 3·5–4·5 m (12–18 ft)
A beautiful hybrid crab with masses of single purple-crimson flowers in April and May. Other superb varieties include *Malus* 'Profusion' with single, deep-red flowers opening to purple-red – and *Malus* 'Snowcloud', an American double-flowered form with pure white blossom.

Below *The Indian Bean Tree* (Catalpa bignonioides '*Aurea*'), *a beautiful tree of great 'architectural' merit.*

LAWNS

LAWN TYPES AND CARE

Q

Please suggest types of hard-wearing grasses that I should ask to be included in a seed mixture for my lawn.

A

The types you need to ask for are dwarf strains of Perennial Ryegrass (*Lolium perenne*), Chewing's Fescue (*Festuca rubra commutata*) and the Crested Dog's Tail (*Cynosurus cristatus*). Usually, mixtures of seed for hard-wearing lawns are sold ready-mixed, and this is the easiest way of buying them, especially for a small area.

Mixtures of fine grasses based on Chewing's Fescue (*Festuca rubra commutata*) and Highland Bent (*Agrostis setacea*) for more decorative lawns are also sold, as well as mixtures containing Wood Meadowgrass (*Poa nemoralis*) for sowing in shady areas.

Q

I have bought a new house and plan to lay a lawn in my back garden. Is it better to make a lawn from seed or turf?

A

If you want an 'instant' lawn, then turf must be the answer. It is, however, about four times as expensive as seed, and the ground still needs thorough preparation to remove perennial weeds and to break up the top foot or so, to ensure drainage is good and the roots can easily penetrate the soil.

Eventually, lawns from seed are superior to those made from turf, and the type of grasses used can be selected to suit the lawn's uses. Hard wearing mixtures containing dwarf rye grass are the best choice if children are frequently using the lawn as a combat area!

LAWN REPAIRS

Q

When is the best time to apply weedkillers to lawns, and how should I do this?

A

Use weedkillers on lawns only when the grass is growing strongly. This is usually during late spring and summer. Do not apply it to grass that has suffered owing to dry weather. Make sure you do not use weedkiller on a windy day as there is a danger that it will drift on to healthy flowers and plants.

Stretch strings down the length of the lawn, 1 m (3½ ft) apart, and use a dribble bar (a perforated tube) on a watering-can to ensure accurate application.

Ideally, wear gloves for protection while using weedkiller and always wash your hands thoroughly afterwards.

Thoroughly wash the equipment after use, keeping it solely for the application of chemicals.

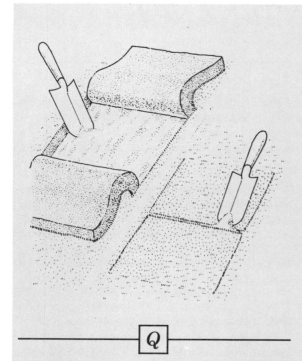

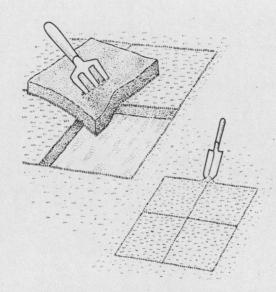

Far left *Bumps and hollows in lawns can be remedied fairly easily. When filling in a hollow, firm the soil well, or when it settles there may still be a hollow.*

Left *Damaged patches can be re-seeded or removed and new turves laid.*

| Q |

My lawn is full of small hollows, bumps and bare areas. Is it possible to rectify each little problem area to avoid digging up the entire lawn?

| A |

Yes, it is possible to level bumps and indentations. Use a sharp edging-iron to cut back strips of turf 230–300 mm (9–12 inches) wide. Peel back these strips – using a turfing-iron or spade – and either scrape out soil or fill in hollows.

Bare areas can be levelled and seed sown over the raked and prepared soil. If the weather is dry after sowing seed, water the soil and then place a sheet of clear polythene over it. Black polythene can be used, but has to be removed as soon as the seeds germinate.

Damaged patches can be re-seeded, or lifted and replaced with new turves. When laying new turves, firm well with a turf beater or the back of a spade. Water thoroughly and keep the area damp for two weeks to help the edges knit together neatly. If the edges of your lawn are damaged, use a sharp flat spade or edging-iron to cut out a piece of turf, then reverse it so that the damaged area is towards the centre of the lawn. Fill the broken area with soil and re-seed.

| Q |

Is there any special system to follow when laying turf?

| A |

Yes. After thoroughly and evenly digging the soil and removing all perennial weeds, tread the soil to firm it and rake it to produce a level surface. When laying the turf, start by laying a row lengthways down one side. Turves can then be laid butting on to this, with the ends staggered so that they are not all in one line. This necessitates cutting some turves in half so the finished result compares with bonded bricks in a wall. Always use a half-moon edger to cut turves, as a spade will leave a scalloped edge.

Left *Turf should always be laid in staggered rows, working from one corner. Ensure that the soil is packed evenly beneath each turf.*

LAWN MAINTENANCE

Q

When should a lawn roller be used?

A

Once a year, to firm frost-lifted turf before the first spring cut. Then put it away. Over-use of a roller quickly compacts the soil, spoiling drainage and restricting aeration which leads to poor root growth.

Q

What is the best way to apply fertilizers to a lawn? I only have a small lawn and no special lawn equipment.

A

Above *To apply fertilizers evenly, stretch string at metre intervals, then space strips of wood at the same distance as you proceed.*

For large lawns a fertilizer distributor is the easiest way. But for small gardens the easiest method is to stretch strings 1 m (3½ ft) apart down the length of the lawn and then use two canes or strips of wood to form 1 m squares. Spread the fertilizer on a calm, damp day at the recommended rate for each square metre, then move one of the canes to form a further square.

Q

Should I use a grass box on my mower, or let the grass cuttings remain on the surface?

A

There are reasoned arguments for both. Allowing the cuttings to remain on the lawn means that mineral nutrients are returned to the soil. Also, the cuttings help to conserve moisture in the soil during periods of drought. However, leaving the cuttings encourages earthworms to make casts on the surface, which may be unpleasant. Also, they tend to encourage diseases to attack the grasses. For a really picturesque lawn it is better to remove the cuttings.

Q

My cylinder-type grass mower produces an uneven cut – in bands across the lawn. What is the explanation?

A

It could be because of either the lawn or the mower. Check that the cylinder is in contact with the fixed bottom blade evenly across the width of the machine. Also, ensure that the cylinder and bottom blade are at a uniform height above the lawn's surface. Or it may be that the lawn is on a slope, and the weight of the machine is not evenly balanced, producing a closer cut on one side than the other.

Q

How can I eliminate lawn moss?

A

There are many proprietary moss killers currently available, usually based on dichlorophen or chloroxuron. Moss usually only occurs on wet, ill-drained lawns, so the best way to prevent the growth of moss is to improve drainage. Once a lawn is established it is difficult to improve drainage; this is why thorough drainage and soil preparation is essential when preparing the site for use as a lawn.

---Q---

What kind of material should I use to top-dress my lawn, and when should it be applied?

---A---

Top-dressing is best done in autumn. First, however, use a garden fork to aerate the soil by pushing it in deep all over the lawn. Alternatively, use a special hollow-tined lawn aerator, which takes out cores of soil. Brush these off the lawn and then use a birch broom or the back of a rake to spread and sweep into the lawn a mixture of clean sharp sand and peat in the ratio of ⅔ peat, ⅓ sharp sand.

---Q---

How do I cope with sloping land that I wish to form into a lawn?

---A---

As long as your land can be sloped evenly, differences in height over the entire area do not matter. Of course, it must be visually attractive and have adequate drainage, but there should be no problem in cutting the grass if you use a hover-type mower. Hand-pushed mowers and those with traditional motors tend to slip off steeply-sloped banks, whereas a hover-type can be trailed over the slope.

PESTS AND DISEASES

Q

The leaves of my chrysanthemums are revealing black areas between the veins, and some of the lower leaves have turned completely black and shrivelled. Have you any idea what is causing the trouble?

A

The problem is caused by chrysanthemum leaf and bud eelworm, a pest that is most persistent and lives in dead tissue for many months. This microscopic worm-like creature penetrates the stems and leaves of chrysanthemums and also attacks many other ornamental plants. Its eradication is difficult and infected plants are best dug up and burned.

Infested plants should not be used for propagation. On a home gardener level there is, unfortunately, little one can do to control this pest, other than buying in healthy plants and growing them on a clean, fresh site. Whenever buying new plants make sure they are clean and not infected. Specialist growers use chemicals not available to home gardeners, as well as special propagation techniques that create healthy stock from which cuttings can be taken.

Q

The flowers on both my dahlias and chrysanthemums are being chewed, but I have never seen any pest on the flowers. What can it be?

A

The flowers of these two highly decorative garden plants are prone to attack from earwigs. They feed mainly during warm evenings and nights, and will chew the leaves as well as the flowers. A general insecticide based on pyrethrum or pirimiphos-methyl, applied every fortnight, will control them.

Alternatively, to trap the pests, half-fill a pot with straw and invert over a cane or support among the flowers. Each morning shake the sheltering earwigs out of the pots into a bucket of boiling water to kill them.

Q

The edges of my rhododendron leaves are being eaten away. What is causing this damage?

A

The culprits are vine weevils, which chew the lower leaves, which are left looking tattered. They also eat the stems of ornamental shrubs. These weevils are small beetles with pronounced snouts. Spray at fortnightly intervals with a general insecticide such as pirimiphosmethyl or pyrethrum.

Q

Some of my herbaceous plants are covered with frothy-like spit around the leaf joints. What is causing this?

A

This frothy substance – known as Cuckoo Spit – is created by the young forms of the common froghopper to protect them from birds. The adult attacks a wide range of plants, including roses, geum, solidago and lavender, and causes stems to wilt and to become distorted. The pest

Above *Rhododendron leaves damaged by Vine Weevils.*

Above right *A Common Green Capsid Bug, an agile, bright green insect, not easy to spot among foliage.*

Right *Cuckoo Spit, froth created by Common Froghoppers. Plants can be considerably weakened by their feeding activities.*

GREENFLY

Many of my chrysanthemums, dahlias and roses are covered with a mass of small, greenish insects which cluster around soft shoot tips and buds. What are they?

A

They are most certain to be Greenfly, often called aphids. They attack the soft tissue, causing a weakening of the plants in general and distortion of all sucked tissue. They also transmit virus diseases that cause further problems. Use general aphid sprays based on pirimicarb, pirimiphos-methyl, or pyrethrum every ten days so that any insects that hatch since a previous treatment are killed. Sprays based on the insecticide pirimicarb will kill the aphids, but will not harm beneficial insects such as ladybirds, lacewings and hoverflies that feed on the aphids.

also transmits virus diseases. Spray with an insecticide such as permethrin, dimethoate or pirimicarb as soon as the pest is noticed. If the trouble persists, spray again after ten days.

Q

My dahlias' young leaves are mottled and puckered with light, irregular spots.

A

The insects causing this are the extremely active Common Green Capsid Bugs. They attack a wide range of plants, from chrysanthemums and dahlias to apples and currants. One aid to controlling these pests is to destroy all rubbish and weeds on which they can overwinter. Spray affected plants regularly throughout the summer with insecticides containing fenitrothion or gamma-HCH. Unfortunately, however, the pest has often departed from the plant before the damage becomes apparent.

Because of their soft-textured stems, leaves and flowers, dahlias are prone to attack from many pests and diseases. Leaf Spot or Smut produces circular brown spots on the lower leaves of bedding dahlias, which eventually turn black and shrivelling. Even the soft shoots at ground level can be attacked by Leafy Gall, becoming a mass of lumpy and distorted shoots. Infected plants are best dug up and burned.

SAFETY PRECAUTIONS

1. Read the instructions on the container and follow them to the letter. Do not add one for the pot.
2. Always wear rubber gloves when handling undiluted chemicals. Wash your hands and face afterwards.
3. Spray at the time indicated on the container, and also at the recommended intervals.
4. Spray in the evening or on dull days when bees and pollinating insects are not active.
5. Mix only as much spray as you can use. Flush surplus amounts of spray down the lavatory and dispose of empty containers by capping them tightly, wrapping them in a polythene bag and placing them in the dustbin.
6. Always use hand sprayers which are kept specifically for insecticide and fungicide application.
7. Do not spray garden chemicals on windy days or in bright sunshine, and do not spray into open flowers.
8. Store all chemicals in their original containers in a secure cupboard out of the reach of children and pets.
9. When spraying edible crops, always allow the recommended interval to elapse before harvesting.
10. Always wash all fruits and vegetables thoroughly before eating to remove all possible traces of chemicals.

DISEASES AND THEIR CONTROL

DISEASE	SYMPTOMS	CONTROL
American gooseberry mildew	Stems, leaves and berries covered with fungus growth, white at first then dark brown. Shoots stunted. Sometimes affects currants	Benomyl. Cut off affected shoots in August and burn
Apple and pear scab	Black round spots or blotches on the fruit and black or brownish-green blotches on the leaves. Worst in wet seasons	Bupirimate and triforine (systemic) – use for apple only; thiophanate-methyl (systemic); mancozeb
Black-spot	Black spots on leaves of roses	Bupirimate and triforine (systemic); copper compound; dichlofluanid; mancozeb; thiophanate-methyl (systemic); thiram
Botrytis	Decay of soft plant tissue, followed by a fluffy grey mould. Affects many crops including lettuce, strawberries and tomatoes	Copper compound; dichlofluanid; TCNB (tecnazene) smoke (for greenhouses); thiophanate-methyl (systemic); thiram
Canker	Oval ragged wounds on bark of apples and pears	Copper compound. Cut out areas affected with a sharp knife as soon as noticed; then paint wound with a wound dressing
Celery leaf spot	Leaves develop brown spots with tiny black dots	Copper compound. The disease can be spread by seed; treated seed is sometimes available
Chocolate spot	Chocolate-coloured spots on leaves, rapidly increasing in size. Affects mainly broad beans	Copper compound. Improve drainage
Club root	Large gall-like swellings on roots of cabbage family	Calomel dust. Liming helps
Coral spot	Orange spots on dead twigs of shrubs and trees	Cut off affected shoots below last affected leaves
Damping-off	Seedlings decay at or near soil level, the seedlings toppling over	Cheshunt compound; copper compound
Downy mildew	Mealy-looking or furry growth on leaves and stems. Leaves sometimes die from the tips and shrivel	Copper compound; mancozeb; thiophanate-methyl (systemic); thiram
Honey fungus	Infects and kills roots of shrubs and trees. Honey-coloured toadstools appear	Dig up old stumps; treat soil with formalin
Peach leaf curl	Contorted leaves, red swollen areas	Copper compound; mancozeb
Potato blight	Black patches on leaves. Also affects tomatoes	Copper compound; mancozeb
Powdery mildew	White powdery patches on leaves of roses and many other plants	Bupirimate and triforine (systemic); dinocap; thiophanate-methyl (systemic); thiram
Raspberry cane spot	Young canes develop small circular spots in May or June. These become elliptical and the centres become whitish-grey	Benomyl; copper compound; dichlofluanid
Rust (carnation, chrysanthemum, rose)	Orange pustules on undersides of leaves	Copper compound; mancozeb; thiram
Tomato leaf mould	Yellow blotches appear on upper surface of leaves, with velvety brown or purple mould growth at the back	Mancozeb; thiophanate-methyl (systemic)
Tulip fire	Brown patches or streaks on foliage. Stunted growth	Dig up and burn seriously affected tulips. Dust with thiram

PESTS AND THEIR CONTROL

PESTS	DESCRIPTION	CROPS AFFECTED	CONTROL
Ants	Immediately recognizable, but there are many species. Can be a nuisance, and encourage aphids	Most plants infested with aphids; ripe fruit	Gamma-HCH; pirimiphos-methyl; pyrethrum; trichlorphon
Aphids (greenfly, blackfly)	Tiny insects, usually found in clusters; some are winged, some not. May be green, black or grey, depending on type	A wide range of plants, indoors and out, including vegetables	Dimethoate (systemic); pirimicarb; gamma-HCH and menazon; fenitrothion; formothion (systemic); malathion; oxy-demeton-methyl aerosol; pyrethrum and resmethrin; permethrin and heptenophos
Cabbage root fly maggot	Small white grubs that eat the roots of brassica crops. The plants are severely checked. Wilting and a blue cast to the leaves are symptoms	Brassicas such as cabbages, cauliflowers, broccoli, Brussels sprouts, radishes and turnips	Bromophos
Capsid bugs	Whitish or greenish insects, rather like largish aphids. There are several types. Plants become weakened and leaves distorted	Many ornamental plants and fruit such as gooseberries and currants	Fenitrothion
Carrot fly maggot	Small white maggots in roots. Leaves of affected plants often turn bronze	Carrots, celery, parsley and parsnips	Bromophos
Caterpillars	Well known to all gardeners. Many different kinds, most belonging to moths	Brassica crops affected by cabbage white butterfly caterpillars; many crops, including gooseberries, by moth caterpillars	Carbaryl; rotenone; rotenone and quassia
Cockchafer	A large beetle about 25mm (1in) long, with black head and thorax and reddish-brown wing cases. Eats leaves; grubs eat roots	Ornamental trees and shrubs, soft fruit, potatoes and herbaceous plants	Bromophos (for grubs)
Codling moth	The small white caterpillar eats its way into apples. Not to be confused with the apple sawfly, which usually attacks about a month earlier in May or June and generally causes the fruit to drop	Apples	Fenitrothion

PESTS AND THEIR CONTROL

PESTS	DESCRIPTION	CROPS AFFECTED	CONTROL
Cuckoo spit (frog hoppers)	Resemble tiny pale yellow grasshoppers. Jump if disturbed. Greenish-yellow larvae protect themselves with a covering of froth	Many garden plants, especially in herbaceous border	Malathion
Earwig	Well-known pests, with distinctive forceps, those of the male being rounded like callipers, those of the female straight	Many, but dahlias and chrysanthemums are especially vulnerable	Gamma-HCH; pirimiphos-methyl
Leaf hoppers	Pale yellow insects resembling aphids and capsid bugs. Cause white mottling of leaves	Many plants, outdoors and in. Roses attract one species	Pyrethrum and resmethrin
Leaf miners	White 'tunnels' in the leaves are a tell-tale sign of these small larvae	Chrysanthemums, holly and certain other ornamentals, and celery	Malathion
Leatherjackets	The larvae of crane-flies. Resemble dark grey or black caterpillars, but have no legs	Grasses, herbaceous plants and vegetables. Worst on old pasture or newly-cultivated land	Gamma-HCH
Mealy bugs	Troublesome greenhouse pests. The small whitish insects protect themselves with a waxy substance	Greenhouse plants and houseplants	Malathion
Onion fly maggot	Small white maggots attack onion bulbs at or just below soil level. Foliage droops	Onions, leeks, shallots	Bromophos
Raspberry beetle	Small yellow-brown or grey beetle, eats buds and flowers. White grub hatches in the raspberry fruit	Raspberries, loganberries and blackberries	Fenitrothion; rotenone; malathion
Red spiders	Actually mites, not spiders; tiny and brownish-red. Can just be seen with naked eye. Under a magnifying glass can be seen to have eight legs. Affected leaves become mottled and bronzed. Worst in greenhouses	Greenhouse crops such as perpetual carnations, houseplants; outdoors may sometimes be found on apples and strawberries	Formothion (systemic); malathion; pirimiphos-methyl; rotenone
Sawflies	Larvae of several fly-like insects resembling caterpillars. The white maggot of the apple sawfly tunnels into young apples; other species eat the leaves of plants such as roses or gooseberries	Apples, roses, gooseberries, plums, and other plants, depending on species	Fenitrothion; rotenone
Scale insects	Small sucking insects, covered by a scale. The scale is about 3mm (⅛in) long, the colour varying from brown to grey or black, depending on species	Houseplants and greenhouse plants; or fruit trees, aucubas, yew (*Taxus*) and beech (*Fagus*), among others, in the open	Malathion; permethrin and heptenophos
Slugs and snails	There are various species of these well-known pests. The type that live below ground are more difficult to control	Almost all crops, but seedlings are most vulnerable	Metaldehyde; methiocarb
Thrips	Small, narrow insects, from pale yellow to black in colour. Flower buds often badly affected	A wide range of plants outdoors and indoors	Gamma-HCH; malathion; pyrethrum and resmethrin; rotenone; rotenone and quassia
Turnip flea beetles	Small black beetles that make small round holes in brassica crop leaves, especially seedlings. The beetles jump when disturbed	Turnips, cabbages, broccoli, Brussels sprouts, and allied crops	Gamma-HCH; rotenone; carbaryl
Weevils	Beetles with an elongated snout. There are many species; the vine weevil grub attacks vine roots, bulbs, corms and tubers, and other roots. The adult beetles eat the leaves	Besides crops mentioned, some favour roses, some apples, others peas and beans	Carbaryl; gamma-HCH
Whiteflies	Tiny white flying insects, sometimes rising when disturbed to form a white cloud	Tomatoes in greenhouses, cabbage family outdoors, ornamental house and greenhouse plants	Bioresmethrin aerosol (for greenhouses); dimethoate (systemic); malathion
Wireworms	Larvae of click beetles, yellow-brown and hard-skinned. Segmented body; up to 25mm (1in) long	Roots of many plants	Bromophos; gamma-HCH; diazinon
Woodlice	Grey, hard-coated creatures, some of which roll themselves into a ball when disturbed. Often found under stones or rotting wood. May damage seedlings, and can be a problem in a greenhouse, but not serious outdoors	Live mainly on decaying material, but seedlings may be eaten	Gamma-HCH; pirimiphos-methyl; carbaryl
Woolly aphis	Most obvious indication of this pest is the cotton-wool-like excretion with which it surrounds itself	Apple trees	Malathion; dimethoate (systemic)

WEEDS AND THEIR CONTROL

Name	Main method of spread	Control, natural	Control, chemical	Remarks
Bindweed (perennial)	Roots	Dig out roots	Glyphosate, dichlobenil	Destroy lifted roots
Black medick (annual)	Seed	Hand-fork, remove before flowering	Paraquat	
Buttercup, creeping (perennial)	Runners with plantlets	Dig out, mulch heavily and completely	Glyphosate, dichlobenil	Improve drainage of soil
Chickweed (annual)	Seed	Hoe out seedlings, dig in before flowering	Paraquat	Treat before flowering
Cinquefoil (perennial)	Runners with plantlets	Dig out roots completely	Glyphosate, dichlobenil	Rootstock brittle and breaks easily
Clover, white (perennial)	Creeping stems rooting at joints	Reduce alkalinity of soil	Glyphosate	
Coltsfoot (perennial)	Creeping underground stems	Grass down; remove flowers before seeding; dig thoroughly	Glyphosate, dichlobenil	Improve soil drainage and nutrition
Couch grass (perennial)	Rhizomes	Dig repeatedly and thoroughly	Alloxydim-sodium	Destroy rhizomes
Daisy (perennial)	Runners with plantlets	Remove with two-pronged hand fork	Glyphosate	
Dock (perennial)	Seed	Remove flower spikes before seeding; dig out roots completely	Glyphosate, dichlobenil	Dig out early in spring
Ground elder (perennial)	Rhizomes	Mulch heavily and completely; dig thoroughly	Glyphosate, dichlobenil	Destroy the brittle rhizomes
Groundsel (annual)	Seed	Hoe out seedlings, hand-fork young plants, destroy before flowering	Paraquat	
Horsetail (perennial)	Deeply penetrating rhizomes	Grass down; dig and remove top growth repeatedly	Severely suppressed by dichlobenil and glyphosate	Destroy rhizomes; improve drainage
Japanese knotweed (perennial)	Rhizomes	Remove top growth repeatedly; dig out rhizomes	Glyphosate	
Nettle (perennial)	Roots, seed	Dig thoroughly; hoe seedlings	Paraquat to seedlings; glyphosate, dichlobenil	
Oxalis (perennial)	Bulbils	Grass down; hand-weed thoroughly	Dichlobenil or glyphosate, following manufacturer's instructions	Destroy all parts of plant
Pearlwort (perennial)	Creeping stems rooting at joints; seed	Hand-fork	Paraquat, glyphosate	
Speedwell (annual)	Creeping stems rooting at joints; seed	Hoe seedlings; hand-fork; mulch heavily	Paraquat	Improve soil drainage
Thistle, creeping (perennial)	Creeping roots	Dig thoroughly; grass down	Glyphosate or dichlobenil	Destroy roots
Yarrow (perennial)	Creeping stems rooting at joints	Dig, or cut through stems in a criss-cross fashion and remove; repeat if necessary	Glyphosate, dichlobenil	

INDEX

INDEX

ACKNOWLEDGEMENTS

The publishers thank the following for providing the photographs in this book:

A-Z Botanical Collection 175 above, 258 below, 276 right; Bernard Alfieri 189 centre, 220 above, 237, 255 above, 270; Heather Angel/Biofotos 2, 8, 10, 42, 48 above, 173 below, 176-177, 202, 212; Autogrow 192-193, 193 above; Barton Grange Garden Centre 215; Peter Black 174; Pat Brindley 11 right, 25 above, 55, 165 top and centre, 166 top and bottom, 168 centre, 170 right, 171, 172 above and below, 175 below, 182-183, 186 below, 245, 255 below, 263, 276 left, 281 below right, 283; Robert Corbin 291; Dulux 36; Marion Furner 25 below, 28, 221 below right, 275, 285; Derek Gould 87 above, 97 below, 124 above, below left and right, 131 left, 133, 140 inset, 142, 266; Susan Griggs Agency (Michael Boys) 69 right, (Stewart Galloway) 11 left; Iris Hardwick Library 264; Jerry Harpur (Magnus Ramsey) 17, (Heslington Manor, York) 18, (John Vellam) 20, (Hinton and Hillier) 27, (Yeomans) 34, (Jenkyn Place) 70; John Harris/Greenhouse Magazine 193 below right, 199; David Hoy Publications 290, 292; George Hyde 220 below left and right, 221 above right, 294; Leslie Johns 278; Marley Greenhouses 154; Tania Midgely 254; Margaret McLean 6; NHPA 219 above; Roberts Electrical 158, 159 left; RHS Wisley 201 right; Harry Smith Photogaphic Collection 12, 14, 22, 23, 24 below, 29, 30, 32 below, 35, 39, 49 below, 57 top and bottom, 61 above and below, 62, 65, 66, 118, 119 above left and right, 122 above and below, 123 above, 130 below, 143 above and below, 144 above, 155, 157, 164 top, 165 bottom, 168 above, 169 centre and bottom, 177 above, 178 left, 179 above, 184 above, 186 above, 187, 188 above, 189 top, 190, 191 above and below, 204, 207 below left, 219 below, 221 above and below left, 222, 225, 226, 230, 233 above and below, 234, 240, 243 above right and below, 252, 257, 258 above, 261, 265, 281 above and below left, 287, 289, 295; Spectrum Colour Library 167, 181 right, 256; Sutton Seeds 164 below; Michael Warren/Photos Horticultural 4, 16, 19, 21, 24 above, 26, 31, 36, 40, 41, 45-46, 48, 52, 53, 63, 127, 128, 130 above, 131 right, 134, 135, 136 right, 137, 139 below, 145, 152, 160, 169 top, 181 left, 189 bottom, 229, 243 above left, 250, 259, 260, 269, 282, 284, 286; Elizabeth Whiting and Associates 67, 146, 148

The following pictures were taken specially for Octopus Books:

Michael Boys 45 inset, 57 centre, 79, 81, 85, 91, 98, 99, 102 right, 112 above, 115, 119 below left and right, 121 right, 125 below, 129, 135 below inset, 141 above, 183 right, 184 below, 185, 207 above and below right, 262; Michael Crockett 159 right, 161, 198, 200; Melvin Grey 166 centre; Jerry Harpur 32 above, 47 below, 49 above, 58 above, 74 right, 75 above, 77, 80, 83, 84, 86, 87 below, 89 left and right, 92, 102 left, 107, 108, 110, 112 below, 113, 116, 117 above and below, 126 below, 132 above and below, 136 left, 138 below, 140, 141 below, 170 left, 206, 239, 242, 244, 246, 267, 268, 271, 293; Neil Holmes 50 above and below, 51, 56, 123 below, 125 above, 144 below, 149, 173 above, 176 left, 179 below, 180 above; Octopus Library 178 right, 235, 237; Peter Rauter 164 centre, 238; John Sims 201 left; Paul Williams 248; George Wright 59, 74 left, 75 below, 78, 82, 93, 94, 106, 114, 121 left, 133 inset, 135 above inset, 138 above, 139 above, 180 below, 188 below, 247, 288